PEKING

A HISTORICAL AND INTIMATE DESCRIPTION OF ITS CHIEF PLACES OF INTEREST

by

JULIET BREDON

Peking : A Historical and Intimate Description of its Chief Places of Interest. © 2008 Soul Care Publishing

All rights reserved. No part of this book may be used or reproduced or transmitted in any manner whatsoever, transmitted electronically, or distributed by any means without the written permission of the publisher.

Library and Archives Canada Cataloguing in Publication

Bredon, Juliet
    Peking : a historical and intimate description of its chief places of interest / by Juliet Bredon.

Includes index.
ISBN 978-0-9680459-8-5

    1. Beijing (China)--Description and travel.
2. Beijing (China)--History. I. Title.

DS795.B73 2010   951'.156   C2009-907122-3

Published by Soul Care Publishing, Vancouver, B.C. Canada
Cover design by Liang Ning
Printed in U.S.A

In Memory of My Father

TABLE OF CONTENTS

I.	Peking—A Historical Sketch	1
II.	The Wonderful Walls of Peking	13
III.	The Legation Quarter And Modern Peking	29
IV.	The Picturesqueness of the Past	45
V.	The Forbidden City	63
VI.	The Wings of the Forbidden City and the Coal Hill	98
VII.	The Sea Palaces and the Mongol Throne Hall	113
VIII.	The Temple of Heaven and the Temple of Agriculture	132
IX.	Three Temples of Three Faiths	152
X.	Temples of Many Gods	176
XI.	Temples of the Tartar City	185
XII.	Temples of the Chinese City	202
XIII.	Temples and Tombs Outside the City	212
XIV.	The Summer Palaces and the Jade Fountain	240
XV.	Temples of the Western Hills	271
XVI.	Temples of the Western Hills—(Concluded)	296
XVII.	The Great Wall and the Ming Tombs	329
XVIII.	The Hsi Ling and the Tung Ling	353
XIX.	Peking—The Old Curiosity Shop	371
XX.	The Fun of the Fair	397
XXI.	Western Landmarks	420
XXII.	Appendix I The Dynasties of China	445
XXIII.	Appendix II - The Principal Festivals and Fairs in Peking	449
XXIV.	Index	455

ACKNOWLEDGMENT

(For the Third Edition)

The Author desires to express her indebtedness to the many friends, both foreign and Chinese, who have assisted her in collecting material for a new edition of Peking, or permitted the reproduction of their photographs, maps, and plans. Special thanks are due, and gratefully tendered to Mr. F. J. Chapman, of the American Legation, who kindly assisted in the preparation of the Chinese characters for the Index and the romanization of Chinese names throughout the text, to Baron de Stael-Holstein, Dr. J. C. Ferguson and other scholars who contributed valuable information from original sources. Also to her husband, Monsieur C. H. Lauru, whose inspiration and general help have made possible the revision of former editions of this book.

Publishers Note:

To view the maps of Peking originally published in this book please visit
www.soulcarepublishing.com

Marble "Pai Lou"—Ming Tombs

PREFACE

Several books have been written about Peking by foreigners, but among these only two are comprehensive —Monseigneur Favier's monumental work Peking and Father Hyacinth Bitchurin's *Description of Peking*[1] both, alas, somewhat out of date from the modern visitor's view point, since much has altered in the city of late years.

The paucity of accurate accounts is chiefly due to obstacles in the way of collecting precise information. The more one studies this fascinating city, old, proud and secretive, the more one realises the tantalising difficulties of learning, even from the Chinese themselves, anything but the merest outline of its history and monuments.[2] A proper appreciation of Peking is, indeed, scarcely in the power of a Westerner to offer since it pre-supposes a thorough knowledge of China's past, an infinite sympathy with Chinese character and religions, an intimate familiarity with the proverbs and household phrases of the poor, the songs of the streets, the speech of the workshop, no less than the mentality of the literati and the motives of the rulers.

With many misgivings, therefore, and craving the indulgence of the readers, this book appears at the suggestion of some who think that a description of Peking covering a wider field than the usual "Guide," and yet without solemn scholarly pretensions, may prove interesting to the average person. Its purpose is simply to play the part of a friend to resident and visitor alike—a friend (in whose taste you perhaps have

---

1 The little book of Father Hyacinth Bitchurin was for many years the only-reliable description of Peking by a foreigner. Its accuracy is unquestioned. Bretschneider and other sinologues recognised it as an original authority and drew largely upon it for their own works.
2 The standard Chinese work dealing with Peking is the *Jih Hsia Chiu Wen K'ao*, an official publication dated 1774. It was largely drawn upon for a second edition of the *Shun Tien Fu Chih* (a description of the metropolitan prefecture, first published in a.d. 1593), brought out in 1S86 by order of Li Hung-chang. A third book, the *Ch'en Yuan Shih Loh* (1788), was the foundation of Father Hyacinth's *Description*. While these and other Chinese accounts contain many important data, they nevertheless often fail to give a cohesive summary of details which appeal to us as essential.

confidence) to take you by the arm for a stroll through the city and its suburbs.

I have no intention of giving long lists of temples or palaces which ought to be seen as quickly as possible—lest the promised pleasures change into an endless vista of labours to be fulfilled, and the hours spent in Peking become hours of endurance rather than enjoyment. Too often the traveller is confused by accumulated misty glimmerings of historical facts, by shadowy ideas concerning this Prince. or that Emperor, this General and that Monk, and stumbles about in a haze which, from insufficient interest and the absence of books of reference, he has no means of clearing up.[3] Better far to leave half the monuments unseen and to see well the rest; to see them not once but again and again; to watch them in many lights and moods till they become part of life and life's recollections. Thus only can the true atmosphere of the city, so powerful and yet so illusive, be absorbed into mind and spirit. From the experience of many years I can truly say that the more intimately the scenes of Peking—by far the finest city in all China—become known, the more deeply they are engraved on the affections. It is not a hurried visit to one or two sights which will enable anybody to feel their spell, but a long and familiar friendship that endears them to us, and gives each a motive and a significance entirely unrecognised and unsuspected by the passing eye.

Who can forget the soft enchantment of Buddhist temples, the green peace of tombs haunted by fearless things, "doves that flutter down at call, fishes rising to be fed?" Or the grandeur of past Imperial splendours? At first it is difficult for the Westerner to grasp the full meaning of these glories of ancient Chinese civilisation— far more difficult than those of Italy, for example, because, as Howells says in his *Tuscan Cities,* "a prime condition of our immediate sympathy with any

---

[3] Books of reference are suggested now and again for such readers as care to pursue a subject further. The majority of works mentioned have been chosen because easily obtainable; many of the older books are out of print, and therefore impossible to consult except in the library of a specialist.

life, or epoch, or civilisation is that we always, and every instant, find our dreary, tiresome, unstoried, unstoriable selves in it"—and we can more easily imagine ourselves taking afternoon tea with Lorenzo the Magnificent or even Caesar Borgia, than with Yung Lo or Ch'ien Lung.

Yet, if we would profit by Peking to the uttermost, we must put away all prejudices of our civilisation, and we must believe that it is not in one class of interests alone that much is to be enjoyed. Archaeology and history should combine to form the noblest impression of Peking, but observation of the life of the people at work, at prayer or at pleasure, with all the symbolical strangeness of Far Eastern life, is needed to complete the picture.

This, then, is my introduction to you, the reader, as one willing to pilot you about the city that I have lived in and studied for years, talking with you, as it were, as I have done with many passers-by who feel they are strangers in a strange place of which they have seen much but know not much, until they have been with one who is Peking's familiar comrade.

J. B.

I. Peking—A Historical Sketch[4]

Cities, like people, have their individualities. Some are commonplace and soon forgotten, others make a striking impression on even the passing stranger. But although what pleases one often fails to interest another, the majority of travellers agree that Peking has an unusually rich and attractive personality.

Something of this is due to the grand conception of the builder's plan, the nobility of surrounding walls and gates, the splendour of palace squares, the vivid colours of Imperial roofs, but still more depends on the general atmosphere of picturesqueness, the striking contrast to accustomed things, and the curious mingling of old and new.

The history of Peking is the history of China in miniature, for the town, like the country, has shown the same power of taking fresh masters and absorbing them. Both have passed through dark hours of anarchy and bloodshed. Happily both possess the vitality to survive them.

More than two thousand years before our era, when the first Chinese settlers began spreading from the upper reaches of the Yellow River over the northern provinces of the future Celestial Empire, the district of Yen, including the site of present day Peking, appears to have invited colonisation "as a very pleasant land, of streams and meres stocked with fish, and where roamed deer, elephants, tigers, leopards and bears."[5]

---

[4] For fuller details on the early history of Peking, see *Recherches Archeologiques. et Historiques sur Pekin et ses Environs*, by Dr. E. Bretschneider, translated by V. Collin de Plancy, and *Peking, Histoire et Description*, by Alph. Favier. Those who are interested in the history of China may consult *A Sketch of Chinese History*, by F. L. Hawks Pott, the best condensed outline for an introductory study, or *Outlines of Chinese History*, by Li Ung Bing, a fuller treatment from the point of view of a Chinese writer. See also the classical histories of de Mailla, Macgowan, Boulger, etc.

[5] "The Early History of Peking," by T. W. Kingsmill, in *Peking*, by Fei-shi.

Juliet Bredon

Historians mention a town called Chi, occupying almost the same site as modern Peking, as far back as 1100 b.c. (about the time of the Siege of Troy). Two miles north of the present Tartar wall, near the Bell Temple, a yellow-tiled pavilion covers a marble tablet on which the Manchu Emperor Ch'ien Lung wrote: "Here stood one of the gates of the ancient city of Chi." This is interesting and valuable testimony to the existence of the semi-mythical town at that place, since all traces of it have disappeared.

Chi, according to Chinese chroniclers, enjoyed a few centuries of importance, judged by the standards of those rough times, as the capital of the Principality of Northern Yen. Its remoteness from the main currents of national development in the Yellow River valley gave this State a measure of independence out of proportion to its actual strength, and it was almost the last of the seven great fiefs of feudal China to succumb to the empire builder Ch'in Shih Huang Ti, the genius who was the first ruler to unify the country.

This monarch took and destroyed Chi in 221 b.c. When his commanding personality was removed by death, the dynasty founded by him in cruelty and blood quickly collapsed. It was succeeded by that of the Hans (206 b.c.—ad. 220) whose name is still a synonym for Chinese nationality, and whose work in consolidating the foundations of the Chinese State, in extending its frontiers and its influence, in establishing intercourse with foreign countries, and in crystallising the achievements of Chinese civilisation, may be compared to the work performed by Rome for Western civilisation.

A new town was built under the Hans a little to the south of the city of Chi. It included a small part of what is now the Tartar City and a larger part of the Chinese City, and was destined for many years to remain an obscure provincial centre. The fateful struggle between the Han dynasty and the Hsiung Nu (a people related to the Huns) does not appear to have seriously involved the Peking district, but we can judge how rapidly it grew in importance with the growing influence of the Northern Barbarians from the records of alien rulers (of

Tunguzic or Turkish origin) who controlled portions of North China after the fall of the mighty Hans.

Under the T'angs (a.d. 618-907), restorers of Chinese political unity, the ancestor of modern Peking still remained a provincial town under the name of Yu Chou. It had already become, however, the residence of a military Governor-General. While occupying this post, the notorious An Lu-shan—a Turk by origin—made the love of an empress the stepping stone to a career which culminated in a redoubtable insurrection, and started the decline of the T'ang Sovereignty.

After the T'angs there followed a succession of ephemeral dynasties. None of them exercised control over the whole of China, and "we may compare this period," says Hawks Pott, "with that era in Roman history, during the decline of the Empire, when the Imperial power fell into the hands of victorious generals." It was Peking that gave China the righteous Chou Kuang-yin, whose ancestors had for several generations occupied prominent positions in Yu Chou. Chou Kuang-yin was the founder of the Sung dynasty at K'ai Feng Fu, and succeeded in reuniting the greater part of China—all but the northern regions, which had meanwhile fallen an easy prey to the conquering Liaos, or Khitan Tartars (a.d. 915-1125). The Liaos were the first to create a metropolis where Peking now stands. They destroyed Yu Chou but built a new and larger city on the same site and called it "Nanking," or Southern Capital, to distinguish it from their other capitals in Manchuria—also "Yenching," or "Swallow Capital"—a name still surviving in literature and commemorated in the name of Yenching University.[6] After each conquest the town rose again from its ashes more splendid than before. At this time it already had a circumference of twelve miles, contained an Imperial palace worthy of a capital, and was surrounded by walls thirty feet high with eight gates.

---

6 "Yenching was only an honorific name chosen on account of the fact that Yen was the early name of the district in which the dynasty decided to locate its capital."—See *The Ancient Capital of Yen*, by John C. Ferguson. See *The China Journal*, Vol. XU, No. 3, March 1930, pp. 133-135.

These defences, however, did not prevent the overthrow of the Liaos by the Chin, or Nuchen, Tartars (a.d. i 125-1234), whereupon a new master came into possession and the place was re-named Chung Tu. The Chins showed themselves comparatively humane conquerors. Instead of destroying, they simply enlarged what they conquered, adding a new town to the east of the old one, building another palace within the new fortifications and a summer palace with pleasure gardens beyond them, approximately on the site of the Pai T'a (White Dagoba) in the Pei Hai. Side by side, though each enclosed within separate walls, the two cities together now formed a large rectangle with a perimeter of twenty miles, defended by walls pierced by twelve gates. These walls stood intact until the present Chinese city was built in the middle of the 16th century, and fragments of them may still be seen near the Po Yun Kuan Temple, the present race course, and in the neighbourhood of Fengtai.

The Chins in their turn were overthrown by the Mongols under Genghis Khan, whose generals took Chung Tu in a.d. 1215, but not before they had laid siege to each of the cities separately and, finally, to the two fortified palaces, which were strongholds within strongholds. Old chronicles describe how they were conquered at last "with glorious slaughter." Reading between the lines, we can picture "those fearful days of carnage and the barbarous wholesale massacres always repeated at the passing of dynasties. No mercy was shown, none expected. The point of view of the man in the street, the humble, plunderable citizen, was of little account in an era when savage conquerors staked the fortunes of an empire on a single desperate throw. A pitiful feature of these conquests, to our modern way of thinking, was the complete lack of resistance on the part of the non-combatants and their fatalistic acceptance of the brutal dominion of the soldiery who converted the city into a shambles, while their terror-stricken victims, often men of far higher mental and moral attainments, awaited death and worse with abject helplessness and accepted it as an established feature of the sorry scheme of things."

Peking – A Historical Sketch

In this particular instance the sins of the rulers were visited more directly than usual upon the people, for the Great Khan brought his forces across the border at the invitation of the Chins themselves, since the latter wanted his help to get rid of the Sung dynasty in Southern China. Their short-sighted policy cost them not only their northern capital but their empire and their throne. The Mongols, once they had ousted the Sungs, betrayed their hosts and, after fifty years of fighting, conquered the country themselves and established their own dynasty. Peking played a decisive role in the history of the Mongols. They inherited with it the services of the faithful Yeh-lu-ch'u-ts'ai, a Khitan by origin, whom Genghis found in charge of the Chin capital, and who later became one of the chief councillors at the Mongol Court (see "Summer Palace" chapter). It is known that two different opinions warred at Karakorum after the death of Genghis: should the Mongol rulers decide to reap the fruit of their conquests in the East, or in the West? No Western country could compare with China in their eyes— China which, since the days of Ptolemy, travellers and geographers agreed in describing as the best organised and richest country in the world, and which for milleniums appeared to the children of the wilderness as something scarcely less desirable than paradise. But the Mongols, perhaps instinctively, felt the difficulty of maintaining their prestige over a people so much superior to them in the arts of peace. The "Chinese party," however, headed by Yeh-lu-ch'u-ts'ai, finally won the day after many efforts and discussions. Kublai Khan moved down from Mongolia and built (a.d. 1264-1267) a city a little to the north of Chung Tu, taken and destroyed by his grandfather (the site including that of the ancient city of Chi), calling it Khanbalig, or City of the Great Khan. Now for the first time it became the capital of all China— of a China, moreover, which the Mongol conquests had drawn into a more intimate contact with the West than hitherto, and that was to reap the benefits of this contact and of a brilliant administration in the form of unprecedented security and wealth.

Juliet Bredon

Kublai chose Peking as the most convenient central point from which he could control not only the provinces of China Proper, but also his domains in what are now Mongolia, Manchuria, Korea, Siberia and Turkestan. A vigorous and magnificent prince, he laid out his new capital in a manner suited to the prestige of a Supreme Ruler—not in the usual Chinese style with "narrow, twisting streets, but with long wide roads through which horsemen can gallop nine abreast." We are fortunate in having Marco Polo, the famous Venetian traveller who visited the Far East in the 13th century—a chronicler worthy of his subject—to describe the Mongol splendour and enable us to form an idea of Khanbalig in its glory.[7]

Fresh from Europe, which in his day was far behind China in civilisation, his admiration for the Orient, however, sometimes led him to exaggeration and inaccuracy. Thus his descriptions are at variance with those of contemporary Chinese historians, who also differ among themselves about the size of Khanbalig and the site of its walls. If we sift down conflicting evidence, it seems probable that the east and west ramparts of what is now known as the Tartar City (so called because the Manchu-Tartars at the beginning of their dynasty drove out the Chinese into the suburb which has since become the Southern or Chinese City) stood almost where they stand to-day, but the Mongol capital had eleven gates instead of nine. A few ruins of its mud walls may still be traced outside the An Ting Men and near the Bell Temple. Unfortunately these fragments and part of a wall in the Winter Palace enclosure, easily distinguishable by the difference in the bricks, are practically all that remain of a grandeur which the modern world knows only by tradition, if we except those two fine monuments, the Bell Tower and the Drum Tower, both in the northern part of the Tartar City. The former has been moved from its original site further east, repaired, and is now irreverently used as a cinema. The latter, actually the original structure built in a.d. 1272, has become an educational library and propaganda centre.

---

[7] See *The Book of Ser Marco Polo*, by Yule-Cordier.

Peking – A Historical Sketch

In a.d. 1368, Chu Yuan-chang, Buddhist priest, administrator and fighter, shattered the last remnants of the greater Mongol Empire by his successful rebellion against the degenerate descendants of Kublai Khan, who returned to their plains and nomadic life. He then established the Ming (Bright) dynasty.[8]

The first emperors of the new line, jealous perhaps of the Mongols and their works, transferred the capital to Nanking on the Yangtsze River, and degraded Khanbalig to a simple prefecture with the name of Pei P'ing Fu. Thus for some years its prestige was destroyed and even its area reduced by moving the north wall two miles to the southward. This humiliation lasted until a.d. 1409 when Yung Lo again made the city his seat of Government, and from that time until 1928 when the Nationalists once more established their capital at Nanking, it was known as Peking, or Northern Capital.[9]

There is a curious legend that when he was only a prince and Governor of the District of Yen, the future Emperor Yung Lo laid the foundations of Peking according to a secret plan given him by a Taoist priest who had a great affection for the young man, exiled, through Court intrigues, to what was then a barren wilderness.

Later when he ascended the throne, this wise and illustrious ruler established himself in the newly-built city "whose beauty and strength were loudly praised by the people," and made it his chosen capital.

More ambitious even than Kublai Khan, he built walls "fourteen miles in circumference, fifty cubits in height and fifty in breadth—the whole circuit having battlements and embrasures—and constructed a Forbidden City, containing many superb buildings, seventy-two wells and thirty-six golden tanks, in style of exceeding splendour."

---

8 For the history of the changing fortunes of China's dynasties in greater detail see *Annals and Memoirs of the Court of Peking*, by E. Backhouse and J. O. P. Bland, and *The Chinese and Their Rebellions*, by Meadows.

9 The proper transliteration of the Chinese characters is *Pei Ching*, *pei* meaning north, but, following the southern Chinese pronunciation, it has become generally known as *Peking* or still more inaccurately, *Pekin*.

Juliet Bredon

Peking's finest monuments, her stateliest bridges, the Coal Hill, the lovely gardens and lakes of the Sea Palaces, the Altar of Heaven and the Altar of Earth, are equally due to Yung Lo. In fact, with the exception of a few repairs and some imitations by the earlier Manchu sovereigns, who apparently possessed no original architectural ideas, the plan of the Taoist monk, faithfully followed by his Imperial disciple, has scarcely been changed from his day to ours. Moreover the conception of this amateur architect who visualised a great city on a site he had never seen—a conception worked out even to the minutest details—doubly compels our admiration when we remember that in his time no man had planned, and none dared carry out, such an elaborate design. When the Forbidden City was built, Versailles was an insignificant shooting lodge, the Kremlin still surrounded by a wooden palisade, and Hampton Court not yet begun.

Had all the Mings been of the metal of Yung Lo, the whole course of Chinese history might have been changed. "The swift decline and pitiful end of the dynasty were primarily due to the corruption and incompetence of the later monarchs," as one historian puts it. "Sunk into ignominious and miserable decadence, they were unable to cope with the serious disorders in various parts of the empire, or to combat the rising power of Nurhachi and his Manchu armies. But their fall was due indirectly to a woman and to an instance of that romantic passion supposed to be unknown in China."

The position of the Mings became desperate when in a.d. 1641 the rebellion led by the ruthless soldier Li Tz'u-ch'eng (whose forces had been fitfully active for ten years) assumed formidable proportions and, sweeping northwards, carried everything before it. If Li Tzu-ch'eng, when he took Peking in a.d. 1644, nad not captured there the favourite mistress of Wu San-kuei, the great general to whom the last Ming Emperor Ch'ung Cheng sent for help against the rebels, and if Wu in his despair and fury at the loss of his beloved, had not thrown over his allegiance to his own people and, abandoning honour and loyalty, joined the Manchus to punish Li, these strangers might never have seated themselves on the Dragon Throne. So the Manchus "owed their dynasty, under Heaven, to the little singing-girl known to contemporary chroniclers as Lady Ch'en, the Round Faced Beauty."

In course of time the descendants of the hardy and energetic Nurhachi succumbed to the flesh-pots of the capital and became no less degenerate than the later Mings. Peking, the long-suffering city, twice expiated at the hands of foreign invaders the evil deeds of incompetent Manchu sovereigns—the first time in 1860 when Hsien Feng, a depraved and irresolute monarch, was forced to flee to Jehol while his capital was desecrated by the presence of the Allied armies, his summer palace burned and his treasures looted. Again in 1900, when evil counsels prevailed at Court and the Legations were besieged, swift punishment overtook the city. Kuang Hsu, the puppet Manchu sovereign of the day, and his masterful aunt the Empress Dowager Tz'u Hsi, narrowly escaped losing their throne. But the Powers hesitated to depose them lest in their fall they drag the whole fabric of Imperial Government to the ground—a thing the Allies wished to avoid, for feeble as that Government was, nothing stood between it and hopeless confusion at the moment.

As a matter of fact, the course of the dynasty was almost run. Eleven years later (October 1911) the Revolution which led to the establishment of the Republic broke out because, as Macgowan puts it, "the ruling house had ceased to display those moral qualities without which no power will long be tolerated by a people like the Chinese." Accepting the inevitable, the Manchus quietly abdicated and Peking, for once, was spared the excesses of rival soldiery.

In November 1911, Yuan Shih-k'ai made his dramatic entrance into the capital as self-imposed mediator between Republicans and Monarchists, and on February 12th, 1912, was elected President of the new Republic.

But it soon became obvious that Yuan had availed himself of popular discontent to break the back of the Manchus only for the purpose of furthering his own ambition. He gradually made

Juliet Bredon

himself autocratic ruler of Peking, and of China. Supporters, well-prompted, urged him to assume the Imperial Title and, like another Caesar, dazzled by the glitter of a crown, he graciously accepted, choosing to ignore the sullen mutterings of discontent throughout the country. But the magnificent ceremonies planned for his formal installation on the Dragon Throne were destined never to take place. Yuan was obliged to postpone them indefinitely and to direct that the petitions urging him to establish a new dynasty be returned to their authors for destruction. A disappointed and a broken man, death soon put him beyond the reach of further intrigue, and again Peking escaped the horrors of party strife within its walls.

Although since 1900 no great calamity has overtaken the city, there have been many minor disturbances and panics during these comparatively calm years. The clash of political factions, the ambitions of opposing statesmen, and the fall of cabinets still periodically disturb the peace.

Thus history repeats itself in Peking with extraordinary fidelity as it has for the last 2,000 years. Governments change, dynasties rise and fall, but the motives which set them up or throw them down are deep rooted in the structural character of the race, and that character changes only by the slowest processes of evolution. Shaped and tempered by the experiences of the past, it is only by a study of the past and its monuments that we may hope to have a sympathetic understanding of the soul of Peking.

Seen from a little distance with its walls and gate towers sharply defined against a background of hills, the city still appears what it was when it first became the capital of China in the Middle Ages, a Tartar encampment in stone, "a fortified garrison of nomad bannermen surrounding the palace of the Great Khan." Looking on temples, walls, tombs, or palace halls, we are reminded of changing religions and martyrdoms, of bitter sieges, of Tartar, Mongol, Manchu or Chinese conquests, of Persian, Indian and Jesuit influences, of gorgeous pageants, of traitors like Wu San-kuei, of soldiers of fortune like Chu

Yuan-chang, "the Chinese Haroun Al Raschid," of Kublai Khan who made Peking the Capital of one of the largest empires the world has ever seen, of Yung Lo, the great builder, of K'ang Hsi, contemporary of the "Roi Soleil," of Ch'ien Lung, soldier, administrator and model sovereign, and of Tz'u Hsi, the woman ruler, strong as the strongest man, who twice fled from the city before the Allied armies of the West.

Many of the oldest monuments have disappeared, as a glance at Father Hyacinth's map will show, because the Chinese have been too indifferent to preserve them. It is a thousand pities that posterity can never know this vanishing world of Eastern splendour at its height. But let us not forget that in its best days all that was most worth seeing was rigorously forbidden to the public. Peking, like Lhassa, remained for centuries a place of mysteries, of closed gates and barring walls. Unlike those of Lhassa, however, the secrets of China's capital did not prove disappointing when they were revealed. Rather the wonder and delight of the temples and palaces, so long inaccessible, surpassed all expectations.

Without doubt the majestic impression of Peking is due to its noble proportions. Nothing is petty, nothing small or insignificant. It is a city of long vistas, spreading over such a vast area that for many years geographers thought it the largest city in the world. Various authorities estimated the population at from two to four million and to their statements the inaccuracy of the Chinese census gave support. We know now that these figures were absurdly high. Peking, in spite of its large circumference, is not closely built over, and the majority of houses have only one story. Therefore we may safely set down the number of inhabitants at about a million.

Though no longer Capital of China, Peking remains one of the oldest "living" cities in the world and reverence is due to its ancient glory for, as Pliny says, "old age, venerable in a man, is sacred in a city." To those who respect history, Peking will ever remain Peking and not Peiping as it is now officially called.

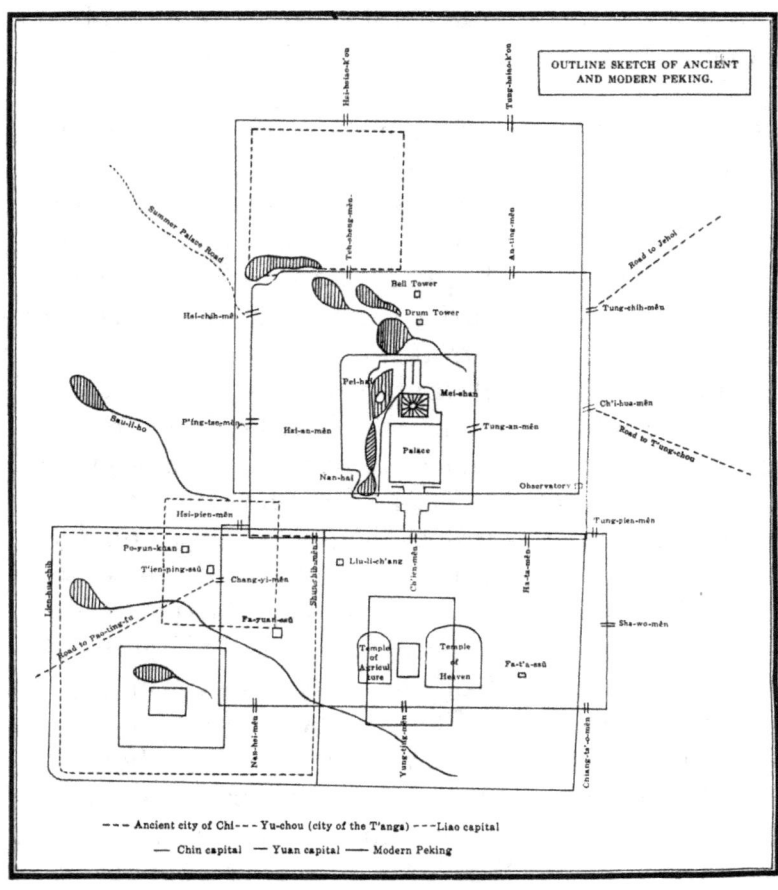

II. The Wonderful Walls of Peking

Walled cities exist all over China, grim reminders of the conquests and calamities against which their inhabitants sought to protect themselves. Few, however, can compare with Peking. The exceptional height of her crenulated walls, the grandeur of her many storied gates, recalling days of romantic warfare, awe and impress the spectator.

Kublai Khan first outlined the ramparts of the Tartar City in beaten mud during the 13th century. But the conquering Mings, mindful of the lessons of history and their own success in storming Peking, rebuilt these walls (a.d. 1421-1439) in their present imposing proportions and faced them with brick that in time has become durable as stone. Nevertheless, as defences they failed again. The Manchus broke through in 1644 by treachery, the Allied armies in 1860 and in 1900 by weapons no masonry could resist, and finally the Republicans in 1911 by the force of ideas against which nothing is impregnable.

Towering forty feet about the Manchu-Tartar City, higher than a two-story building, broader than Fifth Avenue, these noble battlements encircle the city. The moral effect on those who dwell within them is curious. Strangers they impress painfully at first with a sense of imprisonment. But in time this feeling changes to one of soothing security—to the comfortable sensation that the massive grey arms can keep out the rush and worries of the restless world.

For many generations no one was allowed to mount the ramps lest he overlook the Palaces.[10] It was only after 1860 that Prince Kung, anxious to propitiate foreigners, gave the order permitting them to walk on the walls— a privilege more precious then than now, as the streets of those days were unpaved and generally impassable, either ankle-deep in mud or dust according to the season.

---

10 This, according to Chinese ideas, would have been irreverent. Hence the police long forbade the construction of high buildings in Peking.

Juliet Bredon

Delightful views of Peking may be had from the top of these fortifications. On a clear day the plan of the four cities is easily traced. In the centre lies the Forbidden City—the innermost heart of them, shrouded in history and mystery, and surrounded by two miles of massive, pink-washed walls of its own.

Outside this is the Imperial City (Huang Ch'eng), formerly a fashionable residence quarter for Manchu and Chinese officials. It covers an area of nearly two square miles and used to be encircled by another set of walls. The Hsi An Men gives access to the western section, the Hou Men (Ti An Men) or Rear Gate, to the northern section. The Tung An Men on the east side balances the Hsi An Men on the west, and the place of the southern gate, which corresponds to the Hou Men on the north, is taken by the approaches to the Palaces.

Outside the Imperial City again is the Tartar or Manchu City. As its literary name, "City of the Nine Gates," indicates, it has nine entrances.[11] But it is commonly known as the Nei Ch'eng or Inner City in contradistinction to the Chinese or Outer City (Wai Ch'eng). When the conquering Manchus took Peking they relegated the people they defeated, as we have seen, to this Outer City where they were permitted to live and trade. The Tartar City was reserved as a garrison for the troops charged with the defence of the capital—the Imperial Guard or Banner organizations.

---

11 The gates in the south wall are the Ch'ien Men, facing the Palaces, the Hata Men and the Shun Chih Men; in the north wall, the An Ting Men and the Te Sheng Men; in the east, the Ch'i Hua Men and the Tung Chih Men, and in the west, the P'ing Tse Men and the Hsi Chih Men. (The literary, or official, names of these gates are respectively: the Cheng Yang Men, the Chung Wen Men, the Hsuan Wu Men, the An Ting Men, the Te Sheng Men, the Ch'ao Yang Men, the Tung Chih Men, the Fu Ch'eng Men and the Hsi Chih Men). A new gate, the Ho Ping Men, has lately been cut in the Tartar city wall between the Ch'ien Men and the Shun Chih Men. It is, however, a simple passage-way for the convenience of traffic and has no tower above it. According to old tradition, an army starting on a campaign must leave the city by the Te Sheng Men, or "Gate of Victory," and return by the An Ting Men, or "Gate of Peace."

The Wonderful Walls of Peking

GATE TOWER—TARTAR CITY

Juliet Bredon

To one of these Banners every Manchu belonged, as well as those Mongols and Chinese who assisted in the conquest of China. The colours of the banners were supposed to represent the elements. A superstition older than the Manchus had already divided Peking into quarters, each of which was thought to be influenced by one of these elements, so that the arrangement fitted in nicely with popular prejudices. The Yellow Banners stationed in the north of the city represented earth, said by the Chinese to subdue the element of water. The White Banners held the north-east and north-west of the City immediately to the south of the Yellow Banners: they represented metal, which is supposed to subdue the element of wood. The Red Banners occupied the district in the centre from the Ch'i Hua Men to the P'ing Tse Men: they represented fire, which subdues metal. Lastly, the Blue Banners were quartered at the extreme south of the Tartar City: they represented water, which subdues fire. Just as each element was supposed to neutralise the other, so those wise old sovereigns (profiting by the lesson of mutinous troops and rebellious generals) argued that their armed units, thus subdivided, would, in the event of insurrection, subdue one another. In any case the principle of harmonious distribution which even the modern servant pursues in the smallest household details— so deeply is it ingrained in the Chinese mind—was satisfied.

The southern wall of the Tartar City serves also as the northern wall of the Chinese City. To the east, west and south, however, it has lower walls of its own, pierced by seven gates and built (1553-1564) in the reign of Chia Ching by his Minister Liu Po-wen,[12] who utilised for them some of the stones of the

---

[12] The names of these gates are the Chang Yi Men (or Kuang Ning Men) and the Hsi Pien Men on the west; the Yu An Men (or Chiang Ts'o Men), the Yung Ting Men and the Tso An Men (or Yan Hsi Men) on the south and the Sha Wo Men (or Kuang Chu Men) and the Tung Pien Men on the east. Notice near the Yung Ting Men a curiously shaped brick-mound on top of which is a stone tablet with the character for "fire" engraved upon it. When the city was built, this mound served as a triangulation point from which the survey of Yung Lo's future capital was made.

Chin Dynasty (a.d. 1125-1234) palaces. More picturesque and more dilapidated than the grander defences of the Tartar City, they enclose a curious combination of town and suburb. Sometimes they look down upon the busiest commercial streets of Peking and again, perhaps half a mile beyond, on fields, vegetable gardens, or groups of farm houses as peaceful as a country village.

One of the finest *coups d'œil* of Peking is from the Ch'ien Men (Front Gate),[13] so sacred that formerly no corpse was allowed to pass through it. Here the visitor commands the wonderful prospect of the Palaces, the leading feature in every view of Peking, so that the eye is always returning to rest upon them. Because of the vast sweeping lines of their roofs, they look larger even than they are—look mountainous. Their yellow tiles, shining against the dark background of the hills, remain the supreme memory of the city—a picture changing, yet ever beautiful, beneath every caprice of hour and light, whether the noonday sun shines down on them so heavily that it seems to raise about them a swimming golden halo, or they lie under a blanket of glittering snow—whether the moonlight softly touches them with silver figures, or the storm wraps them in copper clouds. A symbol of the colourful past, they dominate the city, and always will, however much may change about them with the times.

The proximity of the hideous railway stations somewhat spoils the effect of the Ch'ien Men tower, and the masses of ugly foreign-style buildings, dotted here and there over the town, mar the harmony of the general view. That wonderful vista of the state entrance to the Palaces with the tree-covered Coal Hill in the distance was still more picturesque when Peking was untouched by modern influences. At the same time, since the outer gate-tower has been repaired, the squares tidied up and the whole avenue paved, the magnificent buildings beyond have approaches more worthy of them than formerly.

---

13 Men means gate, therefore it is tautology to refer, as people sometimes do, to the Ch'ien Men Gate.

Juliet Bredon

Immediately below us, as we stand looking down from this point of vantage, is the front door of Peking. The actual entrance as we see it now has been greatly enlarged and improved. Before the two wide passages were pierced under the wall, the main traffic of the city poured through the single bottle neck of the inner tower— a most inadequate inlet to a busy metropolis. The central doorway of the outer pavilion, which might have helped to relieve the congestion was only used by the sovereign under the old regime. After the establishment of the Republic, the Sacred Entrance became a general thoroughfare to mark the disappearance of Imperial prerogatives. It remained open for three days but was closed again for a short time by popular demand after the mutiny of February 29th, 1912.

Both towers of the Ch'ien Men are modern, the original ones having been destroyed by fire in 1900. The outer *lou* (tower) was then connected with the inner by curving walls; A typical Chinese bazaar where caps and cap buttons, belt buckles of worked brass and gold, pipes and snuff bottles, jade and enamels, matches and cheap kerosene lamps were sold, ran between the gates. When the Boxers fired these booths in 1900 as a punishment for selling foreign goods, the flames caught the great rafters of the tower. Dry with the dryness of ages, these beams that the Mings brought centuries before to Peking ignited easily. Columns of smoke and flame shooting skywards, met and mingled in an enormous black and orange whirl—a barbarically splendid sight. A few months after the Siege the scene was repeated when the inner tower accidentally caught fire, some say through the carelessness of Indian troops.

The Chinese, fearful of ill-luck overtaking the city, hastened to rebuild both towers. The construction of the inner one— requiring nearly five years to complete— was a remarkable sight. Its eight-storied bamboo scaffolding astounded Western architects. Not a nail, saw, or hammer was used. Poles and bamboos were lashed together with overlapping ends, thus permitting any height to be reached without waste of lumber and with the minimum of labour in construction and removal,

The Wonderful Walls of Peking

while a sloping gangway of boards tied together allowed the workmen to carry up the bricks and mortar in cloths according to their custom. Finally the painters were ordered to paint false muzzles of cannon on the wooden shutters as before. In the face of their recent lesson from the genuine guns of the Allied artillery, this shows how little the Manchus learned from adversity.

On the south side of the Ch'ien Men we see, close under the gate, two small yellow roofs which, though seemingly insignificant, cover two important temples.[14] Neither contains anything worth seeing from the artistic point of view. Each boasts only a single altar. But though many of the larger and finer shrines were never visited by the sovereign, he did not fail to stop here whenever he sacrificed at the Temple of Heaven or the Temple of Agriculture or whenever he returned after an absence from the capital—such as the flight in 1900.

The temple on the east side of the gate is of lesser importance—a shrine dedicated to the Goddess of Mercy (Kuan Yin). What gives it an interest for Westerners is the fact that in its tiny courtyard—a space scarcely larger than a ship's cabin—American soldiers killed on or near the wall in 1900 were temporarily buried.

The western temple, or Kuan Ti Miao,[15] is dedicated to Kuan Ti, a Han dynasty hero who opposed the usurper Ts'ao Ts'ao, the classical villain of the Chinese stories. While nobly attempting to do his duty, Kuan Ti was killed and afterwards decapitated in a.d. 219. His head was buried at Loyang (a former capital) in Honan by his enemies, who greatly admired his courage, and his grave may still be seen there. His body, but with a golden head added to it, was buried by his supporters in Hupei province. "Kuan Ti has been styled the patron saint of the Manchu dynasty, and indeed there are legends which, if they could be converted into history, might be held to justify his

---

14 Roofs covered with yellow tiles always meant that a building was either Imperial property or under Imperial patronage.
15 Sec Chapter XI. Also "*The Cult of Military Heroes in China*," by R. F. Johnston (*New China Review*, 1912) upon which this account is based.

claim to that position."... According to one of these stories, Kuan Ti issued from his temple in Peking during an attack on the Forbidden City by a band of rebels in 1813, and intervened so vigorously on behalf of the Imperial House that the rebels were soon put to flight. Several other miracles of a similar nature are attributed to him. No wonder then that "every Emperor of the Manchu dynasty from Shun Chih to Kuang Hsu showed favour to the cult of Kuan Ti, and showered honours upon him, since they so often needed his support to prop the insecure fortunes of the reigning house." Various temples were erected to him in the capital including a private chapel in the Coal Hill grounds, where even the last Emperor deputed one of the princes to perform religious rites at certain seasons.

But Kuan Ti's most famous and most popular shrine in Peking is undoubtedly the one at the Ch'ien Men, built for him by a Ming Sovereign in 1387. It is on record that the Emperor Ch'ung Cheng, the last of that line, accompanied by his Prime Minister Chou Yen-ju, paid a nocturnal visit to this little temple and called upon the resident soothsayer to summon the spirit of the great warrior. While His Majesty was burning incense at the altar, Kuan Ti suddenly materialised himself and went down on his knees, as though he were a minister of state being received in audience by his sovereign. The Emperor saluted him in return, and questioned him about the national and dynastic prospects. "There is no hope," was the spirit's reply, "too many baneful influences are at work." Here the Prime Minister broke in with the remark: "What baneful influences do you mean?" The spirit smiled faintly and answered: "You yourself are worst of all." It was not long after this incident that Chou Yen-ju, a corrupt and incompetent official, was impeached for ten heinous crimes and sentenced to commit suicide—too late to avert disaster from the monarch whom he served so badly.

The Wonderful Walls of Peking

GATEWAY IN TARTAR CITY WALL

21

Kuan Ti still ranks next to Confucius in the spread of his worship which was connected with the Official Cult, and a shrine to him used to be an accessory of public buildings, not excepting Buddhist, and even Lamaist temples like the Yung Ho Kung. Moreover his name is a household word for valour and patriotism and "time has raised him to a pitch of popularity... independent of his position in the official roll of divinities, and... hardly affected by the total withdrawal of such recognition."

For his good advice and assistance in time of trouble, many high-sounding titles have been bestowed upon him, including the quaint appellation of "Demon Queller of the Three Worlds" which was accompanied by a special patent, or golden warrant, and the presentation of an embroidered robe and state cap, deposited in this very temple under the Tartar walls.

Every emperor down to the days of Kuang Hsu showed his appreciation of the popular hero by offering "small sacrifices" at this his central shrine, rebuilt in 1828. Let into the wall of the reception room, where Their Majesties rested behind the tiny sanctuary, is an unusually thick slab of old jade carved in a bamboo design. The leaves are cunningly arranged to form the characters of a poem, and an inscription attributes the picture to the brush of Kuan Ti himself. The tablet was brought to Peking from the south under the early Manchus with Kuan Ti's iron seal which disappeared in the Boxer convulsion.[16]

No one should leave Peking without taking the walk along the wall from the Ch'ien Men to the Hata Men,[17] the next gate to the east.

---

[16] Among his other offices, Kuan Ti held the honorary and invisible presidency of the well known "Heaven and Earth Association," or Triad Society, an organisation akin to the Boxers. "All lodges," says an authority on this much-dreaded secret society, "have shrines to Kuan Ti... whom the members seem to regard as their tutelar deity."

[17] Popularly so-called after the Hata Wang (prince) whose palace used to be in this neighbourhood. Outside this gate is a curious old well, fed by a spring said to be connected with the sea. Many years ago when floods threatened Peking, the people closed this well-mouth with the effigy of a turtle (in cast

The "Fox Tower"—Tartar City Wall

iron) at the same time promising this animal that it should be released at the signal for closing the gates, the beating of a gong. The wily inhabitants, however, who wished the turtle to stay in its place, used a bell instead of a gong so the poor creature still remains on duty at this post. There is a well-known old Pekingese saying referring to this incident: "The city has nine gates, eight gongs and one bell."

Juliet Bredon

From this vantage point the Chinese bombarded the Legations in 1900, and foot by foot the besieged garrison contested it. The remains of one of the barricades, constructed of bricks from the wall itself, are still visible above the Water Gate, where some of the bitterest struggles of those memorable days took place and the guns of the Relief Column shelled the Palace in just retribution.

After the Siege the Powers demanded this portion of the wall handed over to them to be patrolled by their troops as a measure of protection to the Diplomatic Quarter, lest such a commanding position might at any time again prove a menace to its safety. To defend it, adequately iron gates were put up, loop holes made, subterranean passages constructed, and a wireless mast erected by the Americans in order that no subsequent uprising should ever cut off the Legations from communication with the sea.

Later the paved walk from gate to gate, a favourite promenade of Peking residents, was made. Smooth and free from vegetation, this strip is kept neat, unlike the remaining thirteen miles of wall under Chinese control where a narrow pathway, rough and uneven, meanders between the shrubs and grasses that spring up after the summer rains like a luxuriant jungle, forcing their way through the brick pavement from the rich mud below.

From one side of the wall we look down upon the Legation Quarter where many men of many minds have constructed an inharmonious whole, contrasting unfavourably with the dignified unity of the Palaces beyond. Truly the Chinese understand better than we how to adapt their buildings to the surrounding landscape—the frame to the picture, and the picture to the frame. Below the other parapet lies the Chinese City. In summer when all the trees—of which almost every little courtyard contains one or two—are in leaf, it gives the impression not of a town but of a huge park dominated by the blue dome of the Temple of Heaven which rises like a graceful stone flower above the foliage.

The Wonderful Walls of Peking

The Hata Men, or Gate of Sublime Learning, is typical of all the other towers; 99 feet high, it allows free and uninterrupted passage for the good spirits who soar through the air, according to the necromancers, at a height of 100 feet. The system of double doorways connected by walls which extend in semi-circular form— the convex side towards the country as a double protection to the inner Men that opens directly into the city—is common to most of the gates. So are the archways of solid granite, the painted cannon on the portholes and the heavy wooden doors that, until a few years ago, were closed at night. The brass cannon, which under the last Mings and early Manchus flanked the city gates, have disappeared long since. It is odd to see the enceintes, for so. many centuries filled with armed men and noisy with the blare of trumpets and gongs (for to terrify the enemy by deafening him was half the battle according to the old Oriental idea) now devoted to peaceful industrial purposes such as coal yards, or open air bazaars where cheap pottery is sold.

From the south-east corner of the wall beyond the Hata Men one could look down upon the canal and the ramparts of the Chinese City in the days before the Republican Government forbade this liberty. The East pavilion was worth inspecting. The Chinese call it the Fox Tower and believe it to be haunted by a fox for whose ghostly comings and goings its doors are left open. This was the tower shelled by the Russians in 1900, and we can see where the huge hole in the splendid roof has been economically but inadequately repaired with pieces of zinc. The large pillars and cross-beams which form the skeleton of the tower, the ladders covered with a velvet carpet of dust leading from story to story, were, fortunately, uninjured. An abode of bats and swallows nowadays, the tower in its perpetual dusk evokes an eerie feeling. Little imagination is required to believe it indeed haunted. But the ghosts we see there are the ghosts of Mongol or Ming or Manchu warriors in velvet and satin uniforms, holding in their shadowy hands bows and arrows, twisted pikes, or clumsy jingals.

Juliet Bredon

The most important landmark of the east wall, however, is the Observatory, called by the Chinese the "Stargazing platform," built on a buttress higher than the wall itself. The tall tower of the Persian astronomers[18] erected here by Kublai Khan about a.d. 1280 stood at what was then the south-east angle of his capital, which did not extend as far south as the present Tartar City. When the Ming Emperor Yung Lo tore down the southern wall and extended the city to the present line of the Hata Men and Ch'ien Men, he also repaired this building and appointed native astronomers to serve the crude bronze instruments of the day. Thus long before the Jesuit Fathers brought Western knowledge to China, we find that Orientals had worked out an astronomical system of their own. They believed the earth was the centre of the universe and that the sun, moon and stars revolved around it.

In 1685, when six Jesuits came from France, they brought with them a large bronze celestial globe as a present from Louis XIV to the Emperor K'ang Hsi. At that time the famous Father Verbiest was in charge of the Board of Astronomy in succession to the great Father Schall. Verbiest controlled the Observatory until 1688 and introduced Western mathematical precision in the science of astronomy instead of the old approximate methods. The Chinese proved themselves apt pupils. They soon learned to compute eclipses, but when the moment of the eclipse arrived, the Members of the Honourable Board reverted to their old superstitions. Arrayed in official robes, they assembled in the courtyard and frantically beat gongs to scare away the dragon about to swallow the sun or moon.

It was from the elegant designs of Father Verbiest that Chinese artisans cast and modelled handsome dragon-wreathed bronze instruments to replace the older instruments made, at the order of the Mongol Khan by Huo Shou-Ching, a Cantonese astronomer of the 13th century, and still preserved in the courtyard below the Observatory platform. Some of these were removed after 1900 by order of the Kaiser to impress the

---

18 It is curious to observe that among the astronomers here we find at that time a Byzantine called "Gaisue" (Yule, *Marco Polo*).

The Wonderful Walls of Peking

Chinese with the terrors of German vengeance and at the same time to decorate the terrace of the Orangerie at Potsdam. According to one of the stipulations of the Peace Treaty between the Allied Powers and Germany (1919) Verbiest's masterpieces have now been returned.[19]

Though historically their site is of the greatest interest, the actual buildings of the Observatory are modern. The octagonal tower of the Mongols and the Mings was replaced about 1800 by a wooden structure which in its turn has been superseded by the substantial brick terrace of to-day.

The Imperial Granaries and the Examination Halls used to be in this section of the city. The former, on the east side near the moat, served as store-houses for the tribute rice that constituted part of the Bannermen's pay in kind, and was brought up the Grand Canal from the Yangtze Valley.

Of the Examination Halls, where the hopes of generations found disappointment or fulfilment, nothing now remains. Built by the Ming Emperor Yung Lo they were originally a collection of tiled sheds, suggesting cattle pens, in a large walled enclosure. Though architecturally insignificant, their moral importance was enormous. Every third year thousands of students came from the provinces to be examined in them for literary degrees on the old classical system, and the successful candidates received the plums of officialdom. According to our ideas, it was the competitive system carried to burlesque when men wrote essays on Confucian philosophy as a proof of their fitness to govern. The Chinese, however, took it seriously and the ordeal was severe. Candidates were kept in solitary confinement in their cells for three days and two nights, a board for a seat, another for a table, their only luxuries. If they died under the strain, as sometimes happened, a hole was cut in the wall to allow the removal of the body, for the gates, once sealed by the Imperial Commissioners, could not be opened on any pretext. "In practice, however, this elaborate precaution did not prevent fraud. Essays were often bought beforehand, judges

---

19 For a full list of these instruments and the dates of their casting see *Encyclopaedia Sinica*, p. 403.

bribed to recognise certain marks, and needy scholars, too poor to bribe and too humble to impress, sometimes personated the dunces of great families."

The Emperor Kuang Hsu attempted the modernization of this effete system by his Reform Decrees of 1898. Yet it was only after 1900 that the Empress Dowager Tz'u Hsi succeeded in sweeping away the classical examinations, which she wisely realised constituted the chief obstacle to any effective reform of the body politic, and replacing them by modern educational methods. But she took pains to gild the pill for the *literati* by pointing out that the colleges existing in the time of that model ruler Duke Chou—3,000 years ago—were conducted on lines not very different from the foreign universities of the present day, that in establishing similar institutions China was not copying the West but only reverting to her original system—far older than the one she abolished, which was after all quite a modern innovation, having been introduced for the first time under the Ming dynasty.

The Examination Halls had outlived their usefulness. Empty and neglected, they fell into ruin. Some say that the Legations after the Siege, being in need of repairs and finding difficulty in obtaining bricks, bought the material from these tumble-down buildings for reconstructing diplomatic compounds. Whatever truth there may be in this story, one thing is certain—nothing now remains of the gateway to Chinese officialdom but a memory.

The view from the Observatory at the sunset hour is delightful. The day ends in a glowing brilliance with the western sky all fever red. The violet masses of the hills, which form so conspicuous a background in all views of Peking that they soon assume the aspect of loved and familiar friends, stand out sharply. Then as the light fades, their outlines soften. They seem to withdraw little by little, almost regretfully, into the shadows. Gradually one by one the monuments of the city, the palaces, the Coal Hill, the temples, follow their example, fading away in a soft twilight until, last of all, the gate-towers and the walls themselves dissolve into greyness and—it is dark.

III. The Legation Quarter And Modern Peking

The Legation Quarter is the centre of foreign life in Peking. Within the walls of this little international settlement one finds nearly all the conventional buildings of our civilization—churches, banks, shops, hospitals, clubs and an hotel. Each architect has attempted to bring a fragment of his own country overseas, so that bits of America, of Holland, of Italy and Japan stand side by side, and the effect of this combination of styles and periods surrounded by fortress-like defences is most curious.

Yet even this unromantic looking corner of the city has a romantic history. The streets, whose well-ordered ugliness suggests uneventful obscurity, are full of Siege memories of the dark days of 1900. They were once illuminated by human torches when the fanatical "Harmonious Fists" set fire to native Christians. Their walls still show shell and bullet marks. At least one garden has Boxers buried under the lawns. Even that prosaic ditch, the Jade Canal, has run blood. Its poetical name, so little in keeping with the trickle of dirty water that flows between brick parapets, is due to its original source—the wonderful spring of Yu Ch'uan Shan (the Jade Fountain) fourteen miles beyond the town.[20]

Before the Siege the Jade Canal emptied itself into the moat outside the Tartar walls through a black-mouthed tunnel with a rusty iron grille. This was known as the Water Gate—a place of historic interest because the troops who relieved the Legations crept through its bars in single file. No one who saw that scene will ever forget it—the bullets flying through the air as the Chinese made a last desperate attempt to keep back the foreigners, the white-haired British general quietly murmuring: "Thank God!" as he saw the besieged, whom he had been told half an hour before were all murdered, pouring out to welcome him; the handsome Indian troopers with tears in their eyes.

---

20 See Chapter XIV. A part of the Jade Canal has now been culverted.

Juliet Bredon

The grille was removed when the Chinese" brought the railway inside the city,[21] an underground outlet made for the water, and the wall pierced to allow access to the station.[22]

Dramatic as they were, these Siege days are not the only exciting times the Quarter has seen. How often since have its quiet streets been filled with processions of refugees! The plague scare of 1911 brought foreigners from all the outlying parts of Peking to seek shelter in it. ' But when the Manchus abdicated, when the Republican divisions mutinied in 1912, when Yuan Shih-kai died, when Chang Hsun made his coup for the restoration of monarchy in 1917, and when the leaders of the Anfu party fled from popular wrath in 1920, numbers of Chinese officials also came to take refuge behind the loopholed walls, bringing with them cartloads of valuables and provisions. In 1917 the Quarter had the honour of giving asylum not only to the President of the Republic but also to the trouble-maker Chang Hsun himself, who, when he saw the game was up, claimed sanctuary there.

Before the events of 1900 the Diplomatic Quarter, as such, did not exist, though most of the Legations were situated on or near the Chiao Min Hsiang (Street of Intercourse With the People),[23] so named because here, under the Manchu rule, tribute-bearing envoys like the Koreans, Mongols and Thibetans were given lodgment. However unflattering, it is a fact that the Manchu sovereigns long persisted in regarding Western diplomats in the same category as these messengers from tributary states. Did not so enlightened a monarch as Ch'ien Lung send a mandate to George the Third describing

---

21 Their prejudice against allowing a train to pass through even the outer walls was very strong and, until the Powers insisted on a more convenient arrangement, the nearest station to the capital was at the suburb of Ma Chia Pu outside the Yung Ting Men.
22 Peking is symbolized by a dragon, the Hata Men and Shun Chih Men being its eyes, the Ch'ien Men—its mouth, etc' When a rift was made in the body of the dragon by the cutting of the Water Gate, the wealth of Peking—"the dragon's blood"—oozed out through it, says a local proverb.
23 This is now Legation Street, a macadamized thoroughfare very different from the straggling, unpaved road of pre-Siege days.

The Legation Quarter and Modern Peking

himself as "swaying the wide world" and saying: "You, O King, live beyond the confines of many seas. Nevertheless, impelled by your humble desire to partake of the benefits of our civilization, you have despatched a mission respectfully bearing your Memorial.[24] To show your devotion you have sent offerings of your country's produce. I have perused your Memorial. The earnest terms in which it is couched reveal a respectful humility on your part which is highly praiseworthy.... As to your entreaty to send one of your nationals to be accredited to my Celestial Court and to be in control of your country's trade with China, this request is contrary to all usages of my dynasty and cannot possibly be entertained... "[25]

After the war of 1860 the Manchu Court was forced to allow the establishment of Legations in Peking. But that they were still considered a necessary evil to be kept at arm's length if possible, is proved by the cynical offer of the old Summer Palace site (the buildings of which the foreigners had themselves destroyed) as a diplomatic enclosure, and later another tract of land outside the west wall. Both offers were refused on the advice of Sir Harry Parkes who understood the situation and saw through the ruse for keeping foreigners outside the capital.

The oldest owned foreign property in the Quarter is the Russian Legation compound, though the Russian was only the third flag to be hoisted over a Legation in Peking (July 1861). For 300 years, however, Russia had had relations with China, profiting by the relative sureness of her land communications as compared with the rare and difficult sea-communications of other nations in early days. Chinese historians of the 14th century tell us of Russians resident in Peking at that time and even of a company of Russian Guards in the service of China's sovereigns. Moreover in a.d. 1619, Russian caravans brought the first sample of Chinese tea to Europe. The first Chinese diplomatic mission to any Western State was to the Court of the Russian Empress Anne in 1731, and we read how it was

---

24 This reference was to Lord Macartney's Embassy.
25 See *Annals and Memoirs of the Court of Peking,* by E. Backhouse and J. O. P. Bland, and Lord Macartney's *Embassy to China.*

received with great honour in the Kremlin and performed the ceremony of the "k'o-tow" or prostration, which most of the foreign envoys refused to perform at the Manchu Court and which was a bar to their reception for many years.

The present Russian Legation site was the place of residence of even the earliest Russian special missions from the latter half of the 17th century, including Baykoff's embassy in 1654.[26] Known as the Nan Kuan, or Southern Hostelry, it was designated in 1698 as the lodging of the official Russian caravans, started more or less regularly from that date and continued until 1762 according to the Free Trade stipulations of the Nerchinsk Treaty of 1689.

In 1685, during the early years of the reign of Peter the Great, occurred an apparently trivial episode leading; to permanent Russian representation in China—a frontier fight between the Albazines, a small colony of Russian pioneers who had settled at the fort of Albazin on the Amur River, and the Chinese. After a desperate resistance lasting two years, the Chinese conquered this little colony and captured about fifty prisoners. When generously given their freedom, the Albazines accepted K'ang Hsi's proposal to settle in Peking,[27] intermarried with the natives and, in fact, became Chinese in everything save their religion, which they faithfully preserved.

Some years later (in 1727) the Kiakhta Treaty between Russia and China gave the right of residence in Peking to a Russian ecclesiastical mission which had, moreover, certain semi-diplomatic powers, but was primarily the official recognition of the religious needs of the descendants of the Albazines. The Nan Kuan was then turned into a cloister for the missionaries and so remained until, after the Tientsin Treaty of 1858, the Archimandrite gave up his compound for Legation use and moved to the Pei Kuan in the north-east

---

26 See *Russia, Mongolia, China*, by Baddeley. The same compound was. apparently used by the first Dutch and Portuguese embassies.
27 In recognition of their bravery they were enrolled in the Emperor's own bodyguard and incorporated in the Yellow Banner.

corner of the Tartar City, where the Albazines on their arrival had originally been ceded a small piece of land for a chapel.

The actual church in the Russian Legation (no longer devoted to religious ceremonies) is the oldest foreign building in the Quarter. It was first erected in 1727 by the Manchu Government for the use of the Orthodox Missionaries, recognised that same year by the Kiakhta Treaty, but has frequently been repaired till now little of the original structure remains.

The French and British, who only acquired property in Peking long after the Russians, were nevertheless the first Powers to establish Legations there as one of the terms of the Treaty of Tientsin (1858) ratified after the Allied campaign of 1860.[28]

The French found quarters in the *fu* or palace of the Duke of Chin, famous for its lovely garden. The Chin family, once rich and powerful, had fallen on evil days and the property was half in ruins. When the French took it over, some of the tumble-down out-buildings were full of crickets in small earthenware pots. Now in those days fighting crickets, like fighting quails, was a favourite sport among the Chinese. Champion animals often cost large sums, and the last degenerate representative of this noble family had squandered the remains of his substance on them. The Legation was somewhat enlarged after the Siege, part of the site of Chamot's Hotel being added to it. Of the original buildings, the chancery, formerly the chapel, is the most important which remains.

The British Legation has an equally picturesque history. Originally given as a residence by the Emperor K'ang Hsi to his thirty-third son (whose descendants had the title of Dukes of Liang) this *fu* was also falling into decay owing to the poverty of the noble owners. The British leased it from the Tsungli Yamen (the old Foreign Office) at £500 per annum. For forty years the rent was regularly paid, in silver ingots taken in a mule cart by

---

28 See *Histoire des Relations de la Chine avec les Puissances Occidentales 1860-1900*, by Henri Cordier.

the Chinese Secretary of the Legation to the Yamen every Chinese New Year.[29]

Many of the buildings were beyond repair. Part of the Minister's house, however, is the original palace of the Dukes of Liang and the state approaches guarded by stone lions, the open pavilions (*ting'rhs*) with their red pillars, and the quaint kiosks in the gardens were restored and preserved as far as possible, thereby greatly enhancing the picturesqueness of the Legation.[30]

The British always had the largest ground space of any Legation in Peking—an area still further extended after 1900 when the sites of the Han Lin College and the Imperial Carriage Park were added to it.[31] For this reason the British compound was chosen as the refuge for all non-combatants in 1900. Though the fighting here was never so severe as in the French Legation (most of whose buildings were destroyed) there is, none the less, much within its walls to remind us of a gallant defence. The Councillor's garden, for instance, was turned into a cemetery where hasty funerals were held, often under a rain of bullets. The upper story of the house suffered heavily from shell and rifle fire. Its verandahs became miniature forts defended by barricades of sand-bags—and "a motley collection these sand-bags were, such as probably never had been seen in defence works before." Every colour under the sun and every material was used to make them—silks and satins, curtains, carpets, and embroideries being ruthlessly cut up. Perhaps the hottest corner of the defence in the British Legation overlooked the Mongol Market, where the Children of the Steppes came to barter their turquoises arid skins for the luxuries of civilization. Strongly held by Chinese troops, it was a source of danger to the Legation until finally cleared and

---

[29] After 1900 the property ceased to be owned by the Chinese Government and became British Crown property.

[30] One of these kiosks, still in use, became the bell tower for the chapel. Its bell sounded the alarm for general attacks during the Siege.'

[31] In the Carriage Park the elephants and elephant cars, long used on state occasions by China's sovereigns, were kept. The elephants were sent as tribute from Nepaul and Annam.

The Legation Quarter and Modern Peking

burned in a sortie commanded by Captain Halliday who was wounded and received for his gallant action the only V.C. given for the Siege.

A piece of the north-east wall riddled with bullet holes and bearing the rough inscription (now nearly obliterated) "Lest We Forget," and a small monument near the Legation Gate commemorate the sufferings of the foreign community in that memorable siege.[32]

Once the French and British had established their Legations, other nations soon followed suit. Most of the newcomers rented or brought property near those already installed till at last, within a rectangle bounded by the city wall on the south, were situated all the Legations except the Italian, burnt during the Siege, and the Belgian.[33] The majority occupied approximately the same sites as they do now, except that before 1900 they had considerably smaller compounds and were separated from one another by groups of Chinese houses.

A notable exception to the general rule were the Americans who first occupied the property where the building of the Banque de l'Indo-Chine now stands. The ground was once privately owned by Dr. Wells Williams, the famous author of the *Middle Kingdom*[34] When the American Legation was first definitely established in Peking (July 20th, 1892), the French again proved their long standing friendliness towards America by offering hospitality to the Mission. This was gratefully,

---

[32] The Siege still waits for an adequate historian—someone to do what Trevelyan did for the Siege of Cawnpore. Meanwhile various interesting books on the subject have been published. *China in Convulsion* by Arthur Smith gives a good account of the Siege and its aftermath. *Indiscreet Letters from Peking* by Putnam Weale, though exaggerated and often prejudiced, is the most graphic and best known description of the Siege itself and the subsequent sack of Peking. *The Siege of the Legations* by Rev. Roland Allan is a simple narrative of daily happenings in the British Legation, and *La Defense de la Legation* de France by Eugene Darcy is a straight-forward and dignified story of a most important section of the defence.

[33] The German Legation was established somewhat later than the others on ground bought by the Kingdom of Prussia.

[34] A standard work which still holds an authoritative place among the books on China.

though temporarily, accepted. Later Dr. Williams' property was taken over by Colonel Denby, the new American Minister, who afterwards sold it to the Koreans, and finally it passed into the hands of its present owners.

At the conclusion of the Siege, the American diplomats moved for a time into the San Kuan Miao,[35] now the office of the American Military and Naval Attaches, while waiting for their present quarters to be completed in 1905. Congress appropriated $60,000 for the new buildings on the present site, taken over from Chinese owners, and these buildings were, with the exception of the Legation at Bangkok and the Embassy at Tokio, the first Legation buildings owned outright by the United States Government.

Near the first Legations were presently established the Inspectorate of Chinese Customs under Sir Robert Hart, "several banks, a post office, the little hotel kept by a Swiss named Chamot, a brave man with a fearless wife, whose courage and forethought materially assisted in provisioning the Legations for the Siege, and, last but not least important, Kierulff's shop. The opening of this store raised much objection on the part of the Chinese, because Peking was then, and still is, officially closed to foreign trade, and though a crack in the door of their seclusion had been made, the Chinese were very jealous of this crack being widened. The foreign Ministers proved, however, that the shop was necessary to supply their wants and gained their point. Accepting the inevitable, the Chinese themselves became the largest customers for Western

---

[35] The San Kuan Miao was once a Buddhist temple with a great reputation for sanctity among the Chinese. Tablets still standing in the courtyards record the various prominent men who earned merit by repairing it. A legend connects it with the last Ming Emperor. When he heard the rebel Li Tzu-ch'eng thundering at the gates of his capital, he sent a messenger to the gods at the San Kuan Miao asking what to do. The answer came back bidding him draw lots in the Chinese fashion with the bamboo sticks. If he drew the longest, he should boldly attack the foe. If he drew that of medium length, he should await the enemy in his palace, but in case he drew the shortest, he should commit suicide. Fate put the short stick in his hand and he accordingly committed suicide on the Coal Hill.

goods, especially the Palace eunuchs. Consequently Kierulff in early days did a flourishing trade in darning cotton, biscuits, condensed milk, saddles, cigarettes, painted watches, saucepans, insect powder, mirrors, etc.

When the Quarter was laid out in its present size and form (1901) it included the sites of all these buildings (most of which had been either partially or completely destroyed) besides additional land needed to enlarge the Legations and provide barracks for guards. The Italians and Japanese divided the Su Wang Fu where 3,000 native Christians had been lodged during the fighting (the leaves and bark of its fine old trees supplied them with food for the last ten days) and the T'ang Tzu, the mysterious Shaman shrine of the Manchu dynasty. The Belgians also obtained their present site, formerly the residence of the Boxer protagonist Hsu T'ung.[36]

The reserved area became an international settlement. Its business affairs are directed by an Administrative Commission. It has its own police force, its own electric light, and paved streets named in some cases—like the Rue Labrousse—in memory of those who gave their lives to defend them. Since the Legations re-built, they are surrounded by cleanliness and order, and the diplomats now live in a manner compatible with their own civilisation and with a reasonable assurance of dignity and safety.

Like a small island in a vast lake, the Quarter lies in the midst of the city of Peking—but a Peking much changed since pre-Siege days. The upheaval of 1900 affected the Chinese quite as much as the foreigners as far as the destruction of property was concerned. In their search for Christians, the Boxers did not discriminate where they set the torch; and the soldiers, once they joined in the melee, looted with an impartiality worthy of a better cause. Historic houses and handsome shops

---

36 One remembers him as the fierce old Imperial Tutor "whose ambition was to have his cart covered with the skins of Foreign Devils, and whose loathing for Europeans and all their ways was so uncompromising and carried to such an excess that, for several years before the Boxer uprising, he made it a rule to leave his house on Legation Street by a side door leading to the wall rather than set foot on the foreigner's road."

went up in smoke and with them art treasures that cannot be replaced. Much suffering inevitably resulted. Princely fortunes were lost, and later, in the re-arrangement of boundaries, many fine estates divided up.

But Peking has and always has had, a certain quality of immortality. Dominated, defeated, she can rise again like a phoenix from her own ashes. Upon the ruins of her venerable edifices and her ancient customs she can re-build a new life with new energies. Though the upheaval of 1900 was a heavy blow to the city, order was gradually restored. Frightened people crept back from their hiding places, raked over the debris of their homes, then timidly started to reconstruct. The cleansing fires, so cruel to the individual, benefited the community as a whole and municipal improvements began.

Edicts issued by the Empress Dowager Tz'u Hsi on her return to Peking after her flight to Sian-fu did much to pave the way for needed reforms, and to prepare the conservative populace for changing times though even she, with her unusual capacity for seeing how things were going, had no idea how far they would ultimately go. But the real credit for cleaning up the city must be given to Yuan Shih-k'ai and, under him, to the Republican Government.

The first and greatest innovations that altered the face of Peking—and to a large extent its life—were the modern paved streets replacing the old-fashioned dusty highways full of ruts and crowded with a chaotic traffic of camel trains, donkeys, mule litters, and sedan chairs. A macadamised road from the Hsi Chih Men to the Summer Palace for the convenience of officials going to and fro for audience, was the first example of a modern thoroughfare to be built. It followed a route that had existed for centuries and part of the original stone block pavement may still be seen purposely left on either side for the heavy, springless carts—antediluvian vehicles gradually giving place to motor cars and buses.

Since that initial experiment—nearly abandoned, by the way, when the first taxi to use the new road frightened a Grand Councillor's mule and spilled the dignitary into a ditch—many

The Legation Quarter and Modern Peking

miles of highways have been constructed —to the Western Hills, the Tangshan Hot Springs, to Tungchow on the Canal, etc. Within the city itself new streets are constantly being opened. Those past the Coal Hill and along the southern walls of the Forbidden City permit "close up" views of the palaces and the moats which stir the imagination.

Meanwhile a new police force, reasonable and courteous, is instilling some notion of necessary traffic regulations into a people who have no "rule of the road," but little idea of the difference in speed between a wheelbarrow and an automobile, and such scant respect for tram cars that funeral processions refuse to move off their tracks.

Had the first modern improvements not been carried out with discretion and due regard to popular prejudices, they would have aroused bitter resentment. Even though tactfully undertaken, alterations to the square in front of the Ch'ien Men were long opposed by the ultra-conservatives who objected to walls being pierced for railways, to electric light chimneys—in a word to all innovations which might spoil the *feng-shui* (luck) of the city. Strong protests were made against moving the stone lions outside the gate. Now these lions are very old. They are undoubtedly the same creatures which Sir George Staunton, who accompanied Lord Macartney's embassy to China, quaintly described as "Figures so unlike what they are meant to represent, that they might almost be mistaken for knights in armour with periwigs such as were worn in the time of King Charles."

The Peking populace feared that if these venerable beasts were disturbed—as was absolutely necessary for the re-paving of the square—they would be displeased. What was to be done? The problem was finally solved in a truly Chinese way. The lions were blindfolded by tying blue cloth bandages over their eyes—a curious concession to superstition in the 20th century— and then dragged, unresisting, to their new positions.

The scheme of changes included the opening of the Dynastic Gate in front of the Palace—a gate closed for generations. When the workmen removed the tablet of the Manchu Dynasty preparatory to putting up the new Republican name, Chung Hua Men, they found beneath the Manchu characters, and only half obliterated, the title of the Ming Emperors. Indifferent and unimpressed, they put this dynastic tablet in a convenient cupboard near by. But one of the first things Chang Hsun did on attempting to re-establish monarchy (July 1917) was to hang it up again, thus showing its enormous importance in the eyes of Chinese officialdom.

About the same time that the new Republican Government opened this Imperial Doorway for thoroughfare, it also admitted the public to much else that had long been closed and forbidden, as a sign that the city, like the country, now belonged to the people. Those quarters of the Palace Enclosures not actually needed for the residence of the President or the deposed Emperor became accessible by permit. A part of the former Imperial Pleasure Gardens was turned into a public Park, then called Central Park; likewise the grounds of the Temple of Heaven, the Temple of Agriculture and the Altar of Earth.[37]

With the advent of the Nationalist Government, still more drastic changes came to Peking, which ceased to be the capital of China and was officially re-named Peiping, as once before in the early days of the Ming dynasty. At the same time an attempt was made to impose the cult of Dr. Sun Yat-sen, the new national hero, on the city. His portrait and his "Principles" were painted in blue on the walls of the Palaces, Central Park was christened "Chung Shan Park" after his birthplace, and certain street names, reminiscent of monarchical tendencies, were changed to something less unpleasant to revolutionary ears.

But Peking has always had the strange power of receiving the impress of men and events and absorbing them into her own spirit—taming the wild Mongols, and civilising the fierce Manchus till they were fierce no longer. Untouched, untouchable, she remains herself while the winds and the rains slowly wipe portraits and principles" from her rose red walls,

---

[37] See Chapter XI.

The Legation Quarter and Modern Peking

and storms upset her Thrones. Made impotent politically, she leads in the Renaissance of Ideas.[38] Deserted by officialdom, she becomes the cultural capital of China. Conservative by reputation, she tranforms herself into one of the most modern cities in the country.

A striking new landmark, situated west of the Pei Hai and overlooking the lake, is the building just completed for the National Library. Inspired by the throne halls of the Forbidden City, it is one of the finest monuments of "Modern Peking" and a striking proof of how well the leading features of Chinese architecture can be adapted to suit the most up-to-date requirements of a public building.

Successor to the old Ching Shih Tu Shu Kuan, the foundation of which was authorised by Imperial Edict in September 1909, the present Library contains a Stack Room with shelves for 350,000 volumes, besides smaller rooms for special collections from the archives of the Jehol Palace, Yuan and Sung dynasty editions formerly preserved in the Nei Ko (Grand Council), a portion of the books saved from the Han Lin Yuan fire in 1900, etc., besides well-lighted reading rooms and other conveniences for scholars.

Yet this is but one of five libraries in Peking including a Children's library. In addition, there are thirteen centres where lectures are given daily to people unable to read. They form part of a national organisation "to spread general information and the ideas the Government wants its citizens to have."[39]

Perhaps because Peking has always been the place where the highest literary examinations of the land were held, the city maintains its position as an educational centre despite the many changes of recent years. There are three universities within its walls, the most important being the Peking National University (popularly called "Peita") owing its origin to the Reform Movement of 1898 and, therefore, one of the oldest

---

38 It is interesting to note that the Student Movement actually started in Peking on Sunday, May 4th, 1919.
39 See *Peking, A Social Survey*, by Sidney D. Gamble, m.a., Chapter XU, Education.

41

modern universities in China with a faculty boasting such famous men as Dr. Hu Shih, Baron Stael-Holstein and Professor Grabau. The biggest, but the most recently founded university, is the Peiping National University (popularly called "Pingta") comprising eight colleges formerly independent of each other but merged together by order of the Nanking Government.[40]

Peking can also claim a number of primary and middle schools, Technical Colleges, vocational schools, and special schools for the Blind,[41] for the Police, for Actors, for Industrial Apprentices, etc. Considering that prior to 1900 there were practically no modern schools in China worthy of the name and that the "Renaissance Movement" with its slogan "Save the country though scientific education" did not really begin until 1905, the building up of the new educational system in Peking stands out as a great achievement, particularly in years disturbed by civil wards and political turmoil.

"Next to ignorance," says Gamble in his valuable *Peking, A Social Survey,* "poverty is a the most serious of Peking's problems." But this, like so many other practical need of the community, is being attacked by the Municipal authorities. Quite lately an attempt was made to get the beggars off the streets and provide them with adequate food and shelter. General poor relief, though still far from adequate, has begun. Various philanthropic institutions —official and unofficial— in the city now run soup kitchens where hot meals are served, shelters for ricsha pullters during the cold months, orphanages and homes for the added. Poor houses, asylums for the insane (not normally found in Chinese cities), and hospitals with free wards, are indications that the authorities feel a new sense of civic responsibility. Though much of the help given to the sick and destitute root or remove the causes of poverty and misery, doubtless as China develops, as education becomes more

---

[40] For educational institutions due to foreign initiative, see Chapter XXI.
[41] The first Blind School was founded by E. G. Hillier, Esq., who, himself sightless, devised a system of Chinese Braille.

widespread, and as there are more and more industrial opportunities, it will do so.

A modern prison situated near the Temple of Agriculture is a hopeful step towards remedying one of the most crying evils of old China—the barbarous and filthy methods of treating and torturing criminals. A Community Service Group, a Lithographic Bureau for the printing of Bank notes, an Agricultural Experiment station which aims in course of time at the afforestation of the barren western hills—all are modern innovations. Likewise a new Industrial Museum, with a factory attached, employing six hundred workmen, where glassware, rattan, lacquer furniture, woollen, silk, and embroidered fabrics are made and sold.

A Municipal Fire Brigade controlled by the Police replaces the private fire associations of olden days. A "street cleaning force," dressed in special blue uniforms, spreads ashes on the main highways in icy weather, and sprinkles them in summer to lay the dust. The men work in pairs, carrying a large tub between them and throw water alternately by means of a willow basket at the end of a long pole. Strangers never fail to be amused and amazed at this unique method of street-watering done so neatly in the midst of a constant stream of traffic that passers-by seldom get a wetting, and regret that these picturesque "human sprinklers" are being gradually replaced by modern "watering machines."

Admirable and interesting as all this modern progress is, the big problem for the future of Peking, as for China, is to adapt the new standards to the psychology of the Chinese people. Days of transition often bring mistakes and "hurry up" modernity risks depersonalising everything. Between the two poles of the very old and the very new the pendulum swings to and fro. To hasten its movements without disturbing its balance is the difficult and delicate task which the thinking people of China have set themselves to do, well knowing one thing is sure—that morals and ethics have to keep pace with knowledge, or all is lost.

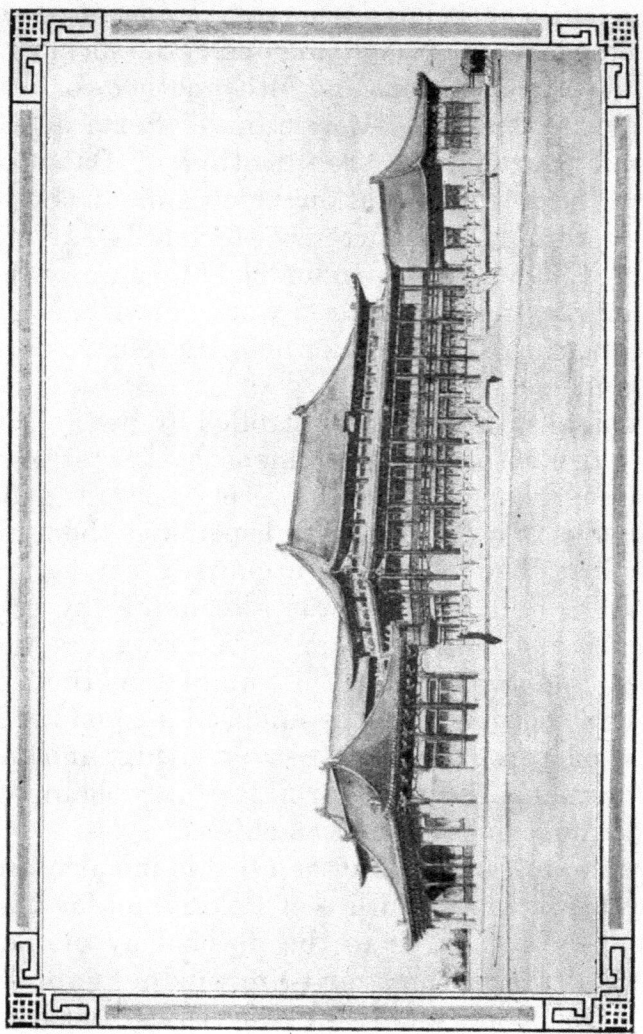

The National Library

IV. The Picturesqueness of the Past

Modern Peking is interesting because all development is interesting, but the greatest attractions of this old town are the ever-present reminders of a yesterday more strange and fascinating than to-day—a yesterday when there were no factories or railways to disturb the dreamy peace of Asia.

Now Peking has always been a city of strident contrasts and even before it ceased to be the capital, its life was no less variegated than the architecture of its buildings—the great blocks of German-inspired offices crowding up to the stately lines of the Palaces. On the one hand, the throbbing activities of industry gave life to the City. On the other hand, the political conservatism of an ancient seat of monarchy—traditional, loyal, and picturesque— still retained for its older quarters, the peace and romance of an English Cathedral town. For the visitor both worlds were—and still are—of compelling interest, doubly so because Peking's dead past is alive, and strangely tangled up with, its progressive present. Telegraph wires carry the world's news to papers printed in a mixture of Chinese and Western characters. Limousines pass camel caravans. Shop signs in gilded hieroglyphics are interspersed with those bearing announcements in quaint attempts at English. Tin-roofed offices are the neighbours of beautiful temples, and the establishment of a modern photographer stands beside the shop of a maker of Buddhist images. What remains of the older civilization is so picturesque that the traveller who arrives to-day in a period of social upheaval from a feudal past to a democratic present, is liable to regret the beauty of things mediaeval and desire to look back on the colourful life of olden days.

The Mings, as we have seen, were capable of planning a magnificent capital. We can still trace and admire the symmetry of the original design in the broad highways that cut the Tartar Town at right angles, three running north and south, three east and west, with handsome wooden *p'ai lous* at the crossings.[42]

But those thoroughfares so grandly planned were originally mud causeways divided, like all Gaul, into three parts. A central raised highway, forerunner of the present macadamised road, served for the lighter traffic, and deep gulleys on either side (since filled up) for the heavier carts. Being of loose earth, unpaved, these roads soon wore into holes where refuse collected and black pigs and scavenger dogs gathered for a banquet. Rain turned the lower levels into dangerous, swift-flowing torrents. The Chinese, however, argued "Once a road—always a road," and, persisting in the principle that what was made by their forefathers was good, attempted no improvements. The same "misguided spirit of reverence for the past left the excellent system of drains designed by Yung Lo untouched till it fell into disrepair and only broken culverts, traceable to this day, remained.

But discomforts were philosophically accepted by a public long ago grown accustomed to them. Physically, even the wealthy were not pampered either at home or abroad. Rooms were seldom heated in winter, except for the brick *k'ang*, or bed platform. Chairs were hard, carts springless. The climate was extreme. When travellers were not sticking in the mud ruts of the rainy *fu-t'ien* (period of greatest heat), they were stumbling through snow in the bitter ta-han (period of greatest cold), or else groping their way in the sand storms which the spring winds bring down from Mongolian deserts to spread like a dirty

---

42 Like the torii in Japan the *p'ai lou* is found all over China. The architectural principle, originating in the torans of the Hindoo *stupas*, is identical whether the material used be wood, brick or stone. Lofty columns, two, four or six according to the size and importance of the structure, support a rooflet more or less elaborate, the peculiarity of construction consisting in the way the great weight of this roof is balanced on supports comparatively light, and mainly on a single cross beam. The *p'ai lou* has no religious significance, as many people imagine. In ancient times any man who did a good or wise action, or any virtuous widow who refused to remarry, might have one erected to his or her memory, but the street p'ai lous of Peking appear to have been built simply for decoration.

The Picturesqueness of the Past

hand across the face of the sky and wipe the brightness from the sun. People whom necessity forced out of doors in the season of "yellow winds" covered their faces with cloths, giving them a ghostly appearance as they moved through the mustard coloured cloud. Feeble efforts were made (as they still are) to lay the dust by sprinkling the streets, by means of tubs and ladles, "but the contents of the tubs, not being water in those days but sewage," only added a sickening odour to other torments.

Still, though in old times men were less comfortable than at present, they had the consolation of a certain happy-go-lucky personal freedom. No police regulations enforced neatness and order. The streets were the living rooms of the lower classes who, unaccustomed to privacy, did not want it.[43] If a man found his shop crowded and desired more room, he encroached upon the sidewalk. A householder threw his rubbish outside his front door if he felt so minded. A peddler, driving a bargain, might block a small lane for hours with his portable stall, unrebuked.

These peddlers, some of whom still remain, were a feature of the life of old Peking—a feature and a necessity. In the days when circulation was difficult and women kept in greater seclusion, housewives did their shopping at their front doors. Only tea, rice and drugs were not peddled. But the purchase of cloth such as was not woven at home, of toilet articles and knicknacks, and of meat and vegetables was all made in the street.

Most of the hawkers had special musical calls like the fish sellers of London or the *Marchands des Quatre Saisons* of Paris—calls that may sometimes still be heard in the evening quietness. Many made known their coming by the sound of some primitive musical instrument. The blast of a shrill brass

---

[43] It is a significant fact that the Government of China, unlike that of old Japan or even of the Greek States or the mediaeval Italian cities, interfered comparatively little with the habits of the people. What a contrast between the sumptuary regulations of Japanese society where every detail of existence was fixed by law, or the Florentine statutes dictating even the number of a man's garments, and the pleasant toleration of old Chinese life gently guided by custom and convenience!

trumpet announced the knife-grinder, the twang of a rude Jew's harp, the barber. The fruit vendor went his rounds clanging two brass cups. The sound of a gong never failed to attract a crowd of idlers to see the performance of the trained sheep, the little dog and the wizened monkey, and at the beat of a certain drum all the children ran down the street after the toy and sweetmeat seller whose stock-in-trade, worth only a few cents, was a constant source of delight to them.

Late at night the "hot sweet potato" seller with his musical call, "Better than pears," catered to the gamblers and opium smokers, or the ricksha coolies working on night shifts and unable to go home for regular meals.

Not only shopping, however, was done in public. Horses were shod outside the blacksmith's door (as they are even nowadays), refractory mules given medicine on the sidewalk. The shoemaker sets down his portable last wherever a customer appeared. The porcelain mender would rivet a plate together anywhere. The pipe seller squatted in the shadow of a temple gate and, drawing his materials from the boxes that he carried suspended from a bamboo pole over his shoulder, fitted new stems into the metal pipes of the neighbourhood. Unfortunately among the picturesque, repulsive sights were common. Masseurs, butchers and chiropodists plied their trades in the open while passers-by obligingly made a detour to leave them room. Barbers shaved their customers on any convenient doorstep. Lepers and lunatics wandered about unchecked displaying their nakedness and their wounds.

When the curfew[44] sounded from the Bell Tower, most people went to bed. There was no prohibition against going out after dark, but, in the absence of street lamps, those obliged to do so carried a lantern. If the light blew out, as sometimes

---

44 One of the great bells weighing 23,000 pounds, cast to the order of Yung Lo, sounded the curfew, while the sonorous drum of the Drum Tower regularly beat out the watches of the night. The clepsydra, or water clock, that once measured the hour of the Rat, the hour of the Ox, the hour.of the Tiger, etc., giving the time to the whole city, disappeared after the Boxer outbreak. The big bell no longer hangs in the tower but stands, useless, in the street below.

The Picturesqueness of the Past

happened, they risked a fall into a ditch, but in olden days it was no disgrace to lose one's way in the most familiar places.

No police force existed then, but a night watch, reminiscent of Shakespeare's Dogberry and his men, patrolled the city fitfully. In addition, private enterprise supplemented government control, for life formerly was lived on the communal system involving collective responsibility—relic of a still older civilization. Shopkeepers and householders protected themselves and each other by guardians, and at night the city was musical with the noise of these men going their rounds, clapping two bamboos together "to let the thieves know they were coming." Indeed this sound, seldom heard nowadays, was as characteristic of old Peking as the smell of brandy is of Cognac.

As no system of water works had yet been installed, each householder drew his supply from his own bitter alkali well, or from his neighbour's by arrangement. Or, if sufficiendy rich, he bought "sweet water" from a hawker who brought it from a distance on a wheelbarrow.[45] The water carrier's barrow still makes the rounds of the outer city, squeaking abominably. But the rasping noise seems to tickle the Oriental ear agreeably, for the Chinese, like Helen's Babies, "wantsch to hear wheelsh go wound."

Were it not for the glorious sunshine and the dryness of the atmosphere, the population of Peking could never have survived the lack of sanitation. But thanks to these healthy climatic conditions, the city has always been comparatively free from the epidemics which prevail elsewhere in China, though from the look of the filthy streets of old Peking one would certainly have inferred otherwise.[46]

The squalor reached to the Palace gates. Even the open space around the Ch'ien Men was neglected, untidy, and

---

[45] A well known Chinese official admitted to me that his supply of "sweet water" from the springs of the Western Hills used to cost him 300 dollars a month.

[46] The temperature varies from 104 deg. Fah. to 20 deg. below zero; yet Peking is in the same latitude as Madrid, Naples and Philadelphia.

littered with refuse. Weeds pushed their way between the uneven flagstones of the pavement. Grass grew on the roof of the Dynastic Gate. Fallen pillars left gaps in the railings. Sometimes a rude attempt was made to close them by sticking up the broken stones and tying them in place with string. But it was easy enough to push a way through and not a few lazy pedestrians did so in order to avail themselves of a short cut across the square. This Sacred Enclosure, in theory rigidly forbidden to all, became the resort of idlers and beggars who sprawled there in the sun out of the way of traffic. Thus was typified the old Chinese tradition of splendour beside hunger, sung by the poet Po Chu-yi: "At the Palace door the smell of meat and wine. On the road outside one who was frozen to death."[47]

The greatest loss to the picturesqueness of Peking came with the passing of the Empire and the impoverishment of the Manchus. During the old regime all Manchu males were, theoretically at least, soldiers at the disposal of the Emperor and received allowances whether on active service or not. Many of them had ample means to satisfy extravagant tastes, while some were connected with the Court and enjoyed the prestige of official positions.

The old-style Manchu Mandarin was a striking figure. Tall and dignified in his official hat with jewelled button, his long robes of silk or sable, and his richly embroidered under-gown belted in at the waist with a carved jade or gold clasp from which hung his embroidered spectacle-case, his ivory chop-stick holder and his enamelled watch surrounded by pearls or diamonds, he had the gratifying effect of being an ancestral portrait of himself. And when he went to or from the Palace in his green sedan chair with extra bearers following behind, or in his closed Peking cart with a handsome mule caparisoned in red, and surrounded by outriders shrieking to clear the way for their master, no wonder the simple folk looked on him with respectful awe as he passed! How the whole patchwork of idlers—the bent old men and the pretty children with their

---

[47] *170 Chinese Poems*, translated by Arthur Waley.

slanting eyes and miniature pigtails sticking out in the five "Cardinal Directions," made haste to press themselves flat against a wall or slip into a sheltering doorway to watch his procession go by! The sight of his grandeur was an event in their dull lives—a kind of Lord Mayor's Show, pleasantly frequent and arousing not envy but pride.

Alas, many of these Manchus, shorn of their fine feathers, are now in actual want. Unable to conceive that their allowances would ever be reduced, they were unfitted to earn their living in a country where competition is bitterly keen, when caste privileges were withdrawn. Too long they had been taught to despise work and neglect scholarship; too long abandoned even their favourite pursuit of arms, their archery and riding, which once made them a vigorous race and for centuries sustained their vigour. As for the higher classes, they made the mistake of forgetting that it was necessary to be men as well as noblemen.

Their women, in the days of prosperity, lent a charming note of colour and vivacity to the grey old capital. Though the Manchu men in unofficial dress were only recognizable from the Chinese by a close and familiar observer, the women-folk have to this day a distinctive costume and coiffure—the long straight gown and waistcoat of bright pink or lavender, the quaint shoes with the heel in the middle of the sole, and the hair done in a high knot or mounted on a satin covered board which stands up cross-wise and ends in prominent wings. This odd and, one imagines, uncomfortable arrangement (part of which is often false and detachable) is decorated with bands of beadwork, handsome pins, and real or artificial flowers—sometimes with fringes of pearls. Its chief charm is the way in which the hair is made to serve as an elaborate frame, well suited to the Manchu type of features, and throwing into relief faces heavily powdered and rouged in remembrance of the supposed white origin which they claim. The unbound feet of the Manchu ladies contributed to an emancipation very striking when contrasted with the seclusion of other Oriental women. They were constantly seen in public, walking with stately grace accompanied by their servants. They gathered in groups, like birds of bright plumage, to gossip at temple fairs. They paid their visits or went to Court in carts or chairs, and a pretty face or a brilliant headdress might frequently be glimpsed through the window of a passing vehicle.

The number and variety of conveyances were among the sights of Peking in olden days, and from the exterior of a chair or cart the rank of the owner could be accurately judged. A reigning emperor or empress had the right to a yellow covered vehicle, an Imperial concubine to one of orange colour. Mandarins of the first and second degrees used the green sedan, those of the third and fourth the blue with four bearers. Humbler people sometimes employed a two-bearer chair, far lighter and less pretentious. Cunningly designed on a simple framework of bamboo rods not much thicker than a thumb, it was strong with the strength of yielding things. The Quaker colouring of its grey or steel blue cover was relieved by little touches of brilliancy peeping out at unexpected corners— ornamental knobs of wrought brass or arabesques of fine bamboo set in delicate patterns against a narrow frieze of red cloth. Sedan chairs gradually disappeared from the town with the advent of paved roads, but sometimes we still meet one of these frail little booths, like a suspended sentry box, in the suburbs, borne on the shoulders of two strong-footed and enduring coolies.

The mule litters, now so rarely seen, were once quite common. Before the days of railways, men from mountainous districts used them on their journeys to the capital. Wheelbarrows were also a familiar feature of the streets, bringing in country produce—rosy loads of radishes or dripping cabbages freshened for market in the filthy water of the moats. Under the walls strings of camels, far more numerous then than now, carried coal into Peking or bore merchandise away with slow measured step, perhaps to the plaintive lilt of a Mongol song. The ricksha, at present so ubiquitous, is a comparatively modern conveyance in the city, almost unknown until after 1900. Men and women rode far more in the old days

The Picturesqueness of the Past

and the variety of mounts was astonishing. Donkeys, with cloth pack-saddles, stood waiting for fares at street corners like cabs or taxis in the West. Mongols had their own riding camels whose paces were intolerable except to their masters. Manchus and Chinese preferred mules. Indeed the mule in North China is a magnificent animal, much finer than the commonly used Mongol pony—arid a handsome mule was a luxury of the wealthy. Surrounded by a group of mounted retainers, some splendidly attired young prince might often be seen riding one of these fine animals on a. high wooden saddle, studded with brass or silver and set on a saddle-cloth of velvet. Ultra-fashionable young men about town paid as much for such mounts as we would for a well bred hunter.

Besides all these methods of locomotion, there were a dozen different kinds of carts. The ordinary passenger cart—the Chinese "cab"—was a two-wheeled vehicle with heavy iron-studded wheels, and a body covered with blue cloth, descended from the rude "kibitka" of the steppes.

The Chinese open freight or omnibus carts remind one of the antique vehicles that may still be seen in certain parts of Italy. They are drawn by a mixed team of different animals, five in the traces, if it is a "full team," and a sixth following behind to do his share when required. Rope harness passed through iron rings loosely attaches the happy family which may include a cow pulling beside donkeys, ponies and mules. Neither brakes nor reins are used. The driver, who lives and sleeps with his beasts, scorns such aids. Walking beside his cart, or sitting on the edge, he seldom has recourse even to his long whip. His voice alone guides and encourages the animals and his Rabelaisian allusions are as picturesque as himself. Needless to say, only a Chinese driver can get any work out of these Noah's Ark teams, as the Allies found to their chagrin in 1860, when the native carters of the Expeditionary Force bolted.

The sensation of the unfortunate passenger forced to journey any distance on such a cart bumping along through deep ruts "like two lines of sunken rails," can only be compared to that of the man travelling across country on a gun carriage.

Juliet Bredon

Yet no other conveyance could have transported him and his goods over the abominable roads leading to the old capital. Many of them were highways made of blocks of stone loosely set together—a form of pavement (reminiscent of Roman roads) which the Chinese themselves say is "good for ten years and bad for ten thousand."

Though railways and motor buses have caused a decrease in heavy cart traffic, the caravan roads converging on Peking continue in use to some extent.

Outside the Hata Men, where most of the carters' inns are situated, it is interesting to watch the loading and unloading of the freight, still transported by men and beasts. A more dirty, cheerful and healthy-looking lot of fellows than the followers of the "open road" with their dusty hair wrapped in cotton cloths, and their long pipes between their teeth, would be difficult to find anywhere. From dawn to daylight's end they have journeyed over rough country with never a complaint, and when at last they reach the city, unload, and tie the tattered nosebags on their beasts, you will find them enjoying a copious dinner of cabbage and macaroni at some neighbouring stall, whose brass crescent proves the cook a Mohammedan co-religionist. Meanwhile such merchants who chose to join the caravan as passengers have dispersed (after a liberal gift of wine money for their safe transport) to fine private homes hidden behind non-committal walls.

A whole volume would not suffice to describe the famous and historical houses of Peking—the residences of high Chinese, Manchu, or Mongol officials who have lived in splendour and often ended in degradation. But mention may be made of one typical property in the north city belonging to the late Prince Ch'ing—a house which in the day of his glory sheltered over a thousand persons.[48] Originally the Ch'ing estate was half the domain of Ho Shen, the Grand Minister of

---

48 'In all Oriental countries the Turkish proverb: "If only a man have honey, the flies will gather," applies. The family system is the life-principle of the social structure, and every great man supports all his relations and connections as a matter of course.

Ch'ien Lung whose wealth, estimated roughly at 900 millions of Taels, was sufficient to excite the cupidity of an emperor, the greedy Chia Ch'ing. No wonder! "The flower garden presented to his favourite by Ch'ien Lung was one of the marvels of the capital in its day. It contained 64 pavilions, some of them decorated with Imperial yellow tiles, and had high towers at the four corners after the design of the Palace precincts, which was undoubtedly inviting disaster. The list of curios in his principal residence reads like the furnishings of a palace in the Arabian Nights. Thousands of sable garments, dozens of pearl necklaces, screens of solid gold, dinner services of jade, soup bowls of topaz, trees of coral, several hundred large rubies, several thousand fine sapphires, lacquer furniture inlaid with gems—these were only a few of his treasures."

"Now to be very rich is always dangerous under an Oriental Court. This is a truth learnt at the dear price of living over and over again. Yet the hoarding instinct is usually stronger than the fear of death itself in a race in which the horror of poverty seems, through ages of the fiercest life struggle, to have accumulated the blind force of unreasoning instinct.

"Ho Shen proved no exception to the rule. He was condemned to death on a trumped up charge after having been repeatedly and severely beaten to make him disclose the total amount and hiding places of his wealth, and all his treasures were scattered. Like the hypocrite he was, Chia Ch'ing issued a memorial explaining his motives in condemning his father's favourite: 'Now be it known that the only object in confiscating a Minister's property is to provide a solemn warning for the guidance of grasping officials... The actual amount of Ho Shen's treasure is a matter of supreme indifference to Us: We are only concerned to vindicate the principle of official honesty.' *Qui s'excuse—s'accuse.* Between the lines of this interesting document we read Chia Ch'ing's determination to deprive Ho Shen of his fortune and his power from purely vindictive and avaricious motives. But had the Emperor chosen, he might have impeached his Minister honestly, since he was, in truth, the canker eating into the heart of the great inheritance left by Ch'ien Lung."[49]

The history of Ho Shen's palace—the western half of which was given to the Ch'ing family, who were imperial clansmen—has become part of the history of Peking.[50]

Yet the passer-by can judge nothing of its splendours. It is always so in China. The finer the home the more carefully it is hidden behind high walls. Even when the front gate is opened, the view of the house within is impeded by a Spirit Screen which ensures additional privacy—that rare privilege of the rich and powerful in the East—and protect from evil influences. Our idea of a house as simply a lodging and a shelter from weather is quite foreign to Orientals. Moreover they value a residence rather for the size of its courtyards and the beauty of its gardens than the height or grandeur of its buildings. The amount of ground space of a fine Chinese establishment is, therefore, always large, and affords its owner the sun, silence, and verdure, so keenly appreciated by the Pekingese, who, in the days before public parks existed, spent much time in their own gardens.

As all compounds look alike from the outside, being simply longer or shorter lengths of wall, there is a puzzling similarity in the smaller streets—devoid of striking landmarks—which makes it very difficult for a foreigner to find his way about Peking. Over 4,800 *hutungs* (residential streets) wind and twist their way through the city. No wonder the first feeling that assails a visitor is bewilderment when his ricksha dives blindly into this maze![51]

---

[49] See *Annals and Memoirs of the Court of Peking*, by E. Backhouse and J. O. P. Bland.

[50] By the irony of fate, its glory was restored by the famous Prince Ch'ing, who played such an important role in the reign of Tz'u Hsi and built up his fortune by corrupt practices as notorious as those for which Ho Shen lost his head.

[51] The word hutung is, strange to say, not a Chinese but a Mongolian name originating under the Yuan or Mongol dynasty. The correct characters for hutting are formed from hu, an ancient name for Mongol, and t'ung a passageway (in other words, a Mongolian thoroughfare), but what the

The Picturesqueness of the Past

There seems to be no key to this Chinese puzzle apparently composed without design or forethought. But if you keep the main thoroughfares that cross each other at right angles in mind, Peking will no longer seem a muddlesome place. Then familiarise yourself with the points of the compass—by which all Chinese answer inquiries regarding direction—and you will be surprised how soon you can find your way about. It is not easy at first, however, to hold north, south, east and west clearly in your head amid the twistings of "Velvet Paw Lane" or "Fried Fish Alley."

Many of the old historic names of the huttings have been changed since the establishment of the Republic in order to do away with memories of former dynasties—a matter of regret to the historically-minded and to lovers of the picturesque. Thus *Huo-ch'iang* (Pot's Bottom) *hutung* is renamed "The Country Is Strong" street; "Turtle Shell" (*Wang-pa-kai*) has become "Ten Thousand Precious Umbrellas"; and of the two "foul smelling hutungs," the one in the east city is now called "May you live to be as old as the Southern mountains" (a classical allusion), and the other, in the west "Rank Conferred."[52]

Nevertheless a few of the smaller lanes still keep their original names, reminding us of old associations. In the *Tung Ch'ang Hutung*, the profligate eunuch Wei Chung Hsien[53] concocted his wicked schemes; in the *Ch'eng Hsiang Hutung* ('*Hutung* of the Prime Minister"), that cruel monster Yen Shih-fan, son of the chief of the Six Wicked Ministers of the Ming dynasty, died of starvation while still in the possession of wealth. After Yen Sung's property was confiscated "he was left with only a silver bowl with which he went about collecting alms"—obviously up and down the neighbouring *hutung* of "The Silver Bowl." But so deep was the popular hatred of this corrupt

---

Chinese probably did was to write down the Chinese sounds from the Mongol name Wu t'rh. See "The Hutungs of Peiping," by C. L. Arlington in *Guide to Peking*, published by the Leader, also "The Hutung and Its Inhabitants" in *Sidelights on Peking Life*, by R. W. Swallow.
52 For a more detailed explanation concerning these and other curious street names see L. C. Arlington's article, *The Hutungs of Peiping*.
53 See Chapter XV.

official that no one would give him anything or buy his last treasure.

Hindrances to traffic—especially in the old days— increased the stranger's difficulties in finding his way, often obliging him to make long detours. The poor beggar frozen at the street corner, the furniture movers bent under their heavy loads, the droves of pigs or sheep being herded to the butcheries, the lazy dogs asleep in the middle of the road, all contributed to force pedestrians into taking a round-about road to their destinations. But the long lines of wedding or funeral processions were the most serious impediment to traffic in the *hutungs*, often blocking them completely and for hours at a time.

Such processions may still be seen—the last patches of bright colouring left in the streets—and on certain days fixed by the soothsayers as "lucky,"[54] they follow one another at frequent intervals.

We Westerners long ago simplified our rites. Not so the majority of Chinese who cling to old traditions and customs despite the new Government's decree that in future "Red and White Ceremonies"—weddings and funerals—"should be conducted on principles of economy, simplicity and appropriateness."

Some of the "younger set"—especially returned students from Europe or America—break away from established conventions, however, when they marry. A short service in a public hall, or a friend's house, replaces the "drinking of the sacrificial wine" in the nuptial chamber. There are no "k'o-tows" to the Gods of Heaven and Earth, no prayers to the protecting Spirits of the Bed. Instead of sitting shyly in her room after the ceremony and allowing the guests to "tease her" with, rude

---

[54] The Chinese allow their every-day activities to be guided by the advice of fortune tellers and astrologers, and these seers have always been, in camp and court, a vital factor in shaping their destinies. When the Dictator Yuan Shih-k'ai wanted to consolidate his position by marrying his daughter to the Ex-Emperor Hsuan T'ung, the soothsayers found that the cyclical signs under which the young people were born did not harmonise. Yuan dared not push the point, and the alliance was abandoned.

The Picturesqueness of the Past

jokes, the modern bride, in a semi-Chinese gown of a pale colour (but not white because that would suggest mourning) drives to her new home beside her frock-coated bridegroom in an open landau wreathed with paper flowers. Before leaving the reception the young couple may even go so far as to be photographed together, the groom seated stiffly, hands on knees, the bride standing rigid beside him, both looking rather sheepish and ashamed of themselves.

"Very advanced, very advanced," the older ladies murmur as they take leave of their hostesses, the two mothers-in-law—a little shocked, and firmly determined that when *their* daughters marry, it shall be in the good old-fashioned way with "Dragon and Phoenix" engagement papers, and the red chair.

More expensive the old-style wedding may be, but who cares if one has to scrimp and pinch to make a good show before the neighbours? Besides the contributions of the guests can be counted on to pay for the marriage feast. The heaviest expense is the dowry that must be carried through the streets on open trays or tables for all to see—the clothes, enough to last for at least a year, and the wadded bed quilts embroidered with the figures of the "Hundred Boys," emblems of many sons.

Then on the great day the red bridal chair followed by the green chair of the "marriage dame" starts out for the bridegroom's home accompanied by bearers carrying lanterns and banners, a pair of geese (emblems of connubial felicity), musicians, etc. Unseeing and unseen in her tightly closed "flowery chair" what, we wonder as we watch her pass by, are the feelings of this young girl going blindly to the home of a man she has probably never set eyes on? Love, as we understand the word, has no part in them. It is a luxury forbidden to a respectable maiden whose wishes must be subordinated to those of her parents and relations. Personal desires would not only entail misery for the individual but strike at the root of the family system. Even should they exist they cannot, therefore, be considered.

Though an old fashioned wedding is an important and expensive ceremony, a funeral is ten times more so, for to economise on a funeral or attempt to modernise it, except in small details, shows a lamentable lack of filial piety and means "loss of face" in the community. There is a curious similarity—very strange to our ideas—between Chinese wedding and funeral processions, so much so that until the red chair or the catalfaque come in sight, we may easily mistake one for the other. There are the same tatterdemalion bearers carrying flags and banners, the same groups of musicians drawing melancholy sounds from gilded instruments like gigantic garden syringes. There are the same beaters upon gongs, round and yellow as full moons, that whenever the drum-sticks touch their thin and quivering surfaces, wail out volumes of protests.

But here the similarity ends. Instead of tables of gifts, the mile-long procession includes an empty sedan chair, like the riderless charger of the West, groups of priests, a white cloth shrine with a portrait of the deceased, lions and phoenixes made of evergreens, scrolls presented by relatives and friends, and paper effigies of servants, also models of carts, horses, books—in fact of everything the dead person used in life—to be burned at the grave.[55] According to popular belief, the dead must take with them all they require for a journey and a sojourn in another world and the only way they can do this is by having paper models made of their necessities. These, being consumed by fire, will follow them in smoke.[56]

Mourners dressed in sackcloth and staggering along under a sackcloth canopy supported by servants, immediately precede the coffin. They, like the rest of the procession, are directed by an official Master of Ceremonies, who at intervals signals for the music to stop and the wailing to begin. When he says, "Gentlemen, it is time to weep," a melancholy moan rends the

---

[55] These are undoubtedly survivals of the "living sacrifices" of antiquity, like the pottery figures and utensils found in Han and T'ang dynasty tombs.
[56] Lately, at the funeral of a certain man, a progressive, this old custom found ludicrous expression. Among the things carried for burning were imitation bottles of beer of which the old gentleman had been very fond in his lifetime. Also replicas of certain sick-room appliances which cannot be named here.

The Picturesqueness of the Past

air, and when he says, "Gentlemen, it is enough," the sobbing ceases.

The bier itself is an enormous wooden framework over which are draped gaudy red satin embroideries. But the coffin hidden beneath them is of plain wood or lacquer and far more dignified and seemly than "the loathsome dapperness of our burial caskets." Owing to its great weight, the number of bearers is always considerable. For an Imperial funeral over one hundred may be required. But 12, 24, 40 or 96 are commonly seen. The fact that these pall-bearers are unwashed beggars in torn, dirty green robes and battered hats—lent them for the occasion—does not detract in native eyes from the impressiveness of the cortege, all very gay and dishevelled in the best Chinese manner. The coolies are in charge of a foreman supplied by the undertaker. He walks in front of them and, by striking two sticks together, gives the signal to change the heavy poles from one shoulder to another. His two assistants throw into the air the circles of white paper supposed to represent cash, a bribe to appease evil spirits who might obstruct the path of the departed.

Under the Empire, the funeral processions of high officials were gorgeous affairs costing hundreds of thousands of dollars. How a great man lived was important to his moral standing, but how his family buried him could make or mar the reputation of that family. When a high dignitary reached an advanced age, his sons and grandsons were expected to present him with an expensive coffin, elaborate burial clothes, and a set of jade ornaments to be placed on his body[57]—pieces to fill the mouth, to close the ears, to lay upon the lips and hold the robes in position. Yet all these extravagances were nothing compared to the drain on the family finances of the actual funeral which

---

57 Jade was supposed to have the special property of preserving the body from decay, and we know that jade amulets were buried with the dead as far back as the Chou dynasty. Couling says—see *Encyclopaedia Sinical*—that in the Han period an amulet in the form of a cicada was placed on the tongue of a corpse, the cicada being an emblem of resurrection, while the pieces placed over the eyes were in the form of fish, symbol of watchfulness.

might entail several days travelling with the coffin to distant ancestral tombs.

Such wastefulness appears shocking to the new Nationalist Government. Hence the decision reached at a meeting of the Committee on Ceremonial Rites and National Costumes that "in future funerals must be more democratic." The old picturesque ceremonial has been proscribed and the Peking Undertaker's Guild warned to discard garish trappings, just as the people as a whole have been warned that in the choice of national costumes, the principles of simplicity, beauty, convenience, hygiene and economy must be emphasised.

However good Republicans we may be, however much we may admire "modern Peking," we must admit, and admit it sadly, that we regret in many ways the picturesqueness of the past. Life—and death too—without the stimulus and extravagance of a Court, is becoming drabber. Alas, that Progress must go hand in hand with ugliness! Or must it? Peking, like China, stands at the cross roads where "the old and the new meet and mingle." Will it not be possible some day—when the transitional period is over—to combine the best Chinese traditions with the necessary modifications of western civilisation? May not the metamorphosis take place without giving century-old grey brick walls for new red brick barracks, graceful silk garments for vulgar semi-foreign clothes, poetic legends for marketable facts, and quaint harmonies of splintered tones for blaring jazz music?

Meanwhile Peking—a true-born royal city—gives an impression of patience and philosophy, accepting where she must, clinging to beauty where she can.

V. The Forbidden City

The Forbidden City[58] which lies, like the kernel of a nut protected by a triple shell of walls, in the centre of Peking—is by far the finest sight of the old capital, both artistically and historically speaking—a haunted city of loveliness peopled by the Imperial ghosts of vanished emperors. What poetic suggestion in the very name—a Forbidden City of palaces reserved for a Son of Heaven! What dignity in the conception of a sovereign hidden away in a secret place from the people of a vast empire whose profound reverence willingly accepted his seclusion! What noble idealism in the immense spiritual and temporal power placed in his hands, in the tradition of his divine descent, and the immemorial dignity of his office!

To have seen the home of these God-Emperors, therefore, is to have seen something much more significant than a group of imposing buildings, even though they stand on the same site—or nearly—as the dwellings of sovereigns have stood for a thousand years. But continuity is a contributing factor to the profound symbolism that links the Peking palaces into a perfect unity "based upon the fundamental principles of Chinese civilisation with its unique conception of Kingship—the Ruler combining in his person the powers of Heaven, Earth, and Man, attributes derived from the Builder of All Things."

Not until the Ming Dynasty, however, did the Forbidden City assume anything like its present appearance or

---

58 The expression "Forbidden City," though used by foreigners, is seldom employed by the Chinese themselves. "Reserved City" they generally call the Imperial domain, or else such literary and symbolic names as "Sacred City" or "Violet Enclosure" (Tzu Chin Ch'eng). The word tzu, meaning violet-purple or deep red, does not refer, as is commonly supposed, to the colour of its crenulated walls, but comes from a literary allusion to the Polar Star believed by Chinese astronomers to be the centre of the celestial world as the Imperial Palace was the centre of the terrestrial world. "The analogy dates back several centuries before the Christian era when the Polar Star (called in Chinese Tzu Nei Hsing, or Star of the Red Myrtle) was considered the animistic correlative of Shang Ti, the Supreme Being, whose Vicar on Earth was the Chinese emperor."—Vissiere.

proportions, earlier palaces being "scattered and surrounded by dusty, unkempt, barren spaces." It was Yung Lo, patron of Peking, who built the Forbidden City as we see it to-day, expressing with a magnificence hitherto unknown, the old conception of high authority. Moreover his architects were bidden to construct according to fixed principles in which astronomic and geomantic considerations held primary importance. They were to seek "harmony with the Universe and obey the Laws of Space and Direction." Hence all important throne halls face south, their colours symbolise the elements, and even the steps that lead to them conform to the sacred numbers. Completed, Yung Lo's palace city was an awe-inspiring combination of mathematics and aesthetic beauty for which the genius of this Imperial Builder planned a suitable setting. Lakes were enlarged, artificial hills constructed, canals dug, and landscape gardens laid out in a manner to remind him of the verdant south, his birthplace.

When the Manchus assumed Imperial Power, they wisely made few attempts to alter what they could not improve, simply re-building on the same model, halls and gates destroyed by fire, and adding yellow tiles to the palace roofs, since yellow was not only the dynastic colour but the symbol of Earth, and therefore, according to their ideas, suitable to cover the dwellings of the "Lords of the Land."

A foreigner visiting the Forbidden City for the first time is surprised and overwhelmed. He can make nothing of it, cannot grasp it at all. With little knowledge of China's historical and ethical background to warn him of what to expect, he is prepared to see a palace in the western sense of the word—one large building with perhaps a few dependencies, like Fontainebleau or Windsor. But instead he enters the mazes of a city within a city and is conducted up and down a network of streets to groups of throne halls or living quarters, each group separately surrounded by walls, and giving the impression of a nest of square boxes fitting one within the other.

Why, he wonders, are the buildings all so much alike, why are there so many of them, and why are they so carefully

The Forbidden City

divided from one another? A little knowledge of Chinese psychology supplies the answers to these questions and helps to a comprehension of the Forbidden City as a whole.

Let us first of all visualise the complicated machinery of living required by a sovereign and his Court, consisting of several thousand persons, shut away entirely from the outside world: the throne halls for state ceremonies and ritualistic purposes, the living palaces, the theatres, temples, libraries, storehouses and dependencies. If these buildings are usually more or less alike—larger or smaller editions of the same model—it is because the Chinese seek harmony rather than variety. Having evolved a type of building (adapted from the tent) suited to their needs and blending with their landscapes, they stuck to it instead of trying further experiments.

As for the habit of surrounding each group of palaces with its own walls, this was doubtless done for two reasons: to ensure double protection in case of internal revolt, and stress the atmosphere of sanctity and aloofness surrounding the sovereign. Orientals well know that isolation commands respect where familiarity breeds contempt.

A glance at the plan shows the Forbidden City clearly defined as a rectangular enclosure carefully laid out according to the points of the compass with its state entrance facing south, because the Emperor's exits and his entrances must be in accordance with "lucky" astronomical influences. It is surrounded by an outer rampart seven metres high, once painted a Pompeian red but faded by time and weather to a soft greyish pink, the lovely shade of ashes of roses. This rampart is pierced by four gates, the Wu Men, or Meridian Gate, on the south, the Hsi Hua Men on the west, the Tung Hua Men on the East, and the Shen Wu Men on the north.

The long stone-paved avenue leading from the Chung Hua Men, or Dynastic gate (opposite the Chien Men or "Front Gate" of the Tartar City) right up to the Wu Men, forms an impressive approach to the mighty throne halls. Closed for centuries—except for the passage of the Sovereign and for Foreign Envoys when presenting their credentials—this

Juliet Bredon

Dynastic Gate (re-named the Gate of China) is now open to the public and one can walk straight through to the T'ien An Men, Gate of Heavenly Peace, flanked by two carved marble pillars supposed to have originated from the totem poles of aboriginal tribes.[59]

Through the dark throat of the T'ien An Men the same road leads straight on, like an arrow pointing at the heart of sovereignty, to the impressive Wu Men, or Meridian Gate. Notice the marble sundial and grain measure standing within its shadow. Both are important symbols. The former, being round, represents the perfection of Imperial virtue patterned upon the sun, whose light shines equally upon rich and poor. The latter, being square, stands for the full measure of justice and mercy meted out by the sovereign to all without fear or favour.

The Wu Men itself, the principal ceremonial gate of the palaces, is an overwhelming structure with its massive fortress walls, its mighty towers, and heavy wooden doors intended to swing open slowly and solemnly on great occasions. In former days the central archway was reserved for the exclusive use of the Emperor when he left the Palace in his dazzling golden chair to sacrifice at the Temple of Heaven, the Altar of Earth, etc.

By the immemorial custom of the East, a custom dating back to Ur of the Chaldees, more than 3,000 b.c, "the Supreme Judge sat in his gate to give Judgment." It is not astonishing, therefore, to find the terrace of the Wu Men used as a stage for impressive functions. Seated upon its high platform, the Ruler of China received his troops when they returned from victorious

---

[59] In ancient Mesopotamia and among the Hittites of Asia Minor similar pillars, but made of wood and pierced with a bull's horn, were erected before the palaces of kings. Poles not unlike them are still to be found in some Chinese villages outside temples or public offices. Another explanation declares these marble pillars a "survival of the Fei Pan Mu (Boards of Criticism and Detraction) instituted by the Perfect Emperor Yao and placed by him and his successors outside the Palace Gates in order that anyone might write upon them an opinion as to the acts of the ruler, or suggestions for improvements in the government."

The Forbidden City

wars, pompously bestowed presents on vassals and ambassadors, and distributed the calendar for the Empire at the New Year.[60] ' Behind the Wu Men there is a large open space through which flows the "Golden River," a canalised stream winding picturesquely between marble parapets. Five[61] bridges lead to the T'ai Ho Men (Gate of Supreme Harmony), a huge open porch supported on red lacquered pillars where the enthronement of Shun Chih, first sovereign of the Manchu dynasty, took place in a.d. 1644.

This gate opens directly into an immense stone-flagged courtyard, one of the most impressive sights of the Forbidden City. The majesty of its proportions, the splendour of the surrounding buildings set on high marble terraces that glitter in the radiant sunshine—the most precious gift of the Gods to North China—and the contrasting masses of cast shadow, are indescribably grand.

Directly facing the Supreme Harmony Gate across this square where many a historic pageant has been held, is the "Supreme Harmony Throne Hall" (the T'ai Ho Tien, re-named since the Republic the Li Tang or Ceremonial Hall) a lofty structure 110 feet high, 200 feet long and 100 feet wide.

With its golden roof like a shining helmet, its painted eaves and carved doorways, this glorious hall represents the highest expression of the grandeur of the Forbidden City. Largest and finest of the palace buildings, it was once the formal centre of the ceremonial life of the Empire and considered so sacred that no woman, not even the powerful Empress Dowager Tz'u Hsi, ever dared set foot there.

---

60 The central pavilion above the Wu Men is now used as a historical Museum.
61 Five, like nine, is one of the Chinese sacred numbers. Hence the five bridgse, the five openings in the Wu Men, etc.

Tien an Men and Carved Marble Pillar

The Forbidden City

A glowing jewel, unsurpassed and unsurpassable, the T'ai Ho Tien rises from its lofty marble terrace, poetically called the "Dragon Pavement." Five flights of carved steps lead, tier on tier, to this platform, where gilt bronze cisterns and incense burners stand, and the sundial and grain measure symbols are repeated. Every conception is intensely formal, every detail regulated by sumptuary law. Even the pillars of the marble balustrades follow the sacred numbers.

Finally, in order to accentuate the nobility and severe splendour of a palace used only on occasions of great ceremony—an enthronement, an Imperial birthday, or a New Year Reception—the architects doubled the roof of the T'ai Ho Tien and introduced an interior dome, or "lantern," in the centre, a height-giving device most effective from within, yet invisible from the outside. Golden hooks with chains attached, (supposed to act as protectors against lightning) adorn the crest. The flaming tiles are set in mortar mixed with a subtle poison which prevents wind-blown seeds from taking root, and the grotesque animal forms that decorate the hips are beautifully made.[62]

Mark well also the slight ripple in the main sweep of the roof lines, though they appear from a distance perfectly straight and square. This deviation is not accidental but expressly introduced to charm the eye without detracting from the purity of the original design.

---

62 The mythical animals placed on palace roofs are supposed to be the escort of the Emperor Min Wang of the Chou dynasty (1122-255 b.c.) a sovereign so cruel that the people sentenced him to be burned to death by the sun on the roof of his own dwelling. A complete procession includes Min Wang riding a fairy hen, a Dragon, a Phoenix, a Lion, a Heavenly Horse (messenger of the gods), a Sea Horse, a Fish, a Long Haired Lion, a Unicorn, a Cow and a Monkey. Whether these animals are fanciful adaptations of the weights that were placed originally on tent roofs to keep them steady in the wind, it is impossible to trace. Neither have we been able to discover why they accompany a monster like Min Wang; why he, or they, came to be considered protectors of a building, nor why the figures must always be in odd numbers—no fewer than three and no more than eleven.

Juliet Bredon

Two lesser throne halls stand upon the "Dragon Pavement" behind the T'ai Ho Tien[63]: the Chung Ho Tien, or Hall of Central Harmony, and the Pao Ho Tien, or Hall of Exalted Harmony, whose high sounding names are characteristic of all palace buildings. In the former—a square building topped by a gilded sphere— the Emperor used to inspect the yellow agricultural implements prepared for his "ploughing ceremony" at the Temple of Agriculture every spring. And every autumn he blessed in the Chung Ho Tien the harvest produced by his work as "First Farmer."

The Pao Ho Tien, third and last of the imposing trinity of throne halls known collectively as the San Ta Tien, was formerly used for the reception of vassal princes, ambassadors and scholars applying for those high literary degrees, once the key to official positions throughout the Empire.

Standing before these magnificent buildings and looking back on all they represented, one cannot help thinking that a whole civilisation was smashed to pieces when China suddenly became a Republic. Once the Empire crashed, a President responsible to a Parliament received in the sacred T'ai Ho Tien in the place of a Son of Heaven accountable to a Heavenly Mandate.[64] The old Chinese New Year, set to the rhythms of the Moon and celebrated with such pomp within these walls, was frowned upon, the literary examinations abolished because no one needed such preparation to be an official any more. But as long as the Monarchy lasted all roads in the Forbidden City led to the San Ta Tien, as in ancient Europe they led to Rome.

---

63 *Tien* is the word used to designate a "first class palace," generally a throne hall. *Kung* is a group of palace buildings with dependencies used as a residence. *T'an* is a small hall and *T'ing* an open pavilion. Certain "second class palaces," often with an upper story, are called *Ke*.

64 It was in this building that the foreign representatives officially recognised Yuan Shih-k'ai as President of the Republic of China in 1913. Foreign envoys were sometimes received in the "Three Great Halls" in the 17th and 18th centuries.

The Forbidden City

"Pillar of Victory"—Entrance to the Winter Palace

Juliet Bredon

Chinese and Manchu officials, however, were not permitted to enter for audience through the "Dynastic gate." That was the Emperor's own. Subjects used either the Tung Hua Men or the Hsi Hua Men, east and west side gates opening on to the garden strip just behind the Wu Men. Civilian officials, taking precedence over military colleagues in land where soldiers were less respected than scholars, used the east gate, the east being the more honourable direction, and the Wen Hua Tien, the waiting palace, near it. This now forms part of the National Museum and its three halls are devoted to an interesting exhibition of Chinese paintings of all periods.

Near the West gate, a corresponding palace, the Wu Ying Tien, where army and navy officers once waited their turn to be received, contains bronzes, porcelains, etc., formerly kept in the Mukden and Jehol Palaces. The gems of this collection are the porcelains and especially the monochromes, masterpieces of that brilliant artistic renaissance which distinguished the reigns of K'ang Hsi, Ch'ien Lung and Yung Cheng. Every colour of the rainbow was triumphantly reproduced in many shadings—the silver white, the blue white, the ivory white; the luminous yellow of sunshine, the dead gold tint of autumn leaves; the hundred blues, turquoise, moonlight, and the elusive "sky after rain"; the purple of the grape; the crackled green of ancient ice, the tea colour with its metallic lustre, the onion and camellia greens, the blacks, lustrous as the pupil of the eye; the pinks of the peach blossom, and the whole gamut of glowing reds—shades, which, though perfected by the Chinese 600 years ago, no one is yet able to imitate.

In addition to these treasures, we find displayed a group of beautiful things recalling the gorgeous and elegant life fostered by Imperial patronage that once existed in China: bronze chariot ornaments,[65] golden horse shoes, carved stirrups, finely woven saddle cloths, curved scimitars with hilts and scabbards ornamented with precious stones, carpets of silk and gold tissue, satin throne cushions and brocaded robes enriched by

---

[65] The Chinese held chariot races and were addicted to all sports of horsemanship, including polo, before the Christian era.

medallions of ivory and coral. All these trappings created with a splendid technical mastery and adorned with every ornament that warms the imagination, attest stateliness and power, high intercourse with kingly and beautiful humanity, proud thoughts and splendid pleasures, throned sensualities and powerful affections, in one blaze of earthly magnificence. Indeed the splendour of these past ages dazzles the eyes of moderns like ourselves, accustomed to sack coats and soft collars, and we cannot but exclaim—as de Goncourt did at Versailles—"What a pity that such works of art should be consigned now to the cold tomb of a museum, and subjected to the careless glance of the stupid passer-by!"

It seems almost a lack of taste to stare at these intimacies of the life of long ago. But curiosity knows no reverence and when we reluctantly leave this Museum, we even pry into the small building near-by—the Hammam bath house built by order of Ch'ien Lung to please that same capricious favourite, the Stranger Concubine, for whom the infatuated emperor constructed the mosque that once stood opposite the Hsin Hua Men.[66]

The fourth gate of the Forbidden City, the Shen Wu Men, Gate of Military Prowess, faces the Coal Hill. This was really the "Household Gate" through which all domestic necessities passed in and out. It was formerly reserved also for the use of the Empress and the ladies of the Court, just as the Wu Men was for the exclusive use of the Emperor. Unfortunately the Shen Wu Men, whose high sounding name suggests victory, has twice been the scene of calamity and defeat—once when the Emperor Kuang Hsu and his aunt, the Empress Dowager Tz'u Hsi, escaped through it disguised as peasants in their swift, hustled flight in 1900, and again when the "Little Emperor Hsuan T'ung" passed its half-open, gold-studded doors in the darkness of the early morning on November 5th, 1924, leaving behind him forever the gorgeous spendours of his Imperial home.

---

66 See Chapter VII

Juliet Bredon

	殿泰交		門左康長
A	Chiao-tai Hall.	U	Chang-kang Tso Gate.
	殿暖西		門西苑瓊
B	Hsi-nuan Hall.	V	Chiung-yuan Hsi Gate.
	殿暖東		門東苑瓊
C	Tung-nuan Hall.	W	Chiun-yuan Tung Gate.
	殿德弘		門則端
D	Hung-te Hall.	X	Tuan-tse Gate.
	殿仁昭		門化基
E	Chao-jen Hall.	Y	Chi-hwa Gate.
	門右內		門福增
F	Nei-yu Gate.	Z	Tse-fu Gate.
	門左內		門祥永
G	Nei-tso Gate.	A′	Yung-hsiang Gate.
	門義遵		殿和中
H	Tsun-i Gate.	B′	Chung-he Hall.
	門祥仁		門右後
I	Jen-hsiang Gate.	C′	Hou-yu Gate.
	門右光近		門左後
J	Chin-kuang Yu Gate.	D′	Hou-tso Gate.
	門右和咸		門右中
K	Hsien-he Yu Gate.	E′	Chung-yu Gate.
	門彩鳳		門左中
L	Feng-tsai Gate.	F′	Chung-tso Gate.
	門左光近		門貞順
M	Chin-kuang Tso Gate.	G′	Shun-cheng Gate.
	門左和咸		殿安欽
N	Hsien-he Tso Gate.	H′	Chin-an Hall.
	門光龍		門寧坤
O	Lung-kuang Gate.	I′	Kun-ning Gate.
	門右成廣		門福隆
P	Kuang-cheng Yu Gate.	J′	Lung-fu Gate.
	門左成廣		門和景
Q	Kuang-cheng Tso Gate.	K′	Ching-he Gate.
	門右成大		門華月
R	Ta-cheng Yu Gate.	L′	Yueh-hwa Gate.
	門左成大		門精日
S	Ta-cheng Tso Gate.	M′	Jih-ching Gate.
	門右康長		門清乾
T	Chang-kang Yu Gate.	N′	Chien-ching Gate.

The Forbidden City

	儲秀宮		傳心殿
O'	Chu-hsiu Kung	j	Chuan-hsin Hall.
	翊坤宮		治性殿
P'	I-kung Kung	k	Chih-sheng Hall.
	隅樓		集戒殿
Q'	Corner Tower	l	Chu-i Hall.
	閣樓		本仁殿
R'	Pavilion	m	Pen-jen Hall.
	體元殿		金缸
S'	Ti-yuan Hall	n	Chin-kang (Golden-Jar)
	養心殿		嘉量
T'	Yang-hsin Hall.	o	Chia-liang (Good Measure)
	長春宮		鶴
U'	Chang-chun Hall.	p	Crane
	佛堂		絳雪軒
V'	Fo Tang (Buddha's Hall)	q	Chiang-hsueh Pavilion.
	中正殿		香雲亭
W'	Chung-cheng Hall	r	Hsiang-yun Pavilion.
	寶華殿		獅子
X'	Pao-hwa Hall.	s	Lion
	景陽宮		廚子
Y'	Ching-yang Kung	t	Small Shrine.
	齋宮		宦官住宅
Z'	Chai Kung.	u	Residences of Eunuchs
	雨華閣		日圭
a	Yu-hwa Pavilion.	v	Jih-kuei (Sun-Dial)
	永安寺塔		龜
b	Yung-an Temple Stupa.	w	Turtle.
	萬善殿		寶鼎
c	Wan-shan Hall.	x	Tripod Incense Burner.
	内務府		千秋亭
d	Nei-wu Fu	y	Chien-chiu Pavilion.
	咸安宮		華表
e	Hsien-an Kung.	z	Hwa-piao.
	主敬殿		象
f	Chu-ching Hall.	a'	Elephant.
	文華殿		井屋
h	Wen-hwa Hall.	b'	Well.
	文華門		
i	Wen-hwa Gate.		

75

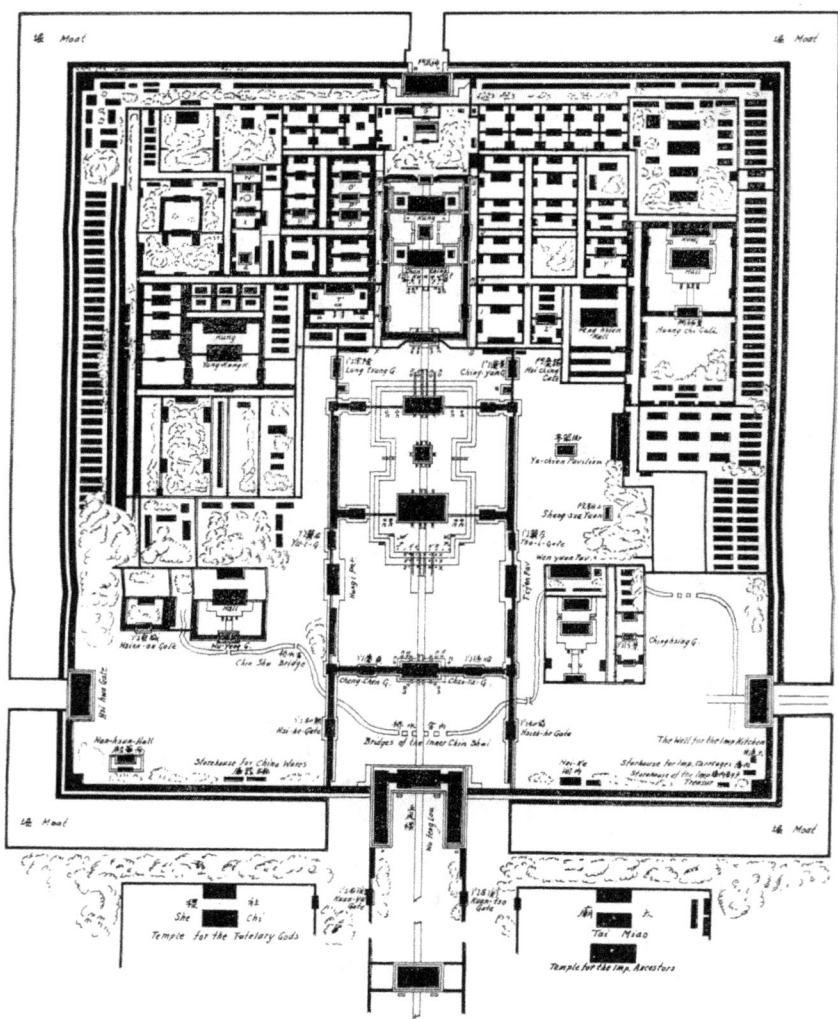

The Forbidden City

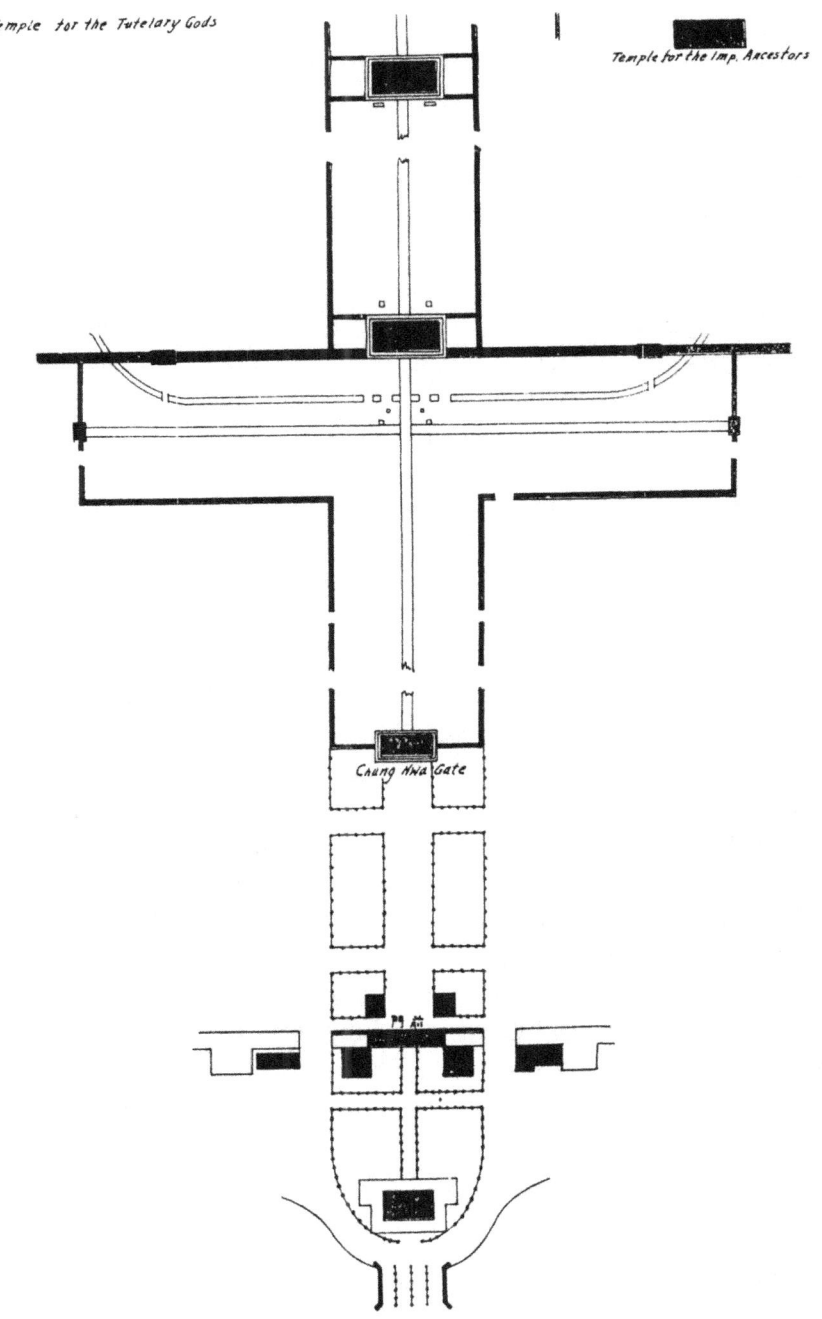

Juliet Bredon

Fate is often pleased to be cynical. To-day a ticket-seller sits in the "Gateway of Military Prowess" and admits tourists to the Inner Courts of the Forbidden City now open to the public as the "Palace Museum" (in contradistinction to the National Museum behind the Wu Men).

"Immediately after the late Emperor was forced to leave the Imperial Palace, the Regency Cabinet... organised a Commission for the custody of Manchu House property... and in view of the prevailing disorder and confusion, decided to seal up temporarily all important buildings in the Inner Reserved City. This was accordingly done with the co-operation of the Cabinet officials, the Headquarters of the Peking Garrison, the Police Commissioner and members of the Imperial Household. Later an inventory of all articles remaining in the Palace was begun... and by the end of 1925 the Central and Western sections were completely catalogued and separate check lists for each palace building were published in book form.... Meanwhile the Commission—a non-political and non-partisan organisation—received numerous requests to open the Forbidden precincts to the Public... and this was done gradually, more and more halls being shown as the inventory work progressed."[67] Plans for further extending the Museum are already a-foot and when time and funds permit, will make the entire Forbidden City a unique treasure house of beauty and culture.

At present, for convenience sake, and because even the Inner Courts[68] as a whole are far too large a morsel to be digested at one time, they are divided into three sections, Eastern, Western, and Central, and opened separately so many days a week—an excellent system which automatically prevents the too hurried tourist from trying to swallow the entire Forbidden City at one gulp.

---

[67] Quoted and abridged from the pamphlet issued by the Palace Museum Committee.
[68] The "Inner Courts" constituting the true "Reserved City," stretch from the Shen Wu Men in the north to the Ch'ien Ching Men on the south.

The Forbidden City

The Western section of the palace is perhaps the most interesting to the general visitor because of its associations with the last Manchu sovereign Hsuan T'ung, familiarly known as the "Little Emperor."

The Western Garden near the entrance was used by him for a playground when, as a small, unhappy lad, he was placed upon a tottering throne. To the "misty minded," as the Chinese call superstitious folk, this bare space left after a fire destroyed the buildings that stood in the enclosure, seems ill-omened. Moreover its neighbour is the "Mourning Palace," distinguished by a roof of blue tiles—blue, like white, being a Chinese mourning colour. Here his Imperial predecessors, who suffered the misfortune of losing a parent, retired in grief, which in olden days meant abandoning affairs of state, bowing before the coffin and wailing for twenty-seven months, going un-shaved and unwashed, and offering food and drink to the spirit of the deceased five times between sunrise and sunset.

Further to the north is the palace where Ch'ien Lung was born and lived as a child. Strange how closely woven is the pattern of birth and death in this Forbidden City, how the bright threads and the dark are intermingled, how coffins and thrones are neighbours! Strange too, how small and insignificant buildings hang on to the skirts, so to speak, of magnificent palaces, and often have an important share in historic events!

The imposing Tz'u Ning Kung—one of the oldest buildings in the Forbidden City—is a case in point. In the enormous central hall converted into a Buddhist temple by the devout Empress Dowager Tz'u An— colleague of the energetic Tz'u Hsi—this gentle lady expired, rumour says, after eating poisoned cakes sent by her rival.

In an insignificant side wing, K'ang Hsi, disillusioned by the quarrels of his turbulent sons, sought peace and security for his old age, and finally died of a broken heart.

In the Gardens opposite the Tz'u Ning Kung, poetically known as "The Gardens of Dispossessed Favourites," those ladies of the household[69] who had forfeited the favours of the Son of Heaven, lived obscurely in the low buildings on either side—buildings whose tired, gentle colours contrast curiously with the vivid tints of the newly restored temples in the garden.

It is regrettable that the public is so little to be trusted in historic places that wire netting has to be nailed across the doorways of these sanctuaries. Because of "Mr. Willard B. Untermeyer" (and his ilk)[70] who could not enjoy the Altar of Heaven "without writing his undistinguished name upon it," more respectful visitors are obliged to glimpse frescoes and Buddhist images from a distance.

Overlooking these poetic gardens, loveliest, perhaps, in autumn when the fallen leaves of the Ginko trees weave a golden pattern on the paths, is the Yu Hua Ke, "Tower of Rain and Flowers," the highest building in the Forbidden City and one of the most striking with its golden roof dragons and dragon-wreathed pillars. It is a triple shrine with three altars and legend says that one was used by K'ang Hsi as a private oratory.

The tall shadow of this pagoda-like structure falls upon the living palaces where the "Little Emperor," his Empress, and his single secondary wife spent their few years of glory.

All these buildings are closed, thanks no doubt again to Mr. Untermeyer "who sought to attach his fleeting personality to the recollection of a grandeur of which some dim rumour had reached him... and thus in his crude way aimed at immortality." Nevertheless we can peer into the royal apartments through dusty glass windows, at all the intimate possessions of this ill-fated young couple who, when they lost the sovereignty of power, gained, as Queen Victoria once said to the Empress Eugenie, "the still higher sovereignty of misfortune." Here is the Imperial bed made of bronze with a mosquito net woven of gold threads. Yonder a dining room,

---

69 The Emperors of China were polygamous like the majority of Oriental potentates.
70 See *On A Chinese Screen*, by Somerset Maugham.

The Forbidden City

furnished in the most commonplace foreign style, strikes a jarring note amidst the beauty of these oriental surroundings.

In the boudoir of the "Little Empress," her round mirror, symbol of conjugal happiness, still stands upon her dressing table and her books are scattered about her private study in pathetic disarray. The window curtains are a little soiled. There is a spot of ink on the carpet beside a chair whose cushion is flattened as if some one had just been sitting in it. A half eaten apple, a faded chrysanthemum in a vase, an open magazine, prove how hastily, and in what perturbation, these unhappy refugees fled from their royal home. Such trifles, accentuating poignant memories, make one realize not only the fickleness of fortune and the fragility of empires, but also that it is no light thing to tear human beings up from roots deeply buried in rich soil for centuries.

Through no fault of their own, the tragic weight of destiny pressed upon these two puppets and held them helpless in the grip of Fate. When the Little Emperor was taken at midnight from his father's house in floods of bitter tears and made a sovereign by order of the Empress Dowager, it was already too late to save the Manchu dynasty. Indeed for him power was never more than an illusion and he sensed under the still shining mirror surface, the queer, dangerous realities—floating but submerged objects of menace for himself and his house.

With the fateful decree of Abdication signed February 12th, 1912, he ceased to be ruler of an Empire any longer. Twelve years later he and his young bride fled from these "Courts of Unhappiness" to retire and live in Tientsin as Mr. and Mrs. Pu Yi, private citizens of China. Thus, whatever their faults, this unhappy young couple, once smothered in beauty, swathed in comfort, and doomed to lose it all, assume the mournful nobility that fate confers on its august victims, and we can think of them only in terms of pity.

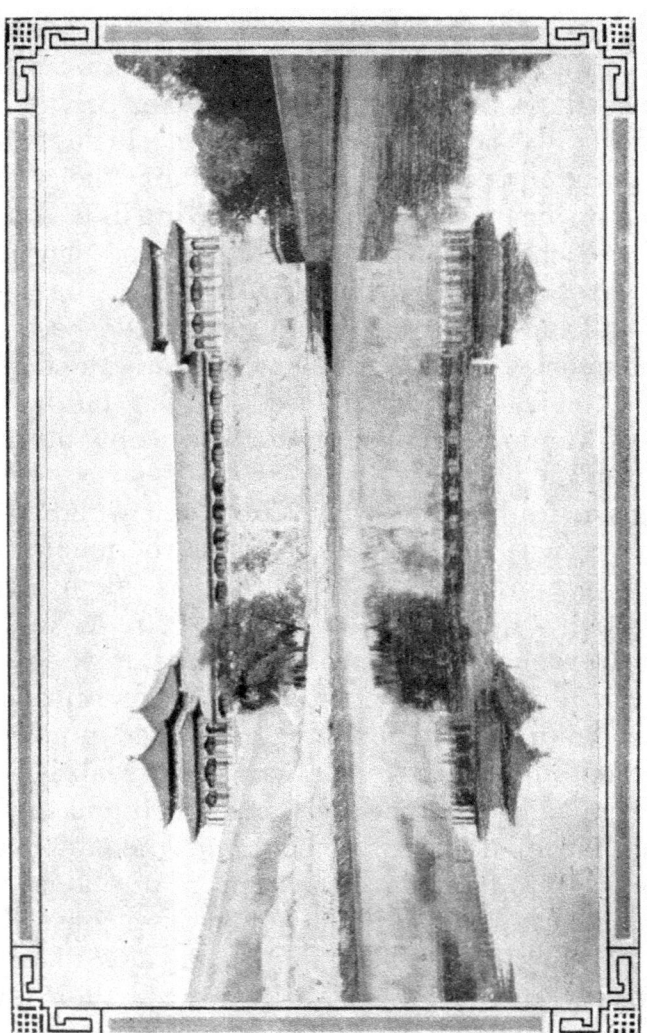

The Wu Men, From the Moat

[Photo by Hartung, Peking]

The Forbidden City

Just as the western section of the Palace is closely associated with the short Imperial life of the "Little Emperor," so the Eastern Section is full of memories of the glorious reigns of Ch'ien Lung and of the Empress Dowager Tz'u Hsi, two of the most powerful and colourful figures of the Manchu dynasty. The "Palaces of the East Road," as they are called, occupy only about a quarter of the space in this section where there is much waste ground devoted to gardens, etc. It is interesting to note that the general plan is similar to that of the Central Section, but carried out'on a smaller scale.

Before visiting the "Inner Courtyards" let us make a detour to the Wen Yuan Ke, the Imperial Library built by Ch'ien Lung in 1776. One of seven libraries planned by this Imperial Scholar, it contains the most precious books extant in his time—a collection of 36,000 volumes entirely written by hand, and many of them the only copies in existence.

Retracing our steps from the library we find ourselves faced by a superb "spirit screen" decorated with nine porcelain dragons, a screen even more perfect than the one of similar design in the Pei Hai.[71]

This leads to the group of buildings collectively known as the Ning Shou Kung, one of the six residential palaces of the Eastern Road corresponding to the six palaces of the "Western Road," for the Chinese with their love of regularity laid out the "Inner Courts" to match one another.

Magnificent as many of these palace groups are, the buildings look so much alike that strangers find difficulty in distinguishing one from another. Only by linking it up with historic figures, and events, does each hall take on an individuality and come to have a meaning for us Westerners.

The Ning Shou Kung, for example, remains forever fixed in the memory once we know it was the personal home of the "Old Buddha," as the Dowager Empress Tz'u Hsi was familiarly called, in her last years. The Huang Chi Tien, the first and the largest building of this group, was the official throne hall where

---

71 See Chapter VII

she held audience after 1900, pending the restoration of the Sea Palaces,[72] which she preferred to the stiff formality and high walls of the Forbidden City, especially after their "desecration" by the foreign barbarians.

In the smaller courtyards behind are her private apartments; her informal throne room divided from her sleeping alcove by handsome red doors with carved and gilded rooflets—a unique decorative device. Small and strikingly simple is this home of the woman who ruled for so many years over one-third of the human race. On the north side of the little room, scarcely larger than a hall bedroom, is her built-in bed with its embroidered curtains, its yellow satin mattress and, above, a low gallery that served as her private oratory where a golden Buddha and tall candlesticks shining with pearls and rubies enriched the altar. Opposite the hidden stairway leading to this chapel, is a k'ang, or raised platform, such as we find in the homes of all northern Chinese. Here eunuchs sat on guard while Her Majesty slept. Beside this brick sofa stand a few tables with rows of clocks, the collecting of which was the Dowager's special hobby.

How picturesque but how uncomfortable, from our point of view, was the life of this autocratic ruler who "had to rise at midnight, winter as well as summer, dress in full regalia in these small ill-lighted rooms, proceed to a dark, dreary throne hall heated only with brass braziers, and there, because she was, after all, only a woman, sit behind a curtain that hung between her and an empty throne, while listening to the reports of the high officials who came to her audiences."

The Ning Shou Kung was built by Ch'ien Lung who grew so fond of this palace that he retired here in his 86th year to pass his last days in peace—a peace well earned after his long period of conscientious rule.

A side gate leads to the garden enclosure in the northeast corner of the Forbidden City which was specially beloved by him and, out of respect for his memory, never used by his successors. What a quiet, restful, shadowy retreat is this old

---

72 See Chapter VII

The Forbidden City

garden with its moon doors, its mosaic walls of different coloured marbles, and its surrounding temples to which time seems to have given a velvet quality! Here and there falling plaster drips to the ground like blood from a fatal wound, and many a pillar is bent like an old man carrying a heavy load of invisible memories. To this enchanted spot where Ch'ien Lung in life dallied with his favourites, or retired to pray, they brought his dead body back to await a propitious day for burial in a small low building where the sunshine still basks on the threshold like a luminous, tamed serpent.

Passing on northwards along corridors of stone tablets inscribed with poems written by the tireless hand of the Grand Monarque of the Manchu Dynasty,[73] one enters a series of symmetrical but disconnected halls full of Imperial treasures. All these buildings were the scene of dramatic happenings in former days and if, as they say, walls have ears, it is a thousand pities stones have no tongues! What stories they could tell us if they could only speak, what "tales of joy and laughter, of sentiment and tragedy!" Who would not like to hear of that grand reception Ch'ien Lung gave in the "Hall of the Five Happinesses" to five generations of his descendants? Who would not listen eagerly to the tragic tale of the beautiful "Stranger Concubine," courted in the very room where we see her portrait against a background of lotuses? Who would not like to know the truthful version of the drowning of the "Pearl Concubine"—beloved of the Emperor Kuang Hsu—in the well near-by, and the secret hiding place where the Old Buddha buried her jewels before her flight in 1900?

Alas, such things we shall never know. But as we walk from palace to palace down those long corridor streets imprisoned between the high pink walls which are so characteristic of the Forbidden City, we seem to feel ghosts follow us wherever we go. Phantoms move across the flagstones silently in satin shod

---

[73] There is a curious legend that Ch'ien Lung was not a Manchu but a Chinese, changeling son of a high provincial official who, invited to bring his infant heir to Court, received in exchange the puny female lately born to the Empress.

feet. Voices whisper in the shadows. Surely something remains of those invisible presences—the endless procession of eunuchs, court ladies and serving maids, who, in the days of the Empire, were always passing, passing to and fro?

But now that they have disappeared together with their pompous pageantry, we try in vain to glimpse their vanished figures, to catch the echoes from the past. The Courts are empty save for guides and tourists whose raucous comments on the blessings of democracy quickly break the spell, and the buildings where vanished emperors lived and loved are turned into museums for the treasures they gathered.

Such hundreds of rare and beautiful things belong to the Palace collections, that the mere enumeration of them would require many volumes.[74]

Naturally so great a variety of treasures can never be shown all at the same time. Therefore sometimes one group of curios will be on exhibition, sometimes another. A detailed description of what each hall contains must, consequently, be a waste of time since the picture that hangs on a certain wall to-day may be replaced by another to-morrow, and the porcelains on view this week may not be the same specimens to be seen next month.

It is only possible then, to give a general idea of the Palace Museum exhibits which include masterpieces from every dynasty displayed in a setting that suits them perfectly. Indeed the public owes a deep debt of gratitude to the Palace Committee for its untiring work in classifying and arranging the works of art, and presenting them so discreetly that visitors are satisfied without being surfeited.

In the "Hall of Paintings," hang pictures of the most famous artists of the T'ang, Sung and Yuan dynasties and some rare

---

[74] To give some idea of the richness of the Imperial collections, it is stated on reliable authority that there are 100,000 pieces of jade alone, varying in size from several feet to a few inches in diameter. There are 10,000 maps and portraits, 1,200,000 books and manuscripts, and the porcelains are numbered in millions.

The Forbidden City

scrolls that date back even to the period of the Hans (a.d. 25-220).

Older still is the collection of bronze vessels with specimens made two to three thousand years ago. In fact these represent the earliest Chinese art forms which have been copied throughout the ages in porcelain, lacquer and even in cheap modern brass, and a study of them impresses on our minds the curious continuity of Chinese art. Moreover, bronze vessels, dating from such distant antiquity express the soul development of the Chinese race. Fashioned when very early Chinese civilisation was based upon ceremonies and divination, used on all important occasions of national and family life—"victory over enemies, prayers for blessings and favours, penitence for transgressions, memorial services for deceased rulers and parents"—these chef-d'oeuvres, many of them with inscriptions in the earliest forms of the Chinese written character, give us an epitome of Chinese history. The most thoughtless passer-by cannot fail to look with respect on such ancient works of art whose decorations of clouds and thunderbolts, etc, were inspired by the forces of nature, and are, moreover, scientific evidence of an ancient and vanished civilisation.[75]

Other halls contain wonderful collections of potteries and porcelains—Sung Dynasty pieces unique of their kind, decorative Ming jars and wine cups, and exquisite Ch'ing bowls and plates, even a group of snuff bottles and nut trays, with medallions in the style of Louis XV, painted to K'ang Hsi's order by Castiglione and his pupils.

Still other buildings contain jades (including two large historic blocks representing the "Mountain of Longevity" and the "Sea of Happiness"), carved and tinted ivories, lacquers, tapestries, brocades, ancient weapons, musical instruments (including the famous "porcelain lute"), imperial seals of gold

---

[75] Two of these Palace bronzes which will doubtless be on exhibition more or less permanently are the only relics of their kind preserved in China—the magnificent bronze basin known as the "Nation's Honour" (1000 b.c.) and the Standard "Measure" of the Han dynasty.

and jade, jewelled trees with flowers, fruits and leaves of semi-precious stones, corals, and many other things distinguished by their beauty, rarity, or historic interest.[76]

It is disappointing to find that however carefully we examine them, we cannot remember half of the beautiful things on exhibition. Much of interest escapes us altogether. And when we look back, we are astonished, often enough, to find what best survives in memory. For some it will be a faded picture of a saint that appeals most, for others a porcelain jar, and then again, for one or two, the personal treasures Ch'ien Lung loved will make a deep impression—the little porcelain dove, the golden walnut, the carved shell. What, we ask ourselves, as we leave the last hall of the "Eastern Road," is the secret of selection in our minds? Why is there often a vitality in small unimportant trifles absent from grander things? Why do we forget a masterpiece, and remember a broken lute? The answer lies with the psychologists.

There are no longer living quarters in the Central Section of the Reserved City as there were in the days of the Mings. A part of it is devoted to the "Garden of Earthly Peace," where the sovereigns rested from their labours. Here, where they were off duty, so to speak, the mighty emperors appear as intimate

---

[76] "Many of these palace pieces were made in the Imperial Factories founded in Peking in 1680 by the Emperor K'ang Hsi who brought practised craftsmen from all parts of the Empire to work in them. The list comprised the following departments: 1. Metal foundries. 2. Fabrication of "ju-yi" (sceptres). 3. Glass works. 4. Clock and watch manufactory. 5. Preparation of maps and plans. 6. Fabrication of cloisonne enamels. 7. Fabrication of helmets. 8. Work in jade, gold and filigree. 9. Gilding. 10. Ornamental chiselling of reliefs. 11. Manufacture of ink-stones. 12. Incrusted work. 13. Works in tin and tin plating. 14. Ivory carving. 15. Wood engraving and sculpturing. 16. Fabrication of lacquer. 17. Chiselling movable type. 18. Fabrication of incense-burning sets. 19. Manufacture of painted boxes. 20. Joiners and carpenters. 21. Lantern manufactory. 22. Artificial flowers. 23. Works in leather. 24. Mounting pearls and jewels. 25. Chiselling metals. 26. Armourers. 27. Manufacture of optical instruments. These ateliers which lasted for a century or more, were closed one by one after the reign of Ch'ien Lung, and what remained of the buildings was burned down in 1860." *Chinese Art Handbook.*, by Bushell.

human figures. Here they become life size. They do not crush us as they do on their thrones where they appear too grandiose, too dazzling, for our drab times.

These "rest gardens" are conceived in a truly Chinese manner with complicated rockeries and pagodas and pavilions perched about. They have high peony terraces framed in encaustic tiles, instead of flat flower beds. They have quaintly-shaped, knobbly trees set in carved stone pavements or surrounded by low stone walls so that those who carry burdens shall not knock against them. The shady walks made of pebble mosaics set in intricate designs, lead to rock caverns whose coolness is welcome on hot summer days. One can imagine how time flowed past here like a quiet stream; how in the season of great heat—when even the palace halls were airless—the weary emperors idled in this enchanted garden from morning to evening until the burning sunshine cooled and the moon rose, letting down her ladders of silver among the trees.

Numerous buildings are scattered here and there; tea pavilions, a school room where the "Little Emperor" studied English, a fishing kiosk built over water, a study, a library, a poetry pavilion, and a private chapel used by the Imperial family. The last has four doors facing the four points of the compass. In front of each is a large cypress tree hundreds of years old which is split up from the roots some seven or eight feet, planted with the two halves a stride apart, and grafted together again higher up so that it forms a living arch under which a worshipper must pass to enter the temple.[77]

Beyond these Rest Gardens are various side halls which were once used as schoolrooms for Imperial princelings, residences of Court ladies, nurseries for the Pekingese dogs they kept as pets, etc.

But the really important buildings of the Central Section are a group of three throne halls that stand together on a marble terrace and, though smaller and less impressive, are

---

[77] There is a legend that these trees represent the character for "jen" (man) (人) which they resemble.

practically replicas of the San Ta Tien, or Three Great Throne Halls.

In fact, these six palace throne halls which we see most clearly from a height such as the Coal Hill, stand one behind another on a great passageway which runs through the centre of the Forbidden City from south to north—a passageway about three hundred feet wide, interrupted, it is true, by gates, but nevertheless giving as a whole the effect of a mighty processional.

Under the Ming regime this second set of throne halls was used as residence palaces, but under the Manchus, and especially the later Manchus, there was a tendency to move the living quarters more and more into the east and west corners of the Reserved City—the "Inner Courts"—and to hold audiences, except on the most formal occasions, in the K'un Ning Kung, the Chiao T'ai Tien and the Ch'ien Ching Kung rather than in the more distant San Ta Tien, Three Great Halls.

Continuing on southwards (from the Shen Wu Men) through the Central Section, we pass the K'un Ning Men and reach the K'un Ning Kung, or Palace of Earthly Peace, divided into two parts. The smaller section was formerly the Imperial wedding chamber. Hence its decorations all in red, the Chinese festal colour, and the golden characters for "double joy" painted on doors and scrolls.

The larger subdivision of this hall was the scene of those curious Shaman ceremonies which the Manchus brought with them from their ancestral home and continued to the last days of the Empire. Pictures and stuffed dolls representing the "Guiding Spirits" of this primitive animistic faith, remain upon the altar and beside them hang brocade sacks, known as "lucky sacks" in which the "lucky locks" worn by Manchu children until their marriage and renewed each year, were kept. At the east end of the room is a "holy" kitchen and a long table where the sacrificial animals were cut up, and on the west a curtained alcove where the officiant—a man if the Emperor was present, a woman if the Empress—retired to pray.

The Forbidden City

Outside the door, notice the "Divine Pillar," a wooden mast with a sheep's vertebra still attached to it. Here, according to Manchu custom the bones of the sacrificed animals were hung, and sacred dances took place.

Next in line with the K'un Ning Kung comes the Chiao T'ai Tien, Hall of Fusion and Permeation, a square building (corresponding to the square central hall of the San Ta Tien), with an unusually splendid ceiling. This was once the official throne hall of the Empress, and her symbols, the phoenix and the full moon, appear in all its decorations. Though now used as a storehouse for Imperial Seals, it was formerly the place where the paraphernalia for her Majesty's only official sacrifice to the Goddess of Silkworms, was kept. Here, too, on the eve of her wedding, an Empress-to-be was received by her court ladies and conducted by them to the K'un Ning Kung to meet her Imperial bridegroom.

The third throne hall, the Ch'ien Ching Kung, Palace of Surpassing Brightness, is by far the most interesting and important building in the Central Section. The original Ming structure dated from a.d. 1514. Destroyed by fire like so many of the Ming buildings, it was re-built on the old model in 1797, after having been used for nearly 200 years as the personal residence of the Sovereign, who slept in the west room and received his ministers in the central hall.

During the occupation of the last Ming Emperor, this palace witnessed one of the most pathetic events that history has recorded. In 1644 rebels were actually thundering at the gates of Peking and the Emperor Ch'ung Cheng, eager to take the field against them in person, found that his army existed only on paper. The situation was hopeless. Desirous, therefore, that those dear to him should not fall into the hands of the invaders, the unhappy monarch bade his Empress commit suicide and killed a number of his concubines. He wanted to kill his own daughter also and struck blindly at her with his sword while he covered his eyes with his other sleeve. But he only succeeded in severing her arm. She fell to the ground unconscious and the distracted monarch, thinking her dead, rushed out of the

Juliet Bredon

Palace, passionately denouncing his officials who had fled like rats from the Forbidden City, leaving him to his fate.

It seems rather a curious coincidence that the Ch'ien Ching Kung was used as a mortuary chapel for the first sovereign of the new dynasty (Shun Chih, who died in 1661) and that no one ever actually lived in it again. On the jubilee of K'ang Hsi and again on that of Ch'ien Lung, a "Feast of a Thousand Elders" was given in this hall, when men over sixty years of age, and from all parts of the Empire, were invited to Court and personally served at a banquet by the sons and grandsons of the Ruler, thus marking the national respect for longevity.

In the same building, Kuang Hsu, the liberal ruler and his friend and trusted adviser K'ang Yu-wei, drew up the famous Reform Programme of 1898. Alas, ideas bear no fruit unless they take root in a strong man's mind. Kuang Hsu, though an honest idealist, lacked will-power and when his plans reached the ears of his aunt, the determined Empress Dowager Tz'u Hsi, she promptly quashed them and exiled her nephew to an island in the Sea Palaces.

In more modern times the Ch'ien Ching Kung was the scene of the first reception of the Diplomatic Body as a whole when Kuang Hsu, after the Boxer Rebellion of 1900, consented to give audience to all the Foreign Ministers together.

Finally, in December 1922, this "Palace of Surpassing Brightness" served as a setting for the last great ceremony held in the Forbidden City, the wedding of the "Little Emperor."

Impressive though this reception was, it seemed but a pale shadow of the magnificent pageants staged in the heyday of the Manchu dynasty by extravagant sovereigns like Ch'ien Lung and K'ang Hsi.

Let imagination, the Great Architect, reconstruct for us one of those ceremonies—a New Year reception, for example in the T'ai Ho Tien. It is midnight, and the gate which leads from the Chinese City to the Tartar City—the Ch'ien Men—is opened by the guard to admit a procession of carts. The wailing creak of the hinges mingles with the rumble of wheels and the clatter of the feet of the mules on the stone pavement. Down silent streets the officials proceed to audience with their Ruler. They reach the East and West gates like spectres, sitting tailor-fashion in their fur-lined springless carts, then stiffly descend and make their way to the courtyard in front of the T'ai Ho Tien. According to their rank they take the places indicated for each group by a small bronze triangle in the shape of a miniature mountain. There is no loud talking but a weird sort of tension in the air, as always at Court ceremonies where men stare into one another's faces "their eyes asking questions which perhaps even the questioners do not understand nor know they ask." In the courtyard below tribute elephants stand at the four corners like statues and the gilt bronze cisterns filled with oil blaze like great cauldrons of flame.

Above, the great block of a building is crowded with eunuchs, in embroidered robes and jewelled chains of office, making last preparations and whispering softly among themselves, their solemn expressionless faces etched with queer shadows in the flickering lights of the horn lanterns.

Since the comings and goings of the Sovereign are subject to the stars, the courtiers wait patiently, shivering in their sable robes, for the hour fixed by the Board of Astronomy when the Emperor will appear. Just as the dawn breaks, a courier announces the Imperial procession is about to start and all present fall upon their knees.

Far away in those Inner Courts the cortege gathers, then slowly winds its way past the lesser throne halls and through the Ch'ien Ching Men, opposite the Ch'ien Ching Kung—the true limit of the Reserved City. Ripples of excitement spread through the crowd of courtiers as the criers announce again, "He comes, He comes, the Lord of Ten Thousand Years." One last dividing wall and the magnificent pageant is in sight; the brilliant banners, the stalwart bodyguards, and finally the yellow satin chair with golden dragons.

Then straightway every man falls upon his knees and bows his forehead nine times to die ground, greeting his sovereign with that hoarse shout—a cheer, yet not a cheer— "Ten thousand years, ten thousand, thousand years."

Juliet Bredon

The golden chair is carried up the high steps to the "Dragon Pavement." The Emperor alights. He enters the hall whose panelled ceiling with its five-clawed dragons (emblems of Imperial power and symbol of masculine strength), and rich red and gold supporting pillars, glow sombrely splendid in the dim lantern light. He mounts the platform to the "Dragon Throne" and seats himself in hierarchic attitude, his pale yellow hands upon his knees, his eyes inscrutable. Then princes and dignitaries come forward, prostrate themselves and offer New Year greetings.[78]

The T'ai Ho Tien has been well named the "Stage of Emperors," across which moved the royal puppets of China's dynasties—an empty stage now echoing to ghostly footfalls.

But whoever has seen a ceremony in one of the great throne halls, standing serene in the drawn light, can never enter one of these noble buildings without feeling the pulse of an ancient civilisation which throbbed as mightily in the 18th century as in that dim past whereof these palaces themselves, though already old, are but a modern record. For in these vast halls where every stone recalls that mighty past, there is a greater quality than the purely architectural—an occult quality that must be felt to be appreciated. Centre of an Imperial cult, they have been for centuries the cradle—and the grave—of

---

[78] There are various kinds of dragons in China; dragons of the sea and of the skies, dragons horned and dragons winged. But the five-clawed dragon, the leading decorative motive in the Forbidden City (and the most picturesque and powerful of all animal forms), was reserved for the Emperor of China, like the sixteen-petalled chrysanthemum for the Emperor of Japan.
In fact the Chinese five-clawed dragon was symbolical not only of sovereign power but of all that belonged to the Sovereign. Thus he himself was called the "Dragon's Person," his countenance, the "Dragon's Face," his throne, the "Dragon's Seat," his pen, the "Dragon's Brush" and his children the "Dragon's Seed." See *Chats on Oriental China*, by J. F. Blacker.
According to Dr. Anderson,. the well known scientist, the "Dragon is the amplification of the Yangtsze Valley Alligator, not a reminiscence of a prehistoric beast, nor a cloud motif, nor a borrowing from Mesopotamian carvings." But there are many other theories on the origin of the Dragon too long to quote here.

reputations; the scene "of all those great diplomatic measures and dark deeds transacted by the Emperors of China between: midnight and daylight—not because 'their deeds being evil; they loved darkness rather than light' but because the Sovereign was so eager to serve his people that he must be about their business even before dawn."

1. Wu Men. 2. Tai Ho Men. 3. Tai Ho Tien. 4. Chung Ho Tien. 5. Pao Ho Tien. 6. Ch'ien Ch'ing Men. 7. Ch'ien Ch'ing Kung. 8. Chiao T'ai Tien, a throne hall where the Imperial seals are kept. 9. K'un Ning Kung, Palace of the Empress. 10 K'un Ning Men. 11. Yu Hua Yuan, garden. 12. Shen Wu Men. 13. Hsi Hua Men. 14. Tung Hua Men.

AA. Moats, store houses. B. Yang Hsing Tien, a throne hall in which the Emperor T'ung Chih resided during the whole of his reign. C. Ning Shou Kung, palace of the Empress Dowager Tz'u Hsi, including D. the Huang Chi Tien. E. Wen Yuan Ko, former Imperial library. F. Tz'u Ning Kung, palace of the Empress Dowager Tz'ti An during the co-Regency. G. Wu Ying Tien, a throne hall used at one time as a Court Printing Press, now the Museum. H. Nei Wu Fu, Imperial Household Department. I. Ch'uan Hsin Tien, formerly a memorial hall to Confucius and other philosophers. K. Nei Ko, formerly used by the Privy Council. L. Nan Hsun Tien, a throne hall where the portraits of emperors of former dynasties were kept. S.S.S. Palaces for the chief Imperial concubines. T.T.T. Palaces for the Heir to the Throne and his brothers. J. Hsi Hua Yuan, garden. X. Ch'e jg Huang Miao, temple to the guardian spirit of the city, built in 1726.

The Forbidden City

PLAN OF PALACES, FORBIDDEN CITY.

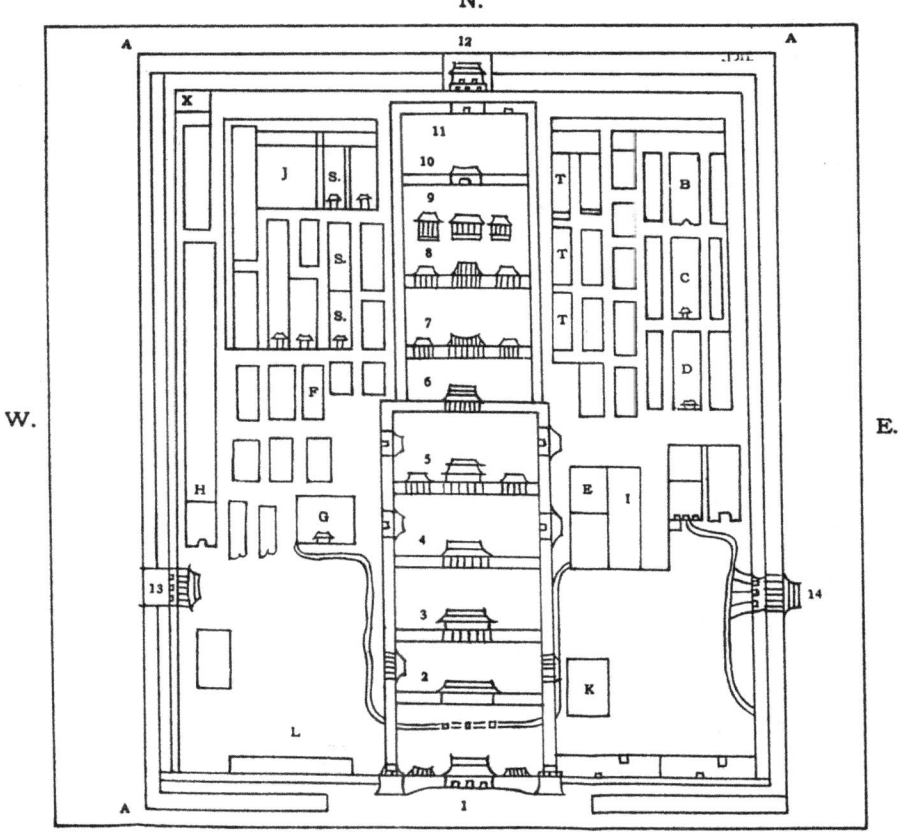

Juliet Bredon

VI. The Wings of the Forbidden City and the Coal Hill

If we compare the Forbidden City to the body of a giant aeroplane, then its two wings are the widespread enclosures attached to it, one on the east side, one on the west. These wings are the T'ai Miao or Official Temple of Ancestors, and the She Chi T'an or "Altar of Harvests," situated in what nowadays is Chung Shan Park. Carrying the simile still further we might call the Coal Hill, behind the Forbidden City (to the north), the rudder, or tail-piece.

Until the fall of the Manchu dynasty, the T'ai Miao enclosure was considered the most sacred place in Peking barring only the Temple of Heaven, because it was the Shrine of the Imperial Ancestors. The Ancestral Cult been since time immemorial deeply embedded in the Chinese race soul. The world of the dead ruled the world of the living, and every individual, throughout his existence, felt himself under ghostly supervision. It was each man's duty, therefore, to offer reverence and sacrifice to the Spirits of his Forefathers as represented by the Ancestral Tablets. In every home, no matter how humble, these simple unpainted strips of wood, symbolising the Souls of the Departed, had their place. Sometimes they stood in rows in a simple cupboard, sometimes a gallery was set aside for them, sometimes they occupied a special hall. But in the case of the Imperial Ancestors, not only guardians of their own clan but, in a broader sense, Protectors of the State, the magnificent buildings of the "Supreme Temple" (T'ai Miao) were alone thought worthy to house them.

These shrines are situated in a glorious old park with avenues of closely planted cedars bent and twisted by their battles with the winds. Such vast open spaces in the middle of a city—so vast that not a sound from the busy world outside penetrates them—serve as fresh evidence of the grandeur of Yung Lo's plan. Not like a miser economising ground did this Imperial Builder conceive his capital. But largely, nobly, with

The Wings of the Forbidden City and Coal Hill

an eye to the Sovereign's dignity, he stretched his walls to enclose great areas never intended to be built upon.

Empty and deserted nowadays, silent as a tomb, the T'ai Miao Park casts a sombre shadow over the spirit which the brightest sunshine cannot dissipate. Few strangers visit this scene of past splendours. The bent old guardian cooking a frugal meal outside his hut in a Standard Oil tin, is slow to answer a knock on the gate. "There is nothing to see here any more," he grumbles, "the buildings are closed. The roads are grass grown. Nobody comes, except the cranes who return faithfully every spring to build their nests in the old trees. For a brief season then there is life. But when their eggs are hatched and their little ones born, they fly south again, abandoning their summer homes at the first hint of autumn."

For any one, however, who cares to lay an ear close to this silent shell of solitude, there are murmurs of past activities. Listen. It is early morning on the day of a "great festival"—let us say the New Year or the "Spring Feast of the Dead"—that mysterious hour just before dawn when "brothers are not yet able to recognise one another." Mists drape a ghostly veil over this habitation of ghosts. By lantern light vague forms move to and fro arranging the tablets in their places—the tablets transported in great state two days before from the private Ancestral Hall in the Forbidden City.[79]

They await the Emperor who comes for sacrifice. Meanwhile His Majesty, to prepare himself for this solemn duty, has fasted all night long in the Hall of Abstinence within his palace walls; the special prayer for the great occasion has been submitted to him, and the Court Butcher reported on his knees that the sacrificial cattle have been slaughtered, their flesh duly prepared, and the "blood and fur buried."

---

[79] The Feng Hsien Tien, near the Wen Yuan Ke, or Imperial library, a hall closed to the public. This was the private "house chapel" of the Manchu dynasty where rites were performed in honour of the Imperial Ancestors on the 1st and 15th of every moon and on various other occasions. Only "official sacrifices" on "Great Festivals" took place in the T'ai Miao. The tablets still remain in the Feng Hsien Tien, each in its own cubicle reposing upon a yellow satin mattress.

And not only the Sovereign but all those Princes and Dukes who took part in the ceremony have been fasting too, refusing meat and wine and all fat dishes, giving up their favourite garlic seasoning. Even the people were forbidden to attend banquets or make music for three days. Moreover, the theatres were closed and the Law Courts ceased to function out of respect for the spiritual Guardians of the State.

A full description of the Rites would be too long to give here. Suffice it to say, they were very beautiful, very reverent, yet very simple. All was severely plain and pure. The wooden spirit tablets, inscribed with the posthumous names of those to whom they were dedicated and held upright in wooden frames, were each placed upon a yellow satin cushion on a throne chair facing a sacrificial table.

It was a purely family ceremony with no outsiders present and no priests. His own kinsmen, the Imperial Princes, conducted his Majesty from one altar to another. There was no favouritism, no varying degrees of reverence. For every ancestor the same offerings were spread— food and wine, of which the souls enjoyed the "spiritual substance." To each the same prayers were said, and the Emperor, in his role of humble descendant, bowed nine times and reported the successes and failures that befell his House. A victorious campaign against enemies, the treachery of a Minister of State, the choice of an Empress—all such events affecting the Imperial family were considered of as much interest to its spiritual founders as to its living descendants.

Slowly the Emperor made his way down the long line of Altars. There were eleven. As he reached the last, the sun rose; a cloud of white pigeons, wheeling above in the blue sky, settled on the sloping roof tiles. The candles guttered in the horn lanterns. The hour of sacrifice was past and the Imperial procession re-formed to carry His Majesty back to more material duties.

The picture fades as the light brightens. It seems fantastic now in broad daylight to suggest that ghosts might linger here. Nevertheless the visitor who can say farewell to the T'ai Miao without being moved must be singularly unemotional. Returning from the "Supreme Temple" through the park, few feel a taste for normal conversation. A word now and then, a forced laugh. For the rest meditative silence. A dog barking near the caretaker's hut makes one start. How could it be otherwise when so many strange spiritual influences stir imagination to its depths? Seeking instinctively an epitaph suited to ghosts long served and now neglected, one recalls the lines from the Book of Revelations, "For the former things are utterly passed away." True, but the old awe remains!

In striking contrast to the silence and deathlike atmosphere of the T'ai Miao, is the cheerful human gaiety that ebbs and flows on sunny days around the old "Altar of Harvests " (She Chi T'an), now surrounded by public gardens, though once it, also, had a solemn character.

Under the Empire, the She Chi T'an (not to be confused with the altar connected with the same ritual, in the Temple of Agriculture outside the Ch'ien Men) played an important part in the "Nature Cult" of which the former Emperors were high priests. Here, as at the Temple of Heaven, only a reigning sovereign had the right to sacrifice to the She and Chi spirits controlling the productive forces of the Earth.

Before a ceremony, this square open altar—a two-storied platform faced with stone and framed by four marble arches—was sprinkled with five different coloured kinds of earth; yellow, black, red, white and blue, supposed to represent the five cardinal points of the Chinese compass; north, south, east, west and centre. And strange to say one can still find, despite the wear and tear of centuries, traces of these coloured sands. But the holes dug in this platform, in which the food offerings to the Earth Spirits were buried, have long since disappeared, and the stone tablet that was driven into the ground to commemorate the She and Chi is nowhere to be seen.

In monarchical days this altar, built by Yung Lo in 1410 and re-built as late as 1756, represented "the independence and integrity of China." The surrounding park was only intended for a setting, and a very fine one too, laid out in what ancient

Chinese books on landscape gardening call the "Imperial Audience Hall style." The placing of every artificial hill, the curve of every walk, the shape of every pond, well and duly considered, result in a harmonious landscape of great dignity and stately charm.

The present Government, as if to underline the fact that the Altar of Harvests is out of date, uses this ancient platform for firework displays or boxing bouts. The buildings nearby have also been devoted to practical needs. In the great hall where formerly musical instruments for Palace Ceremonies were kept, funeral services for Dr. Sun Yat-sen and other modern patriots have been held, whereas the smaller hall, once used by the Emperor as a robing room, is now a public library.

Indeed the sacred character of the whole enclosure disappeared once the Earth Cult, sacred from time immemorial, was discarded like a worn-out garment. Nevertheless, strong opposition came from conservative officials when Yuan Shih-k'ai, ever daring, decided to turn the She Chi T'an into a public park in the Fourth year of the Republic. "Who wants parks in Peking anyway?" they grumbled. "We had none for centuries. The courtyards of our Buddhist and Taoist temples are always open. There, people can pray and play at the same time—those who have leisure. But the majority work all day long and seven days a week. Why, then, desecrate a holy place where none desire to go?"

But these prophecies proved wrong. Crowds flock to Central Park, where in keeping with its present character of a public playground, restaurants and cafes have been opened, swings for children, and bowling alleys for grown-ups installed, and even studios where fashionable folk are photographed "in a painted boat upon a painted ocean."

Such modern innovations, however, cannot spoil the unrivalled picturesqueness of the Imperial setting. Neighbour of Palace buildings, this former royal domain s is unique among the parks of the world. Nothing could be more imposing than the combination of avenues of bronze green cypresses, leaning most of them, but all the more beautiful for that reason; the

The Wings of the Forbidden City and Coal Hill

double red outer walls; the summer houses with their pointed eaves, and the unexpected glimpses of yellow tiled roofs in the distance. The whole makes a picture worth travelling many miles to see—a picture that once stamped upon the mind can never fade.

When the Nationalists took over the management of Central Park, they washed the outer walls a brilliant blue to represent the blue field of the Kuomintang party flag—a political gesture designed to impress the masses that the millenium had arrived. But a few dust storms sufficed to tone down the violent contrast of colour which no longer shocks the eye as one enters the main gate.

Opposite stands the "Victory Monument," very white against an avenue of dark, sentinel cypresses. This marble arch erected to the memory of the German Minister, Baron von Kettler, shot by a Chinese soldier while on his way to the old *Tsungli Yamen* (Foreign Office) in June, 1900, originally stood on Hatamen Street, opposite Lockhart Hall. After the Allied Powers defeated Germany the monument was re-erected in Central Park to commemorate the Victory of "Right over Might."

Under the trees beyond which, judging from their size must have been growing for seven or eight centuries, philosophers sit and argue, poets dream, or politicians discuss, while the more energetic bobbed-haired flappers and their beaux wander about seeing the sights. The tiny "Water Pavilion" of the island is a favourite resort of Chinese honeymoon couples who sit there hand in hand on moonlit evenings. The collection of goldfish, including fan-tailed specimens worth hundreds of dollars attracts amateurs. Scholars pause at the Yao Yen T'ing, the marble belvedere called "Arbour of Woods as Good as Medicine." Gift of a Chinese Christian gentleman, Mr. Ya Yung Tao, who has donated most of his large fortune to Peking charities, its walls are engraved with the maxims of Confucius and other Chinese sages. Children romp up and down the long covered corridor, so typical of Chinese gardens, or chase one another around the rockeries at the base of the artificial hills, while their parents sip tea at a fashionable restaurant.

Although flowers have no "official existence" in a Chinese landscape garden, blossoming trees and shrubs are often introduced for the sake of colour provided they do not interfere with the balance of the design. Thus at different seasons of the year Central Park will be gay with fruit blossoms, lilacs, wisteria, peonies, or lotus.

First to attract those crowds of sightseers who follow the "flower calendar" are the pale pink buds of the flowering fruit trees. Towards the end of March these suddenly burst open as if to remind the Peking populace that spring is here at last, after the cruel frosts and snow showers of the long winter. Now the Park, bleak and deserted through the cold weather, becomes a scene of bustle and activity. All the cafes prepare for guests, setting out tables under the trees. On a holiday afternoon, if the weather is fine, every seat is taken by pleasure seekers.

In April the lilacs reign supreme. Against a background of walls and buildings toned by the hand of time to mellow hues, the haze of purple and white blossoms is most effective—exquisitely fragrant too, and the happy hunting ground of Humming Bird Moths and Swallow Tailed Butterflies who seem to know instinctively how well their glossy black wings show up against the flowers.

The last petals of the lilacs have scarcely fallen when the wisteria opens. One day the gnarled and twisted vines appear grey and dead as if they had given up their struggle and capitulated to winds and snows. The next, answering joyously the call of the sun's warm rays, they suddenly come to life again and burst into bloom. Their pendant flower clusters, hiding all traces of the stem, give the distant effect of mauve smoke rising among the trees.

No one knows better than the Chinese gardener how and where wisteria should be planted to show off the long purple trails of blossom to best advantage. Always, we find male and female vines set side by side to perfect their blooming, and usually they are planted near a dead tree or a summer-house so that they may clamber to the top and transform stark branches into bouquets of pale mauve, or hang wreaths upon the azure tiles. But the wisteria, capricious as a woman, will often disdain one support and choose another, or, not content with covering a single tree, throw down long trailers to the ground, take new roots, and rise again to clasp a grey rockery in its arms and smother it with blossoms.

Towards the end of May the peonies burst into bloom in all the beauty of their rainbow colourings. The favourite flower of the Chinese, sometimes indeed called the "National Flower," its popular appeal is very great. News that the heavy, curling petals are unfolding brings crowds of admirers to the peony terraces, those raised platform's that only the expert masons of Peking know how to build. Children clap their hands in sheer enjoyment of the blossoms and many a poet stands, charmingly unselfconscious, beside one especially beautiful bud composing verses in its honour.

Last of the summer flowers is the lotus. It opens in the season of greatest heat when the cicadae sing the livelong day and frogs croak hoarsely from twilight to sunrise. Undaunted by the sun's fierce rays, this "flower of Buddha" continues to bloom until the first cool breezes of autumn, which bring new life to human beings, sound the death knell of the lotus.

The north side of Central Park borders on the Palace moat. Since the old dividing wall was taken down, it is here that visitors throng for "lotus viewing." By the end of June the broad lotus leaves are already floating above the water, swaying gently in every breeze. If a shower comes, these jade green goblets catch the rain pearls, rocking their treasure tenderly till it becomes a load too heavy to be borne, then reluctantly pouring it back into the moat. Finally, at dawn on some hot July day, the big pink buds open with a soft and characteristic whisper. Noon and the flowers close again, their petals curling up with the overpowering heat. Therefore true lotus lovers come in the very early morning to view their favourite flower in full beauty and, sipping a tiny cup of pale green tea at the water's edge, admire the dew drops that still sparkle like diamonds in the leaf chalices.

Facing the northern Palace moat with its entrance opposite the Shen Wu Men, or Northern Gate of the Forbidden City, stands the Coal Hill (in Chinese "Mei Shan"), a curious, indented mound shaped like a Chinese pen rest. Most people think it is called "Coal Hill" because of the legend that a provision of coal is buried under it for use in case of siege.[80]

But the truth is the expression Coal Hill comes from a popular misuse of the word "mei" which in Chinese means "coal" and also "beautiful," depending on the tone in which it is pronounced. What the scholars named "Beautiful Hill" the people, unable to read the written character, erroneously christened Coal Hill. They then invented a legend to explain their mistake, and the wrong name stuck.

When first built by the early Mongol emperors this artificial height was doubtless intended to serve as a lookout station. Theirs were troublous times necessitating men constantly on watch against invaders. But in the more peaceful days of the Mings the Coal Hill lost its war-like character. No longer needed as a defensive work, it was regarded vaguely as a protection against the evil influences of the north. In reality it became the tailpiece that rounded off the Forbidden City, and seen from the Inner Courts, it gives the effect of a theatrical backdrop which completes the view.

When Chia Ching, in the 16th century, commanded those five airy pavilions placed upon the heights, courtiers began to frequent them in order to look down upon the city where these prisoners of luxury were forbidden to wander.

As they grew more and more decadent, more and more careless of their duty, sovereigns and their eunuch officials, idled whole days away on this picturesque hill. Pleasure alone appealed to them, pleasure as thoughtless, reckless and extravagant as in the days of Marie Antoinette. *Après nous le*

---

[80] Colour is lent to this legend by the example of a T'ang dynasty emperor who did actually store coal under a mound behind his palace at Sianfu, in Shensi, many centuries before the so-called Coal Hill existed in Peking.

deluge was as much the motto of one regime as of the other, and led to the same fatal end.

Nevertheless, deaf to all warnings, the dissolute Mings wandered under the trees whose leaves, when the sun shone on them, looked like emeralds from the treasury of some tributary king, or reclined upon rich carpets with silken cushions to support their elbows. Some amused themselves by painting, others, summoning their attendants to bring ink tablets and writing brushes, inscribed upon a stone verses in praise of some famous Court beauty:

> "Like floating clouds her silken robes,
> Like swaying willow-boughs her grace.
> But may I even dare compare,
> The dazzling sunshine to her face?"

The ladies of the seraglio, wearied of their embroidery or of performing upon their reed flutes, likewise came with mincing steps and swaying grace to while away the interminable hours of their idle lives in the park.

There was often a whispering of silks, a weight of perfumes in the summer houses, of the titter of soft laughter as the painted damsels peeped through latticed windows or screens of leaves at the roadway below the wall, the Street of Everyday Life that skirted the Imperial Pleasure Hill. With proud indifference, yet with childish curiosity, these favourites of fortune, who thought the main business of living should be laughter, fun and happiness, watched the hungry beggars crying for coppers to passers-by, watched the carts toiling through the dust.

No doubt they pitied the insignificant and humble traveller in his dull blues and greys. Not for such as he the sumptuous splendour of yellows and reds, the richness of dragon robes, the lordly magnificence of pleasure parks. Then one day an Imperial edict, written upon perfumed yellow silk, commanded a Court painter to decorate the walls of a pavilion. The painter hastened to the palace immediately, brush in hand, prepared to begin his work. A prince received him courteously. "Serve us well and we shall know how to reward you," he said. "Meanwhile, have you any requests to make? What models do you desire, O famous painter?" For in the imagination of the prince, the picture was to be of some gorgeous court pageant.

But the Master advanced slowly to the doorway of the pavilion and pointed out the city at his feet, the gate towers, the temples, the trees, the carts, the horses and mules, the men and women passing by.

"These, Your Highness," he made answer, "are my models."

"But this is not beauty, only drab monotony."

"Pardon, Your Highness—this is life."

And the prince, turning thoughtfully away, let the artist have his will.

Fate, that grim jester, staged the tragic end of the last Ming Emperor Ch'ung Cheng on this very scene of his extravagant pleasures. More sinned against than sinning, this pitiful sovereign struggled manfully for years to re-build his government on a substantial foundation, changing Prime Ministers forty-seven times in his despairing efforts. But towards the last he was reduced to palace eunuchs as advisers, and these corrupt rats and foxes finally caused the downfall of himself and his dynasty. As dawn was breaking on the day of doom, "the bell rang in the palace for the morning audience but none attended. The emperor then... removed his long Imperial robe, donned a short dragon-embroidered tunic and a gown of purple and yellow. His left foot was bare.

Accompanied by one faithful eunuch, Wang Ch'eng-en, he left the palace by the gate of Divine Military Prowess, the Shen Wu Men, and entered the Coal Hill enclosure. Gazing sorrowfully upon the city he wrote on the lapel of his sleeve a valedictory decree: 'I, feeble and of small virtue, have offended against Heaven; the rebels have seized my capital because my ministers deceived me. Ashamed to face my ancestors, I die. Removing my Imperial cap and with my hair dishevelled about my face I leave to the rebels the dismemberment of my body. Let them not harm my people.' Then he strangled himself in

The Wings of the Forbidden City and Coal Hill

the pavilion known as the Imperial Hat and Girdle Department, and the faithful eunuch did like wise.[81]

It is a great temptation to linger in the pavilions on top of the Coal Hill, to look down upon the site of this pathetic suicide and beyond upon the Forbidden City drowsing in the sunshine, while high up in the sky a black cross hangs—an eagle surveying on motionless wings a deserted kingdom. History can suggest few contrasts more dramatic. One lingers sipping tea in the very summer house that Catherine the Great of Russia, thrilled by the accounts of her admiring Ambassadors, copied at Tsarskoe Selo. One harks back to the days when Rebellion still had some romance to redeem it and soldiers in velvet uniforms set the torch to the city until clouds of bitter smoke enveloped this Pleasure Hill.

Reluctantly then we follow the steep path that leads downward to the Shou Huang Tien close to the north wall. Four wooden archways face this venerable hall, These are curious because their supports rest in stone sockets carved like lions curled flat on the ground as if asleep. Bronze deer, storks and handsome incense burners decorate the high marble terrace, flanked by gnarled pines whose aching roots are imprisoned by carved stone railings. The building itself is a replica of the Feng Hsien Tien, or Private Ancestral Hall, in the Forbidden City—proof that it was connected with the Cult of the Dead.[82]

Ancestral portraits of the Manchu Sovereigns still stand in this their private chapel where supplementary offerings were made to these pictures after the sacrifices to the Spirit tablets.[82] Each emperor, painted life size and in ceremonial robes, occupies the central panel of a dragon-framed tryptich somewhat like an immense screen, with his two empresses, one on either side, and an altar table with vessels for food and

---

81 *Annals and Memoirs of the Court of Peking*, by E. Backhouse and J. O. P. Bland. The usual account that he hanged himself to a tree is incorrect, though until lately the chain he was supposed to have used was suspended from one of the pines.

82 Also to be seen in this hall are the musical instruments formerly used in the Confucian ceremonies—the jade gongs, brass bells and long, lacquered lutes.

drink in front. When, as in the case of T'ung Chih, Kuang Hsu, etc., there was only a single "official wife," the third panel contains a picture of a red phoenix instead of the portrait of a lady.

Many of these portraits are most arresting and well worthy of study. Nurhachi and T'ai Tzu, father of Shun Chih, founder of the dynasty—what sturdy men they look, tanned and weather-beaten by the hardships of the plains! Chia Ch'ing and Yung Cheng wear moustaches, a most un-Chinese habit. Ch'ien Lung bears the stamp of greatness; but pitifully feeble in comparison with their sturdy forefathers are the blank and boyish faces of T'ung Chih, the dissolute lad, and Kuang Hsu the semi-invalid. It is plain to be seen that the Manchus were wearing out. The Old Buddha is the last striking personality of her race and her powerful features contrast curiously with the dreamy countenance of her inefficient colleague, the Empress Tz'u An. In fact but one woman of Tz'u Hsi's line would seem to surpass her in strength— Yung Cheng's wife, that wonderful mother of a wonderful son (Ch'ien Lung)!

The vitality of these pictures despite their flat faces without shadows and very small hands without bones or muscles, is the more remarkable when we consider how ancestral portraits are painted in China. Even in the case of non-royal persons, the artist never saw his subject. Summoned only after his model's death, he appeared with his "Book of Faces" in which the types, both male and female, were numbered. Then the relatives gathered in solemn conclave, and, advised in Chinese fashion by their servants, chose from the book such features as they believed most nearly resembled those of the dear departed. Thus the death portrait became actually a mathematical problem. Nose 1, plus Mouth 6, plus Ear 22, plus Eyes 13, equals grandfather. Incredible as it sounds, this method gives a striking individuality to Chinese posthumous portraits. Somehow suggestion of resemblance is achieved, and no two are alike.

Whoever sets out sightseeing with a time table in Peking will bitterly regret it. Even places like the Coal Hill—a mere bagatelle compared to the Forbidden City-have a way of dissipating the hours. It would be a pity to miss, for instance, the group of low buildings to the west of the Shou Huang Tien, in appearance so ruined and insignificant that they might well escape the attention of the hurried visitor. Now falling to pieces, they can scarcely be called a sight any longer, yet this tumble down place (the Kuan Te Tien) was once a mortuary chapel where the bodies of emperors lay awaiting a lucky day for burial, often for months at a time. It is on record that K'ang Hsi came here in sackcloth to mourn his father and his lamentations were heard by the "common people respectfully listening outside the walls."

No one can fail to notice the series of stately *p'ai lous* and yellow-tiled pavilions that trim, so to speak, the south side of the Coal Hill enclosure. But unfortunately few strangers know where to find the entrance. A side gate to the west of Coal Hill admits us to this Temple of the Most High, the Ta Kao Hsuan Tien—from the rear. Originally a small detached palace built in 1550 the main hall was transformed into a temple dedicated to the Yu Huang or Jade Emperor, the Supreme Taoist divinity. Here China's sovereigns came to pray for rain, after first confessing their sins and admitting that the drought was due to their own lack of virtue. The rain tablet, now removed to the Forbidden City Museum, used to stand under a circular dome carved and gilded between two magnificent dragons chasing the fabled pearl.

The phoenix of the exceptionally fine spirit stairway leading to the smaller hall behind—the Cho Tien Ying Yuan—indicates that this building was for the use of the Court ladies. It was in fact a schoolroom where girls chosen to serve at court were taught etiquette "and the various arts respectable for their sex." "Every seventh day of the seventh moon," says Father Hyacinth, "they present the results of their skill for the inspection of the Emperor."

There are some trivial episodes which memory insists upon associating with certain places though it allows to drop out of account events more momentous that occur in the same settings. This cameo of shy maidens beginning in these monastery surroundings careers whose rich prizes were open to beauty and ambition, is the one that always comes to mind in these quiet courts.[83]

---

[83] For several months in 1900 foreign soldiers were quartered here because the place had been a Boxer stronghold, but the temple remains in remarkably good preservation and is now used as a branch library of the Palace Museum.

VII. The Sea Palaces and the Mongol Throne Hall

Ch'ien Lung was the last of the Manchu sovereigns to travel extensively in their Empire. His successors, lacking the energy and interest to see conditions for themselves, went no further from the capital than the hunting palace at Jehol. In truth, the Dynasty, like a valuable but mended vase—a thing that still looked to the casual glance whole and fine but was too flawed to stand any test—maintained an impressive appearance but lost touch with the Nation.

Behind the impenetrable calm of rose tinted walls, the later Ch'ing emperors, too apathetic for effect, too soft for hardship, varied the monotony of their dull, if gorgeous lives, by moving from the Forbidden City to the Sea Palaces, a ten minutes journey by sedan chair.

Though such close neighbours, the Sea Palaces were conceived in an entirely different spirit from the "Inner Courts." They have the charm of informality, lower walls without fortress gates or moats and larger gardens, permitting a simpler life. Their buildings border on the artificial lakes begun as small ponds under the Chins (who brought water to feed them all the way from the Jade Fountain) and enlarged by Yung Lo into the Three Seas; the Southern Sea (Nan Hai), the Central Sea (Chung Hai), and the Northern Sea (Pei Hai). Like the builders of Versailles, Yung Lo knew instinctively how to compose a landscape. He understood the charm of surprise and contrast, the value of artificial hills in a flat landscape and of artificial water on a dry plain. Consequently the elaborate setting of the Sea Palaces aims at a reproduction of nature in her many moods, but the general design is so contrived that all the separate scenes work into a harmonious whole.

When the Republic was established, the Sea Palaces were the first part of the Imperial domain to be taken over by the new Government and the Nan Hai, or Southern Sea Palaces, became for a time the "White House of China." After 1925 when the Provisional Chief Executive, Marshal Tuan Ch'i-jui moved out, taking with him both the Presidential and Cabinet offices, all three Sea Palaces were opened as Public Parks.

There are several entrances to these enclosures, each convenient for different groups of buildings. But in order to get a general view down the lakes, it is best to visit the Nan Hai and the Chung Hai (both within the same walls) first, and, for sentiment's sake, to enter by the Hsin Hua Men, the gate formerly used by the President and by his invited guests when he gave a garden party.

This gate has a romantic history far older than the Republic as it was erected by Ch'ien Lung's order for his Mohammedan favourite, a captured Princess of Kashgaria. Neither his devotion nor the gifts he showered upon her, contrived to make this homesick beauty, whom custom forbade to leave the palace once she was installed there, forget her husband and her distant home. Therefore the Emperor commanded that a double-storied pavilion be built, in order that from its upper verandah she might look towards her own land beyond the hills and hear the Muezzin's call to prayer from the Mosque across the road. And in this pavilion, still called by the Chinese the "Home Looking Building," this lovely lady known as the *K'o*, or Stranger Concubine, lived and mourned until she died by her own hand.[84]

The ruins of her Mosque stood, until a few years ago, just outside the wall of the Sea Palaces. "Services were held there by a Chinese Mohammedan who had made the pilgrimage to Mecca, an aged man supported in his crumbling shrine by a handful of the faithful; but he died in 1908 and thereafter the inner walls and pillars fell, so that the place, still beautiful in the last stage of ruin, remained a pathetic monument to the splendour of bygone days. It was pulled down by order of Yuan Shih-k'ai, ostensibly because it had become unsafe and because the site was required for the erection of barracks, but really because its tower dominated the Palace grounds at a point near

---

[84] According to her last request her body was taken back to Kashgar where her tomb may still be seen outside the city.

The Sea Palaces and the Mongol Throne Hall

the President's residence, and might have been used by mutinous troops for sniping purposes."[85]

The Nan Hai, or Southern Sea, begins almost at the foot of the "Home Looking Gateway" and as we follow the paved walk along its eastern shore, spreads out like a fairy vista before us with the Ying T'ai Island floating in the middle distance, and the white Dagoba of the Pei Hai standing like a sentinel against the dark masses of the distant hills. But climb the artificial mounds above the path and you get a very different outlook. Beyond, to the south, lies the city, in summer a bouquet of green leaves with the Temple of Heaven, like a single blue blossom in the centre; in winter, rows of naked, shivering houses with stark branches whipping in the wind above them. For never was a city like Peking for changing in appearance with the seasons, sometimes all rich and verdant, nearly tropical; sometimes all bare and grey and shrivelled with the cold.

From this height the Empress Dowager Tz'u Hsi watched the fires started by the Boxers on the fateful night of June 15th, 1900, watched them with satisfaction since they were a sign she would soon be rid of the hated foreigners.

Then, in the best of humours, she climbed down again and walked on to the boat-house where her state barges were always kept in readiness because Her Majesty was fond of water excursions. Indeed she gave orders to stop the bombardment of the Legations (in 1900) for an afternoon so that she might enjoy a picnic undisturbed by the noise of guns. These barges, shorn of their trappings and sadly in need of a coat of paint, now convey tourists across the lake and the rowers standing to their oars are a strange survival of a vanished regime when no subject could sit in the presence of Majesty.

Close to the old boat-house is a pavilion with an upper story for "lake viewing," and just beyond on the very edge of the water, a tiny look-out arbour facing the island. Then comes a

---

85 *Annals and Memoirs of the Court of Peking*, by E. Backhouse and J. O. P. Bland.

little garden, with buildings once used as a library (now a school) and near its gate the marble bridge that separates the Nan Hai from the Chung Hai, the water flowing from one "sea" to the other through a wide canal. The opposite bank, the western bank, bends like a curved arm to meet this bridge and in the crook are the ugly, red, foreign-style buildings put up by Yuan Shih-k'ai and used by him as Presidential offices. Just alongside them are a cluster of low Chinese houses, nothing much to look at in themselves but enclosed by a wall with picturesque doors and windows shaped like vases, tea pots, leaves, etc.—fantastic designs peculiar to Chinese architecture. The carved brickwork surrounding the window frames and over the tops of doors is as fine as any wood carving, whose delicacy it imitates.

Opposite is the narrow bridge leading to the island, for all its beauty a place of melancholy memories. Here the Emperor Kuang Hsu found his St. Helena, with only a few yards of water between himself and liberty. But the "Old Buddha," his implacable aunt who sentenced him to banishment, saw to it that the eunuchs on guard were changed daily lest they grow to sympathise with their prisoner and assist him to escape.

Unhappy idealist, too weak to carry out his ideas, he lacked even the driving force necessary to protect himself against the perpetual intrigues of Oriental Court life! Hour after hour, day after day, therefore, he sat on the broad terrace beside the lake gazing towards the Forbidden City, waiting, hoping perhaps that his last appeal to his fellow reformer K'ang Yu-wei might bring release, —waiting for two long years after his fatal *coup d'etat* in 1898.

When the Court returned to Peking from Sian-fu in 1902, Kuang Hsu returned to live on this same island with its tiny palace built out into the water among the lotus, but this time under less restraint and probably, owing to his timid and retiring disposition, by his own choice. Rumour says he died here and the room where "he mounted the dragon and ascended on high" is pointed out to visitors, a small room simply furnished but with large glass windows. Idly, with hands

The Sea Palaces and the Mongol Throne Hall

clasped in his lap, this frail and melancholy failure looked out to the last with pleasure on his little world of beauty. He had come to love the perfection of its dwarf proportions, the bright colours and variety of the roof tiles unusual even among Peking palaces, and to listen with philosophic pleasure to the lapping sound of the water that once held him prisoner and finally lulled him to his last dreamless sleep.

Leaving the island and following the path that leads along the western bank of the Chung Hai, or Middle Sea, we find ourselves in the famous rock gardens where the Empress Dowager used to give fancy dress parties, appearing herself, on one notable occasion, dressed as a Buddhist angel with the notorious eunuch Li Lien-ying in attendance.

A side gate from these gardens leads to a little theatre whose miniature stage gives the place an air of cosy intimacy absent from other palace playhouses. Across a strip of water, intended to soften the voices of the actors, is the royal box connected with the theatre by a gem of a marble bridge at one side. This box is actually a good sized room. When a play lasts several days—as Chinese dramas sometimes do—the spectators need space to move about. Only intermittent attention to the actors is given, or expected. It was, in fact, quite customary for the Sovereigns to retire into the side alcoves of their commodious *loge*, for a meal, a siesta or the transaction of state business.

The unsightly grey brick, foreign style building almost overlooking the theatre has a curious significance. The first time that the Empress Dowager Tz'u Hsi found it politic to receive the ladies of the Diplomatic Corps in the Sea Palaces, her own apartments were thrown open to them. But the guests whose rough manners failed to measure up to her exquisite standards, offended Her Majesty by fingering curios and draperies. "Henceforth," the Old Buddha declared as she ordered everything they had touched removed from her sight, "these clumsy barbarians shall be entertained in their own vulgar surroundings, not in my own home." That is why she, an artist to her finger tips and a lover of beauty in all its forms,

Juliet Bredon

deliberately caused this "house of ugliness" to be built. Let us forget it as soon as possible, pausing only for a moment to glance at the curious bronze figures with animal heads[86] beside the steps, and then go on by the Old Buddha's favourite walk along the lake, where once a light railway[87] ran, to the garden palaces she loved.

Indeed every nook and corner of the Sea Palaces is so closely associated with the Empress Dowager Tz'u Hsi— the extraordinary woman who held the Imperial system together long after it was rotten at the core, by her political sagacity and the strength of her remarkable personality—that wandering about them, one forgets their earlier owners. Everywhere her memory dominates. This was the domain she loved (far better than the stately precincts of the Winter Palace) and loving made her own. Here she felt free. Here she could escape from some at least of the myriad duties she had to perform—state duties and domestic duties too, as "official mother of a household comprising not only her descendants, the Emperor and Empress, but sixty Concubines,[88] several thousand eunuchs and a great number of Court ladies and maid servants on all of whom she must keep her watchful eye."

How often must she have paced the covered galleries of that zigzag bridge winding to and fro across the water—the "Bridge

---

[86] These figures represent the twelve signs of the Chinese Zodiac; the Rat, the Ox, the Tiger, the Hare, the Dragon, the Snake, the Horse, the Sheep, the Monkey, the Fowl, the Dog and the Pig. Such figures, in miniature of course, are placed upon the Altar decorated for the Star Festival and used in other household ceremonies. They also give their names to the two hour periods into which the Chinese formerly divided day and night. For a full explanation of these cyclical signs see *The Moon Year, A Record of Chinese Customs and Festivals*, by Bredon and Mitrophanow.

[87] It was built with the Empress Dowager's consent by progressive officials who wanted her support for some railway scheme. They got the desired permission for the commercial line but were told to promptly remove the sample from the Palace grounds.

[88] The system of concubines was to guard against the possibility of there being no heir—a calamity in any Chinese family and doubly so, of course, in the Imperial House. Lack of sons to carry on the line and sacrifice to the Ancestral Tablets meant nothing less than heavenly annihilation.

The Sea Palaces and the Mongol Throne Hall

of Ten Thousand Years"—on rainy days! How often must she have loitered with her ladies in that curious wall-less pavilion built over a spring that trickles slowly through a narrow channel in the pavement cut in the semblance of a Chinese ideograph! This intricate arrangement was designed to impede a rapid flow, for fond as the Chinese are of introducing water in the form of lakes and pools into their gardens, they do not care for quick flowing water near their dwellings. Indeed old fashioned folk still believe that a running stream carries good luck away with it.

Surely the Old Buddha picnicked in the blossoming season under those quaint twin *ting' rhs* with double roofs of soft blue tiles draped with wisteria vines! Nor, lover of flowers that she was, could she fail to visit the peony terraces in the late spring when the heavy pink and red blooms of the "King of Flowers" form a brilliant contrast to their setting of grey rocks.

Entwined with traditions of Her Majesty, are souvenirs of Yuan Shih-k'ai, the fatal President, who planned to mount Her throne and, during his short career as head of the state, also lived in the Southern Sea Palaces. He used as his waiting room the hall facing an oblong strip of water so like a Venetian Canal, with a finely carved ceiling and a floor paved with squares of marble, alternately black and white. He built that strange tabernacle with red doors studded with gilt knobs and carved balustrades copied from the Temple of Heaven, to contain the "golden casket" (simply a gilded safe) in which he placed the names of the three candidates for his succession, thus following, in his Imperial ambition, the precedent of an Emperor—K'ang Hsi—who made no public choice of an heir but hid the name of the one to rule after him in a sealed coffer.

Yuan's game was deep, his strategy subtle. While at heart he hunted with the Imperial hounds, he pretended to run with the Republican hare. Hence the small obelisk he erected in the Palace grounds. Its inscription says: "Set up to mark the opening of the first Parliament in China." But the date on the stone is only four months before Yuan Shih-k'ai dissolved that Parliament and the inconspicuousness of the Monument would seem to indicate that the Dictator was not over anxious to advertise a necessary commemoration. The light of after events explains much that seemed inexplicable at the time.

What a curious coincidence that this monument to a democracy she despised, should stand at the very gates of the Old Buddha's own palace—a group of buildings near the lake protected by a "Spirit Screen," or Wall of Respect (such as one sees before the entrance of nearly every big Chinese house or temple to ward off evil influences which must enter in a straight line or not at all) and guarded by a pair of blue cloissonne lions!

"Ten Thousand Years"—another name for the Empress Dowager—built this palace for her own use and Yuan Shih-k'ai spoiled it by roofing over the courtyard in front of her throne room and turning it into a hideous modern hall, where he received foreigners. The charming rooms behind now form a kind of dais to the new building, like an elevated stage divided and subdivided by carved partitions of rich brown sandalwood exuding a delicious fragrance. The frames of the round openings in these partitions, though sometimes six inches thick, are carved completely through with extraordinary richness and variety of design different on both sides.

Tradition says that in this regal setting the Empress Dowager breathed her last and that she died, as she lived, dramatically. Ill and worn, with the premonition that she was near her end, this indomitable woman courageously rose from a sick bed to give audience to the Dalai Lama. Seated on her throne in hieratic pose and full ceremonial robes, she impersonated for the last time the dignity and power of her mighty ancestors as the doors were thrown open and the Buddhist Pope, in his gorgeous yellow vestments, entered and bowed before her. But the solemn silence was broken by a deep sigh as the proud head of the woman who had attempted to dominate Death, fell back. The terrified eunuchs scattered. All feared a sudden tragedy, yet none dared verify their fears. Finally the Dalai Lama himself mounted the throne dais... and confirmed them. Within twelve hours of the Old Buddha's

The Sea Palaces and the Mongol Throne Hall

passing, but whether before or after remains an unsolved mystery, the Emperor Kuang Hsu also departed for the "Shadowy Land."

This double tragedy deeply shocked the world. But for the old Dowager's foresight in "placing upon the throne an Emperor, though only a child, about whose succession there was no question," before her own strength failed, a most difficult diplomatic problem might have arisen. Concerning this dark chapter of history few know, and none dare tell, the truth. The eunuchs say that "the fire in the Emperor Kuang Hsu's kitchen was out first"; officials affirm that the Dowager left for the "far country" two hours before her nephew. Did one or both depart from natural causes and which really preceded the other?

Wondering, guessing at the hidden intrigues, we linger to gaze across the lake at the larger temple where the Dowager so often went to pray, like all strong natures, that her will might prevail, and at the smaller shrine which seems to float raft-like, upon the water. Then we go on to the last important building in the Central Sea Palaces, the Tzu Kuang Ke.

This "Throne Hall of Purple Effulgence," easily distinguished by its high roof of green and yellow tiles, was originally built by one of the Ming emperors to receive his Mongol subjects and hence became popularly known as the "Hall of the Mongol Princes," though generally used for the reception of all strangers, including foreign diplomats, until 1900.

From its marble railings to the overhanging eaves that trim it like a rich valance, this palace, while not comparable to the Great Throne Halls of the Forbidden City, is built on a scale sufficiently grand to impress tributary vassals about to enter the presence of Majesty.

The interior forms one vast, lofty apartment whose bare simplicity increases the effect of size. The eye, undistracted by secondary ornament, instinctively seeks the platform with its two curious black marble tablets inscribed with Manchu and

Juliet Bredon

Chinese characters and the splendid carved and gilded throne of archaic design.

When Yuan Shih-k'ai gave his famous garden parties in the Sea Palaces, visitors were conducted to the "Mongol Throne Hall" to view the collection of Imperial portraits[89] hung there for the occasion. They then left the Palace grounds by the gate near the marble bridge which divides the Southern Seas from the Northern Sea.

The Chinese poetically call this the "Jade Rainbow Bridge" (built in a.d. 1392) because scholars refer to it as the point from which hangs the "Great Jade Rainbow," and the lake beyond they call the "Golden Sea" or "Pool of Great Secretion." (T'ai I chih).[90] Under Yuan Shih-k'ai's regime this bridge was divided lengthwise by a red wall which spoiled the view of the three lakes, though it prevented the public overlooking his quarters in the Southern enclosure. Fortunately this barrier has been removed and one of the loveliest views in Peking is free to all. "Whoever enjoys a thing possesses it." Therefore this beauty is ours so long as we choose to linger here—ours the reflections on the lakes, ours the noble silhouette of the White Dagoba with the golden halo of the sunset, ours the thrill of the rising moon as she dips her long finger into the water.

Before entering the Pei Hai, or Northern Sea enclosure, let us pause at the Ch'eng Kuang Tien, the circular structure so like a fortress, that stands at the eastern end of the "Rainbow Bridge." A heavy arched gate and a flight of steps lead to the high brick platform of this "Round City," to give it its familiar

---

89 These portraits or some of them, are now in the T'ai Ho Tien. The pictures of the Emperors of the older dynasties, with the exception of one or two Sung originals, are of course copies, though some of them purport to be authentic likenesses of sovereigns who lived from 3,000 to 500 b.c.

90 So named from a famous lake adjoining the palace of the Emperor Han Wu Ti, near Ch'ang An. Old records refer to this lake as the "Great Saliva Pool" (referring to the saliva of the Yang and Yin, or male and female principles of the universe) in which were placed the three "Islands of the Immortals," thus symbolizing the spiritual nature of the pool. Like so many names in Chinese gardens, these were derived from Taoist philosophy and have a significance intelligible to Chinese scholars but not to ordinary people.

The Sea Palaces and the Mongol Throne Hall

name, which was used as a palace under the Mongol Dynasty. But it is probably much older, for that reliable authority, Father Hyacinth Bitchurin, speaks of a white barked pine tree in the courtyard which was one of three known to have been planted by the Chins (a.d. 1125-1234).

No records of their tenancy remain. The dominating figure connected with this curious place is Kublai Khan, the most distinguished man who ever lived there. Both Marco Polo and Friar Odoric have left descriptions of what the "Round City" was like in his day. They say it was the "most beautiful palace in the whole world," which may well have been true in Mongol times but sounds ridiculously exaggerated at present, especially if we compare it to the Forbidden City. Probably when these old chroniclers waxed so enthusiastic, much existed that has since disappeared. They speak of "many buildings of large size with glazed tiled roofs, dragon-entwined columns and whitewashed walls," whereas now only one big hall remains, built in the unusual form of a Maltese Cross. It is empty save for the famous "Jade Buddha" with the "Mona Lisa" smile, a figure more -curious than beautiful and not really made of Jade at all but of Italian alabaster.[91]

The Nottingham lace curtains at the windows are a sorry substitute for "hangings of white sable and draperies of rich red leather." The rough bare floors and dingy walls no longer boast their "carpets of black sable and hangings of yellow cat." What has become of the "precious hardwood furniture carved to the fineness of cobwebs" that once stood in Kublai's apartments? And of the wonderful decorations of his throne hall, "enriched with different coloured marbles and shining with jewels"? Gone is his barbaric throne covered with cloth of gold and inlaid with precious stones, vanished no man knows where the clepsydra of

---

[91] Legend says this image was presented to Ch'ien Lung by a King of Cambodia. Obviously it came from abroad, as neither material nor workmanship are typically Chinese. The small "Jade Buddha Temple," just inside the Hsi Chih Men contains a picture of this image, proof perhaps of special sanctity.

Juliet Bredon

gold and pearls with the little golden figure appearing before the dial to announce the hours of the great feasts.[92]

On such occasions we are told, silver trumpets heralded the entry of the Great Khan among the guests. Vassals who served him wore "silken kerchiefs bound over their mouths and nostrils so that no breath nor odour from their persons should taint the dish or goblet presented to the Lord." Whenever he raised his cup to drink there was a burst of music, and the assembled company bowed low before the Emperor as he quaffed his wine. In those days none blushed to be thirsty and the huge pearl-tasselled jade vessel,[93] "two paces in height and exceeding the value of four great towns, was emptied from golden goblets by the riotous crowd of revellers as fast as pipes could bring the liquor flowing into it."[94]

Not only did wine flow freely at these old Tartar feasts but merriment was unrestrained. Mechanical peacocks contributed to the fun and the retainers of the Khan "in order to amuse their Lord," as Friar Odoric says in his quaint phrases, "go after one another and clap their hands, upon which the peacocks flap their wings and make as if they would dance. This," he adds naively, "must be done by diabolic art or by some engine underground."

After such feasts the noble host and his guests would adjourn to the Pei Hai Gardens to witness the lascivious "mysteries of Gopi" in honour of Krishna Gopi, the Herdsman, when sixteen maidens and eleven musicians danced and sang.[95] Or they might choose to row upon the lake in the Imperial

---

92 Was this perhaps the clepsydra, crowned by a lofty porcelain tower, which the "Beggar Emperor" Hung Wu of the Ming dynasty had razed to the ground to remove an evidence of useless waste?
93 To-day this giant punchbowl stands under a blue tiled pavilion built to shelter it. After the fall of the Mongol dynasty it was relegated to a temple in the West City and used by the monks for storing pickled cabbage. Finally Ch'ien Lung bought it back at a heavy price and added a description testifying to its antiquity.
94 *The Book of Ser Marco Polo, Cathay and the Way Thither*, by Yule Cordier.
95 A Ming dynasty ode describes these "Mysteries" and gives details of tie costumes worn by the participants.

The Sea Palaces and the Mongol Throne Hall

Dragon Boat with moving tail and flapping fins, or wander through the gardens where Kublai Khan ordered his henchmen to plant "a certain blue flower," brought from the Mongolian plains, as a reminder to his clansmen of the birthplace of their ancestors.

In those days the vast acres of the Pei Hai were a paradise for game, and many wild creatures roamed there undisturbed—"white deer and fallow deer, gazelles and roebucks, also fine squirrels of various sorts... so tame that the admiring guests might caress them."[96]

"If the Mongols, instead of amusing themselves with trifles, had applied their energies to the task of contenting the people" as the "Beggar Emperor" Hung Wu of the succeeding Ming dynasty, cynically remarked, "they might have preserved the sceptre in their family."

But Kublai Khan and his hard drinking followers ended by loving their golden ease too much. Nomads by birth, accustomed to the sane and simple life of the steppe, the luxury of a settled civilisation undid them. They have been dust these hundreds of years. Nevertheless the romance of their revels still clings around the Pei Hai, as the memories of the Old Buddha's fetes still seem to animate the Nan Hai.

Facing the south entrance gate rises the "Jewelled Island" crowned by the Pai T'a, or White Dagoba, which foreigners irreverently call the "Peppermint Bottle" because of its shape—a mighty monument glowing in the sunshine like a phantom lotus bud. There is a quaint tradition concerning the hill on which it stands. Once a miraculous mountain in Mongolia, known as the Hill of Bliss, its possession assured supreme power. A monarch of the T'ang dynasty offered a princess of his family as a bride to an Uigur[97] prince in exchange for it. The offer was accepted. But the mountain was large and difficult to transport. The Chinese, however, prayed to the God of

---

[96] "A few deer still remained in the Pei Hai under the early Manchu emperors." *Russia, Mongolia, China*, Baddeley.

[97] The Uigurs were once a powerful tribe in Central Asia. Our word "ogre" is said to be derived from the name of these dreaded barbarians.

Hindrances and Obstacles, whose face is dark. Then they built a fire around the hill and poured vinegar over it, whereupon like Cleopatra's pearl, it dissolved, and the pieces were easily removed to China.[98]

Scarcely less poetic is the story of the buildings that have stood on this enchanted height. Long, long ago in the days of the Liaos, the famous Empress Hsiao, the same who built the now ruined temple of Po Wang Shan on the eastern spur of the Western Hills,[99] erected here a little palace known as the "Powder Tower." But the vanities of women gave place to the chanting of monks when, by order of Genghis Khan, the site was handed over for a monastery to Ch'ang Ch'un,[100] the holy Taoist teacher (buried at Po Yun Kuan) whom he summoned to his Court to advise him on government and religion.

The present Dagoba was built by the Emperor Shun Chih in a.d. 1652 when the first Thibetan Pontiff to be confirmed in the title of Dalai Lama came to Peking and, probably as a delicate compliment to the illustrious guest, the form chosen was that of the Buddhist "chortens," or reliquaries, common throughout Mongolia and Thibet, which symbolise by their five sections—base, body, spire, ornament and gilded ball—the five elements, earth, water, fire, air and ether.

The Chinese have a superstition that this landmark visible throughout the city casts no shadow to the west, though on the east the huge mass of brickwork is always mirrored in the lake.

The ascent to the White Dagoba is fatiguing. But we are repaid for our efforts at every platform where we halt for breath. Here is the Temple of Silkworms dedicated to the Empress who taught Sericulture to the Chinese people 4,500 years ago, yonder a picturesque shrine encircled by a miniature city wall. It has, alas, been turned into a tea-shop. Further up

---

98 As a matter of fact this mound, like the Coal Hill, was probably the result of the excavations from the lakes. The Mongols carried a stream up to the top of the mound by primitive pumping machinery—a stream which poured from a dragon's mouth into a square basin. Their fountain has, however, long since disappeared.
99 See Chapter XVI.
100 See Chapter XIII.

The Sea Palaces and the Mongol Throne Hall

we get a glimpse of roofs whose vari-coloured tiles cover a Lama sanctuary with a quaint group of prostrate bronze figures representing the demon leaders of heretical sects, held down, at the Command of Buddha, by geese and other animals. Then one last steep flight of steps and we stand upon the highest platform. Between us and the huge Dagoba towering larger than all anticipation, is a single shrine of encaustic tiles each made in the shape of a Buddha's head. Some, unfortunately, have been defaced by tourists with a mania for souvenir hunting. But the triple-headed, many-handed Lamaist idol with a necklace of skulls remains intact. And no vandals can spoil the glorious view.

We climb down again to visit the famous Yi Lan Tang Palace on the other side of Jewelled Island—the most important building in the Pei Hai. Two paths round the island start from the Marble Bridge and lead to the narrow terrace of the Yi Lan Tang, or Hall of Beautiful Waves. On this curved balcony along the water's edge the "Old Buddha" loved to linger, looking down upon the lotus plants that, in the blooming season, appear as an unevenly woven brocade with a raised pattern of pink flowers. Leaning against the marble balustrade one summer afternoon in 1900, they say Her Majesty took the momentous decision to attack the Legations.

To-day this terrace has been transformed into a restaurant usually crowded with visitors, since for some reason the Pei Hai is more popular as a playground than the Nan Hai. Skaters flock here in winter, and in summer, families hire canoes and row up and down the open lanes of water roped off among the lotus plants.

Barges or sledges, according to the season, leave the landing stage just below the "Hall of Beautiful Waves" to carry visitors across the lake. They land us at the Wu Lung T'ing, or Five Dragon Pavilions, situated on a peninsula that juts out into the water like a sleeping dragon. Built in a.d. 1460, these arbours were a favourite resort of poets, inspiring many a sonnet. Formerly a gentle shadow of decay added a note of pathos to their beauty. But the restorations of 1925 spoiled the "atmosphere." New paint is a poor substitute for the carved dragons that once decorated their roofs, and glass windows divorce the modern sonnet writer from intimacy with whispering waters lapping against moss grown stones.

Little thrill is left nowadays in these Poet's Pavilions where chattering crowds sip tea or dine on doubtful tablecloths, and an attendant in a soiled coat pesters foreigners for "cumshaws." Yet far away from this too modern restaurant there are delightful old buildings and gardens where few visitors penetrate; deserted precincts asleep like the enchanted palaces of some fairy tale, and haunted by ghosts of the past.

When we have seen "The Curtain Wall of Nine Dragons," the centre of attraction for all tourists to the Pei Hai, and dined in the open air cafe near by with the fashionable Chinese crowd (so amusing to watch) that goes there because its chef was once head cook to the Old Buddha and his dumplings are famous, let us wander about those half-ruined temples.[101]

For the sake of sentiment it would be a pity to pass by the "Little Western Heaven" where plaster images of the saints stand among the hills and valleys of the Land of Unlimited Happiness, the paradise of the gentle Buddha Amitabha. Alas, nothing is left of the Wan Fo Lou Temple whose giant image, larger and finer than the one in the Yung Ho Kung [102] was destroyed by fire in 1919.

---

[101] This magnificent structure built of Imperial tiles with its nine dragons of different colours, fired and carved in high relief, disporting themselves on a ground of blue rocks and green sea waves, once served as a spirit screen to a temple. All traces of the latter have disappeared, however, and it now faces a grey brick gateway opening on a public playground, first made for the sons of Yuan Shih-k'ai.

[102] See Chapter IX.

The Sea Palaces and the Mongol Throne Hall

"White Dagoba"—Pei Hai

But it is pleasant to wander through the peaceful precincts of the Monastery of Ch'ang Fu Ssu amidst whose grass grown courtyards a Sanscrit printing press once existed, as the inscriptions on stone tablets tell us. A temple with two bronze pagodas flanking its deserted altar is equally of interest and we should not miss the "Precious Hall" behind it—a wonderful shrine faced with green tiles each made at a kiln several hundred miles distant from the particular place it was to occupy. Delightful too is the garden of the scholar Tsang Yuan who, having passed first in the highest literary examinations, entertained therein the Emperor of his day; and curious the little dock that Ch'ien Lung built when, like Peter the Great of Russia, he started making boats after his visit to the Hangchow Lake.

One palace in the Pei Hai remains closed to visitors. Formerly used by the Foreign Office for entertaining distinguished guests, this group of buildings situated in the midst of landscape gardens with ponds, rockeries and splendid old cedars, is now devoted to quarters for the Institute of History and Philogogy. In these secluded and inspiring surroundings where ladies of the seraglio used to walk followed by fat eunuchs with high pitched voices, Chinese scientists are doing valuable and constructive research work completely disassociated from political dissentions and upheavals.[103]

Far more than in these buildings, however—lovely as they are—the charm of the Northern Sea Palaces, lies in a setting which age has mellowed.[104] Indeed the atmosphere of these forgotten corners of Kublai Khan's Pleasure Park is indescribable, especially for those who have time to linger there in those early morning or late afternoon hours, when the public does not intrude. The poetic spirit of the Pei Hai, half ruined,

---

[103] This Institute forms part of the Academica Sinica, or National Central Academy, founded in 1927, with branches in the three cultural centres of China, Peking, Shanghai and Nanking.

[104] The Pei Hai is the oldest part of the Peking Palace enclosure and its beginnings date back to the Norman Conquest of England, perhaps earlier.

The Sea Palaces and the Mongol Throne Hall

silent and deserted, is like a savour that must be tasted, a perfume inhaled, a colour seen through sympathetic eyes. It is in the gnarled branches of old cedars and the reflection of willows bending over the lake. It is in the grey stone embankment curving along the shores. It is in the flight of ducks towards the south, the song of frogs in the rushes. It is in the flowing weeds creeping to caress the broken marble balustrades and the tender shrubs pushing their way through a yellow roof. It is in the shadows of the tiles on blue waters, and the purple tints of crows' wings on mauve gateways. It is in the solitary heron standing in the sunset on a rock, motionless as a bronze figure upon his pedestal. It is, in fact, the remembrance of the past staring at us wistfully, and the desolation of the present softly veiled by gilded dust.

Juliet Bredon

VIII. The Temple of Heaven and the Temple of Agriculture

Second only to the Palaces in splendour and surpassing them in holiness is the magnificent group of altars, collectively known as the "Temple of Heaven," situated in the Chinese City (the old "Southern Suburb" of Peking) within a walled enclosure three miles in circumference.

The total area of this beautiful park is a little over 700 English acres—about twice as large as the Legation Quarter—and were it not for the curve in the northern wall, would be almost a perfect square. This curve, however, was considered necessary, like the semi-circular brick screen behind Chinese graves, to prevent the ingress of evil influences from "the Northern abode of Darkness."

The arrangement of the "buildings, altars and broad avenues constitutes a lasting memorial to the consummate ability of the Chinese to utilize large spaces to the best possible advantage. Indeed the whole plan is very striking, especially as seen from the air, when the blue tiled roofs, white altars, red walls and borders of dark cypress trees stand out with a remarkable symmetry of arrangement."[105]

Without exaggeration we may say that no other sanctuary on earth has a more profound or grandiose conception, or more adequately expresses the instinctive desire of humanity to show reverence for a Power above and beyond its puny self. The open marble altar, radiant in its isolation, is a survival of those primitive altars on which the Perfect Emperors offered sacrifice 4,000 years ago, or which Abraham erected in his wanderings. It is one of the few remaining relics of the original Chinese monotheistic faith—the old, old belief that God is everywhere, invisible and all-seeing, "dwelling in a house not made with hands"—held in Asia before the gods were personified and their images enshrined in temples.

---

[105] Quoted from "A Mason's Survey of the Temple of Heaven," by Harold Cushing Faxon, p.m. Published in the *Peking Leader*.

The Temple of Heaven and the Temple of Agriculture

The Ch'i Nien Tien—Temple of Heaven

Juliet Bredon

One man and only one, the Emperor, Son of Heaven, was thought fit to ascend this worshipping place and, under the dome of the sky which covers it like a hollow turquoise, to make obeisance to the Supreme Being.

By reason of his divine descent, he alone could represent the "invisible power resident in the visible Heavens," and therefore his most honourable prerogative was to perform the annual sacrifices to the Ruler of the Universe.

Though the exact origin and meaning of these sacrifices became gradually lost in the mists of antiquity, the fact of their continuity for more than 4,000 years lent them a special moral significance. But with the passing of time the worship also grew to have a political importance, because the duty of performing it belonged by right to the reigning sovereign, and from a dethroned monarch the right passed on to his conqueror whose success was considered evidence of the call of Destiny, making him the representative of God on earth. "The public offering of sacrifice to the Creator was therefore regarded as the chief evidence of the authority to rule, and partly on this account the practice was strictly observed and jealously guarded by the sovereigns all down the ages."[106]

As the father of his people, sole fountain of power and honour, the Head of the State must not only be worthy to stand as the Pontiff-Supreme before the Deity, but bear the nation's sins upon his shoulders. The responsibility of the sovereign was acknowledged by the "Emperor T'ang (1766 b.c.) who said: 'When guilt is found anywhere in you (the people) occupying the myriad regions, let it rest on me, The One Man.' Again, when a human sacrifice was suggested as a means of propitiating Heaven in a time of great famine, he declared: 'If a man must be the victim, I will be he.' The ruler then fasted, cut off his hair and nails, clothed himself in rushes like a sacrificial victim, and, in a plain cart drawn by white horses, proceeded to a grove of mulberry trees where he prayed, asking to what error or crime of his life the calamity was due. That was in the

---

106 *The Original Religions of China*, by John Ross, D. D.

The Temple of Heaven and the Temple of Agriculture

18th century before Christ. In the 19th century after Christ, a prayer[107] very similar in intention was offered up by Tao Kuang (1832)" when drought scourged the land. Again in 1903, Kuang Hsu besought that rain be not withheld on account of his sins.

The Great Sacrifices[108] at the Temple of Heaven, where the Emperor gave formal expression to his function of Supreme Intercessor and consecrated Sin-bearer of his people, took place annually at the Summer and Winter Solstices, the latter on the same day as the old Druidic and Teutonic ceremony from which Christmas originated. Indeed the Chinese rites were a form of nature worship similar to that practised by our own ancestors thousands of years ago.

No foreigner has ever beheld the Emperor officiating in his capacity of High Priest, but the Altar has been seen prepared for the occasion; the huge horn lanterns hoisted on poles, the gilt dragon-entwined stands holding the jade gongs, and the shrine to represent "Heaven" placed upon the highest platform facing south, with the "tablets of the Imperial Forefathers ranged on either side "so as to form a rough nonagon."

---

107 *My Chinese Notebook*, by Lady Susan Townley.
108 The sacrifices at the Temple of Heaven belonged to the category of Great Sacrifices, which also included those to Earth, the Imperial Ancestors, the Gods of Land and Grain, Confucius and the Protectors of the Dynasty, as distinguished from the Medium Sacrifices and the Small Sacrifices to the Sun and Moon, the patrons of Agriculture and Silk Weaving, Mountains, Rivers, and Great Men. The special features of the Great Sacrifices were the open altar and the whole burnt offering—essential requirements which remained unchanged from the time of the Perfect Emperors (3000 b.c.) to the Manchus— though the accompanying rites were elaborated gradually. Twenty-six centuries before the Christian era there was already a Master of Ceremonial Ritual in China showing the importance attached even in those early days to forms. In the Book of Rites (Department of Sacrifice) of the Manchu Dynasty, the Worship of Heaven is prescribed with minute detail. The accompanying plan gives a list of the offerings to Shang Ti, the Supreme Deity, and of the persons present (among whom it is worthy of notice that no priests appear) to assist the Emperor. The reader is once more referred to the book of Dr. Ross for a translation of the full Ritual and many picturesque and interesting details too long to quote here. See also *The Moon Year*, by Bredon and Mitrophanow, for a detailed description of the three classes of "Sacrifices."

Secondary shrines to the Sun, the Moon and the elements stood on the second terrace, while incense bearers, musicians and official assistants in ceremonial robes occupied the lowest platform.

The Imperial visit to the Temple of Heaven was announced beforehand by the following Edict published in the official *Peking Gazette*:

"On the ____ day of the ____ moon of the ____ year, being the winter (or summer) Solstice, We shall reverently sacrifice to the Great Ruler of Imperial Heaven at the Altar of Heaven on behalf of you, Our people. The purity of the ministers depends upon their hearts, their righteousness upon the determination of each to exalt his office, lest by neglect to discharge their duties calamity be visited upon the State. Be reverent. Let there be no carelessness." A notice was sent to each Legation warning foreigners not to approach or attempt to look upon the Imperial procession. Chinese were ordered to remain indoors and to put up their shutters along the route, while the side streets were closed off with blue cloth curtains.

The day before the ceremony the Emperor left his Palace by the Wu Men in a yellow sedan chair borne on the shoulders of sixteen bearers, attended by his Master of Ceremonies, a cavalry escort armed with bows and arrows, mounted eunuchs in gorgeous robes carrying paraphernalia for the sacrifice, and standard bearers in velvet uniforms holding triangular flags. Escorted by this brilliant retinue, the Emperor slowly passed on his way to the "Great Lofty Shrine," located three miles south of the Palace because it had ever been the custom to worship Heaven in the outskirts of the capital. The central gate of the Ch'ien Men was opened to allow of His Majesty's passage, the picturesque marble "Bridge of Heaven" cleared of booths and beggars, and the street smoothed where it had been worn into ruts by the serrated wooden tyres of carts, and paved with sand.

The city seemed to hold its breath, awed by the deep solemnity of the occasion. In absolute silence, the sovereign made his journey and his sacrifice. Lest even the whistle of a distant train break the impressive stillness and thus profane the rites, there was no railway traffic in or out of Peking from the time he left his palace until his return to it.

The Son of Heaven awaited reverently in the Chai Kung, or Hall of Abstinence, the coming of that mystic hour before dawn which was to assemble round him the spirits of his ancestors. Then he ascended the marble platform bearing the round jade tablet (*pi*), an ancient symbol of sovereignty. He knelt humbly before the only Master he acknowledged, and, as the smoke of the whole burnt offering—a bullcalf of unmixed colour and without flaw—rose to Heaven, with trembling voice gave expression in the name of his people to the loftiest idea of worship they knew, a worship which, "recognising as sole divinity the spirit of the great blue dome overhead," discarded, for the occasion, all the idolatrous and superstitious practices of an essentially pantheistic race.

Very strange to Western eyes were the shapes of ritual objects, the actions and attitudes of the Imperial High Priest and his assistants. Each movement was regulated by tradition, and to perform well the functions even of an assistant necessitated a long disciplinary preparation. Officiating, the Emperor seemed rather a statue than a man, an image directed by invisible hands, his every gesture full of mystic significance, while the immemorial hymns of peace were chanted and the mimes performed the sacred dances with rhythmic steps.

When the Republic was established, the question of who should worship Heaven disturbed the conservative element of Chinese officialdom until Yuan Shih-k'ai, a man strong enough to make his own precedents, quoted the old, unwritten law that the public offering of this sacrifice "was the chief evidence of the right to rule," and claimed, as the head of the new Government, the prerogatives of Official Intercessor. The ceremony actually took place, but it was a pale shadow of the former sacrifices, grotesquely modernized by the presence of a cinematograph operator. Even Yuan Shih-k'ai himself realised that, without the prestige of Imperial descent, what should have been reverent became meaningless because the majesty and the sincerity of the worship had departed. It was therefore abandoned as un-republican, and the nation, indifferently transferring allegiance from Emperor to President, gave a remarkable example of how the Chinese will sometimes suddenly accept the overthrow of their traditions.

The Temple of Heaven has been alternately opened and closed to foreigners for many years—closed sometimes through their own impious behaviour as, for example, when vandals danced on the marble altar. After 1860 entrance to the grounds was easily gained by a small tip to the gatekeeper, but when the privilege was abused, the domain was once more rigorously shut. In the eighties a few foreigners entered by riding through a broken wall. But after 1900 the Allied troops forced their way in, and the First Bengal Lancers and a Punjabi regiment were quartered there, the officers' mess being installed in the Emperor's Robing Room (the Hall of Abstinence). Though military necessity was the excuse for the invasion of these mysterious solitudes, the Chinese were deeply shocked by it. The defilement proved an additional pretext for neglecting necessary repairs to the temples, which in a few decades threatened to present only a heap of ruins, overgrown with grass and weeds.

The place remained open for several years, shorn by events of much of its romance. A corner of the outer park was used for a time by the foreign community as a polo ground. Later, sports were held in the enclosure, and, on the establishment of the Republic, the Chinese themselves devoted part of it to an agricultural station of the Forestry Bureau. Yuan Shih-k'ai also opened the temples for three days to the general public, and for the first time the populace walked freely through the sacred precincts and Chinese women ascended the Altar of Heaven. Worse sacrilege still, General Chang Hsun camped his troops there in July 1917. When he attempted to re-establish monarchy, the holy enclosure was the scene of a battle between his men and the Republican soldiers. Walls were loop-holed and shells burst over the blue domes of the buildings, fortunately doing little havoc.

The Temple of Heaven and the Temple of Agriculture

Some efforts were made after the collapse of the Chang Hsun affair to repair the damage of time and of man— luckily, since the neglect of a temple so inspiringly beautiful is a world tragedy. Both in the inner and outer park new roads were made, gates opened to allow of finer vistas, spacious courtyards cleared of grass, and the public admitted everywhere for a small entrance fee. That barracks, a Wireless Station and a Bureau of Preventive Medicine were also part of the new scheme of things proved, alas, how nowadays utility is ousting reverence. But happily these modern innovations are not conspicuous from the temples of the inner enclosure which is divided by a second wall from the outer park.

Though a shrine dedicated to the Invisible Deity existed in China from very early times, most of the buildings used for the Worship of Heaven in Peking date originally from the reign of Yung Lo,[109] the Grand Monarque of the Ming Dynasty. The Chai Kung, or Hall of Abstinence,[110] where the Emperor used to keep the vigil that sanctified him for the service on the morrow, while his attendants camped in the spacious courtyards, is an exception, being a comparatively modern palace. Once it contained an Imperial throne and a handsome carved wooden screen, but these have disappeared now like the famous bronze statue of Silence.

A short paved avenue shaded by cypresses leads to the great white Altar of the Most High God. It stands open to the sky in the centre of a square court surrounded by dull red walls pierced by four marble archways. Four flights of steps facing the four points of the compass mount to the three shining terraces, surrounded by richly carved marble balustrades. The middle stone of the highest platform was considered by the Chinese to be the hub of the Universe. Moreover, every detail of

---

109 Like Louis XIV in France and Peter the Great in Russia*this long-lived, energetic sovereign has associated his name closely with his capital. Something of his mighty presence lingers in every monument, for, as a great patron of the acts, he left traces of his taste, and his generosity everywhere. Indeed no monarch since Yung Lo has enjoyed the proud privilege of stamping his individuality more strongly on the city than its founder.

110 A similar palace, for ceremonial fasts, exists within the Forbidden City.

this magnificent monument—the last word in majesty—had a deep significance. Conceived with geometrical precision, it was, like the Forbidden City, the combined work of architects, astronomers and doctors of magic.

The Altar we see to-day is not, however, as originally built by Yung Lo, but a reconstruction carried out under Ch'ien Lung whose Edict on the subject is worth quoting:

"The Space upon the Altar of Heaven is too small for the accommodation of the tabernacles, sacrificial vessels, and various other articles to be arranged thereon. In planning to substitute a new altar the surface of the three terraces, while still preserving the numerical relation of nine by five (both sacred numbers in China), should be enlarged so as to enable those officiating to have more room to move about and show proper reverence. You officers should carefully consider and memorialise. Respect this."

This remarkable document called forth a no less extraordinary reply from the officials to whom it was addressed:

"In compliance with the Edict, we have consulted and found that the measurement of the old Altar of Heaven... of the Ming Dynasty shows a very slight connection with the 5 by 9 numerical relation... We now propose that according to the correct standard—the musical pipes—the Altar be made to contain by ancient measurement in the first terrace a diameter of 9 *chang*, or 1 times 9, in the second a diameter of 15 *chang* or 3 times 5, and in the third terrace a diameter of 21 *chang* or 3 times 7, so that the heavenly numbers 1, 3, 5, 7, and 9, will all be represented, and the diameter of the three terraces added together will make a total of 45 *chang*, thus expressing the numerical relation of 9 times 5... "

Evidently Ch'ien Lung and his officials attached the greatest importance to the preservation of these interesting numerical sequences in the only altar in China dedicated to the worship of the One Supreme Deity. Multiples of nine appear in the flights of stairs of nine steps each, in the total number of the balustrades (360) and on the uppermost terrace which

The Temple of Heaven and the Temple of Agriculture

contains nine times nine or 81 stones, the figure nine squared being the symbol of completeness to the Chinese.[111]

South-east of this remarkable Altar at the distance of an arrow's flight, stands a furnace for the flesh offering. It is nine feet high (again the sacred number) with three flights of steps and faced with green tiles. The bullock was placed inside upon an iron grating under which a fire was kindled. The rolls of silk, which also formed part of the offerings, were burned in eight openwork metal braziers; likewise the prayers written upon silk, after they had been formally presented and read before the tablets. An urn was added when an emperor died.

Directly north of the altar and facing it is the small building with a round roof of black enamelled tiles, known as the "Imperial World" (Huang Ch'ing Yu) where the spirit tablets of the Ch'ing Emperors were kept.[112] A paved causeway behind leads to the Ch'i Nien Tien, or Temple of the Happy Year, whose triple roof is a conspicuous landmark all over Peking. Nothing could be lovelier than the approach to this hall—the raised marble avenue in the centre with the out-jutting platform for the Emperor's yellow resting tent; on the right and left groves of sombre firs, throwing into relief the white pavement. The avenue ends at a gate with a curved and gabled roof. Beyond this we stand face to face with the noblest example of religious architecture in the whole of China. "Springing upwards from a three-tiered marble terrace, the Temple of the Happy Year rises 99 feet into the air, a magnificent triple-roofed, azure-tiled, gold-capped shrine." In all the decorations it is the blue of the celestial vault, bending tenderly over this masterpiece of human aspiration, which triumphs. So it was meant to be, for the colour was deliberately repeated in the

---

111 Quoted and abridged from *A Mason's Survey of the Temple of Heaven, Showing the Importance of the Numerical Sequences Upon which the Famous Altar was originally Erected*, by Harold Cushing Faxon, p.m.

112 Until 1913 these ancestral tablets stood here enclosed in wooden shrines placed on low stone tables, four on the east side and four on the west side of the circular hall. They were removed in 1913 to the T'ai Miao or Temple of Ancestors and their places are now occupied by tablets to the Spirits of the Sun, Moon, Stars and other Forces of Nature.

porcelain of sacrificial utensils that the Emperor used, in his own robes and those of his assistants. Even the light that fell upon the sacred celebrations was softened tc the delicate shade of a cloudless sky by thin glass rods strung together in cords and hung over the tracery of doors and windows.[113]

There is a legend that the "Temple of the Happy Year" was struck by lightning when it burned to the ground[114] in 1889. The Chinese believed that this disaster happened because a centipede dared to climb the gilded ball, and attributed the series of calamities that afterwards befell the Empire to the wrath of Heaven at such presumptuousness. To appease this anger the temple was rebuilt. But the wood of the original columns, probably some kind of chestnut, could not be found. After a long search to fulfil the requirements of tradition, it was agreed to use Oregon pine of which huge logs were imported with much difficulty and at enormous expense.

These columns are one of the most remarkable features of the building. Four, elegantly lacquered, support the upper roof, while the two lower roofs rest upon twelve plain red pillars—all straight trunks of single trees.[115] Phoenixes and dragons adorn the panelled ceiling divided by painted cross-beams lustrous with colour and gold. The windows are covered with openwork

---

[113] "Colour symbolism," says Bushell, "is an important feature of Chinese rites. Just as at the Temple of Heaven all is blue, at the Temple of Earth all is yellow, at the Temple of the Sun, red, and at the Temple of the Moon, white, or rather the grayish blue which is known as *yueh pai* or moonlight white, pure white being reserved for mourning. The changing seasons have likewise a mystic significance which is reflected in the Imperial robes."

[114] The fire was really due to carelessness, not lightning at all, and thirty-two officials and guardians lost their heads for it.

[115] The great weight of Chinese roofs always necessitates the multiple employment of the column which is thus assigned a function of the first importance, as the stability of the whole structure depends upon the framework. The walls, filled in afterwards with brickwork, are not intended to figure as supports. The space, in fact, is often occupied by doors and windows carved with elegant tracery of the most flimsy character.... The old Chinese buildings are therefore curiously analogous to the modern American buildings with their skeleton framework of steel filled in with dummy walls.—Bushell.

The Temple of Heaven and the Temple of Agriculture

wooden screens of graceful designs—designs in which the Chinese excel, more than seventy different patterns being known. Brass hinges, beautifully worked, and gilded bosses ornament the handsome doors which open to—emptiness. Only a throne screen with (curious modern note!) an electric bracket, and the shrines for the Ancestral Tablets, stand lost and lonely in the shadows of the temple. Did the Chinese architects wish to tell us that all pomp and power and beauty lead to emptiness and silence?[116]

A number of secondary buildings surround the central hall. They are closed, no matter for regret, being on the whole of little interest; guard houses, resting rooms for attendants, kitchens where the consecrated meats were prepared according to the ancient ritual, and store rooms where the sacrificial paraphernalia was formerly kept.

What do repay a visit are the long, cool corridors on the east that lead to an old disused well, near which a certain wild asparagus—noted for its medicinal qualities—used to grow, and the nine boulders, carved with clouds that legend assures us were used by the Emperor Yu to close the holes in the sky which caused the Deluge. In this quiet corner where the casual tourist so seldom penetrates, we can gaze with no fear of interruption over the acres of waving grass where sacrificial cattle used to browse, and enjoy the scent of wild herbs and the sight of violets peeping out between old stones.

Let us return, if time be given us, in the early morning when the light is pale and the roofs hang like a faint, faint vision in a milky atmosphere soft as memory, and again at high noon when the full splendour of heaven kindles and sparkles, and yet again when the sun is sinking like a fiery ball behind the Western Hills, touching the marble till it blushes. Let us stand once more on the Altar in the magic moonlight; or when the powdery flakes of snow descend with fairy, transforming touch.

---

116 The first republicans were desirous of making this sacred building the cradle of their laws, and the Committee for drafting the Constitution held sittings here for a short time, but Yuan Shih-k'ai ended the work of this assembly.

Juliet Bredon

When we have seen the Temple of Heaven in many moods, then and only then will we appreciate the full harmony of its proportions; the skilful! blending of noble architecture with the beauty of trees and the spaciousness of the sky, and realize how truly it reflects life and life everlasting. Then we will feel that the sacred groves and buildings stand for wisdom, love and reverence and an all pervasive peace that tempers the divine radiance to man's benighted understanding.

The Temple of Heaven and the Temple of Agriculture

PLAN OF SACRIFICES, ALTAR OF HEAVEN.

This plan, compiled from the Manchu "Directory of Worship," refers to that portion of the Temple of Heaven enclosure in which the sacrifice is offered and its attendant ceremonies performed.

- A. The third or highest platform on which is set the shrine to Shang Ti and the shrines to the Five Emperors. These offerings are placed between the numerals i and 3 of the Plan.
- B. The second platform.
- C. The lowest platform.

1. Position (above the steps) of the shrine of Shany Ti, facing south.
2. The shrines of the Five Emperors facing east and west.
3. The praying place with the table for the Written Prayer.
4. The tsun, or Wine Vessel.
5. The place for the Reciter of the Written Prayer.
6. Large censers for incense (lu).
7. Imperial Guards.
8. Officials in charge of incense.
9. Officials in charge of silks (offerings).
10. Officials in charge of sacrificial vessels.
11. Place for the Reciter of the Prayer.
12. Officials in charge of kneeling cushions.
13. Officials of the Censorate.
14. The Kuang Lu, or officials who present meat and drink to the Emperor.
15. Officials in charge of placing the shrines, etc.
16. Officials of the Board of Rites.
17. Place of the Emperor.
18. The official Assistants of the Emperor—the Sacrificial Court and the Prompter.
19. Officials in charge of kneeling cushions, etc. (Same as 12).
20. Officials of the Censorate. (Same as 13).

21. Shrine to the Sun. (On second platform).
22. Shrine to the North Star.
23. Shrine to the Five Planets.
24. Shrine to the Twenty-eight Constellations.
25. Shrine to the Host of Stars.
26. Shrine to the Moon.
27. Shrine to the Clouds.
28. Shrine to Rain.
29. Shrine to the Wind.
30. Shrine to Thunder.
31. Place for the Princes.
32. Place for the Censors.
33. Place for officials of the Board of Rites.
34. Place for the Ushers.
35. Place for the Director of Ceremonies.
36. Place for the subordinate attendants who sacrifice to the Secondary Deities.
37. Place for the Pei Tzu and Dukes.
38. Place for the musicians and dancers.
39. Place for minor officials assisting.
40. Place for the singers.
41. The furnaces (liao) for burning the silks, etc.
42. The place for officials in charge of this burning.
43. The great furnace for the whole-burnt sacrifice of the bull.
44. The ceremonial place whence this burning of the sacrifice is witnessed.
45. Assistants.
46. Place for minor officials to witness the burning of the sacrifice.

Reproduced from The Original Religion of China, by John Ross, D.D.

The Temple of Heaven and the Temple of Agriculture

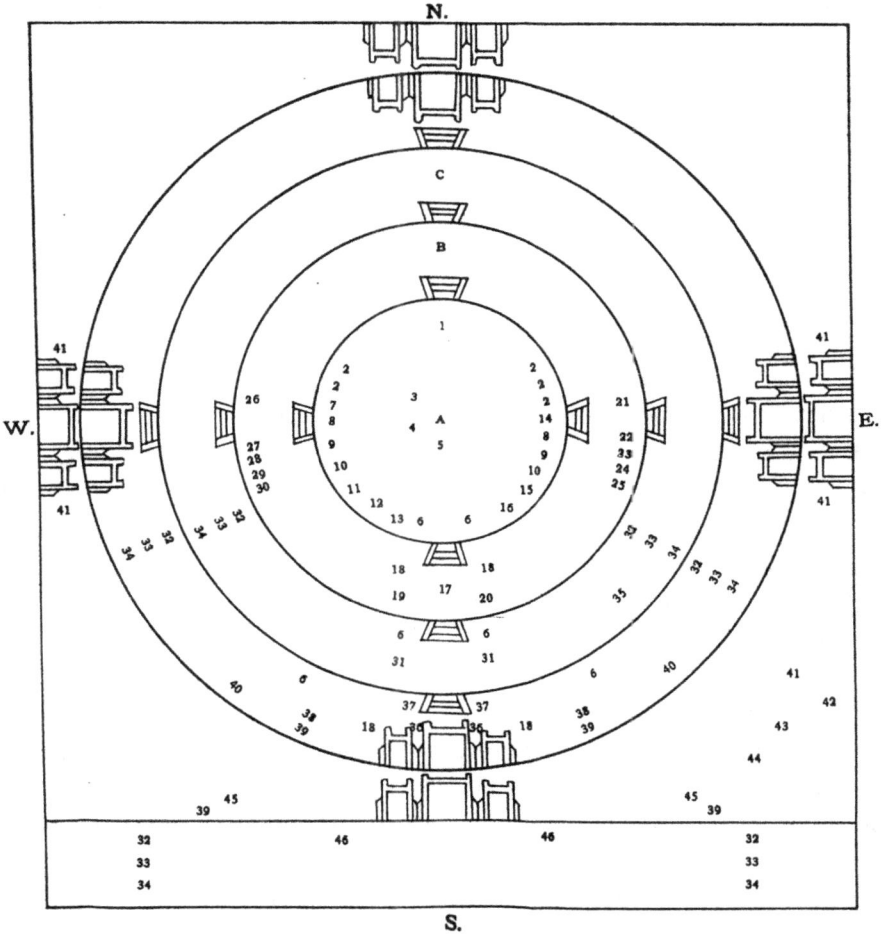

Juliet Bredon

On the other side of the broad street leading from the Ch'ien Men to the Yung Ting Men stands the Temple of Agriculture (Hsien Nung T'an)—a counterpart of the Temple of Heaven but on a smaller scale—dedicated to the cult of Shen Nung, a prehistoric emperor known as the First Farmer, whose "special talents enabled him to understand the cereal world and exercise great influence over it," and to whom are ascribed the invention of the plough, the discovery of the medicinal properties of plants and the establishment of the first markets.

This temple also has a deep significance in a country primarily agricultural where, as Emerson says, the people believe that "all trade rests at last on the farmer's primitive activity" and honour his calling;[117] where the sovereign himself confirmed the high, idealistic position of the cultivator of the soil by offering solemn worship to the fruitfulness of the earth. Here each year on the first day of the second period (*fu*) of spring he came with a numerous suite, including three princes and nine high officials, and sacrificed to Shen Nung's tablet in the large hall near the Hsien Nung T'an, or "Altar to the Inventor of Agriculture." He then went into the field set aside for the purpose and ploughed with his own hands a furrow from east to west, coming and going three times, thus setting an example of industry to his subjects, and dignifying the toil of the meanest field labourer. The chief of the Ministry of Finance stood at the Emperor's right hand flourishing a whip, the Viceroy of Chihli province on his left holding the seed, which a third official sowed in the furrow behind His Majesty. When the Sovereign's task was finished, he retired to a resting place, the Ch'in King T'ai, where he watched the princes and dignitaries finish the field. The ground was afterwards tended by old and skilled labourers chosen from among the farmers, and the crop, gathered in autumn, kept in storehouses and used for special offerings. Following the Imperial example, the heads of provincial governments, the prefects and district magistrates

---

[117] In China the farmer is classed only after the scholar and before the merchant and the artisan, these being the four estates into which the people were divided.

The Temple of Heaven and the Temple of Agriculture

all over the empire went through a similar ritual on the same day. But the rank of the Chief Actor rendered the ceremony most imposing in Peking.

The other large buildings in the Temple of Agriculture are the T'ai Sui Tien, or Temple to the Planet Jupiter, the Shen Chih T'an, or Altar to the Spirits of the Sky and Earth, and a palace, the Ch'ing Ch'eng Kung. To the north of the altar stand four grey stones engraved with the dragons of the clouds. Sacrifices were offered here to the Sacred Mountains. Yonder two more stones, carved to represent rivers, have hollow receptacles at their bases for libations to the Spirits of the Waters.

Though the present Temple of Agriculture was only built in the Chia Ching reign of the Ming dynasty (about a.d. 1520), the worship of the Emperor-God of Husbandry is infinitely old. We have a description of the ceremonies as practised under the Yuans and records tell us how, under the Mings, eunuchs assisted the Emperor. But, like the Worship of Heaven, the cult of Shen Nung has been abandoned since the establishment of the Republic.

The enclosure, forbidden to visitors till after 1900, when it was occupied by American troops, is now open to the public, the outer park intersected by broad roads. The inner precincts, where the buildings are situated, has been made into a public garden with neat railed walks, benches under the trees, and cages for deer. But the main hall, re-decorated by Ch'ien Lung, and the storehouses where the Emperor's yellow ploughs were kept, are closed and sealed. A trivial wooden summer house now stands upon the principal altar, which is square to represent earth, as the T'ien T'an (Temple of Heaven) is round to represent the heavens.

Hall in the Temple of Agriculture

The Temple of Heaven and the Temple of Agriculture

Those who knew the Temple of Agriculture before the tidying up process destroyed its originality and character —a process very different from artistic restoration and repair of beautiful old buildings—will always regret the peace, the loveliness of the place as it was; a wild waste of grass land carpeted in summer with mauve wild turnip flowers, where the bronzed, bent guardians cut rushes and piled bundles of fragrant herbs, where silence, broken only by the cawing of rooks or the song of a meadow lark, reigned, and one felt drawn close to the secret wonders and charities of the earth.

Juliet Bredon

IX. Three Temples of Three Faiths

Apart from the worship of Heaven and of Earth - official rather than popular rites—there were many religious cults in China and many temples to different faiths in Peking.[118] That these existed so peaceably side by side was due to the innate toleration of a people not given by nature to strong religious convictions or antipathies and willing to let each man seek truth in his own way. In fact, "China enjoys a unique position in religious thought," as Parker says,[119] "because samples of all religions have been presented to her in turn, and it is surely very much to her credit that at no period of her history have the ruling powers 'in being' .... refused hospitality and consideration to any religion recommended to them purely as such." Official sanction was given to various forms of Buddhism, to Jesuits, Dominicans and Franciscans, to Orthodox Missions from Russia, to semi-religious philosophical and ethical systems like Taoism and Confucianism, even to Mohammedanism, most militant of all faiths, which (perhaps in return for this recognition) showed itself less aggressive in China than elsewhere.

The Mohammedan Rebellions must not be regarded as religious wars. They originated in political rivalries or mercenary disputes and were crushed by the Government because they interfered with state policy and public order. Though tens of thousands were slain in these bitter struggles, the survivors suffered no religious persecution. Their faith—the Faith of the Prophet— remains to this day a living force in China, with deeper roots than any other foreign teaching

---

118 According to recent statistics published by the Bureau of. Social Welfare of the local Municipal Government, there are 1,968 temples and monasteries in the 15 police districts into which Peking is divided. Of these 1,048 are administered by the representative of the different religious orders to which they belong; 723 arc in charge of civilian trustees, while 135 are practically deserted.
Connected with these temples are 2,133 Buddhist monks and nuns, 605 Taoist monks, 149 Lamas and 160 Moslem priests.
119 *China and Religion*, by E. H. Parker.

Three Temples of Three Faiths

introduced into the country, save only Buddhism, and the last Manchu Emperors ruled almost as many Moslem subjects as the Sultan of Turkey and the Shah of Persia together.[120]

Over 10,000 Moslems live in Peking. The brass crescent of the Mohammedan meat seller may be seen on many a butcher's stall, while the followers of the Prophet still have almost a monopoly of the caravan trade to and from Peking.

For their spiritual needs we find many mosques scattered over the city—the Chinese say forty, but this is probably an exaggeration. The most famous and one of the oldest (built in a.d. 1764 by the Emperor Ch'ien Lung for his Mohammedan concubine) formerly stood on the Ch'ang An Chieh facing the Presidential Gate.[121] Its worshippers claimed descent from the Prophet himself, through the Khoja of Kashgar and Hi, and were brought to Peking as prisoners of war after the famous campaign of Ch'ien Lung's general Tsao Hui in Chinese Turkestan. The best known "Li Pai Ssu"[122] or "Temple of Ritual Worship" still standing, is the one in the Niu Chieh (Cow Street), south-east of the Chang Yi Men in the Chinese City. It well repays the trouble of a visit, preferably on Friday, the Mohammedan Sabbath, when the principal service is held at two o'clock in the afternoon.

---

120 "It is a remarkable thing that the Chinese histories record not a single word about the introduction of Mohammedanism. We only know in a general way that Islam spread over Asia in the ninth and tenth centuries and had already established a firm foothold in China in the time of Kublai Khan who... issued a decree requiring that Mussulmans and other persons of foreign religions should do their share of military duty."—(Parker). There is a legend that the first mosque in China, "The Mosque of Holy Remembrance," was built at Canton by the maternal uncle of Mohammed. Among the best reference books on this interesting subject are: *Islam in China*, by Marshall Broomhall, *Origine de I'lslamisme en Chine*, by Deveria, *Le Mahometisme en Chine*, by De Thiersanr, and *China and Religion*, by E. H. Parker.
121 See Chapter VII.
122 The word "Li-pai" for "worship" was first used by Mohammedans and was then adopted by Protestant Missionaries who introduced this expression for "Sunday" and for "a week."

Juliet Bredon

The Moslems who crowd the lane dress in the same blue cotton robes worn by the bulk of the population. Likewise their mosque from the exterior appears like any ordinary Chinese temple. This is disappointing to the visitor, who may be expecting a sanctuary resembling St. Sophia on a smaller scale. But in China native influence invariably modified what was borrowed from other nations, hence domes are replaced by Chinese roofs and minarets by square towers.

We enter by a small gate, passing an open mortuary with stone slabs where the bodies of the Moslem dead lie wrapped in winding sheets, awaiting burial.[123] Polite attendants, some of whom show distinct traces of Arab blood, lead us to the Hall of Prayer, a Ming building, repaired and redecorated. A venerable old man, who might be mistaken for a prophet, requests us to remove our shoes and ushers us in, holding up the heavy blue door curtain. After the full blaze of the sun, the filtered light from the *musharabieh*-screened windows, reminiscent of mosques in Spain, is dim as moonshine. For a minute or two we distinguish nothing but gleams of gilding in a soft gloom. Then we perceive rows of wooden pillars dividing the room into naves and at the farthest end, facing the entrance and looking toward Mecca, the *mihrab* or "Wang yu lou" (the altar)—a small platform with symbolic globe-shaped boxes on either side. In the right hand corner a flight of steps leads to a pulpit on which stands a coffer containing the Koran. The walls and arches, especially on the west side, the Mecca side, are adorned with sentences from this Sacred Book written in Arabic script, since it has never been translated into Chinese.[124] Glass and horn lanterns hang from the low ceiling to light services held before dawn and after dark. The severe simplicity of this dignified interior contrasts strongly with the sanctuary of a Buddhist or

---

[123] The Moslem Chinese are the only Chinese who bury without a coffin though coffins are on hire at the mosques to carry the body to the grave in the same way as a hearse is hired in Western countries.

[124] The translation of. the Koran into any language is forbidden. So is the use of any human or animal symbol in the decoration of a mosque. The tortuous, bewildering curves which surround and embellish the texts are therefore adaptations of leaf and flower forms.

Three Temples of Three Faiths

Taoist temple full of gilded images, dusty offerings and gaudy hangings. The single piece of furniture in the place is a Chinese wooden table near the entrance with the conventional "Set of Three" (San Shih), the triple incense burning apparatus consisting of the tripod urn, the round box and the vase, in front of an Imperial tablet with the inscription "wan sui, wan wan sui"—"a myriad years, a myriad myriad years." The presence of insignia smacking of idolatry surprises us, till our guide says that such were prescribed for every temple, no matter what the doctrine, as a pledge of the loyalty of the worshippers, and constituted the "official permit" to worship.

While we examine these things, the faithful straggle in from the side rooms where they have performed special ablutions—men only. Women are not admitted, as their presence is contrary to Mohammedan tenets. Does not the Koran say: "No woman, save her husband of his goodness bring her, shall enter into the Kingdom of Heaven," thus depriving her of a separate identity in matters religious?

In long gowns and white turbans, or green conical caps which the owners have earned the right to wear by making a pilgrimage to Mecca, the congregation follows the service in Arabic, with a devotion and solemnity very different from the careless worshippers at other Chinese temples. At frequent intervals the faithful bow, then kneel and touch the floor with their foreheads. Again, standing with fingers outstretched and thumbs on the lobes of their ears, with hands clasped on the breast or laid upon the knees, they resume their prostrations, proving that, though the Arabian sects rather despise these co-religionists for practising a debased form of the pure belief, still they are devout in their fashion.

The main hall is faced by a square tower where the Muezzin follows the beautiful Moslem custom of calling to prayer. Side rooms are reserved for the priest and his little scholars. In the pretty courtyard the pupils romp, and many happy childhoods are spent there under the kindly eye of the teacher who is a teacher only, and not, in the English sense of mastery, a master. Year after year the little ones play till they grow too big for games and leave the shelter of the courtyard to begin the bitter work of life, and to become the fathers and mothers of children whom they send to play in their stead.

Quite another order of religious faith is embodied in Lamaism, a decadent, yet picturesque form of Buddhism imported from Thibet.[125] Though there are no Chinese Lamas, all of the sect, including Living Buddhas, being Mongols or Thibetans, there are several Lama temples in Peking.

The most interesting is the Yung Ho Kung, one of the famous sights of the capital, situated in a sheltered and sunny corner of the city at the end of the Hata Men street near the north wall. Commonly known as "The Lama Temple," the proper word to describe it is really monastery or "gompa"—a Thibetan word signifying "Solitary Place"—which we should translate as cloister, for it is not a temple in the true sense of the term, since the public does not worship there. Before 1900, to enter the precincts was difficult and to depart from them harder still—especially for foreigners. One Russian did indeed visit the Lamasery several times, using a box of Huntley and Palmer's biscuits, of which the Living Buddha of the day was very fond, as a passport. But even he had gate after gate shut in his face when he tried to leave, whilst fierce monks jeeringly asked how much he would pay to get each opened.[126]

An exception was made at the yearly festival of the Devil Dance (held on the 30th of the first moon) when the "gompa" was open to all comers. On this occasion a huge crowd still gathers. After a long interval of waiting, patiently endured, several beings, half-human, half-devil, suddenly hurl themselves into the midst of the expectant throng. Their costumes are weird, resembling those of Red Indian medicine men. Death's head masks cover their faces, painted flames lick

---

[125] Lamaism has been broadly described as "a compound of black magic, nature worship, and Tantric Buddhism."
[126] Endless stories were told of the brutality and effrontery of the priests, some of which form the basis of that thrilling romance, *The Swallow's Wing*, by Hannan, which reads so very like truth to those who penetrated within the Yung Ho Kung prior to iono when it was thrown open to the world by the armies of eight nations.

Three Temples of Three Faiths

their limbs from foot to knee, and in their hands they carry long-lashed whips to be used in clearing a space for the dance. With demoniacal yells they dash about, pushing back the crowd and beating the unwary till they have made sufficient room. Then from the temple emerges a strange procession of dancers. They wear vestments of many colours and huge masks of bird or beast. To the slow and measured cadence of bronze trumpets and drums they advance in fours, bowing and circling, their heads lolling from side to side with the time and the movements of their bodies. The performance lasts for hours to the immense delight of the crowd that, regardless of the attentions of the long-whipped devils,[127] draws closer in its eagerness to see the cutting up of an effigy of the Evil Spirit which ends the ceremony.

To-day the mystery of the Yung Ho Kung, so long guarded by the Lamas with all their material and spiritual resources, is unveiled, and visitors are admitted on payment of a small entrance fee. Though the inevitable attraction of the taboo no doubt did much to establish the reputation of the monastery among foreigners, this reputation had other more solid foundations. As the former residence of a Living Buddha, a God Incarnate from the Lamaistic point of view,[128] as the home of a large community of priests (about 1,500 resident and nonresident) belong to the Yellow or orthodox sect, the place possessed great religious importance, while its political prominence was also considerable owing to the official patronage of the Chinese Emperors who granted the monks many privileges, such as permission to speak with the Sovereign face to face, besides lands and revenue. The Throne hoped to profit in return by the goodwill of the Order whose influence throughout Thibet and Mongolia is enormous, and to strengthen its hold thereby over those distant provinces.

---

127 Though unpleasant, it is considered lucky to be struck by the whips.
128 The Yung Ho Kung is now ruled by a Thibetan Abbot specially appointed by .the Dalai Lama of Thibet. Only monks who have had smallpox are given the post because a Dalai Lama died in Peking of this dread disease during Ch'ien Lung's reign. See Chapter XIII.

The days of prosperity are gone now. Imperial grants have ceased. The fixed tribute from the Mongol Banner Corps in Peking no longer pours its golden stream into the temple coffers. The Republic gives but a meagre pittance in support of the monks.

Nevertheless we must not conclude from outward signs of ruin that the old monastery is without consideration. Far from it. In the dilapidated guest rooms many a Mongol prince lodges when he comes from the steppes, and the temples remain, even in their decline, a spiritual and social centre of Mongolian life in the former Chinese capital.

Originally the Yung Ho Kung was the palace of the Emperor Yung Cheng, transformed for religious uses on his accession (a.d. 1722) in accordance with the Chinese precedent that the birthplace of a sovereign shall never afterwards be used as a dwelling. The spacious grounds, the fine halls, each divided from its successor by handsome courtyards, are worthy of their traditions, no less so the entrance avenue with its yellow-topped *p'ai lous*. Here, in the shade of spreading trees, where magpies and big black crows hold their parliaments, monks walk to and fro telling their beads. From the dwelling quarters—the low buildings on the right—one dashes out to offer us a figure carved in wood from Thibet, so he says, at five times its value,[129] and, to our surprise, urges us to buy in a few words of broken English. Greed has stimulated these Mongols, who do not trouble even to learn Chinese, to find a means of communication with the foreigner. We can read in their disagreeable accents and vulgar gestures that the priests are lazy, ignorant and of low social standing. Yet men who know the community well, scholars who have the freedom of the library of the monastery, assure us that it includes some shining exceptions—Lamas of genuine religious feeling and vast erudition, who are consulted and held in good repute.

In the first courtyard at the end of the avenue stand two bronze lions, the male with a ball under his paw—for the

---

[129] The real treasures of the temple are carefully labelled and numbered to prevent the priests from selling them to tourists.

Chinese lion like the English gentleman, is never happy unless he has some kind of ball to play with— the female with a cub, both renowned specimens of casting.¹³⁰ They guard the first of the prayer halls where sits Pu Tai, the Laughing Buddha, once a monk and the friend of little children. His cheerful face is familiar, for there is hardly a temple where this popular god is not worshipped in China or in Japan.¹³¹ Enthroned in the vestibule of the monastery, Pu Tai is the herald of more serious gods. Passing through his ante-chamber, we cross a courtyard containing a large tablet with the history of Lamaism inscribed upon its four sides in four languages— Chinese, Manchu, Mongol and Thibetan—and a celebrated bronze incense burner eight feet high.

In the two halls beyond—immense rectangular apartments filled with the sweet scent of incense—gilded bronze figures of Celestial Buddhas are enthroned, with flaming aureoles and hands uplifted in blessing, or clasped in prayer. Their shrines are enriched by many treasures— by fine Ch'ien Lung cloisonne, by splendid Yung Cheng enamels, by beautiful silken carpets made at Ninghsia beyond the wild Ordos country, by numbers of Thibetan and Mongol pictures of mitred saints seated on polychromatic clouds—pictures spirited in design, and in colouring very like the Italian Primitives.

---

130 Such semi-mythical monsters, carved in stone, cast in bronze or fashioned in cloisonne, are commonly found before the entrances of important buildings in Peking. Their living prototypes, both male and female, are supposed by the Chinese to secrete milk in their paws. Hence the representation of the female holding a cub underfoot to feed it. The male, free from maternal cares, is said to occupy his leisure and preserve his manly strength by playing with the ball. Within the last fifty years, the primitive inhabitants of the mountains of Korea, like the early Chinese, placed silken spheres near the supposed haunts of these monsters at night, returning next day to gather them up and distil from the toys, which the lions had obligingly rolled to and fro with their paws, the "lion's milk" so valued as medicine.

131 In the latter country he appears as Hotei, the merry monk with the hempen bag from which he takes his name, endowed with national traits in that spirit of playful reverence which characterises the Japanese artist.

Juliet Bredon

What may be called the main sanctuary lies still further back, in the heart of the enclosure. We go in expecting to see huge and splendid effigies—only to find ourselves face to face with one gilded image of a Thibetan saint wearing a pointed cap, and a miniature Buddha draped in a yellow satin cape and hood. He is not impressive like the larger idols, but he is exceedingly sacred, the most sacred image within the walls. Many years ago he appeared in a dream to an emperor who thereupon sent a holy monk to the borders of Thibet to find him. But when the monk reached the designated temple, it was empty. Presently he heard a faint voice speaking. "Here I am," it said, directing him to a wall. The monk then removed the bricks and freed the Buddha. Fearful of losing the precious image, he tied it upon his back and started on his long journey homeward through Siberia. Now the people of that country spoke a strange language which the holy man could not understand, and at first he was often puzzled how to ask his way. The little god, however, easily learned the difficult tongue to help the friend who had released him, and when they reached the great capital at last, the monk recounted how he had received miraculous aid. Thus the image became known as the "Little Buddha Who Speaks Russian." The gods forget nothing, so the priests tell us, and he has kept his talent to this day. Try him and see!

Three Temples of Three Faiths

Incense Burner—Yung Ho Kung

Juliet Bredon

Services open to visitors are held in this hall every afternoon. The Lamas and Lamalings make a picturesque group as they walk out from their cells into the sunlight in their yellow helmet-shaped caps, supposed to have been originally copied from the sacred peak of the Central Asian mountain, Chin Shan, and their orange or brick-red vestments which set off so well the bronzed Oriental flesh tints. Slowly they file into the sanctuary and take their places. When the abbot, who sits in the centre of the community, lifts the bunch of peacock's feathers from a vase by his side, there is a sudden burst of strange music, a clashing of cymbals, a beating of drums, a blowing of trumpets and conch shells. He intones a kind of Gregorian chant, and the monks, facing each other like singing-men in a choir, recite the litany moving their hands and fingers in various mystic ways meanwhile. The endless repetition of the same prayer is supposed to have a beneficial effect in withdrawing the mind from worldly thought, but does in fact seem rather to deaden and hypnotise it, rendering the participant incapable of any serious meditation whatever. As the monks sway rhythmically, slouching on their kneeling-cushions, it is plainly evident that the appearance of the visitor in the doorway thrills them far more than their devotions. Still, despite their drowsy inattention due to the drugging effect of constant repetition, the service is impressive, especially on great festivals, when the magnificent litany of the Maidari is sung by the monks in perfect time and with extraordinary low tones, acquired when the voice is breaking.

Three Temples of Three Faiths

The deepest bass of the West could not reach the notes on which the high priest chants the opening phrases of the magic formula enabling the "Sor"[132] to overpower the Spirits of Evil:

"O Sor, who turneth to dust all those who have sinned!
O Sor, who turneth to dust all the detestable enemies of the Faith!"

Then, when he lifts the pyramid high above his head the first time, the chorus answers in his name:

"I, the Yogatsari, I throw the Sor,
The awful Sor that is sharper than the point of a spear,
Whose dreadful force surpasses even the thunder!"

Again the abbot lifts the pyramid, again the chant recommences:

"I, the Yogatsari, I throw the Sor!
That which I throw is not for the Gods that dwell in the Worlds above,
Neither for the Dragon Kings that dwell in the Worlds beneath,
Nor for the Spirits that float in space twixt earth and heaven,
Nor for the Lords of the land and the waters—
I, the Yogatsari, I throw the Heavenly Sor
To crush the fierce foes who rend our souls
And place obstacles before the mighty Faith,
To paralyse the demons who trouble our spirits!"

And when, at last, having lifted it for the third time, he casts it upon a flaming pyre, the Lamas conclude with the terrific peroration which might pour from the lips of some old Hebrew prophet:

---

132 The "Sor" is a pyramid of dough, painted red and decorated with flame and flower motifs. On the top is a representation, also in dough, of a human skull. The whole constitutes a talisman against evil (the Manchu Emperors, for instance, sometimes had the "Sor" incantations read before starting on military expeditions)—also a mystical offering to the Buddha-Maitreya.

Juliet Bredon

"I, the Yogatsari, have thrown the dreadful Sor!
O, Keepers of the Gates, fling wide your doors!
Yea, they have been opened, and the truth marches out like a triumphant army.
Guardians of Hell, seize and imprison all our enemies that have form and substance!
Keepers of the Doors of Hell, close the doors upon them,
Yea, close even the crevices therein I—
Now the Doorkeepers have closed the smallest cracks
And imprisoned all spiritual obstacles—to set us free!"

The service as a whole reminds one superficially of masses in St. Peter's or other Roman churches.[133]

Most famous among the sights of the Yung Ho Kung is the huge gilded Buddha of the Resurrection (Maitreya) carved from the trunk of a single Yunnan cedar. His gigantic figure towers up through three stories and is by actual count seventy-five feet tall, though according to the Lamas he is the height of seventy elbows, the stature which they believe, we shall all attain at our perfect reincarnation.[134]

"Big Buddha, see Big Buddha," says a noisy, impudent Lamaling as he pushes one into the hall and holds out his hand for a tip, though well aware that visitors are expressly asked not to expend more than the price of their entrance ticket. In

---

[133] In outward forms there are certain striking resemblances, which it would be interesting to trace to their beginnings, between the Roman Catholic Mass and the Lama service. "The Lamas have the crosier, the mitre, the cope, the service with responses, the censer, the blessing with outstretched hands on the head of the faithful, the rosary and the processional. I have even seen Lama priests administer absolution to pilgrims. After having purified himself by prayer in the court of the temple, the penitent is admitted to the altar, and there a Lama marks his breast with a square seal with Sanscrit characters."-Choutze. *Tour du Monde*, 1876.

[134] "One difference between Lamaism and the ordinary form of Chinese Buddhism is shown by a characteristic detail—their discordant conception of Maitreya, the Coming Buddha. The Chinese usually represent him as an obese figure of small stature. The Lamas on the contrary, portray him as a colossal figure, robed as a prince, with the jewelled coronet of a *bodhisa*."—Bushell.

Three Temples of Three Faiths

the semi-darkness the cruel and vindictive countenance of Maitreya looms above us with the lamp over his head—formerly lit when the Emperor visited the temple—and the silk scarf in his hands presented to him by the Empress Dowager Tz'u Hsi. How remote and unsympathetic he seems, how detached from the worship that goes on around him!

A crooked, rickety staircase leads to a high gallery on a level with the head of the huge image. From the verandah there is an unusual view over the beautiful roof of the main hall, with dormer windows diversifying its lines. A gigantic prayer wheel attracts attention. This is simply a cylindrical chest full of written prayers and revolving on an axis. One turn of the wheel is considered equivalent to reciting the thousands of petitions it contains —a labour saving device that appeals strongly to the indolent devotees of an inert belief.

Behind this sanctuary we come to the last of the central temples. It contains images of the three "Taras," or Goddesses of Wisdom. "They are seated upon lotus flowers, the lotus flowers of the Apparitional Birth, and the light grace of their limbs folded within the petals, the suppleness of the fingers numbering the numbers of the Good Law, reflect ideals possibly inspired in some forgotten time by the charm of an Indian dancing girl." According to Lamaist tradition, Catherine the Great is supposed to be one of the re-incarnations of the goddess on the right, and the same legend is sometimes connected with the name of Queen Victoria.

There are many lesser shrines, so many that to enumerate all their deities would only weary the reader unfamiliar with the complicated ritual of Lamaism. But in nearly all these side halls is something worth seeing—in one, for instance, the famous jade and gold Buddha. Notice also the wooden figure behind it, for the priests say that it was taken from the waters of the Pei Hai after an emperor had seen a wonderful light hovering over the spot where it lay hidden.

In another room stands a golden model of paradise, and in a third the likenesses of two hippopotami who tried to kill Ch'ien Lung when he was out hunting—beasts scarcely less fierce and quaint than the statues of four green-faced guardsmen who bested them and saved their sovereign's life.

The fortunate visitor may chance upon a secondary service in one of these side halls conducted for novices who murmur their prayers with wandering eyes and interrupt their devotions by intervals of horse-play. Such chapels are full of tawdry paintings of demons and she-devils, freaks of diabolical imagination, all part of the spurious apparatus of terrorism of a religion whose hold is the hold of fear. Obscene figures of the Gods of Desire that drive the world, draped in yellow silk shawls, stand upon the altars among butter lamps, conch shell trumpets, wine cups made from human skulls, and other strange things of which the priests themselves often do not know the meaning.[135]

Unfortunately among the Lamas, the grosser forms of demonology and superstition, introduced from the dread cult of Siva, have overlaid the nobility of the original Buddhist conception.

From the unwholesome moral atmosphere of the Yung Ho Kung we turn almost with relief to visit the Confucian Temple near by. How different are its quiet courts dedicated to a calm and comfortable philosophy!

---

[135] To understand these symbols and their origins would require years of study and an exhaustive library of rare books to draw upon. Waddell's *Buddhism in Thibet*, however, gives many interesting details on Lamaism, and *The Unveiling of Lhasa* by Edmund Candler contains some picturesque descriptions of life and lamaseries in Thibet.

Three Temples of Three Faiths

COURTYARD IN THE LAMA TEMPLE (YUNG HO KUNG)

Juliet Bredon

Though the "Ta Ch'eng Miao"[136] is called a temple for want of a better name, the term is no more exact than the word "religion" applied to the cult it serves. Confucius, its founder, who lived when the Jews returned from Babylon and Greece was invaded by Xerxes, posed as no Messiah and arrogated to himself no divinity. He even denied any merits of discovery or invention, but taught confessedly and designedly only a system of morals founded on ancient ideals which he re-vivified and arranged in orderly form. Hence his rites include neither priests nor images of gods, but are in fact simply a variation of the cult of ancestor worship—the foundation of many Eastern religions and the cement which held together Chinese society, on the whole sober and law-abiding, through so many vicissitudes.

For us Westerners it is difficult to assign to this great Sage his proper place, and still more difficult to appreciate a power in his principles sufficient to make them an ideal for public and private life in China among the learned and aristocratic, the scholars and officials, no less than among the simple people, for 2,000 years. Probably he should rank with Plato as one of the world's greatest teachers, though Plato's precepts, if deeper and higher, never had the binding force for his disciples that those of Confucius had for his. The latter's influence is doubtless largely due to the fact that he set forth in cultivated form practical solutions for practical problems.[137]

To this day his precepts remain a living factor in China, though at one stage of the Nationalist Movement there was a

---

136 "Miao" is the general term for "temple," "Ssu" being specially applied to Buddhist sanctuaries, and "Kuan" to Taoist shrines. "T'an" means "altar."
137 The subject of Confucianism is too large to be treated here. Those interested should read *China and Religion*, by Parker, Confucianism and Taoism, by Douglas, Professor Legge's *Religions of China*, also his Imperial Confucianism and his master-work *The Chinese Classics*, or *Faber's Digest of the Doctrines of Confucius*. Most valuable of all are the standard translations of Confucius' own works for, though some of his sayings are going out of fashion, his doctrine is still a key to a large section of Chinese thought.

Three Temples of Three Faiths

violent reaction against Confucius and his doctrines, culminating in the destruction of certain temples dedicated to his memory. Millions of Chinese, however, though still good Buddhists or Taoists, follow his teachings at the same time,[138] and every city has a temple in his honour.

The one in Peking, second only in size and beauty to that in Chu-fu—the philosopher's birthplace in Shantung —is very impressive. First built on its present site under the Yuan Dynasty, about the end of the 13th century, it has been remodelled and rebuilt many times. The present great hall is probably Ming.

After seeing so many of the beautiful monuments in Peking partially ruined, it is refreshing to find this holy place kept in good order, showing no material degeneration from its ancient glory. Just as the doctrines have remained undimmed in their passage down the years, so the roofs glisten with perfect tiles, while the painting on the eaves is fresh and clean and the tablet over the door newly gilded.[139] Even the sacrifices in honour of the Sage were held there until three years ago, in the second month of spring and again, in the second month of autumn.[140] The elaborate and reverent service took place at three or four o'clock in the morning, but it was possible to

---

[138] This fact illustrates the conservative vitality of Confucianism without indicating a weakness in the other faiths. The Master, with complete toleration, never discouraged his followers from practising religion. Buddhists and Taoists regard Confucianism as an ethical system only and, for their part, do not forbid their converts to follow its rites. Mohammedanism and Christianity, however, considering their doctrines complete rules of life, will not allow this.

[139] Extensive repairs were made by Yuan Shih-k'ai who appropriated $50,000 for them. Yuan was an ardent supporter of Confucius and did his best to influence the debate in the Chinese Parliament in 1917 as to whether Confucius should be made the God and Confucianism the state religion of China, in favour of his hero. But the motion was rejected. See *Autumn Leaves*, by E. T. C. Werner, p. 248.

[140] The pendulum having again swung back, Confucius has been re-installed more or less, and his birthday is celebrated with official approval. The ceremonies, however, are much simplified from those of former days, marking the fact that "the Master Of All Ages" must now play second fiddle to Sun Yat-sen.

Juliet Bredon

obtain admittance to the rehearsal at a more reasonable hour the day before.

Certain officials used to be designated to burn incense and prostrate themselves before the table of the Sage, while the chief officiant read an address from a scroll afterwards placed in a casket on the altar. Groups of musicians in Ming costumes played the six hymns in praise of Confucius, known as the "Odes to Peace." The Master being in life a great lover and patron of music, his spirit was supposed to find delight in harmonies rendered exactly as they used to be twenty centuries ago, "with hand drums and great drums, small flutes and great flutes and pandean pipes of a form unknown to Western Pan." Many of the instruments were actually hundreds of years old, but their forms are older still. The musical stones hung from carved frames, the drums on stands curiously and beautifully wrought, the lutes with silken strings, the *yueh-ch'in* or "full moon guitar," the *yang-ch'in* or dulcimer, the *sang* or organ flute with thirteen reeds, the "straight flutes," and flutes played with the nose, were invented long before the Sage was born.

Visitors enter the Confucian Temple by a gate at the west side of the enclosure. Near the entrance, among cypresses whose gigantic girth carries us back to the Sung dynasty, stand graceful tablets of stone,[141] erected to over a hundred scholars who distinguished themselves at the Triennial Examinations in the past five or six centuries.

Under a covered gateway are ten black stone drums about three feet high—mountain boulders roughly hewn into this shape. They are supposed to date from the Chou dynasty (1122-255 b.c). For many years these cherished relics of antiquity lay half buried in some waste land in the province of Shensi. A poet, Han Yu, famous in his day, implored that they be moved to a place of safety, and about a.d. 820 they were set up in the Confucian temple of Feng Hsiang Fu. During the period of the Five Dynasties (a.d. 907-960) they were again lost, but a prefect under the Sungs (a.d. 960-1260)[142] found nine out of the ten and

---

141 The oldest dates from a.d. 1351.
142 For fear of further accidents to these priceless relics, Ch'ien Lung

Three Temples of Three Faiths

put them in his house. Finally, in a.d. 1052 the missing one was recovered and when the Sung emperor, fleeing from the Khitan Tartars, made his capital in the province of Honan, a hall was especially built in the palace to contain them. They rested there a few years only, for the Nuchen Tartars sacked the city in a.d. 1126, dug out the gold inlay with which the inscriptions[143] had been filled in (to betoken their value and at the same time to prevent their injury by the hammer when taking rubbings), and carried off the drums to their own capital—modern Peking.

The records on these monoliths have always been of the most profound interest to archaeologists. Chiselled in primitive seal characters, they are said by some scholars to be the oldest relics of Chinese writing extant, but were probably copied from ideographs on still more ancient bronze vessels.[144] The inscriptions comprise a series of ten odes, a complete poem being cut on each drum. Their stanzas in irregular verse celebrate the hunting expedition of a feudal prince about 1000 b.c. when the Aryans were conquering India, when David reigned in Israel, and Homer sang in Greece.

Many sinologues have differed in deciphering what is almost undecipherable, and many poets have given their best

---

ordered exact copies made in marble.

143 "The Chinese obtain facsimile rubbings of inscriptions with sheets of thin, tough, cohesive paper, moistened and applied evenly to the surface of stone or bronze. The paper is first hammered in by a wooden mallet, a piece of felt being interposed to prevent injury to the object and afterwards forced into every crevice and depression by a brush with long soft bristles. It is finally peeled off, imprinted with a perfect and durable impression of the inscription which comes out, of course, in white reverse on a black ground. Very often on old stone tablets one finds dark shadows of ink, showing that an amateur of writing has taken a rubbing of some specially fine characters of the inscription." —Bushell.

144 "Chinese script was undoubtedly ideographic in origin, the earliest characters being more or less exact reproductions of objects: the phonetic element was not adopted till much later, in the same natural course of development which analogous scripts have undergone in other parts of the world. This is indicated by the name of ' picture of the object' given to the primitive characters, which are said to have been invented by Ts'ang Hsien, and to have replaced the knotted cords and notched tallies previously used, like the *quipos* of the ancient Peruvians, for recording events."—Bushell.

inspirations in praise of these three thousand-year-old stones, blackened through repeated rubbings, from the time of Han Yu, who laments that the sixth drum has been hollowed out by some vandal for pounding rice, to the Emperor Ch'ien Lung whose verses in proof of their authenticity are engraved on a large marble tablet.

Beyond the stone drums is a lovely courtyard with six yellow-tiled pavilions containing stone slabs resting on turtle backs. They record the foreign conquests of the Emperors K'ang Hsi, Yung Cheng and Ch'ien Lung.[145] Just as the Emperors of Japan to this day announce their victories before the tablets of the Imperial Ancestors with the happy certainty that the great dead continue their interest in the fortunes of the living, so these old Chinese sovereigns brought to the manes of Confucius the reports of their successes.

Three flights of steps lead from this courtyard to the main building, the "Hall of the Great Perfection," with a renowned "spirit stairway" in the centre.

The proportions of the hall itself give an impression of harmony and intellectual repose. We enter feeling under our feet a softness of coir matting thick as moss. Within all is austere and pure; there are no images, no ornaments, no symbols—except the vermilion lacquer tablet dedicated to "the most holy ancestral teacher Confucius," the four smaller tablets in which reposes the spiritual essence of the Master's Four Great Disciples (Tseng Tzu, who wrote the "Great Learning," the first of the Four Books, Meng Tzu who wrote the fourth, Tzu Ssu, grandson of the sage, who wrote the "Doctrine of the Mean," and Yen Tzu whose conversations with the Master are recorded in the "Analects"), while the Eight Lesser Disciples have smaller tablets in the background. The stately rows of

---

145 The tablets commemorate:
    Conquest of Western Mongolia. K'ang Hsi a.d. 1704.
    Conquest of Eastern Thibet. Yung Cheng a.d. 1726.
    Conquest of the Miao Country. Ch'ien Lung a.d. 1750.
    Conquest of Sungaria, land of the Kalmuks. Ch'ien Lung a.d. 1760.
    Conquest of Eastern Turkestan. Ch'ien Lung a.d. 1760.
    Expeditions to Szccliuan and Yunnan. Ch'ien Lung a.d. 1777.

Three Temples of Three Faiths

massive pillars were formerly hung with laudatory couplets, and the beams with dedicatory inscriptions, one of which was penned by each succeeding emperor in token of his veneration of the Sage.[146] These inscriptions have been removed in deference to Republican susceptibilities. Only the tablet presented by President Li Yuan-hung is left hanging high up, its text of gold shining in the dim light.

Visitors usually go to see the Hall of Classics, or Kuo Tzu Chien, to the immediate west of the Confucian Temple, the same day. Originally a simple school under the Mongol dynasty, it was converted into a national university by Yung Lo. The Emperor went there in the second month to expound the Classics, seated upon a throne in the central hall, or Pi Yung Kung, with a famous screen behind him fashioned in the form of the five sacred mountains. The cypresses in the garden were planted by a teacher of the Mongol era, but the Hall of Classics is not the original Yuan building, having been erected by Ch'ien Lung after the ancient model. It is a lofty square edifice with a double-eaved roof, surmounted by a large gilt ball and encircled by a verandah supported by wooden pillars—the whole standing in the midst of a circular pond[147] crossed by four marble bridges leading to the central doors.

The elegant tracery of the windows, the wide-spreading roof and beautiful arrangement of timbers within, as also the complexity of the highly painted beams outside, make this a fine specimen of Chinese architecture. Unhappily this hall, though indirectly associated with Confucius, has not been restored like his temple. Dust invades it unhindered, dulling the red lacquer and gilded ornaments. "Why do you not at least clean off this lovely throne?" we inquire of the meek-faced

---

146 The finest was composed of four bold characters: "Wan Shih Shih Pao," "The Model Teacher of a Myriad Ages," written by K'ang Hsi and authenticated by his seal. The last of his line, the deposed emperor Hsuan T'ung, like his illustrious ancestor, also contributed his word of praise.

147 This pond used to contain golden carp and fine lotuses. But when the Republic was proclaimed, and a president instead of. an emperor appeared in these old precincts, the flowers and fish died—according to legend. At all events, not one blossom or one carp now remains alive there.

Juliet Bredon

guardian. "Because," he replies, "if I did, tourists would sit upon the sacr.ed seat, whereas, if left dirty, none will be tempted to do so." His knowledge of human nature was. more exact than his excuse.

Laziness, indeed, was the root of his neglect—laziness and pride. A true conservative, he resented the intrusion of the foreign vandal in this abode of Chinese culture, and while he led us around the deserted galleries, with their many hundred stone tablets bearing the complete text of the Four Books and the Five Classics,[148] past the quaint old sundial from which official mean time was formerly taken, to the magnificent porcelain *p'ai lou* on the way to the street—his manner plainly showed, despite his eagerness to earn a gratuity, that he considered us interlopers.

---

148 The inscriptions on these upright stone monuments were engraved by order of the Emperor Ch'ien Lung, in emulation of the Han and T'ang dynasties, both of which had the canonical books cut in stone at Sian-fu, the capital of China in their time. Moreover, they were also intended to form an insurance against the loss of these all-important memoirs of antiquity, and against the whims of a second Ch'in Shih Huang Ti. The text is divided on the face of the stone into pages of convenient size, so that rubbings may be taken on paper and bound up in the form of books.

Three Temples of Three Faiths

"Pai Loo"—Hall of Classics

Juliet Bredon

X. Temples of Many Gods

In addition to these big sanctuaries there are hundreds of other temples in Peking, less known to Westerners, but famous among the Chinese who, with perfect impartiality, have commemorated every sainted hero by a shrine and propitiated every god by an altar. "The higher minds alone can rest content with abstract imaginings; the lower must have concrete realities on which to pin their faith." Therefore, side by side with the pure worship of the Supreme Being, the primitive cults of the lesser deities have kept their humble clientele.

Even remnants of Nature worship from far forgotten ages persist in the deification of the forces of the universe which man instinctively wondered at or feared: the sun, the stars, the thunder, the rain and the wind—all, in short, that he heard, saw or felt, yet could not comprehend. As he progressed in civilisation, he clothed his terrors with forms which resembled the human, appeased them by offerings, invoked them for aid, or thanked them for benefits received.

Each of the Nature Gods had his own distinct personality and his own temple. The God of Thunder was enthroned in the Ning Ho Miao, east of the Forbidden City. Built about a.d. 1770, it has now been diverted from its original purpose and become a prosaic police post. Evidently the thunderbolts of this deity no longer strike terror in men's hearts, since his other shrine, the Lei Shen, or Chao Hsien Miao, on the western side of the Palaces and dating from the same era, is being used for educational purposes. It is rather pitiful and makes one feel as though a revered tragedian had suddenly lost favour with the public. His most magnificent gestures no longer have power to thrill an audience.

The God of Rain fares little better. In the Fu Yu Ssu (near the Chao Hsien Miao) where he once lodged, a rival god listens to the prayers that he has every right to think should be intended for his ears. After being dedicated to him in 1723, the temple was first given over to the Buddhists, and later to the Lama Sect. Though somewhat neglected now, its green and

Temples of Many Gods

yellow roofs are still a handsome ornament of the quarter near the Hsi Hua Men, and about twenty Lamas live on the premises which they share with a Chinese school. The valuable library was removed to Japan in 1900. But what cannot be taken away from this temple are the memories of the days, before it belonged even to the poor Rain God, when K'ang Hsi as a child was sent there with his nurse to avoid an epidemic of smallpox in the Forbidden City. He grumbled, as children do, at being separated from his parents and resented the parting even in his old age. But he left a tablet, a throne and a collection of writings, still on view in the main hall, to atone for his petulance.

In his religious fervour and constructive energy K'ang Hsi also converted what, under the Mings, was a military depot into the Buddhist temple of Wan Shou Hsing Lung Ssu, just opposite Fu Yu Ssu, in a.d. 1700. Gradually this temple grew to be a favourite asylum for the old eunuchs of the Court, and as such enjoyed the patronage of the Manchu Emperors, every one of whom, including the deposed Hsuan T'ung, enriched it with grants and honoured it with inscriptions. The halls, containing interesting Buddhist images—only rarely accessible to strangers by the courtesy of the priests—also serve as repositories for the magnificent coffins of eunuch patrons. A beautiful catalpa tree[149] in the small courtyard, shades an open air theatre where religious plays and pageants are given. The whole atmosphere of the place suggests contemplation, the Oriental's ideal of life. The monks sit in the gardens "when trees are green and bushes soft and wet, when the wind has stolen the shadows of new leaves and the birds linger in the last boughs that bloom," and meditate with that power of perfect abstraction of which the headlong West knows nothing. Content, they dream their lives away "till even the sense of self seems to vanish and at last through the mist-like portal of unconsciousness they float out into the vast, undistinguishable sameness of Nirvana's sea."

---

149 This species of tree provides the favourite and the most expensive wood used for coffins in China.

Juliet Bredon

The winds have their shrine in the Hsuan Jen Miao, identical in appearance with the Ning Ho Miao, and a little further north on the same street. When it was built in a.d. 1738, the southern breezes fanned a handsome altar, and their presence was reverently recognised. But now they come and go unnoticed. Not a single incense stick glows in their honour any more. Empty and forsaken, the buildings remain in charge of an official who turns an honest penny by renting them to needy artisans.

Much stronger devotees of nature-worship than the Chinese were their Manchu conquerors, descendants of tribes inhabiting the gloomy "taiga" (forest)—a wild land of sudden storms and tremendous natural phenomena. The group of yellow-tiled buildings in the south-eastern corner of the former Imperial City,[150] quite close to the Hotel de Pekin, is the only shrine of Shamanism, or the "Black Faith," in Peking, outside the Palaces. Known as the T'ang Tzu, or official Shaman temple of the Manchu Court, it was built to replace the older T'ang Tzu, burnt during the Boxer troubles.[151] Though no stranger has seen the secret ceremonies held there, we know from records that they were the same as those formerly performed at Mukden. During the sacrifice a Shaman ("respectable person"), dressed in a robe adorned with dragons, wearing a "holy hat" with two antelope horns, and carrying brass bells attached to his girdle, read a Manchu prayer to the spirits and then executed a dance from the old Manchu ritual. That this rude form of animism—this strange survival of the primitive faith of the aborigines of Siberia, whence sprung the Tunguz forefathers of the Manchus, should persist in the capital of a highly developed civilisation like the Chinese only shows how deep a reverence for their past must have inspired the first Manchu rulers when they built a temple to the religion of their

---

[150] Since the dividing walls of the Imperial City have been demolished, it is scarcely distinguishable from the surrounding Tartar City into which it has now merged. The original boundaries, gates, etc., may be traced on the map of Father Hyacinth Bitchurin.

[151] See Chapter III.

Temples of Many Gods

forefathers—and the last when they rebuilt it after a foreign invasion of arms and ideas. A staff of Shamans and Shamanesses (the latter to hold services for the Empress), selected from the families of the Palace guards, was maintained till the end of the Ch'ing rule.

Not far from the T'ang Tzu is a Lama temple, also closely associated with the Manchu dynasty. This is the Mahakala Miao (or Pu Tu Ssu) built on a kind of platform fifteen feet above the surrounding houses—an unusual device. The place was originally a Ming palace where the Emperor Cheng T'ung resided on his return from captivity in Mongolia (a.d. 1457) [152] Under the Manchus, it became the property of Prince Jui, the famous Dorgun Amah Wang, fourteenth son of Nurhachi, the most powerful and romantic figure in the Manchu conquest of China. He was the man who entered Peking in triumph, and, according to an agreement with Wu San-kuei, rewarded his own people for their services in helping to suppress Li Tz'u-ch'eng's rebellion by establishing a Manchu dynasty. Like another Warwick, this kingmaker sent for his six-year-old nephew, the Ruler of the Manchu clans, and put him upon the throne under his regency, with the reigning title of Shun Chih.

When Prince Jui was killed in December, 1650 at the early age of 39 whilst engaged in his favourite sport of hunting, the boy sovereign rewarded the masterful captain, who for seven years had been the guiding spirit in his councils, with the

---

152 The Emperor Cheng T'ung, during whose reign China suffered severely from an invasion of the Mongols, was induced personally to accompany an expedition of half a million men against them. It ended in disaster. His army was almost annihilated: the general in command was killed and Cheng T'ung himself taken prisoner. The Mongols held the sovereign for ransom, but although the sum demanded was ludicrously small, for some strange reason the money was never paid, and the Emperor was left in the hands of his captors, his brother Ching T'ai being placed on the throne (a.d. 1450). When the Mongols perceived that they derived no benefit front keeping him a prisoner, Cheng T'ung was finally sent back, but as his brother was unwilling to abdicate, he was forced to retire for a time into private life, living quietly in the Pu Tu Ssu. Afterwards, during an illness of Ching T'ai, he regained the throne by a coup d'etat and ruled over the Empire for another eight years.

highest posthumous titles. Later, through the accusations of rivals, he lost these honours and his name was struck off the Imperial clan roll, but more than a hundred years afterwards the Emperor Ch'ien Lung restored his fame, thus proving that no man's deeds are ever finally condemned in Chinese history.

Prince Jui's picturesque palace long remained haunted in the popular imagination with memories of the great hero and the pathos of its empty walls was sung in a contemporary ballad:

> "I wander through the wood of whispering pines,
> And pass the gateway of a princely house.
> There reigns a heavy silence in the courts
> Where slumbering birds are startled at my voice.
> Through carven windows peep the unchecked weeds,
> And the tall spears of grasses pierce the tiles.
> None seek for favours at the open door;
> The place is but an empty tenement
> Without a host....
> The warrior who for seven glorious years
> Planned glorious deeds within these crumbling walls,
> Is gone to be a guest in heavenly halls."
> *(Wu Wei-yeh: "Tu-shu-wo-shu-shih.")*

The Emperor K'ang Hsi converted the old palace into a Lama temple dedicated to Mahakala, an incarnation of the Hindu god Siva—hence the name Mahakala Miao— and gave the priests the special privilege of holding services in Mongolian instead of Thibetan.[153]

A little Lama boy, seeing visitors approach, appears with the key of the hall which they desire to visit. He leads them across the single courtyard to the sanctuary. It contains many

---

[153] This is the only Lama temple in Peking where Mongolian services are allowed, despite the fact that most of the Lama communities are composed almost exclusively of Mongols. A similar exception was made for two lamaseries in the village of Hai Tien, on the Summer Palace road, and for the one near the Hsi Ling: in all three the sacred books are read in Manchu. The only lamasery in which services are held in Chinese, is said to be at Jehol.

Temples of Many Gods

interesting and curious things. On the left is a fantastic carved stand with bronze bells, each of a different tone. The little Lama points out with a chuckle that some are missing. Perhaps the empty spaces represent good bargains. Further back stand rows of gods looming weirdly in the dusk—Arhats and Buddhas and Bodhisats and the shapes of a mythology older than they. Some are conventional figures seated upon lotus pedestals; others ride upon elephants, tigers or monsters mythical. One sinister and splendid god, blood red, demoniac, and with eyes of delirious fury, tramples upon a human being.

High up, near the ceiling, is a small niche with silken curtains, dedicated to Mahakala. But the golden image is gone, stolen in Boxer times like most of the other treasures of the temple. Empty also is the niche in the model of the holy shrine of Wu T'ai Shan. Its precious Buddha likewise excited the cupidity of some "Harmonious Fist" who mingled greed with his misguided patriotism. The sacred books, stored in cupboards which the guide obligingly opens, were spared. Probably the looters did not know their value as one of the few complete texts written in Mongol, or else they were too bulky to carry away. Some tree trunks of valuable woods carved with scenes from the life of Sakyamuni still stand before the altars, and a handsome stone incense burner, much like an early Italian fount, remains, as well as various painted bronze vessels, scarcely recognizable as such until, on being tapped, they give out the soft note of a muffled bell.

The novice gropes his way into a side chapel where it is so dark that one is unable to distinguish anything but vague forms. With a naughty twinkle in his eye, he takes a candle and, lighting it, climbs upon the altar to lift the draperies of images anatomically too realistic to bear close inspection. Near these crimson and green gods, half man, half beast, typifying hurricane creative power, whose wicked eyes burn in the dark like the eyes of a black cat, stand four swarthy guardians, dressed as men-at-arms. Quaint effigies of Buddha's "Army of animals," symbolising force not far distant from ferocity, surround them.

Juliet Bredon

Among these strange creatures that might have stepped from Noah's Ark, is the armour of the great Dorgun. The dusty satin coat lined with iron plates, the pointed helmet, the yellow ceremonial umbrella falling to shreds, the arrow cases stiff with years, the bow he bent so bravely, call vividly to mind the figure of the warrior-statesman whose skill, prudence and moderation were largely responsible for bringing China under Manchu rule, and whose mediaeval presence kept aglow the princely magnificence of the sanctuary before the gods intruded there.

Even more interesting than the Mahakala Miao is the Lama Monastery of Sung Chu Ssu, a large establishment containing three separate temples: Fa Yuan Ssu, Chih Chu Ssu and Sung Chu Ssu. No record exists of the date of its foundation, but the priests say that in Ch'ien Lung's time the property was bought from the Buddhist monks who then occupied it for the Chang Chia Hutukhtu of that day. He and his successors lived at Sung Chu Ssu in semi-royal state from the 17th century until a few years ago, when the present incumbent moved to Wu T'ai Shan in Shansi.[154]

After his departure the tide of prosperity ebbed at Sung Chu Ssu, now fast falling into disrepair. It is the old, old story of lost prestige and present poverty since the government no longer gives subsidies for the repair of historic places. How strange it seems to us westerners who respect and preserve the relics of our past that the Chinese with their awakening national consciousness, of which we hear so much, should be so careless of their monuments!

"Falling down, falling down," says the old gatekeeper, shaking his head sadly as he leads us to the tottering buildings of Chih Chu Ssu in the western part of the monastery. Unless something is done, and soon, the fine square hall will crumble

---

[154] The Chang Chia Hutukhtu ranks fourth among the pontiffs of the Lama hierarchy which includes about 160 Hutukhtus. His only spiritual superiors are the Dalai Lama, the Pancheng Erdeni Lama of Thibet, and the Cheptsung Tampa Hutukhtu of Outer Mongolia. A Chang Chia Hutukhtu was sent to Peking from Thibet for the first time in a.d. 1691 during the reign of K'ang Hsi and received the title of "First Living Buddha of the Capital."

away into ruins like a hundred other show places that should be carefully preserved.

Fa Yuan Ssu, on the eastern side, is in little better condition. A few fine statues remain, a few handsome frames with high gilt tops for hanging bells, and, in the courtyard, a curious bronze replica on a carved marble pedestal of the Sacred Mountain, Omei Shan—the "Hill That Reaches Heaven."

The central temple appears less melancholy. At least its roof is rainproof. But the empty throne chair of the Chang Chia Hutukhtu once more depresses our guide. "When His Holiness lived here, what a good life we had," he murmurs. "Grand visitors came then to honour the Lamaist Order in His Sacred Person. The prayer wheels turned incessantly, and the sound of coins falling into the money boxes was sweet as music to our ears. Ah, those were the days when there were many monks living here and great ceremonies!"

As our eyes grow accustomed to the dim light of the sanctuary we notice preparations for a festival. "It seems you still hold ceremonies," we remark. "Yes," he grumbles, "but few attend and they are no longer profitable. However, if you are interested, your visit is well-timed, for all is prepared in honour of Jvalamuktu, Goddess of Cholera, whom we worship at the Winter Solstice. This very night, while you are sleeping, the monks will chant a service in her honour."

At our request he explains some of the symbols. The little figure in yellow robes is a portrait of the Chang Chia Hutukhtu, sent to represent him at the ceremony. The table spread with tiny dishes containing grains, vegetables, etc., is an offering of the earth's produce, the "first fruits," so to speak, expected with the spring crops. The dough pyramids, with demon heads or skulls, decorated with painted flames, represent the God Brahma, the Hindoo Creator, and the Four Guardians of the Four Directions of Space. The bull's horns and crossed arrows, laid upon platters, are symbols to counteract evil influences. As for the paper man on a paper horse, he is the Danapati or

Juliet Bredon

"Benefactor of the Clergy" who pays, or is supposed to pay, for this particular ceremony.

"Alas!" adds our guide with justifiable pessimism, "a paper man pays with paper money."

When we place two round silver dollars upon the altar, he smiles at last, the smile of a man who scents a bit of pork in a well filled rice bowl. "Not since the days of the Chang Chia Hutukhtu," he mutters, bowing us out with a very low bow, "not since those days have we eaten our fill."

XI. Temples of the Tartar City

The Tartar City of Peking is particularly rich in temples—relics of the days when there was not the hurry, the bustle, the lack of tranquility of modern life, and men were willing to spend money on the gods instead of on themselves; when to "acquire merit" by building a shrine was more important than to command soldiers and harass the people. Close under the northern Tartar wall (just west of the Yung Ho Kung) stands Pai Lin Ssu, one of the most restfully beautiful temples imaginable—a place which still retains the serenity of the past. Yet from the very ordinary dusty street outside and the blind front of unimposing walls, no one could guess the importance of the monastery hidden away in this quiet corner.

We only realise it once we pass the gate and enter a fine courtyard, nobly planted with trees—trees that intensify the stern secrecy of such places when we look down on them from the city walls.

One or two fine stone tablets dating from the Ming Dynasty—squarer and squatter than the type erected under the Ch'ings—stand before the main building, a fine hall containing a trilogy of slender-waisted and large-breasted goddesses.

Spacious inner courtyards beyond have the usual two storied dwellings for the monks, and, hidden in a little windless corner paved with old flagstones, grows a white pine with a cluster of trunks like a many-branched candelabra.

As Pai Lin Ssu has the reputation of being an exceptionally holy place and the headquarters of famous Buddhist scholars from the South when they visit Peking,[155] so its Abbot has an unusual reputation for sanctity.

"Would it be possible," we inquire of an acolyte, "to see this holy man?"

A faint flush creeps over the young monk's face: "Certainly, he will be delighted to receive you, but not for a few moments.

---

[155] In this temple, also, the important conference with Japanese Buddhists was held.

Juliet Bredon

At present a cinematograph operator is taking his picture on the terrace." Such is the price of fame nowadays—even for saints! Let us hasten to add that the performance, though incongruous, was not undignified. Assistants arranged the Abbot's robes before the camera began to click and removed the black knitted cap which he considered unbecoming. Then, as he walked meditatively to and fro forgetting, apparently, that he was being filmed, a dove, white as a handful of snow, descended from one of the roofs and settled upon his shoulder. The operator smiled at this unexpected human touch. What a caption it would make—"Even birds love this holy man!" Fifteen feet of dove with Abbot and the camera ceased clicking. The young operator bowed very politely, put on his foreign broad-brimmed hat, packed up and left, while the Abbot approached us with a smile wrinkling the corners of his eyes. "Do you not find such modern notes jar upon the peace of this retreat?" we inquire respectfully. "Oh, no," he answers, "when one's breathing is equable, there is peace of mind whatever happens and wherever one may be, whether jostled on the highways or sitting alone in a mud hut." Murmuring a petition that our breathing may be made equable, we take our leave of this serene man and his serene monastery, saying, "Farewell, Your Holiness, your words are in our hearts." Not too far distant to be visited comfortably on this same sunny morning are several small shrines on the banks of the Chi Shui T'an, now a shallow pond but once a lake crowded with barges bringing country produce to the capital along the canal built by Kublai Khan.[156]

---

[156] This canal, still to be seen near the Hsi Chih Men but slow-flowing - through neglect, was originally intended to bring the waters of the Western Hills to Peking, and linked up a whole system of waterways with the Grand Canal. The laying out of the lakes in the Tartar City however, was only completed under the Ming Emperor Wan Li, in whose day there used to be much animation on the banks of the Chi Shui T'an. Many curious ceremonies took place there. On the 12th day of the sixth moon it was the custom to bathe the Imperial horses in its waters, and the animals were led in procession, covered with silken blankets, preceded by grooms waving red flags and followed by a black cow with a single horn "who must on no

Temples of the Tartar City

Our way leads past the Te Sheng Men, popularly called the "fruit gate." In the compounds nearby, wholesale dealers bargain for the fruits that the peasants bring in from their orchards—red apples, golden persimmons and purple grapes which look very colourful spread out in flat baskets a yard in diameter. Picturesque stalls shaded by blue cloth umbrellas are gay with pyramids of apricots in spring, and piles of watermelons in summer, while processions of donkeys, with paniers filled with farm produce, pass under the faded gate tower all the year round. To add to the confusion, peddlers with trays hung from their shoulders, call out their wares from time to time, and groups of men standing in the middle of the street clamourously discuss their business or squabble about trifles.

This bustling scene of activity soon changes. A little further on we come to a peaceful residential quarter, practically untouched by progressive influences and seldom explored by foreigners—a quarter where ancient China still seems to stretch out her hand, laying it gently upon the quick pulse of modern times. Here life is lived much as in Ch'ien Lung's day with only a few telegraph poles to disturb the illusion. Hawkers still sell to women peeping shyly from their doorways. Men bargain for their coffins in the streets, and carry their birds to sing at sunset under, the willows bordering the Chi Shui T'an or make an occasional pilgrimage to shrines like Hui T'ung Tzu, the "Temple for Worshipping Ancestors Beside the Swirling Waters." This quaint little place stands on a hillock which is also an island. Inside there is nothing worth wasting time over, but the terrace looking down on the lake and the old stone monument beside which the women of the neighbourhood do their washing, is a delightful place to linger. Choose, if you can, a balmy spring day, when the hours merge imperceptibly into one another and clocks and calendars fade from memory, and

---

account be allowed in 'front of the horses." A week before, the Imperial elephants were taken for their yearly bath, not here but in the city moat outside the Shun Chih Men, while large crowds of people watched the spectacle. A certain day was also set aside for women to wash their hair, and householders to bathe their cats and dogs.

you will never regret a complete surrender to the lulling spell of this "Temple-of-Lots-of-Time."

Then, when the spirit moves you, meander along the shore to another group of insignificant Ming buildings known as the Kao Miao (High Temple), forever associated with the names of Parkes and Loch. Here these unfortunate Englishmen, treacherously imprisoned in 1860, and cruelly ill-treated in the Board of Punishments, were lodged for many weary weeks. The old priest in charge until a few years ago remembered when the two "foreign devils" were kept in custody in the temple, and pointed out the cramped courtyard where they walked in constant fear of being killed if the Allied armies, camped outside the walls, should attack the city; also the small dark room where they slept, with the square of wallpaper (since removed by loving hands) on which they wrote their names and last messages. Such proofs fix the Kao Miao without a doubt as the place of imprisonment of Parkes and Loch, though a little Yuan dynasty temple, near the lake, claims the captives too.

In vivid contrast to these tiny shrines is the imposing Kuan Yo Miao, a handsome group of buildings originally intended for the Ancestral Hall of the ex-Prince Regent (Prince Ch'un, father of the deposed Emperor Hsuan T'ung), and situated immediately behind his vast palace. As this magnificent temple was only built in the reign of Kuang Hsu, it is still in fairly good preservation and enables us to judge how the older monuments looked when their paint was fresh and their tiles intact. Yuan Shih-k'ai appropriated this property in the name of the Republic, and converted it into a military shrine dedicated to Kuan Ti and Yo Fei.

Kuan Ti, usually called the Chinese God of War, is not "a cruel tyrant delighting in battle and the slaying of enemies; he is the god who can avert war and protect the people from its horrors." Most famous of the great soldiers "who were canonised by their country as unselfish patriots, his is certainly the supremely romantic figure in one of the most romantic periods of Chinese history (the Period of the Three Kingdoms). In fact this hero was first singled out for special honours by the

Sung emperors who set him up as a central figure of a national cult continued by the Mings with regular sacrifices, and developed by the Manchus with special reverence."[157]

As Kuan Ti received exceptional honours from the late Ch'ing dynasty, it would not have been surprising if the victorious revolutionaries had decided to treat him with cold disdain. But the establishment of the Republic could not dethrone a god beloved by all kinds and conditions of men. He even remains, in a sense, a Protector of the State, receiving homage on his birthday according to the ancient decree (promulgated as far back as a.d. 1531) which says that "national events of importance shall be reported to the spirit of the Marquis Kuan in his temple, so that he may not be left in ignorance of his country's fortunes." Perhaps the new generation feels that his miracles may still be useful, and, remembering how on numerous occasions he has come to the rescue of outnumbered armies and beleaguered garrisons by appearing at the head of an irresistible force of demon or angel soldiers (the alleged Mons incident has many a prototype in Chinese annals) has decided to continue not only his grateful but his hopeful worshippers.

Kuan Ti's special position, however, is not quite what it was before 1911, for he is now required to share his quasi-divine honours with another patriot, Yo Fei, who also holds a high place in the affection of the Chinese people. This noble warrior, called the "Chinese Bayard," lived nearly a thousand years after Kuan Ti, during a very unhappy period of Chinese history. He distinguished himself against the Golden Tartars (Chins), at that time engaged in driving the Sung emperors from the plains of northern China. But the reigning Sung monarch (Kao Tsung) was by no means elated at his victories, fearing that this redoubtable general would force the Tarters to send back the Emperor Ch'in Tsung[158] whom they had carried off as a prisoner, in which case Kao Tsung would either have had to

---

157 See Chapter II, also *The Cult of Military Heroes in China*, by R. F. Johnston (*The New China Review*, 1921).
158 See Chapters X and XII.

resign his throne, or fight; against its legitimate occupant. Yo Fei was also unlucky enough to incur the hostility of Ch'in Kuei,[159] a powerful minister whose intrigues against him finally resulted in his imprisonment and death.

In course of time the gradual elevation of Yo Fei to a place among China's patron saints and divinities took place by that curious process of posthumous rehabilitation not uncommon in the East. "A temple was built and dedicated to him, and funds were provided for periodical sacrificial rites. But very little notice of Yo Fei was taken during the Manchu period, and this for an interesting reason. The Golden Tartars against whom he had fought so strenuously were kinsmen of the Manchus... and racial pride, if not filial piety, demanded that the Manchu sovereigns should show respect for the memory of their predecessors on the Dragon Throne. Nevertheless nothing was actually done to injure the reputation of the great soldier who had been the deadliest enemy of the Tartar race, or deprive his spirit of the honours it already enjoyed."

The idea of a "military temple," where formal homage should be paid to Kuan Ti and Yo Fei, together with twenty-four other celebrated leaders and patriots considered worthy to partake in the ceremonial rites (Kuan Ti and Yo Fei were to share the highest honours equally, and the others to be regarded as their spiritual "associates"), originated with Yuan Shih-k'ai and was based on sound considerations of practical statecraft and national efficiency. Its main objects were to encourage patriotic ideals among the people, to raise the profession of arms in public estimation, and inspire the soldiers themselves with military zeal and professional ardour.

"The Hall of Military Perfection," in the Kuan Yo Miao, the "mother church" of the reorganised cult of military heroes, is a handsome building standing in a spacious courtyard. The interior with its fine pillars and richly decorated roof, contains the figures of Kuan Ti and Yo Fei seated side by side, both richly robed; both conveying an aspect of stern dignity combined with gracious benevolence. There is also a model of

---

159 Sec Chapter X

Kuan Ti's famous charger "Red Hare," of his no less famous sword "Blue Dragon" (with which he once struck a rock till water gushed out to slake his thirst) and also of the white horse Yo Fei rode to battle.

"The first ceremony in honour of these two patriots and the other heroes associated with them, took place in this hall in January 1915, when a general deputed by Yuan Shih-k'ai led his officers and soldiers to the newly-established temple, and each man bowed his head as he filed past the effigies or tablets of those who fought and, in many cases, died for their country. Similar ceremonies were continued for a few years but have now been abandoned."

Almost next door to this imposing temple of Heroes is the peaceful old Nien Hua Ssu, with several restful shady courtyards and fine images sheeted with gold. In the rear hall, very dusty despite the big glass case which rovers it, is a bronze Buddha seated upon a pedestal formed of hundreds of tiny images of Buddha—an unusual piece of work. Some lovely gilded lotuses standing in jars upon the altar recall a charming legend of how the lotus became a sacred flower, and why it is so often placed beside the Buddha.

One day, at dawn, Gautama sat meditating when he heard a strange sweet song. As he listened, wonder and joy crept into his heart, for the melody slowly unfolded a "Plan for Salvation"—something he himself had long sought with prayer and meditation. But suddenly the music ceased and he waited in vain for it to begin again.

Hurrying to the edge of the cliff, he peered into the mists of the valley and beheld a devil who turned a taunting face towards the anxious and disappointed prophet. Earnestly Gautama begged for the remainder of the song and the continuation of the Plan. But the devil declared he could sing no more till his hunger for human flesh and his thirst for human blood was satisfied. Then only would he sing of that mystic Secret, giving knowledge of salvation to all mankind.

Hearing these cruel words, Gautama exclaimed, "Satisfy thy hunger with my flesh and quench thy thirst with my blood, but continue, I beseech thee, thy song until every soul is saved." Whereupon casting off his robes, he threw himself down from the rock. A sudden gleam of sunshine lighted the valley below and touched the pool where was floating a lotus with spreading leaves and one unopened bud. As the holy prophet fell through the air, the bud suddenly burst into bloom and on its snowy petals sank softly the One who was to bring to more than a third of humanity a new hope of Salvation, and a faith far better than they had known.[160]

Not far from Nien Hua Ssu stand two other Ming Temples, Yu Sheng Ssu, where an enterprising merchant makes modern copies of old lacquer cabinets leaving them to weather in the courtyard, and Kuang Hua Ssu, where the visitor stumbles unexpectedly upon a splendid specimen of old European furniture, a Portuguese carved wood table presented to the monastery in Ch'ien Lung's reign.

Another Kuan Ti Miao, dating from a.d. 1734, may be seen close by, near the stone bridge between the Hou Men and the Drum Tower. Here once again we have a proof how this patriot unselfishly shares his shrines with others. The God of Riches, always a popular deity, has an altar in the self-same building, and so has the Fire God, who in fact now gives his name to the temple, popularly known as the Hou Shen Miao. His face is dark, blackened by his own smoke and scorched by his flames, and he looks on the whole rather a boorish god.

Probably the oldest temple of the Tartar City—where so many famous temples, like the Ma Shen Miao,[161] Temple of the Protector of Horses (whose site is now occupied by part of the Peking University), have disappeared—is the tiny shrine, supposed to date from the T'ang dynasty, dedicated to Erh Lang, nephew of the Heavenly King, whose famous sleeve-dog

---

160 In Japan, where this legend also exists, the raised centre of the lotus is called a "seat" to this day and, as in China, lotus blossoms, either natural or artificial, are placed before every Buddhist shrine in memory of the assistance given to the Holy One.

161 Built by the Ming Emperor Cheng Teh and later richly adorned by the early Manchu sovereigns. Near it stood the Imperial stables and the department of eunuchs in charge of them, also the elephant stables.

"that howls towards the sky," faithfully aided him to pursue the heavenly monkey. The latter was the guardian of the peach trees of eternal life, but stole the fruit instead of watching it. When Erh Lang discovered this, he immediately gave chase to the thief who, having the power of undergoing seventy metamorphoses (each the basis of a popular legend) baffled him again and again. Once the mischievous monkey entered his pursuer in the shape of a small worm and wriggled about inside him till he saw an opportunity to escape. Again he changed himself into a temple, the gate being his mouth, the front hall his head, etc. Erh Lang detected him on this occasion by noticing that the honorific lantern-pole, which represented the monkey's tail, was behind instead of in front of the temple; that is to say—was in the right place anatomically speaking (for a monkey) but in the wrong place architecturally speaking (for a temple). Luckly Erh Lang was able to undergo seventy-two transformations as compared to the seventy of the monkey, so he finally outwitted the astute animal and chained him up for his misdeeds.

Situated on the Hata Men street, opposite the Teng Shih K'ou, Erh Lang's shrine is known as the "Dog Temple," and numerous ex-votos of Pekingese pugs, little curly, short nosed, fringy-pawed things, are heaped up on the altar. When a dog is sick, the owner offers one of these life-like portraits in felt or fur, but it is considered almost as lucky to steal one from the altar while the priest, who has been blinded by an offering, beats the gong with his back turned to the thief. If, however, the offering is not large enough, he suddenly turns round and catches the would-be pilferer. Then the whole manoeuvre becomes inefficacious.

The discovery that not only Erh Lang, "The True Prince of the Wonderful Tao," could cure the illness of mortals, but that his dumb companion had the power to do the same for his own species, was made accidentally by an old woman. While praying for the recovery of her son, her ailing pet dog, which had followed her to the shrine, was miraculously healed, and her gratitude took the form of the first ex-voto puppy.

Juliet Bredon

When we visited this shrine, a woman was attending to the duties of the absent priest, burning joss-sticks, beating the gong and sewing in the intervals between worshippers. She also assisted visitors to "ch'ou-ch'ien," or engage in divination by the drawing of lots. This was done in the usual way with a bundle of divining sticks, each bearing a character corresponding to a sheet in the "Fortune Book." The seeker for knowledge shakes up the sticks in a bamboo jar, or "pi-t'ung," until the one showing his fate falls out, and the old lady hands him the leaflet prophesying what is in store. Grown men come quite seriously to consult the oracle and his humble priestess. In fact the revenues of the temple are drawn chiefly from this harmless spring of superstition, for throughout the East magic is a recognised and very potent factor in everyday life.

A quaint legend is attached to the Erh Lang Miao. In olden times a butcher owned a thriving establishment in the neighbourhood. One morning he noticed that the best piece of meat left on his stall over night had disappeared, and this happened day after day. Puzzled and annoyed, he accepted his son's offer to watch in the shop after dark, armed with a knife, in the hope of discovering the thief. About midnight the lad was aroused by the appearance of a yellow dog attempting to steal the succulent morsel. He made a stab at the animal, which disappeared. But to his amazement, on following the blood trail, he saw that the creature had gone out through the crack of a bolted door. Next morning he traced the trail to the Erh Lang Miao. Now his family had always been devout worshippers at that temple, and he was therefore shocked to find that there was a deep gash in the effigy of the dog lying at Erh Lang's feet. When from that day the butcher's business failed, and his family were reduced to beggary, he realized that butchers, like other men, may sometimes entertain an angel unawares, and it occasionally pays to give up "the pound of flesh."

On the opposite side of the city, the south-western, are several large temples better known, if less dear to the hearts of the people.

Temples of the Tartar City

Close to the *p'ai lou* on the big street leading to the P'ing Tse Men stands Kuang Chi Ssu, whose unimpressive entrance gives no hint that it is one of the richest Buddhist monasteries in the city with a hundred priests in residence. Part of the large outer courtyard is now devoted to a "Thousand Character People's School," but the bell and the drum in the two handsome towers still sound for services held in the inner sanctuaries.

An intelligent young monk, wearing fur-lined ear flaps, asks if we would care to see the Buddhas. "We would indeed be pleased to see them. Your beautiful courtyards promise much of interest." Proudly he throws open the high doors. We face a trinity of heroic size figures, Sakyamuni, Amitabha and Yao Shih Fo,[162] with their disciples, and an altar adorned with an exceptionally fine set of the "Eight Precious Jewels."[163] We are sincerely impressed not only by the image and treasures but the way this sanctuary is kept in order, and say so frankly. "Thanks for your polite words," the monk replies, "but the look on your faces is one of the best tributes our temple has received. Permit me, please, to show you other things." He conducts us to examine a collection of gilded Lohans, larger than life, and to a group composed of figures of Kuan Yin, Goddess of Mercy, Pu Hsien Pusa, the "All Gracious," and Wen Shu, the Indian Manjusri, mounted respectively upon a tiger, a six-tusked elephant, and a lion.

Fine things these are, unusual things, and in exceptionally good condition. But then the temple is not very old— only a Ch'ing dynasty temple whose greatest patron was the Emperor Yung Cheng, distinguished for his piety, and most generous in his gifts to the gods. Keeping time to the rhythm of the breezes, the many wind bells of Kuang Chi Ssu sound a perpetual dirge for this saintly Sovereign as they swing from the eaves.

On the same street, but nearer to the P'ing Tse Men, are two temples well worth a visit. One, the Pai T'a Ssu, we have often

---

162 For a full description of the various Buddhist Trinities, see *The Moon Year*, by Bredon and Mitrophanow, pp. 271-273.
163 See Chapter XIX

seen from a distance, for its tall white dagoba towers high above the trees, and rivals the white cone of its sister on the island in the Pei Hai.

The dagoba is attached to what is now a dilapidated temple—yet once upon a time this Monastery was rich beyond the dreams of avarice. Built by the Chins in a.d. 1084 to contain relics of Buddha, it was magnificently embellished by Kublai Khan in 1271 as a Lama temple dedicated to Manjusri or the "Buddha of Wisdom" (Wen Shu Pusa). Marble balustrades were added to the stairways, more than five hundred pounds of gold and over two hundred pounds of quicksilver used to decorate the monument itself. The pinnacle, 270 feet above the ground, was ornamented with bronze reliefs beautifully worked, and the body of the dagoba adorned with jasper and encircled with a string of pearls. In 1423, eight hundred little brick pillars were distributed round it tc hold votive lamps, and on some of the iron lanterns half effaced characters indicating Ch'ien Lung's reign are still decipherable.

With muffled step and hollow cough an old Lama guardian approaches, holding the usual rusty key. He has a poverty stricken appearance but a kindly face and his smile of welcome shows how much he needs the little gratuity which it is usual to give. As he opens each creaking door he coughs so badly that we feel if we ever come here another time we shall ask for him in vain.

Little enough is to be seen in the temple—only a few halls with gods whose aureoles are broken and whose altars are bare of offerings. A sad Buddha stands lonely in his folded robe, lifting his hands in a vanity of blessing. The worn hollow steps leading to his shrine tell of dead thousands whose pilgrim feet have trod them, and the old Lama, who has opened these doors for forty years, remembers hearing from men who were old when he was a child acolyte, of the ancient splendours of the temple, of its portrait galleries, of the famous library added in the 17th century, of the last repairs undertaken by the faithful in 1819 and, most wonderful of all, of the Sandal Wood Buddha whose abiding place it once was.

Temples of the Tartar City

Now this statue of Buddha was for centuries the most famous image in Peking—the smallest of three statues supposed to have been made in Heaven, and consecrated by Sakyamuni himself as a representation of his body. It bore the message: "One thousand years after my entry into Nirvana, you (the image) will travel to the land of Chen T'an (China) to bring great bliss to the people and lead them towards Paradise." The figure was transported to the Pai T'a Ssu after many wanderings, all of which are on record. K'ang Hsi interested himself in its history and left a description saying: "The sound of the precious sandal wood of which it is made is metallic like the sound of bronze. It is bright as lacquer and miraculously changes colour according to the light and temperature. Seen from behind, it appears to have the head bent forward in meditation, but looked at from the front, the face seems lifted upwards. One hand is stretched downwards, the other raised in blessing, and the fingers are connected with each other like the webbed toes of a goose."

Unfortunately for the glory of the Pai T'a Ssu, K'ang Hsi's veneration for this most holy image led him to build a special monastery for it, the Hung Jen Ssu,[164] near the Pei Hai, to which it was removed when the Buddha, according to legend, attained the age of 2,700 years. Thus, shorn of its treasure, the Temple of the White Dagoba gradually declined in power and popularity, till now it has become only a place of memories.

Quite close to the Pai T'a Ssu and immediately beside the new Central Hospital is another shrine well worth visiting—the Ti Wang Miao, a memorial temple dedicated to the monarchs of China from the remotest ages to the Manchu dynasty, and to the great men of their reigns. This is, in fact, the Chinese Pantheon. The two stone tablets before the gate are "getting-

---

164 The magnificence of the Hung Jen Ssu impressed all who visited the monastery. Its treasures were priceless—draperies, embroideries, golden altar vessels and jewels presented, for the use of the Buddha and the profit of the priests, by the faithful. In 1900 the place became a stronghold of the Boxers who looted it with zeal and thoroughness. The Buddha disappeared and the monastery itself was burned, the site being now occupied by barracks.

off-horse tablets" such as we see before Imperial graves and buildings of particular sanctity. Their inscriptions, however, are unusual, being in four languages, Chinese, Manchu, Thibetan and the rare Arabic.

The first courtyard is empty. In the second stand several buildings: a main hall in the style of the Palace halls, two smaller side halls, and two "*t'ing rhs*," containing stone tablets—all first erected in a.d. 1522, but enlarged under the Ch'ings, who covered their roofs with yellow tiles.

The worship which took place annually in this temple until the fall of the Manchus was performed by a prince of the first rank delegated by the Emperor to sacrifice in his name to the illustrious dead.

Now the foreign visitor wonders, "Why this curious anomaly of an alien dynasty discharging duties of sacrifice to those it dispossessed?" The answer to such a question involves an explanation of Chinese ancestral worship and the cult of the dead which lack of space forbids.

Yet even without a deep knowledge of these subjects, every visitor is impressed by the rows of simple tablets commemorating men who once ruled the Middle Kingdom.

There are no images. The canonised heroes are represented by spirit tablets only; that is to say by plain oblong pieces of wood each bearing the name of the person it represents. In the place of honour stand the tablets of the "Perfect Emperors," somewhat larger than those of their descendants.

During the propitiatory services, these simple strips of lacquered wood (differing from one another only in the gilded characters indicating the reign and posthumous title) were given honours equal to those accorded their owners in life, since the spirit of the departed was supposed to reside actually in the tablet. Due ceremony required that a newly arriving tablet should do homage to those of its ancestors, and the Master of the Rites, reverently kneeling to. receive it, "invited" the tablet with all solemnity to be pleased to leave its chariot and enter

Temples of the Tartar City

the temple. The precedence in the spirit world was exceedingly rigid, more rigid than at any mortal Court.[165]

Chinese annals, however, are full of instances showing that spirits may be degraded or promoted in the shadowy world. Ghosts might even be excluded from the Pantheon. K'ang Hsi, for example, refused admittance to the tablets of two Ming emperors as having been the authors of the ruin of the Empire, though he included the last one who fell with his throne. The selection of good sovereigns alone recalls to mind the custom in ancient Jerusalem of allowing wicked princes no place in the sepulchres of the Kings. But in China, such exclusion was a very serious step, always attended with bitter discussions, because to condemn a spirit to wander comfortless in the other world might have dangerous consequences to the living.

On the other hand, those who were unjustly shut out might be reinstated, and this applied not only to sovereigns but to the spirits of distinguished statesmen (called by the Chinese "Kuo Chu" or "Pillars of the Land") who were associated with the glory of their masters in the side halls of the Ti Wang Miao. The rule even held good for women of the Imperial family. Remember the case of the Pearl Concubine, said to have been thrown down a well by Tz'u Hsi's orders as the Court fled from the Forbidden City in 1900. When persistent rumours of foul play began to trouble the Empress Dowager, she issued a special decree extolling the virtue and admirable courage of the dead woman "who (according to the Edict) preferred to *kill herself* rather than witness the pollution and destruction of the

---

[165] "A curious example of this careful adherence to rank occurred when the tablet of the Old Buddha was invited to enter the Manchu Temple of Ancestors (T'ai Miao). Before this could be done it was necessary that the tablets of her son, T'ung Chih, and of her daughter-in-law should first be removed from the hall, because the arriving tablet could not perform the usual obeisance to its ancestors in the presence of that of a younger generation. To give an idea of the respect with which the tablet of a reigning sovereign was treated, we may add that the Regent, acting for the child-Emperor Hsuan T'ung, made nine ' k'o-tows' before each of the Nine Ancestors and their thirty-five Imperial Consorts, with due regard to the order of seniority." (See Backhouse and Bland, op. at.).

ancestral shrines." Her praiseworthy conduct was, therefore, rewarded by the granting of a posthumous title, regarded as fulfilling all reasonable requirements of atonement to the deceased, however she met her death. "Alive, a Pearl Concubine more or less might count for little when weighed against the needs of the Old Buddha's policy; once dead, however, her spirit must needs be conciliated and compensated."

Like so many other places towards which the Nationalist Government shows complete indifference because they do not happen to be connected with its own heroes, the Pantheon is neglected, and shorn, perhaps intentionally, of much of its dignity. The side halls which used to contain the tablets of lesser heroes are empty now. To judge from the rows of small paper Republican flags hung up near the ceiling, they must have been used for "party gatherings."

In the central hall, the tablets remain huddled together. Above them hangs the portrait of Sun Yat-sen and a framed copy of his Will, between two Republican flags, the whole effect dingy rather than impressive. Four big characters proclaim the slogan, "Under the Sky All Men are Equal." They appear curiously incongruous in a place once dedicated to those who proved themselves above the ordinary run of mortals.

Behind the modern Waichiaopu building stands another memorial hall much smaller than the Ti Wang Miao but similar in purpose, and modern enough to prove that posthumous honours were accorded to noted patriots even after 1900. One pavilion shelters a monumental stone tablet in memory of two High Commissioners to Thibet in the reign of Ch'ien Lung. Their death at the hands of Thibetan revolutionaries gave rise to the Imperial Decree calling for the building of a memorial hall to express the respect and gratitude of the Throne.

Connected with and behind this pavilion is a second shrine called the "Four Loyalists' Hall,"[166] dedicated to the memory of Four officials who bravely protested in the midst of the Boxer

---

[166] Built by a distinguished Chinese diplomat and Minister of Foreign Affairs, Lou Tseng-Hsiang, who later entered a Catholic monastery in Belgium.

Temples of the Tartar City

madness against the destruction of the Legations—protested "with serious tone and countenance and in fearless and straightforward words." Two of them at least—Yuan Ch'ang and Hsu Ching-ch'eng— voluntarily laid down their lives as a warning, and to point out what they believed to be for their country's good.[167]

"If to meet an undeserved doom with high courage is heroism, then these men were indeed heroes. In reading their memorials, and especially the last of them, one is inevitably and forcibly reminded of the best examples in Greek and Roman history. In their high-minded philosophy, their instinctive morality and calm contemplation of death, there breathes the spirit of Socrates, Seneca and Pliny—the spirit which has given European civilization its classical models of noble fortitude and many of its finest inspirations, the spirit which, shorn of its quality of individualism, has been the foundation of Japan's greatness."[168]

The twin pagodas of the Shuang T'a Ssu, which all who pass through the west city cannot fail to notice, are likewise memorial shrines built in honour of two Thibetan pontiffs. They are connected with a small Buddhist monastery erected by the Chins in a.d. 1200, neglected and forgotten by the Mings, but restored by Ch'ien Lung, to disappear again in modern times. These two pagodas, one nine stories high, the other seven, bear the names of the holy men to whom they are dedicated.

---

167 Their courage and unselfish patriotism was first recognised by an edict of the Regent, Prince Ch'un, who placed their names on the honour roll of National Heroes.

168 A stirring appreciation for the character of these patriots, as well as an excellent and scholarly translation of their memorials, may be found in *Annals and Memoirs of the Court of Peking* and *China Under the Empress Dowager*, by Backhouse and Bland.

Juliet Bredon

XII. Temples of the Chinese City

The temples of the Chinese City are the oldest in Peking. Most of them no foreigner ever visits, some he never even sees because they are hidden in little twisted lanes far from the main streets; lanes "alive or dead," as the Chinese call them, meaning lanes open at both ends or lanes with one end closed. Yet many of these sanctuaries are extremely ancient, with curious legends attached to them, and they appeal to the imagination, even in their crumbling ruin, quite as much as the better known shrines.

"Those people are little to be envied," as Ruskin says, "in whose hearts the great charities of the imagination lie dead, and for whom fancy has no power to repress painful impressions of ruin, to ignore what is ignoble, or disguise what is discordant in scenes otherwise so rich in remembrances."

Several temples in the Liu Li Ch'ang district, which had great historical interest and are marked as large and important on the old maps of the city, have completely disappeared; to look for them now is "love's labour lost." Little by little the fires of devotion burnt themselves out in one after the other, leaving deserted altars where the battered images look like what indeed they are—dusty gods retired from business. A quaint exception is the little Taoist temple, known as the Lu Tsu Miao, dedicated to Lu Tsu, one of the "Eight Immortals," who is a patron chiefly of barbers and actors, but to this day commands also the superstitious devotion of a few "respectable" worshippers. Votive tablets line the corridor leading to this small sanctuary where the air is never fresh—always stuffy, old-fashioned air.

There is more vitality about the P'an T'ao Kung, a Taoist temple on the banks of the canal near the Tung P'ien Men. Translated, its name means "Palace of Trained Peach Trees," and behind the image of the "Hsi Wang Mu" or "Queen Mother of the Western Heaven," may be seen an espalier of intertwined branches covered with paper peach blossoms. Among the Chinese the peach is the symbol of longevity, and to

Temples of the Chinese City

the Taoists, represents the fruit of the Tree of Life. He who by his virtuous conduct obtains the privilege of plucking a peach from the celestial orchard of the Heavenly Mother, takes his seat among the Immortals at a yearly feast celebrated in her palace. Wonderful dishes are served to this illustrious company —bears' paws, monkeys' lips, dragons' livers, and peaches which confer eternal life. In the P'an T'ao Kung all the Gods are shown in an elaborate carved frieze saluting the Hsi Wang Mu who, attended by phoenixes and fairy handmaidens, awaits the guests with the Mystic Peach in her hand. On the "Feast of the Immortals"—the third day of the third moon—a famous fair is held here amid much popular rejoicing. Large crowds congregate along the banks of the canal, where a regular street of shops, restaurants and amusement booths, springs up. Occasionally the rare women-acrobats on horseback give a thrilling performance to which their red clothes and bound feet lend an exotic charm. The festival is particularly popular with old ladies who assiduously say prayers and burn incense before the compassionate Goddess, begging her for long life and asking her to repair the ravages of the years.

In the neighbourhood of the P'an T'ao Kung, near the Tso An Men, stands the old pagoda of Fa T'a Ssu, familiarly known as the "Little Tired Pagoda," because of the legend attached to it. The story goes that many hundred years ago, in the time of the Chins (a.d. 1125-1234) this pagoda was erected in a distant province. But one day it conceived a desire to visit the capital. So it started wandering across the fields and through the villages, and the country people, amazed at the miracle, knocked their heads in the dust as it went by, while the wise men who watched its progress murmured: "Verily the impossible hath been wrought by the strength of desire." At length, after journeying tens and hundreds of miles, it passed the wall of the great city. Then, like a human traveller, it grew weary and rested on the spot where we see it now, having no strength to go farther. Therefore the people called it the "Little Tired Pagoda," and built a temple in its honour. But the temple has long since disappeared, and it stands solitary in the fields like an extinguished torch.

Not far away, near the north wall of the Temple of Heaven, is a very peculiar memorial temple, the Chin Chung Miao, built in honour of Yo Fei—also enshrined in the Kuan Ti Miao—by order of K'ang Hsi, though his reigning House had little reason to revere this Sung dynasty hero, and generally ignored him.[169]

If the gate is shut, knock and you will probably be admitted by a polite man, evidently of the merchant class. "We have hired the place," he tells visitors, "for purposes of trade, but if you desire to see the ancient images of the temple, be pleased to come in." Whereupon he conducts us past a modernised showroom containing rows of cheap clocks, along a crumbling corridor, with two stone guardian lions which have long ago lost their balance, fallen from their pedestals and broken their heads off. In the first courtyard he calls our attention to a battered iron statue, a kneeling figure. "Formerly there were a pair," he explains, "one represented the treacherous Minister Ch'in Kuei, the other his wife, whose wicked intrigues brought about Yo Fei's death. Until recently both stood outside the temple, and passers-by spat upon the traitors and kicked their images. The woman's statue finally fell to pieces and disappeared." "As for Ch'in Kuei," says Johnston in *The Cult of Military Heroes*, "it is not only his iron image that has been subjected to daily insult. His very name still undergoes one of the worst indignities that could well be imagined, for it is used as a synonym for a spittoon, and his posthumous honorific title has been changed to 'false and foul' while, on the other hand, the warrior whom he defamed and slew has gathered fame and honour with the passing of the centuries."

The two halls dedicated to Yo Fei have not been dismantled, but his effigy, surrounded by his valiant captains and his bows and arrows, shares the first with boxes of window glass. In the second he and his wife are seated on chairs of honour among picture-frames.

---

169 See Chapter XI

Temples of the Chinese City

The merchant's admiration for the hero seems no wise dimmed by these sordid surroundings. Rightly judging that the greatest figures of history have appeared at their best in exceptional moments only, he realises that Yo Fei in life must have more than once looked just as dusty as his image among the framed oleographs of "Queen Victoria's Coronation" and "Marie Antoinette On Her Way To The Guillotine." "No theatrical idealism clouds for any educated Chinese the sense of the humanity of his country's greatest men; on the contrary, it is the evidence of every-day humanity around them that most endears their memories to the common heart and makes, by contrast, more picturesque and admirable lives that were not ordinary."

Once upon a time there were also temples behind the enclosure of the Temple of Agriculture, but many famous places, like Hei Lung T'an, have completely disappeared save for the few stone slabs that mark their sites. Such shrines as are left serve chiefly as rendezvous for pleasure parties who, in warm weather, frequent their quiet rooms for dinners, or their terraces for the sake of the air and the view across the rushes that grow in profusion under the southern wall of the Chinese City. An exception, however, is the San Sheng An, a vegetarian nunnery on the road to the Printing Works, near the Ch'eng Huang Miao, (dedicated to the tutelar deity of the city) where the well-known fair in honour of the Ch'ing Ming festival is held in the third moon. The cooks of this nunnery are renowned for their preparation of vegetable food and wealthy Chinese patrons willingly forego meat, forbidden on the premises, for the sake of the specialities of this refined kitchen.

There are a few more temples farther on, near the Yu An Gate, in whose quiet courts life with its pathetic struggles scarcely penetrates, and behind whose walls existence flows slowly and deeply. One of these is Sheng An Ssu, grey with age, drowsing in the fields like an old, old man sitting in the sun and remembering many things. For years no repairs have been made here, and wounded roofs and walls are sadly in need of "first aid." But two or three priests still drone a round of daily services in the single hall before the three large Buddhas, while—

> "Vainly does each, as he glides,
> Fable and dream
> Of the lands which the River of Time
> Had left ere he woke on its breast,
> Or shall reach when his eyes have been closed."

Neither the Buddhas nor the Lohans are remarkable. But the frescoes (probably Ming) of Buddhist figures larger than life, that cover the walls are very striking—both well done and well preserved—and the copy of the Sandal Wood Buddha (Chan T'an Fo), that once stood in the Hung Jen Ssu near the Pei Hai is unique.

The priests claim the last Emperor of the T'ang dynasty, Chao Hsuan Ti (a.d. 904-907), as the founder of their temple, but admit that he left it unfinished at the fall of his house. None can say who completed it, nor when the "Winds of the Five Corruptions" began to blow upon it down the centuries and finally left it poor in revenues but rich in secluded, drowsy felicity.

Not far away is another T'ang temple, Tsung Hsiao Ssu, founded by the great T'ai Tsung, most revered of all the T'ang emperors, after the more famous Fa Yuan Ssu was finished. To honour these, his two favourite shrines, T'ai Tsung gave each a wooden image lacquered in gold from Thibet. An original Wu Liang Fo stands in the main hall at Fa Yuan Ssu, but in Tsung Hsiao Ssu only a replica is enshrined in a stone tablet. Except for a few frescoes on the walls, there are no relics or treasures of interest and no signs of care or reverence for the altars of the gods. The priests are loquacious and greedy— spoiled by visitors who come to see the famous roof of the big catalpa tree, which has been preserved as a curiosity on account of its size and great age. Long ago, to judge by the handsome sotobas of departed abbots outside the red walls, religion was taken seriously here. Now, frowsy priests neglect their masses for the more profitable occupation of gardening. Their peonies are famous and draw crowds of sight-seers in the season. Much work and care is expended on the plants, obviously to the detriment of religious observances, but the collection is indeed remarkable, showing magnificent specimens of wine-red, pink, white and "black" blooms. The most curious and the rarest, however, are the green peonies, whose flowers are only a shade lighter than their leaves.

Tsung Hsiao Ssu, despite its garden, cannot compare with Fa Yuan Ssu, the largest monastery in the Chinese City, situated south of the Liu Li Ch'ang quarter (Lan Mien hut'ung), on the spot where a bone of the goddess Kuan Yin was supposed to have been found in a.d. 645. The mellow loveliness of the old buildings is enhanced by the patina in which Time wraps all beautiful things. There is no artificial colour, but brick and stone have turned, under the action of rain and sun, to different shades of grey, varying from the silvery tone of birch bark to the sombre grey of basalt.

Among the priests we notice with pleasure that the ancient ideals are by no means dead. Unlike the inmates of many Buddhist establishments who do not even pretend to observe their vows, they love their sanctuary, they know its traditions, they are proud of its treasures. One old monk urges us to mount the rickety ladder steps of the bell tower and strikes the bell in order that we may thrill to rich notes that have echoed down the centuries. Another shows us a huge acacia ("huai-shu") said to date from the T'ang dynasty, and many lovely flowering trees—lilacs with trunks a foot in diameter, gnarled plum and cherry trees, great filmy mists of petals in spring time. But he regrets, almost as if he himself were at fault, that the peony plants are still only green shoots sprouting from the earth, and begs us to return in the fourth month when their flowers are the glory of the temple gardens.

Then as the rumour spreads that honourable foreign guests are visiting the premises, a young priest, more highly educated than those we have met so far, comes to acquaint us with the temple history and answer any questions we may wish to ask.

Juliet Bredon

Courteously he deciphers the inscriptions on the stone tablets in the main courtyard. Several are Ming, one being the gift of the last ill-fated sovereign of the dynasty, but a few date only from the Manchus.

"These are mere modern things," he says apologetically. "Now I will show you much that is more interesting." Whereupon he leads us through a small hall to see a statue of the kindly Buddha Who Loves Little Children, with figures of pretty naked babies playing about his shoulders and nestling in the folds of his neck—the same Pu Tai of the Lama Temple, but more sympathetically presented.

Next we mount a high platform where another sanctuary stands. The priest points out the big blocks of its foundations. "They are part of the original temple built by T'ai Tsung," he relates. "The Beloved Emperor erected a pagoda on this site (which was in the south-east corner of the Peking of his day), on his return from his wars in Liaotung and Korea, as a memorial to faithful officials and dutiful sons who perished for the State. Here prayers were said for the repose of their souls and beneath these stones rest the ashes of some of his favourite horsemen, the dead, yet undying, heroes whom the Sovereign himself led to battle, carrying black tiger skin banners—those same warriors who shared his triumphal entries into his capital of Sian-Fu."

"Many great men have been associated with this temple," he also tells us. "There was the Sung Emperor Ch'in Tsung who stopped here on his way from K'ai Feng Fu to his death in captivity in the north as a prisoner of the triumphant Chins in 1126. There was the celebrated Hsieh Fang-teh, a loyal official and well-known scholar of the Sung period, who, on being taken captive and imprisoned here by the Mongol Yuans, refused to eat and so died. There was also the rebel An Lu-shan[170] (8th

---

170 An Lu-shan's fate was sealed at the battle of T'ai Yuan where artillery was first used against him by the troops of Su Tsung, successor of the unlucky Yuan Tsung (712-756), memorable as the founder of the Han Lin College and of the *Peking Gazette*, the oldest periodical in the world. It is interesting to note that the Emperor Su Tsung employed in this campaign four thousand Arab soldiers, lent to him by the Khalif Abu Giafar. The

century a.d.) descendant of a Turkish tribe first conquered by T'ai Tsung, whose redoubtable revolt, when Governor of Peking, began the decline of the T'angs. He and a contemporary rebel general built two high brick pagodas here. But the greatest of all was T'ai Tsung himself, one of the noblest rulers who ever sat upon the Dragon Throne."[171]

Presently the young priest announces that the abbot would be pleased if we would take a cup of tea in his sitting room—an offer we gladly accept. The old man salutes us with that politeness which immediately puts a stranger at his ease, and phrases of courtesy to which we reply as best we know how, expressing gratitude for the unusually kind reception.

---

descendants of these Arabs are part of the Moslem population of Kansu province who preserve a dim legend to that effect. A peculiarly fine breed of ponies and the Lan-chou cats—not unlike Angoras—both show traces of an admixture of the blood of animals brought by these strangers to a strange land.

171 The praise of the priest is justified by historical records. The Great T'ai Tsung (a.d. 627-649), contemporary of Mohammed, shed immortal lustre on the T'ang dynasty founded by his father. The author of the *Middle Kingdom* compares him favourably with Akbar, Marcus Aurclius and K'ang Hsi, or with Charlemagne and Haroun Al Rashid. To him was due the pacification of the Empire after many centuries of disruption. Founder of an army of 900,000 men recruited from a people who had forgotten the art of self-defence, master of the regions from Kashgaria to Korea, including Thibet (with which he was the first to deal, as he was the first to receive an embassy from Byzance, giving shelter at the same time to the last of the Sassanides), patron of arts and letters and himself an author of remarkable works, a mighty hunter and a famous warrior, he realised the ideal characteristics of a Chinese ruler. The splendour of his court and of his pageants reminds one of the dazzling description of Chinese magnificence which we find in the *Arabian Nights*. Boulger in *A Short History of China* says: "His whole figure stands out boldly as one of the ablest and most human of China's sovereigns," while Parker quotes T'ai Tsung as "the only instance in the whole course of Chinese history of an emperor who was, from a European point of view, at once a gentleman and a brave, shrewd, compassionate man, free from priggishness and cant." After his death a reflection of his genius appeared in his concubine Wu Tse-t'ien, the famous Chinese Irene, sometimes called the "greatest of China's Catherines," who later married T'ai Tsung's son, and ruled the empire for twenty-two years, during which, despite her personal immoralities, the people prospered and much glory was added to the fame of the T'angs.

"It is rare," he replies, "that Europeans ever visit this old temple. Would you care to see things that your countrymen seldom see?"

Again we express our thanks and he gives orders that the "holy of holies," be opened and goes there with us, calling our attention to treasures worthy of notice; for example, the queer, lantern-shaped stone box with inscriptions, in front of the sanctuary and the stone tablet within, dating from the 10th century—both valuable historical relics, to the images behind the gilded screen of woodwork and gauze, one of which is that supposed to have been presented by T'ai Tsung, and the "Chieh T'ai" or platform for ordaining priests, of which only three exist in the temples of Peking and the neighbourhood.

We follow him into a pretty courtyard back of the main building, where stands a two-storied temple. Here we admire some pictures painted in the reign of Yung Cheng and copied on older models. The deep blues and rich reds are as fresh as if they had left the brush but yesterday. Figures and faces follow the law of Chinese art in the subordination of individualism to type, of personality to humanity, and we turn from the dignified, passionless countenances of painted saints, and the soft folds of their draperies, to find replicas in the faces of the monks standing about us watching with the same quiet, inscrutable gaze, in robes less brilliant in colour but differing little in form.

Pleased with our admiration, the old man gives an order and a priest brings from a recess scrolls which he tenderly unrolls. "These," says the abbot, gazing at them lovingly, "are genuine Sung pictures. We were lucky to preserve them during the Boxer troubles. But they are not often opened. Once when they were shown to a foreigner, he wished to buy them for a museum and became insulting when we refused to sell at his price or any price. Therefore now they are seldom exhibited."

After we have duly inspected and wondered at these marvels, he adds: "There is just one more thing you may care to see," and leads us to a side altar on which stand tablets such as

Temples of the Chinese City

are used for the spirits of the dead. Lighted lamps are placed before them and pyramids of cakes and fruit.

"These tablets," he explains, "commemorate the soldiers who died in the Great War and the offerings are for the comfort of their souls."

"But no Chinese soldiers were killed on those dreadful European battlefields?" we suggest.

"Certainly, we know that. They are for the foreign soldiers."

"Of course you realise that none of those dead are Buddhists?"

"Yes, but may we not admire the beauty of their sacrifice? And are not all faiths fundamentally alike in that they desire the good of humanity? In your Christian churches do you not pray for the salvation of all and believe in it?"

At a loss to admit that immense kindly toleration such as this is not universal, we remain silent. Therefore, sensing that he has asked what we do not wish to answer, he covers our confusion by remarking: "If you will permit it, this temple desires to set up a tablet especially to commemorate the dead heroes of your country. And we wish to invite you shortly to join us in a universal service of remembrance—for we feel sure you must revere the beauty of Buddha's teaching."

"We honour the faith of such as you who follow it," we answer. Then at the threshold we say our goodbyes, and the abbot and his monks bow very, very low, showing the crowns of their smoothly shaven heads, glossy like balls of ivory.

Juliet Bredon

XIII. Temples and Tombs Outside the City

Scattered over the plain outside the City we also find temples. Some are tumble-down monasteries whose revenues have failed, whose worshippers have fallen away, and in whose solitudes a few infirm priests manage to exist. Such are interesting only to specialists in Chinese antiquities or students of inscriptions, their crumbling gods are of a world incomprehensible without years of familiarity—a world of myths, beliefs, and superstitions about which Westerners as a rule care little. No longer can we call such places beautiful in the ordinary sense of the word, but they have a picturesqueness of their own for those with eyes to see it.

Other sanctuaries beyond the walls of Peking remain as prosperous and popular as any within them, and to this category belong Ta Chung Ssu, Wan Shou Ssu, Po Yun Kuan and the Tung Yueh Miao.

Perhaps the best known to foreigners is Ta Chung Ssu, the Great Bell Temple,[172] renowned for its mighty bell to which clings a touching story of filial piety. This temple lying among quiet farms is an easy and pleasant walk of two miles from the Hsi Chih Men, or an excellent ride of four or five from the An Ting Men across the plain, passing through the old Tartar mud wall, once the northern boundary of Kublai Khan's capital.

A shrine of some sort existed on this site long before the famous bell was moved here from Wan Shou Ssu in 1743, or the red-eaved hexagonal building constructed to house this world's wonder, the greatest feat of bronze casting in China. It swings down to our level from enormous rafters, and the lips, curved like flower petals, are graven with sayings from the Sacred Books. Stand in the pit beneath and marvel at its height.[173]

---

[172] Also called Chueh Sheng Ssu, or the "Temple Where They Understand the Secret of Existence."
[173] By actual measurements, which, however, give no idea of its impressiveness, the bell is seventeen feet high, thirty-four feet at its greatest circumference and eight inches thick. Its weight is variously

Temples and Tombs Outside the City

Then climb the crooked stairway and toss cash through the hole in the top—purposely left to prevent the bell from bursting when struck too hard or when the strokes follow one another too closely—for the coins that fall through the opening bring luck to the thrower.[174]

We wish to hear the mighty voice, but the priests say this is forbidden and has ever been so without an order from the Emperor, who no longer now has power to command. They remind us that it is no common temple bell and relate its history.

Yung Lo himself commanded it to be made in the 15th century, some say as a present to a famous priest, and an inscription records the sovereign's name and the name of the man who cast it. According to the Imperial desire, it was to be of such a size that when struck the sound should be heard for a hundred li (30 miles), therefore the bell was strenghtened with brass and deepened with gold, and sweetened with silver. But though the master-moulder measured the materials for the alloy and treated them skilfully and prepared the fires and the monstrous melting pot for melting the metal, and though the casting was made twice, each time the result was worthless. Whereupon the Emperor grew so angry that he sent word that if the renowned bell-smith failed again, his head would be severed from his neck. "Then the bell-smith consulted a soothsayer who, after a long silence, made answer: 'Gold and brass will never meet in wedlock, silver and iron never will embrace until the blood of a virgin be mixed with the metals in their fushion.'

---

estimated at from 20,000 to 80,000 pounds. Though the big bell of Moscow is larger, this is the largest hanging bell in the world. In order to move it from Wan Shou Ssu to its present position legend says a special canal was dug during the summer. When this waterway froze solid—as canals do in the bitter Peking winter weather—the bell was slid along over the ice to its new home. Where could one find a more ingenious method for moving such a weighty object in the absence of adequate tackle?
174 Like most Chinese bells it has no tongue and is not rung but struck from the outside by a log of wood swung on chains.

Juliet Bredon

"When the beautiful daughter of the bell-smith heard this, she determined to save her father from the fate hanging over him. So, on the day of the third casting, she leaped into the white flood of metal, crying: ' For thy sake, oh! my father.' The whirling fountain of many coloured fires absorbed her and no trace of her remained except one tiny shoe with embroidery of pearls and flowers, left in the hand of the serving woman who sought to grasp her by the foot as she jumped, but was only able to clutch the pretty shoe. When the casting was finished, however, the bell was more perfect in form and more wonderful than any other bell. And when it was sounded, its tones were deeper and finer and richer than the sound of any other bell, so that its voice, like summer thunder, was heard at a distance of twice 100 *li*. Yet, between each stroke, there was always a low moaning which ended in a sound of sobbing and complaining, as though a weeping woman softly murmured: 'Hai!' And when that sharp, sweet shuddering came in the air, then all the Chinese mothers in the many-coloured byways of Peking whispered to their little ones: 'Listen, that is the dutiful daughter calling for her shoe. Hai! That is she crying for her shoe.'" [175]

On the An Ting plain itself stands another well-known temple, the Huang Ssu or Yellow Temple. This large rambling place consists of two establishments, the Eastern and the Western, each of which is presided over by a different sect of Lamas. The buildings of the former, dedicated to Sakyamuni Buddha, were erected on the site of an old Liao dynasty temple by the Emperor Shun Chih in a.d. 1652 as an occasional residence for the Dalai Lama. Those of the latter were constructed by K'ang Hsi about 1720 to accommodate Thibetan and Mongol Lamas in general, and have been the haven of such visitors ever since. All the earlier Manchu emperors took pains to conciliate the dignitaries of the Lama church because they needed their allegiance and feared their enmity. But K'ang Hsi

---

[175] The Ta Chung Ssu bell was the largest of five great bells cast by Yung Lo's order. Another used to hang in the Bell Tower and a similar legend is attached to it. See *Some Chinese Ghosts*, by Lafcadio Hearn.

had particular reason for doing so, as, during his travels, he caused the death of a Living Buddha at Kuei Hua Ch'eng in Mongolia. Hence the large sums this monarch spent embellishing the Huang Ssu while striving to atone and regain the friendship of the Mongol monks.[176]

The splendid marble "stupa" was added by Ch'ien Lung, the Magnificent, in memory of the Thibetan Pan-ch'eng Lama who died of smallpox at Peking in a.d. 1780. The holy man is not, however, buried under the monument. Careful always to keep an eye on the gallery of public opinion, the artist-emperor doubly proved his piety to the world by sending the body of the illustrious priest back to Thibet in a golden coffin and then erecting this beautiful "chorten" over a second precious casket containing his infected garments.[177]

No better example of modern stone sculpture exists near Peking than this pinnacled memorial adhering generally to the ancient Indian type, but differing from it in that the dome is inverted. The spire, composed of thirteen step-like segments symbolical of the thirteen Buddhist heavens, is surmounted by a large cupola of gilded bronze, and the whole monument, with the four attendant pagodas and the fretted white *p'ai lous*, raised on a stone and marble terrace. From its wave-patterned base to the gilded ball thirty feet above, it is chiselled with carvings in relief which recall the Mongol tombs and palaces in Agra and Delhi, scenes from the life of the deceased Lama; the preternatural circumstances attendant on his birth, his entrance to the priesthood, combats with heretics, instruction of disciples and death. A pathetic note is given by the lion who wipes his eyes with his paw in grief over the good man's passing. Unfortunately many of the richly ornamented

---

[176] When K'ang Hsi appeared before the Living Buddha at Kuei Hua Ch'eng, the latter received him sitting upon his throne. One of the Emperor's followers, incensed at such casual treatment of his master, the Son of Heaven, thereupon drew his sword and killed the Saint. a terrible fight ensued with a heavy toll of life on both sides, so it is said, and K'ang Hsi himself just managed to escape by mounting a fleet horse.

[177] Such is the legend, but these robes are also claimed by a small temple in the Forbidden City near the Yu Hua Ke, or "Tower of Rain and Flowers."

sculptures were mutilated by the soldiery quartered in the temple after 1900, who knocked the heads off figures with the butts of their rifles.

The stupa of the Yellow Temple is now walled off in a separate enclosure by order, and at the expense, of the Panshan Lama who proposes, it is said, to further repair this magnificent monastery when funds are available.

Let him make haste, for most of the buildings have gaping walls and broken roofs through which the rain splashes upon their foundations. Strings of coloured prayer flags,[178] which the monks call "galloping wind horses" flutter before altars where the faithful dare not pray for fear of falling tiles, and the two splendid marble monsters[179] near the dagoba sit crooked on their haunches on the uneven pavement.

Even the main sanctuary with the statue of Sakyamuni Buddha, where hundreds of Mongol pilgrims still piously prostrate themselves and deposit their Khadaks (scarves of blessing) on the idols, is full of cracks and rifts. The traveller's palace[180] with its fine lofty rooms and handsome private chapel (reserved for a Living Buddha, and closed to the public) is no longer sound, while the neighbouring temple with the faded but handsome yellow, blue and green columns seems about to collapse, and *p'ai lou*, which formerly faced the stupa, is nothing but a heap of plaster and stone.

---

178 Such flags are made of squares of coloured cloth and the monks believe that, when the winds move them, the gods accept the prayers inscribed on the banners as actually prayed.

179 These represent the "hou" or "king of Beasts."

180 Two Dalai Lamas were received and lodged in this palace; the first in a.d. 1652 with great pomp and state, the second, who arrived in the capital after his flight from Lhassa in 1908, with less formality, as his visit was considered ill-omened by the Empress Dowager Tz'u Hsi, to whom astrologers had foretold that her own death would coincide with his coming—which it did. The richly decorated rooms were also the headquarters of Sir Hope Grant in 1860.

Temples and Tombs Outside the City

Marble "Stupa"—Yellow Temple (Huang Ssu)

Like those of the Yung Ho Kung, the monks of the Yellow Temple are pathetically poor, though the latter supplement their slender funds by the manufacture of bronze images, incense burners and vases. At one time their foundry vied with Dolo-Nor in the manufacture of gods for the "People of the Wilderness" (Mongolia and Thibet). But the demand for Buddhas is no longer what it was, and most of the pieces we see being turned out; nowadays are not destined for temples at all, but for the Peking cloissonne manufacturers, who pay the Lamas a miserable pittance for bronze vessels, later wired and enamelled in their own factories.

The yearly temple festival, which is held on the 13th of the 1st moon and includes a Devil Dance, also brings in some revenue, and morbid visitors are always ready to pay to see the curious but repulsive "T'san T'an" (outside the main enclosure) where dead priests are kept in wooden boxes like gramophone cabinets. The attendant will lift the lids to show the Lamas in various stages of decay— at a price. Two for a dollar represents a reasonable bargain, though one is usually enough to satisfy anybody's curiosity.

At the Black Temple[181] not far away, Devil Dances were also held, and in connection with them cart races and riding exhibitions which used to attract the owners of fast horses in Peking.[182] These have been abandoned. But the place remains an ideal site for a picnic on a sunny day.

Another monument, showing like the Huang Ssu strong traces of Indian influence, is the ruined Wu T'a Ssu, or "Five Pagoda Temple," two miles west of Peking and not far from the Summer Palace road. Supposed to be a copy of the ancient Indian temple of Buddhagaya, it has a picturesque history.

---

181 So called from the colour of its roof tiles.
182 Unlike our clergy, Lama churchmen have always encouraged racing as the Mongols understand that sport, and throughout Mongolia the highest ecclesiastical dignitaries officially patronise it, themselves owning many "favourites."

Temples and Tombs Outside the City

In the early part of Yung Lo's reign, during which a new impetus was given to the intercourse between China and India, a Hindu "sramana" of high degree came to the Chinese capital and was received in audience by the Emperor to whom he presented five golden images of the Buddha and a model of the memorial temple erected on the spot where Sakyamuni attained his Buddhahood. In return the Emperor, himself the son of a monk, appointed him State hierarch, and fitted up for his residence a monastery (founded during the preceding Mongol dynasty) to the west of Peking, promising at the same time to build a reproduction in stone of the model temple he had brought with him to enshrine the sacred images. The new temple was not, however, finished and dedicated until a later reign (Ch'eng Hua's), according to the marble slab with an Imperial inscription set up near it. This specifically states that in dimensions as well as in every detail the Wu T'a Ssu is an exact reproduction of the celebrated "Diamond Throne" of Central India. Only the five pagodas from which the temple takes its name remain, standing on a massive square foundation whose sides are decorated with rows of Buddhas. Worshippers and objects of worship, all have vanished. But the crows perch on the pinnacles waiting for occasional tourists with tea baskets.

Near the Wu T'a Ssu—in fact plainly visible from it— is the lofty two storied hall of the Ta Hui Ssu (Ta Fo Ssu), or "Temple of the Big Buddha." Though partially restored as late as 1910, it is rapidly falling into decay again under the melancholy eyes of a single priest, impotent to save his crumbling buildings. He affirms that this temple was founded by the great T'ai Tsung of the T'ang dynasty, and was subsequently enlarged and restored by the Mings, in proof of which latter statement an incense burner dated Ching T'ai and a Wan Li tablet may be seen in front of the main hall. This contains a tremendous image of a "Thousand Armed and Thousand Eyed" Buddha, surrounded by Bodhisatvas and acolytes of heroic size—impressive figures threatened with destruction by the sagging roofs.

Juliet Bredon

A little further on in the same general direction we reach Wan Shou Ssu ("Temple of Ten Thousand Longevities") situated on the banks of Kublai Khan's canal. First built by the Ming Emperor Wan Li in a.d. 1577, the shrine has been repeatedly repaired and was kept in good condition, so long as the Imperial corteges going by barge to and from the Summer Palace, stopped there to rest. The Empress Dowager Tz'u Hsi liked the place especially—liked its charming suite of detached guest rooms, liked to wander through the old rock gardens, to sip her scented tea under the yellow tiled *t'ing' rhs* and to gaze at the blue demi-lune of the Western Hills from the balcony of the high "Hall of Ten Thousand Buddhas"— a Ch'ien Lung building where prayers were said for the longevity of his mother. Hence the Old Buddha never failed in generous gifts to the monks, which enabled them to keep up their temple for the glory of Sakyamuni and for her pleasure.

More to the north of the city, near the An Ting Men, lies the Temple of Earth (Ti T'an) dating from a.d. 1520, the moral complement according to Chinese ideas, of the Temple of Heaven (T'ien T'an). Like the latter it had great significance as a place of Imperial worship and was jealously closed to the public until the Allied troops entered and camped within its walls in 1860. But, because Earth was second in sanctity to Heaven, the park is smaller, the buildings less imposing, the open altar square, instead of round (since according to the old belief, the Earth was square) and built of yellow tiles, colour of the soil, instead of white marble. The absence of braziers and furnaces is a significant reminder that the sacrifices offered here were buried instead of burned. Little charm, unfortunately, is left to this fine enclosure since Feng Yu Hsiang made it into a public park and noisy children trample the grass-grown spaces, where meadow larks sang at sunset, into dusty playgrounds. One cannot help thinking that sometimes the "hand of democracy is heavy."

Temples and Tombs Outside the City

Wu T'a Ssu

Juliet Bredon

The lesser altars to the Rising Sun (the Chao Jih T'an, outside the east wall near the Ch'i Hua Men) and to the Evening Moon (Hsi Yueh T'an, outside the west wall near the P'ing Tse Men)—both built in the same year of the Ming Emperor Chia Ching—have escaped modernization. Nothing worth seeing remains in either for the hurried globe trotter. But there is enchantment still in these tranquil spaces for leisurely wanderers who have attained that blessed state of serenity which comes of knowing there is no need of haste.

Twenty years ago the last ceremony took place at the forlorn "Altar of the Moon," according to the old caretaker. He saw it himself. He swept the paths the Emperor trod. He watched, from a respectful distance, the offerings being placed upon the quadrangular terrace. "Tell us of that last service," we beg. He is reluctant, as Chinese always are, to speak of old customs to foreigners lest we find them ridiculous. But we persuade him finally with an empty bottle from our lunch basket—the accepted currency for many a priceless legend!

"It was on the evening of the autumn equinox that His Majesty came. When the Harvest Moon shone full on the altar spread with white offerings, white silks, white jades, milky pearls. The Lord of Ten Thousand Years bowed before the creamy tablet with the silvered characters meaning "Place of the Spirit of the Light of Night." Afterwards four animals were sacrificed, a pig, an ox, a sheep, and a deer, while the bell tolled from a near-by tower. Then the emperor changed his sacrificial robes in the pavilion yonder and returned to his palace while we humble folk," he added with a chuckle, "shared the meat offerings with the moon."

Nature worship is practically a thing of the past in China. The Sun and Moon have ceased to be gods. The older, grander beliefs are dimmed by popular cults like Taoism with its host of deities, some angelic, others demoniac, made in man's image.

Even Taoism is itself an example of doctrines conceived in mystic purity and deteriorated into a jumble of superstitions by the masses. If Lao Tzu, its founder, who sought essential,

Temples and Tombs Outside the City

spiritual truth were still alive, he could not trace the smallest resemblance between his own ideals and the polytheistic worship which now bears his name, nor recognise half the gods whose effigies stand in his temples, for the Chinese pantheon "has gradually become so multitudinous that there is scarcely a being or thing which is not... propitiated or worshipped."[183]

About the best example of a Taoist pantheon, with its innumerable images, is the Tung Yueh Miao, a rich sanctuary dating from the Mongol dynasty (a.d. 1317) though built on the site of older structures. It lies half a mile beyond the Ch'i Hua Men (east gate of the Tartar City) opposite the Temple of the Rising Sun, and is dedicated to "He Who Rivals Heaven," namely, the Spirit of Mount T'ai Shan (the sacred mountain in Shantung) a deity ranking in the Taoist hierarbhy almost on a level with the Creator. In the main hall, this mythical figure sits enshrined where shadows meet and whisper and shrink back into deep darkness. A corner of his sanctuary is shared by the God of Writing to whom all those desirous of succeeding in literature bring offerings of pen-brushes and ink slabs. Also on the occasion of the temple festival (from the 15th to the 28th of the third month) the pious, after confessing their sins and reciting their virtues, make gifts of paper, so that the Recording Spirits can write down their good and bad deeds, balancing them against the future judgment.[184] Three religious associations contribute to this festival—the Dusters, who dust the images, the Artificial Flower Makers, who put up an arch of paper flowers, and the Lamp Makers' Guild, which maintains an "everlasting" oil taper.

---

183 See *Myths and Legends* of China, by E. T. Chalmers Werner, Chapter IV, "The Gods of China."
184 Since the God of writing in the mythical period of antiquity elaborated the art of forming ideographs by imitating the footprints of birds, the written character in China has become so sacred that its misuse is a sin and its preservation counted among the meritorious actions. Men are still employed to collect old placards off the walls and every scrap of waste paper bearing characters. Such fragments are then taken to a special furnace attached to a temple, and reverently burned.

Juliet Bredon

The minor shrines of the Tung Yueh Miao are filled with the Deities that control Diseases. Sick people come here to propitiate the Gods of Fever, of Chills, of Coughs, of Consumption, of Colic, of Haemorrhage, of Toothache, for gods exist governing "every part of the body from the hair to the toe nails." To make assurance doubly sure, the ailing conclude their pilgrimage by a visit to the famous brass horse in one of the shrines behind the main hall, which can cure all maladies. Here the scriptural admonition: "An eye for an eye, etc.," is literally paraphrased, for the blind have so long rubbed the creature's eyes, with prayers for their own, that he also is nearly blind—and the rheumatic have worn his shoulders down.

Mental ills and anxieties likewise find their physicians among the shrines. From the dusk of his ghost house, Yueh Hsia Lao Erh, the "Old Man of the Moon," who ties the feet of predestined couples together with invisible red thread at their birth, listens to the prayers of lonely maidens seeking mates. The Prison God once heard the supplication of officials of the Board of Punishment, and took pity on the executioner returning home from his hateful task by forbidding the spirit of the criminal to haunt the instrument of justice. Poor women kneel with pathetic faith before the "Princess of the Coloured Clouds"—Pi Hsia Yuan Chun—daughter of "He Who Rivals Heaven"—to ask her for some favour; a child to the childless, or luck to the unsuccessful. And surely the goddess never could refuse, remembering the re-birth when she was woman and wife, the prayer we overheard prayed before her by a peasant girl:

"I am dark, too dark because I have toiled in the fields, because the sun has shone upon me. For the pleasure of my beloved, deign thou augustly to make me very white—white like the women of the city, Oh! Merciful Mother."

On the wall of the entrance a giant abacus helps debtors and creditors to settle their accounts. With prayer and fasting the disputants proceed to the temple and there spend a night. Then in the morning, none can tell how, the rightful decision appears upon the abacus. The gods have judged and their verdict is above the law.

But the most unusual feature of the Tung Yueh Miao is the open gallery of painted clay devils applying the punishments of the Taoist Purgatory to erring souls destined to be re-born into the world again and again, until, perfected by suffering, they are fit to be transferred to the eternal bliss reserved for the Righteous.

A special temple called the Shih Pa Yu ("Eighteen Hells") a little further along the same street, is devoted to a series of similar torture scenes, surpassing in realistic horror anything in Madame Tussaud's collection.[185] Here a fearsome King of Hell holding the register of Life and Death, presides grimly over the horrible tortures of the damned. A devil in the next compartment is busy sawing a soul in two, pulling his saw towards him, instead of pushing it just like any ordinary Chinese carpenter. Further on a liar, bound to a post, is having his tongue dragged out slowly, with artistic jerks; already it is longer than the owner's body. The face is a nightmare. Several criminals appear with their heads in their hands. A little further on a man is being eaten alive by two monsters having women's faces: one is red, the other blue. "The red has been his wife, the blue his concubine," our guide explains.

We shudder: "Why do your Chinese artists like to portray such horrible things?"

"Oh, we find them good because they point a moral. Probably this man was unable to keep order in his household. Perhaps he was blinded by the infatuation of passion. How, then, could he hope to escape punishment?"

"Now if the foreigners prefer to see comfortable things" —he adds anxious to please.

"Assuredly! Show us comfortable things." Whereupon he obligingly leads us to see good men rewarded— wise, just, and honourable persons bringing offerings of silks and jade, and

---

[185] For a full description of these Taoist Hells, see *Strange Stories from a Chinese Studio* (Appendix) by Herbert A. Giles.

borne on clouds to the regions of Paradise. Thus we are able to carry away a pleasanter impression.

The mother temple and headquarters of the Taoist sect in the Peking district is Po Yun Kuan or the "Temple of the White Cloud" outside the Hsi Pien Men, or "Western Wicket" of the Chinese City. A venerated place already in the days of Kublai Khan, it still remains one of the largest and richest monasteries in the neighbourhood with a community of over 100 monks. Through the palace eunuchs, who endowed it in the days of their prosperity to secure themselves a comfortable retreat for their old age, the temple was intimately connected with the Court. The higher priests were rated among the palace functionaries and exercised no little influence on politics, while at the same time they managed to command popular respect (a rare thing in China where the priesthood is generally held in disrepute) by putting some dignity and form into an indefinite and baffling cult, too often degenerated into wizardry and superstition of the cheapest kind.

Po Yun Kuan is an accumulation of halls with many images, with large suites of guest rooms, a theatre and rock gardens where, as says the Chinese poet, men "wander deep into the shrine of Tao, for the joy they seek is promised in that place."

The oldest part of the temple stands on the site of a T'ang dynasty structure repaired by the Chins in a.d. 1192 when it was *inside* the city. Under Genghis Khan it was renamed the "Temple of Eternal Spring" (Ch'ang Ch'un Kung) because of associations with the Taoist sage Ch'ang Ch'un, the celebrated monk and teacher summoned to the Mongol Court at Karakorum by the conqueror Genghis Khan who wished to satisfy his curiosity about the various Chinese religions. Ch'ang Ch'un belonged to the sect of the "Golden Nenuphar" or "Altogether Holy," and was a master of alchemy, devoting much time to a search for the "philosopher's stone" and the secrets of immortality. Born in Shantung and already famous under the Sung and Chin dynasties whose invitations to court he always declined, he finally yielded to the call of the Mongol Khan on the latter's invasion of China and, although heavy with years,

Temples and Tombs Outside the City

set out to meet him. "I eat the same food and am dressed in the same tatters as my humble herdsmen," Genghis wrote to the Sage through one of his Ministers (for the great conqueror could not write himself). "I consider the people my children, and take an interest in talented men as if they were my brothers. ... To cross a river we make boats and rudders. Likewise we invite sage men ... for keeping the empire in good order. I shall serve thee myself!" But by the time Ch'ang Ch'un reached Mongolia, Genghis had already left for the West and the monk only came up with him on the borders of India.

Recognising the true worth of this distinguished thinker who had undergone great hardships to give his message, for he was wounded in crossing battlefields, a fugitive in rebellious cities, half starving in the desert, Genghis received him royally, supplied him with a fine tent, feasted him and asked him many questions. Fearlessly, the Sage told the Emperor again and again that one who wished to unify States should not engage in killing and plundering. "The true foundation of a government is to serve God and love men. The true preparation for the life everlasting is a pure heart and few desires."

The Emperor, delighted at this wise counsel, declared: "God gives me this good teacher in order to revive my conscience. Therefore write down what he says that I and my sons may always see it."[186]

---

[186] The teachings of Ch'ang Ch'un, as set forth by him to the Great Khan, may have been the foundation of an allegorical work attributed to the prophet's pen—the *Hsi-yu-chi*, or *Travel to the West*, translated by Timothy Richard under the title of *A Mission to Heaven*. This book is not to be confounded with the actual description of Ch'ang Ch'un's journey composed by one of his own disciples, nor the authentic account of a journey to India written by the famous Chinese Buddhist monk Hsuan Tsang of the T'ang dynasty. The latter is known as the *Hsi-yu-chi* or *Description of Western Countries*. Moreover, Ch'ang Ch'un himself became the hero of a subsequent allegory, much after the style of his own, which is also known as the Hsi-yu-chi.

Ch'ang Ch'un's alleged work is remarkable in so far as it contains the message of the greatest prophet of Mediaeval Asia to the greatest military genius the world has ever seen. Further it proves that the author had a mind broad enough to conceive the righteous law of the Universe, which he

Juliet Bredon

When after some time Ch'ang Ch'un returned to Peking, Genghis gave him, as we know, the site of the Pai T'a dagoba in the Pei Hai for a monastery.[187] Whether he actually lived there is uncertain. The temple records show that he died at Po Yun Kuan in 1227 (the very year of the death of his Imperial patron) at the age of 80. A hall dedicated to his memory covers his tomb under the stone pavement. Here his rice bowl, supposed to have come originally from Korea, is preserved with two Imperial inscriptions to testify to its authenticity. Here too, his statue is enshrined, and worshipped.

Six hundred years and more he has been dead, yet every year (on the 19th day of the 1st moon) the people still flock to honour him with a grand procession, somewhat like a Breton "pardon"—in which his sacred image is paraded for all to see. The festival coincides with the "Gathering of the Hundred Gods" when one of the genu of the temple is supposed to appear in its precincts as an official, a young girl, or a beggar, and the Taoist priests spend the night in a vigil under the trees awaiting the apparition. The general festivities, lasting three days, formerly closed with horse races much frequented by the *jeunesse dorée* of the capital.

From Po Yun Kuan it is worth while going on to visit T'ien Ning Ssu, one of the oldest buildings in the vicinity of Peking, outside the Chang I Men. The monks used to offer tea and sweetmeats stamped with the Wheel of the Law in the high terraced guest room of the tumbledown temple whose noble thirteen storied pagoda (6th century a.d.) holds a colossal Buddha with a commonplace gilded countenance. They coaxed visitors to throw cash at a metal plate hanging above the hand of the image for the prosperity of all concerned.

To the west lies Wang Hai Lou, a park with the ruined palace of Tiao Yu T'ai, or the "Fishing Terrace." The remains of pleasure grounds first laid out in the 12th century, this was a favourite fishing preserve of the earlier Manchu emperors. Alas, the picturesque old "Tower Facing the Sea" (built in 1773

---

regards as the foundation of all true religion and above sect.
187 See Chapter V.

Temples and Tombs Outside the City

on the site of an older Chin palace) is now crumbling, and the lagoon choked with rushes which flutter mournfully in the wind. The chanting of the frogs alone breaks the stillness. Their voices seem softer than those of the common croakers of the rice fields; to vibrate almost with the melancholy of muted instruments in deference to the forgotten generations who once visited this overgrown domain. To their accompaniment, the guardian repeats the words of the old Chinese poet:

"With hands resting upon the floor, reverentially you sing your song, O frog. But all the guests being gone, why still thus respectfully sitting, O frog?"

Beyond Wang Hai Lou we can still trace the mud walls of the old Chin city.[188] The whistle of a train passing close by sounds a discordant note as it puffs its way along, practical but unpicturesque, to the Race Course, where the foreign community amuses itself by running the small Mongolian ponies which horse traders bring down from the grassy plains beyond the Great Wall each season.[189]

Our eyes, wandering beyond the reed grown lake,[190] near the track, pick up the stone road that passes close to the ruined temple of Yen Tso Ssu with a fine bronze Buddha fifty feet high. No doubt once the statue was housed in a handsome building. Now only two side walls remain and the image itself stands exposed to sun and showers but for the small modern rooflet, built over it. The place is lonely save for some village children who approach and beg shyly at sight of a stranger.

Still following the white line of the highway along the left bank of the Hun river, we can distinguish the temple of Pei Hui Chi with the statue of the bronze cow whose duty, in which to China's sorrow she often fails, is to watch the river and keep it from flooding the surrounding country.

---

188 See Chapter I.
189 The first race course, used before the present, site was secured, lay near the actual rifle range outside the T'ung Pien Men, close to the tomb of one of the powerful Yu Princes—pillars of state under the early Manchu emperors.
190 The Race Course Lake, the Lien Hua Chih, is mentioned in the Chin Annals as feeding one of the canals belonging to the water system which connected Chihli with Shantung.

Juliet Bredon

Nearer to us, shining white in the sunshine, is the Lu Kou Ch'iao (bridge)[191] spanning the stream beside the picturesque village of the same name. Five long years (a.d. 1189-1194) an army of labourers toiled to make it strong and beautiful, shaping the thirteen (eleven nowadays) stone arches, carving the parapet guarded by stone lions so bewildering in number in bygone years that no man was supposed to be able to count them. Marco Polo crossed and praised it in the 13th century, hence foreigners call it the Marco Polo Bridge, and modern engineers still commend the enduring construction in which technical problems, such as the placing of the piers in a shifting river bed of mud and quicksand, swollen to a torrent during the rainy season, were skilfully solved. Destroyed by a flood in the 17th century, it was rebuilt by K'ang Hsi, and repaired by Ch'ien Lung, as the tablets under the yellow-tiled pavilions at both ends record. The fortified city to the east of the bridge was built by the last Ming emperor in a vain attempt to check the advance of the rebel Li Tzu-ch'eng.

The groups of trees which everywhere catch and hold the eye like oases amidst the khaki-coloured fields generally indicate temples or tombs. More often the latter. These dwelling places of the dead contrast pleasantly with the squalid habitations of the living. How beautiful is the habit of burying amidst the fields, frequently in the very ground where a man toiled during his lifetime, instead of in gloomy cemeteries. It reminds one of touching invocation from the tragedy of *Helen* by Euripides: "All hail, my father's tomb! I buried thee, Proteus, at the place where men pass by, that I might often greet thee: and so, even as I go out and in, I, thy son, call upon thee, father." Such customs prove that a people have no morbid fear of, but rather a tender reverence for, the dead generations which lie under their feet wherever they tread. They like to feel that their lands are haunted by the gentle ghosts who outnumber by myriads the living.

---

191 It was a mutiny of the Chin troops at this bridge which led to the capture of Peking by Genghis Khan in a.d. 1215.

Moreover in China, as in old Greece, to die is to enter into the possession of superhuman might—to become capable of conferring benefits or inflicting misfortune by supernatural means. Yesterday a man was but a common toiler, a person of no importance, to-day, being dead, he becomes a divine power. Small wonder then that the surviving generation honours its dead. Sacrifices to spirits are rooted in the deep ethical feeling of a race which believes that "Devotion to the memory of ancestors is the mainspring of all virtues. No one who discharges his duty to them will ever be disrespectful to the gods or to his living parents. Such a man will be faithful to his prince, loyal to his friends and kind and gentle to his wife and children."

But, partly also, the cult of the dead is pursued for the self interest of the living. Each ghost must rely upon its mortal kindred for its comfort; only through their devotion can it find repose. Given a fitting tomb and suitable offerings, it will aid in maintaining the good fortune of its propitiators. But if refused the sepulchral home, the funeral rites, the offerings of food and fire and drink, it will suffer from hunger and cold and thirst, and, becoming angered, will act malevolently and contrive misfortune for those by whom it has been neglected.[192]

These, then, are the reasons why the best and prettiest sites are chosen for graves in China; why those who are able to afford it spend lavishly to please their departed; and why, wherever we find a neglected coffin peeping half uncovered from its mound, or a broken stone monument, we may know that no heir remains to carry on the ancestral worship, and the greatest tragedy which can occur in a Chinese family has left the spirits without sustenance.

Of the many famous tombs near the Race Course, the most interesting and the best kept are those of the late Empress Dowager Tz'u Hsi's parents. The guardian, an old man with a single tooth rising like an obelisk from his lower jaw, proudly points out the honorific arch and the marble tablet. Like all

---

[192] See *Japan, An Attempt at Interpretation*, by Lafcadio Hearn, also *The Origin of Ancestor Worship*, by Herbert Spencer.

Orientals, Tz'u Hsi took pains thus to advertise her filial piety. She gained further kudos from the orthodox by declining to enter the capital, after her flight in 1900, on the Peking-Hankow Railway, because that line ran close to her parents' sepulchres and it would have been a serious breach of respect to their memory to pass the spot without reverently alighting to sacrifice. As this was not practical she changed her route, arriving from the south at considerable inconvenience but to the great admiration of her people.

Another handsome grave is that of Prince Tse, two miles east of the Sha Wo Men, noted for a famous pine. The tree is scarcely eleven feet high but the branches have been trained outwards and downwards over a framework of poles until they cover perhaps twenty square yards. The trunk is completely hidden by the spreading branches which look like an enormous green hat of the shape worn by peasants in rainy weather.

Speaking of trees there is, south-west of the Tartar City between the Tung Pien Men and the second lock on the Tungchow Canal, a curious tumble-down shrine[193] built over the trunk of a sacred tree so large that a man on horseback could safely hide behind it. We stumbled upon this forgotten site unexpectedly one day when rambling through the country. A creaking ox cart stopped outside and the driver entered with an incense stick in his hand. "Surely this is no temple, Elder Brother," we remark, "why then do you come to worship?" "My child is ill," he replies unwillingly. Perhaps this refusal to tell things is due to the old superstition that it is bad luck to give information concerning your family or your business to a stranger—or to a Government official. But a few words of sympathy and the offer of a cigarette breaks down his peasant reserve. Luckily he belongs to a village close by and knows the legend of the place.

"This is a shrine to a female tree spirit. Look, the inscription carved in the wood says so. Formerly, twice a year, in the 2nd

---

[193] For a very full and scholarly explanation of this shrine and its origin, see *Chen Mou Tch'ang, Le Hangar tin Bois Génie*, by Maurice Adam. *Collection de la Politique de Pekin*.

Temples and Tombs Outside the City

moon and the 8th moon, an Imperial Prince was commanded by the throne to worship here."

"Very curious. But what has that to do with your sick baby?"

"Why, everybody knows that tree spirits cure diseases,"[194] he says with a touch of pity for our ignorance.

As to how or when this mystical Chinese hamadryad entered her tree, he could tell us nothing, nor when it first assumed a sacred character.

What starts a legend that turns a familiar shade tree into a fairy with magical powers anyway? We guess age is a factor, and also any peculiarity that would strike the imagination of the country folk.

In this case the name of the giant now fallen, "The Camphor Tree Whose Top Was Bowed," suggests some fantastic story that no one remembers any more. But it must have been credited at one time since Ch'ien Lung wrote a poem about this tree and praised it, giving what to us seem vague geomantic reasons why it should be worshipped, and connecting the presiding spirit with power over the "Five Directions of Space." Actually it appears that this remarkable log was one of those left over (probably purposely owing to its unusual size and shape) when the palaces were built in the reign of Yung Lo, as we know from Chinese records that a great deal of wood used for the construction of the Forbidden City was gathered in this place.[195] Though some of it was used elsewhere later, this piece which appealed to the superstitious fancy of the local people, became gradually endowed with spiritual qualities, and finally enshrined.

Many of the handsomest tombs in the neighbourhood of the city are situated in the country, known among foreigners as the Happy Valley (which, by the way, is the best riding country near Peking) extending from the T'ung Chou Canal to the Nan

---

194 The superstition exists all over China where sacred trees are not uncommon.

195 As the great timbers used for the throne halls were floated on rafts up the Canal, it seems logical that they should be landed and stored in this neighbourhood.

Juliet Bredon

Hai Tzu, or "Southern Hunting Park," an abandoned and unused domain where for years the "David deer" roamed in herds. The last of these rare creatures, indigenous to China, were killed and eaten by the Mohammedan troops of the Boxer General Tung Fu Hsiang in 1900. In fact no game of any kind is left in the Hunting Park, but good walkers and keen riders will enjoy visiting the attractive remains of the Yung Ho Kung ("Palace of Eternal Peace") in the north-east corner, where the emperor rested after the chase. Unfortunately the pretty Ming Dynasty Temple, locally known as the "Blue Temple" because it was roofed and floored with azure tiles, has disappeared. The southern end of the park is now devoted to utilitarian purposes and contains barracks, a parade ground and aeroplane hangars. An amusing toy railway runs from the Yung Ting Men to the southern entrance of the park.

Among the tombs on the banks of the T'ung Chou Canal, there are new tombs like that of the celebrated Yung Lu, the lifelong friend and devoted retainer of the Empress Dowager Tz'u Hsi, and old tombs whose broken walls show a glimpse of reeling monuments between sober ranks of cypresses.

A favourite haunt of foreigners is the pretty "Tomb of the Princess" just below the second lock. Though a winding cart road will take us there, we choose rather to go by the canal itself for the sake of its associations. Who would not wish to journey along this 13th century waterway that existed long before the streets of Paris were paved, or London had its first public lamp?[196] Certainly no one who knew of the fascinating

---

[196] Do not forget that this Canal is actually an arm of the world famous Grand Canal which it joins at Tientsin thus giving direct water communication between Peking and Hangchow in Chekiang province—a distance of 900 miles or, as Marco Polo puts it "forty days journey long."
"The Chinese engineers, men of science, having reported that vessels from the provinces of Cathay could no longer reach the Metropolis, the Khan gave them orders to dig a great canal... from Khambalig to the ports frequented by ships... This canal is provided with many sluices intended to distribute water all over the country, and when vessels arrive at these sluices they are hoisted up by .means of machines whatever their size and let down on the other side into the water. The Canal has a width of more than 112 feet. Kublai caused the embankments to be faced with stone... and the two sides

Temples and Tombs Outside the City

life along the banks—the picturesque surprises ashore and afloat. In summer, the open air restaurants with stone benches and tables are crowded with country folk, and the cages of their singing birds hang from the mat p'engs (awnings). Truck farmers bring their barrows of vegetables to the water's edge, wading in to freshen them for market. From the mud villages where the peasants raise those fine, fat Peking ducks praised by all epicures, the flocks waddle down to swim among the slow, heavy passenger boats that ply between the locks. At a little distance there is romance in the monotonous tones of the professional story-teller who paces to and fro on the crowded barges, enlivening the journey for the Chinese passengers with his endless historical tale to the accompaniment of two bamboos which he clicks like minstrel's bones—though at close quarters the endless repetition jars on our nerves. Moreover, on the whole scene there rests a charm of light reminiscent of the desert—an extraordinary atmospheric clearness through which the most distant objects appear focussed with amazing sharpness. It is a light that burns out all detail in a landscape, that produces grand splashes of colour, that causes mud walls to glow.

In winter the scene changes. Harsh, gritty with dust, the brown fields lie in the grip of the frost, and the canal is a sheet of ice. The boats lie useless along the banks, anchored with lumps of mud and protected by branches of thorn bushes. Quaint sledges take their place, pulled by one man and pushed by another, while little boys on primitive iron skates circle round them like hungry sparrows, begging coppers from the passengers. The tea houses are deserted then. Only an occasional villager may be seen breaking the ice near the banks to allow the ducks their daily swim. When he has herded the valuable birds back to their shelters, thirsty pariah dogs gather

---

of the road (along the banks) are planted with trees and no one, soldier or otherwise, is permitted to break off branches of those trees."—Yule's *Cathay*, Chapter 13, p. 115.

The Canal, now choked up for much of its length, was repeatedly repaired (even under the Manchus) so long as it served its original purpose—to convey the tribute rice to the capital.

to drink at the water hole, passing the word to distant comrades in some mysterious way.

In this desolate season, the pines of the Princess's Tomb gracefully break the monotony of the sombre landscape— just as the romance of her story agreeably contrasts with the monotony of average Chinese lives.

An inscription dated Ch'ien Lung exalts the virtues of the "Fo Shou Kung Chu," or "Imperial Maiden with the Buddha Hand," that is, with a webbed connection between the fingers— one of the attributes of Buddha.

Tradition says that she was the Emperor's own daughter by a beautiful slave girl whom he met and loved while on a hunting trip in South China.

Now this slave, as the Imperial master discovered when he had installed her as favourite in his palace in Peking, was no mortal woman but a "Shen," or spirit, who by night changed herself into a wild duck and flew back to her home among the southern marshes. And the girl-baby born to her was not mortal either, since her fingers had a fine film of skin connecting them.

When the mother died, the Court astrologers, bade the Sovereign guard this precious child whom the Gods had marked for their own. But alas! the spirit maiden scorned mortal conventions and, forgetting rank and dignity, fell in love with a groom in the Imperial stables for "she was wild of nature, wild as the teal that speeds south like an arrow when the mid-autumn festival is past... and when love called, she became heedless of decorum, unmindful of Imperial solicitude and careless of the counsels of sages."

When Ch'ien Lung, accustomed to be obeyed, discovered the intrigue of the lovers grown careless with passion, he decreed that they must die. "But because she was an Imperial Princess and the daughter of a spiritual being, he commanded a stately tomb to be built for the erring maiden with a marble *p'ai lou* and an avenue of stone animals as befitted her rank.

"Then, all being in readiness, a funeral cortege floated down the canal in barges... But instead of a coffin the bearers carried a closed chair with yellow curtains, and behind the chair walked a figure wrapped in a long cloak such as horsemen wear.

"They say there was no cry from the princess when her attendants led her to the opening of the tomb, and stood aside with uplifted torches. They say the lover leaped the low steps and followed into the darkness like a moth springing towards a flame. They say that while the masons with bricks and trowels laboured unwillingly and in silence closing the opening through which the moonlight slanted, a voice from the gloom within bade them make haste."

They say, too, the peasants whose great-great-grandfathers lived near by, that for three days the lovers lingered alive like another Aida and Radames for their murmured endearments could be heard. And still each spring the trees continue to whisper over their bed of stone, and passers-by hear in the lisping of the maple leaves and the quiver of the many-fingered pines the "song of the builders building the dwelling of the dead."

As we turn from the resting place of the little princess who loved too well, we stop to look at a group of children near the gate. They are playing at funerals, burying crickets who died with the Morning Glories, and pretending to repeat Buddhist "sutras" over the graves. A passing lad sings a song full of queer plaintive modulations, unusually pleasant to hear. We call to him and ask what he is singing about.

"It is an old song," he answers, "the boatmen sing it on the canal":

> "Things never changed since the Time of the Gods,
> The flowing of water, the Way of Love."

Only rarely do we find the love theme in Chinese legends, but the pathetic note is often present in tales about old tombs, for example, with the graves of two dispossessed sovereigns of the Ming dynasty.

The first, Chien Wen (1398-1402) after losing his throne to his redoubtable uncle Yung Lo, became a monk in a Yunnan monastery where he found happiness in spite of his tragic transition. His identity was finally traced by a poem in which he recounted the misfortunes of his early days. Summoned to an honorific confinement at the court of the Emperor Cheng T'ung, he died in the capital, pining for the calm of his retreat.

Legend says that in his last years, a gushing spring from an old well threatened to flood the neighbourhood of Peking. The saintly ex-emperor volunteered to quell the waters, which he did by seating himself upon the spring. His mummy may still be above the same well, now bricked over, in the "T'ieh T'a," a half forgotten turret outside the Tung Chih Men, crowned by the small iron pagoda from which it takes its name. Yet the mummy is still supposed to control not only the rebellious spring, but also to regulate the rainfall in answer to prayer.

At the foot of a hill quite close to the Summer Palace— for in China the neighbourhood of graves was not considered unlucky or unseemly even near an Emperor's pleasure house—lies the tomb of that other unfortunate Ming monarch, Ching T'ai[197] (1449-1457), whose reign was recorded in history as an interregnum and who was denied burial in the official sepulchre of the Mings, the Imperial mausolea to the north of Peking. The Empress Dowager, taunting her miserable nephew Kuang Hsu with the illegality of his succession to the throne (her own doing), threatened his memory with a similar fate.[198] Consequently Kuang Hsu always maintained a melancholy devotion to the memory of Ching T'ai by reason of their common sorrows. From a window of the Summer Palace he would gaze for hours at the grave of his luckless predecessor and, lamenting its neglected state, he persuaded one of his eunuchs

---

197 See Chapter X.
198 There were indeed many curious features of resemblance between the Ming Emperor's destiny and his own. Ching T'ai had also been placed on the throne by command of an Empress Dowager instead of his elder brother—the same who was carried into captivity by the Mongols but who afterwards returned and lived in the buildings now known as the Mahakala Miao. Ching T'ai, after a miserable life, was treacherously murdered by eunuchs whilst performing sacrifice and his reign was expunged from the annals of the dynasty, though eventually restored.

Temples and Tombs Outside the City

to plant new trees about it and to repair the pillars of the main hall of sacrifice, bidding him, at the same time, take care that the Old Buddha should not know by whose orders these things were done, lest she become angry. So the old tomb was no longer forsaken, and Kuang Hsu had at least the comfort of having ministered to a forlorn kindred spirit.

Juliet Bredon

XIV. The Summer Palaces and the Jade Fountain

The habit of building summer palaces and laying out pleasure gardens dates back in China to the highest antiquity. The histories of the Liao and Chin dynasties (10th to 13th centuries a.d.) show that the rulers of that period had country residences near the present Summer Palace. They also record the existence of the spring at Yu Ch'uan Shan (the Jade Fountain) whose supply of fresh water determined the settlement of the Court throughout so many centuries in the neighbourhood.

Though certain ruins are popularly attributed to them, little is definitely proved to remain of the buildings of those early ages. Even the edifices occupied by various sovereigns of the Yuan and Ming dynasties have disappeared, but two pairs of 16th century bronze lions were excavated in 1908 near the Jade Fountain on the site of what is believed to have been an ancient Summer Palace.

We may assume that whatever Ming structures stood in the vicinity at the time of the Manchu conquest, there was nothing worthy of restoration by the reign of the second Manchu Emperor K'ang Hsi as he set about the erection of an entirely new plaisaunce in a.d. 1709. The Scotsman, John Bell, who was on the staff of the Russian Embassy sent to China by Peter the Great (1719), writes that the Ambassador Izmailov and his suite were invited by the "aged Emperor K'ang Hsi to a country house called Tsan Shu Yang (Ch'ang Ch'un Yuan) about six miles westward from Peking," which country house was evidently, from John Bell's descriptions, the one newly constructed, as a part of Yuan Ming Yuan, or what we now call the Old Summer Palace.[199] This is corroborated by the fact that the next emperor, Yung Cheng, lived at Yuan Ming Yuan, and died there in 1735.

---

[199] *Travels from St. Petersburg in Russia to diverse Parts of Asia,* Glasgow, 1763.

The Summer Palaces and the Jade Fountain

His successor Ch'ien Lung embellished and beautified the domain, joining together into a harmonious whole the separate palaces begun by K'ang Hsi. Thrilled by pictures and descriptions of Versailles brought by the Jesuit priests, he planned gardens and buildings on a much more elaborate scale than formerly prevailed in China, even adding copies of European mansions.

Alas, the taste, the talent and the treasures lavished on this favourite residence by Chinese, Italian and French architects and artists were not long destined to be enjoyed by his descendants! Chia Ch'ing preferred Jehol—where he was killed by lightning while taking his ease with a favourite—though we know he lived occasionally at Yuan Ming Yuan, because he planned to receive Lord Amherst, the British Ambassador, there in 1816.[200] Tao Kuang with his pre-occupation about economy, and his housewifely thrift which in old age verged on parsimony, was not the man to enjoy a property so expensive to keep up. He was, however, spared the humiliation of his son Hsien Feng, in whose reign Yuan Ming Yuan was burned by the Franco-British troops.

To anyone with a historic sense there is great glamour in travelling along the highway to the Summer Palace— even in a motor car, even in a hurry, as most people do— because one may. if one chooses, summon for company the shadowy figures that have passed there since those distant days when it was scarcely more than a country lane which the early emperors followed on horseback.

---

200 Lord Amherst never saw the splendours of Yuan Ming Yuan after all. He refused to proceed farther than the village of Hai Tien and missed having his audience with the Son of Heaven on account of the insistence of the Chinese that he should "K'o-tow" to the Emperor as the Dutch Ambassador had done.

The Summer Palace

[Photo by Hartung, Peking]

The Summer Palaces and the Jade Fountain

Before the Ruler left his palace, triangular flags were placed along the Imperial route warning the people that the road was reserved for His Sacred Majesty. When he actually started, a first signal bade them retire into their houses. Every door must be closed, every window shuttered, and at the intersection of transversal streets, silken curtains were hung shutting off the traffic. At the second and third signals, the princes and officials waved back the retainers who were smoothing the yellow sand spread along the Son of Heaven's pathway. At the fourth, these richly robed nobles knelt by the roadside ready to greet their lord. At the fifth and last signal, the Emperor himself appeared on a richly caparisoned horse with jewel-studded stirrups. A thousand men-at-arms surrounded him, raising a cloud of dust that enveloped the procession like a golden powder.

Two or three centuries later the emperors, grown soft and effeminate, ceased to ride in a "cloud of golden powder" but were carried in sedan chairs or floated out lazily by barge along a canal shaded by graceful weeping willows. An Imperial boathouse may still be seen near the Kao Liang Bridge (the first bridge outside the Hsi Chih Men) with which, by the way, a curious legend is connected.

Owing to the abuses that characterised the beginning of Yung Lo's reign—great ruler though he afterwards became—a saintly man possessing magic powers decided to teach the Emperor a lesson, and, if possible, make him repent of his sins, by cutting off the water supply of Peking. This he proceeded to do by filling two barrels, one with sweet, the other with bitter water, from two different wells in the capital, and wheeling them outside the walls on a barrow. A wise counsellor warned Yung Lo of the danger which was menacing his city, and the Emperor, much alarmed, called for volunteers to frustrate the wizard's scheme. None came forward, however, except one warrior named Kao Liang, renowned for his courage and recklessness. Kao Liang received orders te pursue the wizard, pierce the barrel containing the sweet water with a spear, and then gallop back at full speed, but on no account to turn round lest, like Lot's wife, evil befall him. He obeyed, but no sooner had he pierced the barrel and begun to dash off on his horse striking a shower of sparks on the stones, than he heard the sound of a mighty rush of waters behind him. The faster he sped, the louder grew the roaring. Kao Liang had almost reached the city wall when the terrific noise behind him and the sight of a spreading sheet of water rising above his horse's hoofs overcame his precaution. Doubt vanquished faith. Recklessly he turned round and as soon as he did so—the waves swept over him and he was drowned on the very spot where the Kao Liang Bridge now stands. Later Yung Lo discovered to his disgust that the champion, unable in his haste to distinguished between the wizard's two barrels, had pierced the one containing the bitter water. Water thus did come back to Peking, but has ever since been bitter and hard, so that many a traveller, unaccustomed to it, has showered curses, while shaving, on poor Kao Liang and his well-meaning bungling.

Just beyond the village of Hai Tien, formerly an encampment for Palace Guards and a busy centre when the court was in residence at the Summer Palace, we pass broken walls and overgrown parks, once the country seats of princes and high government officials. The modern buildings of Yenching and Tsinghua Universities[201] stand on the sites of some of these old estates, and at the corner where the road forks eastward toward the Old Summer Palace and westward toward the new, is the former residence of the Seventh Prince,[202] father of the Emperor Kuang Hsu, set in a charming garden surrounded by high walls, for the Manchus were ever jealous of their privacy.

---

201 See Chapter XXI.
202 He was the seventh brother of the Emperor Hsien Feng, hence his title of Seventh Prince. The property is now unoccupied and the buildings partly in ruins.

The Summer Palaces and the Jade Fountain

Gateway of the Summer Palace

Juliet Bredon

Few visitors nowadays trouble to visit the Old Summer Palace (Yuan Ming Yuan) and yet, though disappointing to the sightseer, it is a fitting place to meditate on bygone days of pageantry and ceremonial. Shut your eyes and imagine some long procession come winding down that empty road out of the echoing past; men carrying "silken banners that lift to the sun, in patterned embroideries of many colours, the glory of the Emperor and his ancestors; banners round and square, banners blue and crimson, white cylindrical banners whose story never ends, borne by slant-eyed men in silken coats aflare like rainbows. Who are these bringing gifts? In the hand of one is a bowl glazed with the blue of forgotten seas; another holds high a long-necked silver swan, tall in its pride. In the carved box carried by a third is rolled a landscape painted in powder of malachite and lapis lazuli, with the dreams of ten thousand years. A fourth brings a vase pictured with ladies of an ancient reign—court ladies in trellised gardens, with kingfisher-feather ornaments in their hair and rich robes entwining their slow little feet. Others bear precious charms carved in ruby and amethyst and emerald, or little ivory sages in lacquered boxes, or finely tapestried silken panels woven into fables of the phoenix bird. And one lifts high a wonder work of moon-white jade, wrought... into an image of Lord Buddha throned on the lotus, Lord Buddha with eyes fixed in rapture, his right hand extending two fingers to bless the world.

"They must be going to the Palace of the mighty King, these gift bearers, attended by eunuchs in dazzling coats, by guards mailed and sworded and terrible, by musicians ringing bells and beating drums, by hordes of retainers more gorgeous than poppies in the sun. They will turn from the road into a covered walk whose pillared roof, tiled without and painted within, answers with many colours the challenge of the light. Slowly they file between the crimson columns to kneel before the Dragon Throne and lay their gifts around it. The gilded banners salute the sacred roofs of six colours, the roofs orange and green, turquoise and heliotrope, peacock and sapphire, with the little guardian animals at the corners. They begin to ascend the

The Summer Palaces and the Jade Fountain

low white steps of the Hall of Audience.... Why do they halt and delay—a moment, a prayer's length, hour after hour? Why do the courtiers pause motionless, their rich robes and trappings a-sparkle in the sun? Why does the Son of Heaven linger alone in the ante-room, contemplative, absorbed, ecstatic—the Son of Heaven radiant with youth and power, his yellow robe woven with the symbols of might, his brow adorned with the precious pearl?[203] Why does he not rise and go forth to his throne, and take proud possession of his state, while the tribute bearers approach and fall prostrate before him heaping their offerings at his feet?

"The Son of Heaven sits motionless in his yellow robe with its symbols of might, his brow lit by the glow of the precious pearl. Hour after hour he sits thus contemplative while the procession waits. For the Son of Heaven is making a poem—a little poem of four lines that shall give sound and shape to the world."[204]

The illusion vanishes as we reach the entrance gate where once the golden lions stood.[205] Here the hunchbacked and taciturn guardian, who as a child witnessed the sack and burning of the palaces, appears to guide us to the ruins, for Yuan Ming Yuan is an enormous enclosure. He follows a path

---

[203] A sentry patrolling the palace precincts one moonless night suddenly noticed something sparkling in the lake. Digging down at the exact spot where the light glowed he found a large oyster, which contained two pearls joined together in the shape of a gourd. The pearls were presented to the Emperor K'ang Hsi who said that they must have been sent from Heaven for his special protection, so he wore them for a cap button and bequeathed them as a precious heirloom to his descendants. (See Notes by L. C. Arlington, *The New China Review*, 1921).

[204] See In Cathay, by Harriet Munroe.

[205] Colonel Wolseley who came to Peking with the Allied Expedition of 1860 says that, as these lions "were of a bronze colour, none of the foreigners took the trouble to ascertain the metal of which they were composed, assuming them to be the ordinary alloy of which bronze ornaments, so common in China, are usually cast." Some months afterwards, in Shanghai, a Chinese asked an Englishman residing there whether the Allies had removed the golden lions from the gate of Yuan Ming Yuan, and, upon being questioned, he described them accurately as being painted a bronze colour. See *Narrative of the War-with China* in 1860, by Col. G. J. Wolseley.

meandering through the long grass, up artificial hills crowned by wrecked pagodas, down into little valleys choked with the debris of shattered pavilions, over broken bridges of finely dressed stone that span canals bordered with wild iris, to the island with its ruined landing stage and tottering balustrades in the "Fan Shaped" lake overgrown with rushes.

That island was once the jewel of the domain. Unsurpassed and unsurpassable, its palace of a hundred rooms shone with tints which the eye can enjoy but the lips cannot name—shadings as delicate as the subtle subdivisions of tone in Chinese music. "This palace has four fronts," says Father Attiret who visited it, "and is of such beauty and taste as I cannot describe. The view from it is lovely. The rocks of wild and natural form that compose the island itself are fringed by a terrace of white marble with balustrades curiously carved. On this stand at intervals of twenty paces beautiful blue enamel vases with imitation flowers made of the blood, cornelian, jade and other valuable stones."[206] Another Jesuit thus pictures the seigniory as a whole. "In his country house outside the capital the Emperor (Ch'ien Lung) passes the greater part of the year, and he works day and night to further beautify it. To form any idea of it one must recall those enchanted gardens which authors of vivid imagination have described so beautifully. Canals winding between artificial mountains form a network through the grounds, in some places passing over rocks, then expanding into lovely lakes bordered by marble terraces. Devious paths lead to enchanting dwelling pavilions and spacious halls of audience, some on the water's edge, others on the slopes of hills or in pleasant valleys fragrant with flowering trees which are here very common. Each *maison de plaisance*, though small in comparison with the whole enclosure, is large enough to lodge one of our European grandees with all his suite. That destined for the Emperor himself is immense"—as large, the writer adds naively, as his own native town of Dole (in the Jura)—"and within may be found all that the whole

---

[206] From this terrace the Court used to watch naval fights between miniature junks with small brass cannon.

The Summer Palaces and the Jade Fountain

world contains of curious and rare—a great and rich collection of furniture, ornaments, pictures, precious woods, porcelains, silks, and gold and silver stuffs." Finally the good man concludes by saying: "Nothing can compare with the gardens which are indeed an earthly paradise."

It was these gardens that Ch'ien Lung, envious of the pleasure parties of the French Kings, desired to adorn with fountains which he commanded Father Benoist to create, in spite of all the latter's representations of "want of knowledge." The required water was drawn from the Jade Fountain five or six miles away, and stored in a large reservoir to feed the cascades and run a famous water clock with twelve animals who spouted water for two hours each.

At the same time (about 1737) the Emperor charged Father Castiglione to build the foreign pavilions and Chinese workmen, with their genius for copying, successfully reproduced the Rococo ornaments of marble porticos, loggias, and horseshoe stairways for which the Jesuits gave them designs. These Western palaces had for Ch'ien Lung all the charm of novelty. He was delighted when the French Court sent him a set of Gobelins to decorate their walls. Like Marie Antoinette at the Trianon and Catherine the Great in her Chinese pavilion, the unfamiliar surroundings enabled him to indulge the age-old human love of masquerade.

Where are the palaces that once stood in this fairy setting — the Palace of Contentment, the Palace of Floating Clouds, the Pavilion of the Favourite? Alas! Bricks and marble are piles of debris now. Here and there a column still stands, or one lies prone in the long grass. Clusters of majolica flowers, blue, yellow, or violet, as bright as though made yesterday, wreathe fallen capitals. Fragments of friezes and pediments lie buried under the Morning Glory vines. The Sun-emblem of the *Roi-Soleil* (Louis XIV) clings to a tottering wall. A lizard scurries to the shelter of a fountain overgrown with weeds and tares. What a mournful scene, and how doubly pathetic are all things intended for pleasure when they fall to ruin! Justly our guide describes Yuan Ming Yuan as "a palace that has lost its soul."[207]

When the golden fingers of the setting sun fall alike upon these classic reminders of the West and the pointed roofs and pagodas of the new Summer Palace and the Jade Fountain in the distance, few landscapes present a more striking contrast, few rouse in us a stronger sensation of regret. Every contemporary writer speaks with sorrow of the destruction of the old Summer Palace and the treasures it contained. Even the officers who had to set the torch and touch the fuse felt the pity of it. But Lord Elgin and the British Commander-in-Chief decided that some great reprisal should be made for the violation of a flag of truce and the outrageous treatment of foreign prisoners. What more suitable spot, they argued, for such retribution than the place where these captives had been tortured? Let punishment fall upon the ruler alone, rather than upon his long-suffering people, since, however much he wished to do so later, the Emperor could not disclaim responsibility for this crime. True, he was surrounded by the leaders of an anti-progressive party who advised him that treaties with Western nations could be ignored and effectual resistance offered to European armies. But the ready ear he gave to their counsel and his arrogant edicts convicted him, as the following phrases show: "Hereby We make offering of the following rewards. For the head of a black barbarian (i.e. Indian trooper) 50 taels; for the head of a white barbarian 100 taels; for the capture of a barbarian leader, alive or dead, 500 taels; and for the seizure or destruction of a barbarian vessel 5,000 taels.[208]... We now command that all the treaty ports be closed and all trade with

---

[207] It is significant that none of the buildings or fountains are adorned with statues whose absence is noticeable in all the Peking palaces. This is due to a Chinese prejudice. Busts are considered particularly unlucky. When, defying tradition, the Emperor Kuang Hsu's head appeared on the Thibetan rupee, superstitious objectors attributed his subsequent misfortunes to the innovation. The same conservatives foretold Yuan Shih-k'ai's downfall as soon as he allowed his portrait to appear on the dollar.

[208] A tael was worth in those days approximately five shillings, or one gold dollar.

The Summer Palaces and the Jade Fountain

France and England stopped. Subjects of other submissive states are not to be molested, and whenever the French and British repent of their evil way and return to their allegiance, We shall be pleased to permit them to trade again as of old, so that Our clemency may be made manifest." Moreover, Hsien Feng could hardly deny his direct complicity when those prisoners, unlucky enough to escape immediate decapitation, lay on his own palace courts in the burning sun, deprived of every necessity, devoured by vermin and brutally ill-treated by their gaolers, till death mercifully released them from their sufferings.

When the Allied forces reached Yuan Ming Yuan the Imperial family had just left through a side gate, and the fan, pipe, hat and papers that the Emperor had been using were still in his private apartments. This proves how suddenly and in what utter confusion the Court fled to Jehol, though the Annals record a face-saving decree which described the Emperor's departure as an "autumn tour of inspection."

"In spite of strict prohibitions against looting, the foreign soldiers, maddened by the murder of their comrades, carried off most of what was portable; the golden plates from temple ceilings, golden images from the altars, jades and pearls. Not one-tenth of the treasures were saved to enrich the world; five-tenths of the precious fragilities were smashed by the butts of muskets or hurled about by sky-larking soldiers, and the rest were consumed and shivered in the final fire and explosions."[209]

The burning palaces lighted the sky for two nights and sent black clouds of smoke drifting towards frightened Peking for two days, while the work of destruction was pushed to the farthest pavilions in the folds of the hills.

---

[209] *China, The Long-lived Empire,* by E. R. Scidmore.
Two jade and gold sceptres, a complete Imperial costume, a few rings, pearl necklaces, lacquers and porcelains were saved and sent as souvenirs to Napoleon III.

Juliet Bredon

If here and there a pagoda or a shrine was spared by some regretful officer, Time, which deals hardly with Chinese structures of wood and brick, achieved its ruin. Besides, bands of local thieves seized the opportunity to demolish what might have been repaired. Building materials were carried off by them and sold, including thousands of pounds of lead that lined the fountains. Fine old tiles were disposed of to neighbouring farmers for a few cents and used as chimney pots. Marble pillars were broken up for the sake of the iron clamps that held them together, and splendid trees ruthlessly felled for firewood. Truly this place of beauty suffered an Old Testament vengeance!

Later the Chinese, with their talent for face-saving at the expense of the foreigner, explained that the punishment which overtook the Emperor was not really due to the Allies at all but to the Imperial disregard of the warning which Mencius, the great philosopher, gave one of the feudal princes of his day.[210] To this dignitary he said: "You have a hunting park ten miles square and the people complain of your extravagance. Duke Huai has a park twenty miles square, and all his people love him and rejoice in it. For while you shut up your park and enjoy it yourself alone, Duke Huai throws his open, so the more delightful he makes it, the more pleasure they have out of it and the more they love him." Selfishness was indeed the motto of the later Manchu emperors. Not even their highest officials saw anything of Yuan Ming Yuan save the formal halls of audience. All the luxury, all the beauty, was for the Emperor alone and his Court. Here in gilded dalliance the Only Man shut out all thought of painful and disagreeable things till the bloody paw of war rudely shattered his dream and wiped out his treasures.

After the dark days of 1860 and the death of Hsien Feng, the ill-starred palace of Yuan Ming Yuan was abandoned and never re-built. No doubt the place was too full of unpleasant

---

210 Some say that this destruction was a just retribution for the partial despoiling of the Ming Tombs by Ch'ien Lung, who used materials taken from them in the embellishment of Yuan Ming Yuan.

The Summer Palaces and the Jade Fountain

memories for the Empress Dowager Tz'u Hsi, who shared her husband's ignominious flight, ever to wish to live there again. For the first dozen years of the Regency, therefore, the Court was without a summer residence. But when the Old Buddha found herself advancing in years, she grew desirous of a quiet retreat. By this time she had been the *de facto* ruler of the Chinese empire for a quarter of a century. She had tasted the sweets of autocracy, had satisfied all her instincts of dominion, and was anxious to exchange the strict routine of the Forbidden City for the comparative freedom of country life.

At the outset her plans met with opposition, but opposition never deterred her from getting her own way. Her privy purse was empty; this was not sufficient reason, either, to daunt such a determined woman. She solved the problem by appropriating the twenty-four million taels destined for the Navy and using it instead for the construction of her pleasure house. Indeed China's humiliating defeat at the hands of Japan in 1894 was largely due to the diversion of sums needed to strengthen her fleet for what an American writer aptly describes as "a woman's $50,000,000 whim."

The new palace was completed for her 60th birthday. By a curious coincidence, the original buildings which stood on her chosen site were also erected for the 60th anniversary[211] of an Empress, the Lady Niuhulu, mother of Ch'ien Lung—a woman not unlike herself in force of character, and bearing the same name as her own mother. While on a visit to Hangchow with her son, over whom she exerted great influence, the first Niuhulu admired a pleasaunce there, whereupon Ch'ien Lung conceived the idea of copying it for her near Peking. Such was the inspiration of the New Summer Palace, then called Wan Shou Shan.

After Niuhulu's death the place remained unused for many years, -having suffered like all the Imperial property in the neighbourhood of Yuan Ming Yuan during the Allied campaign in 1860.

---

211 An event, according to Chinese ideas, calling for special gifts and honours.

Audience Hall in the Summer Palace

The Summer Palaces and the Jade Fountain

Painted Gallery—Summer Palace

Juliet Bredon

When the Old Buddha decided to rebuild Wan Shou Shan—re-named I Ho Yuan—for her own use, she made it into a really superb domain which was, of course, closed except to her invited guests. Nowadays it is open to all who can afford the entrance fee, and one can imagine the autocratic Dowager turning in her grave as crowds of globe trotters on a "Round the World Tour" besiege her Imperial entrance.212 A guide, like a fat yellow spider, lies in wait for visitors. He will show us everything and tell us everything for a dollar. We assure him we do not want his information, as we have been here a dozen times. He insists we shall lose our way and lowers his price to sixty cents. We tell him we know the place better than he does. He promises to come for fifty cents. We tell him to get out of our sight. Finally he offers, with a wave of garlic and and operatic gesture, to accompany us all the afternoon for twenty cents. We hurl in his teeth a Chinese expression more forcible than polite. Then at last he leaves us in peace, turning his attention to a party of tourists that his keen eye spies in the distance.

Unlike the Forbidden City, the Summer Palace is not a collection of remarkable buildings, impersonal, aloof, almost cold, which seem to look down contemptuously on the tiny ant-like humans that hurry between them. But what I Ho Yuan loses in magnificence, it gains in sympathy. The picturesqueness of the setting, the unerring taste with which sites of temples and pavilions have been chosen, the consummate artistry of the Chinese landscape gardeners in taking advantage of natural features to heighten their effects—these constitute the charm of the New Summer Palace, and form the dominant impression we carry away from this "garden of ghosts."

With her instinct for beauty, Tz'u Hsi included the lovely lake, the bronze pavilions and the "Ten Thousand Buddha Temple" on the hill—all conceived by Ch'ien Lung—in her own plan. She also decided to leave untouched the ruins on the

---

212 The low buildings on the left were used by the Foreign Office for transacting state business when the Court was in residence at the Summer Palace.

north side of the enclosure. With the passage of time, they have grown to blend admirably with their surroundings, and give to her smiling domain the note of gentle melancholy needed to accentuate its charm.

The new dwelling palaces where the Empress Dowager and her nephew, the Emperor Kuang Hsu, actually lived are grouped together at the south-eastern end of the lake. This cluster of buildings also includes the theatre and the Audience Hall, the latter near the entrance gate in order that officials, who came on public business, might avoid passing the private apartments.

Facing the beautiful white marble terrace which follows the southern shore of the lake are the emperor's own pavilions, and a special landing stage with balustrades curled into sea foam and coiled into dragons.

Further on towards the west are the Old Buddha's apartments, a series of verandahed halls, connected by open corridors and built around spacious courtyards. Roofed over in her day with honey coloured matting and thus transformed into cool outdoor living rooms like Spanish patios, these courts were kept filled with rare shrubs and twisted trees. The two cypresses trained into extraordinary shapes were Her Majesty's pride, and she was wont, her attendants say, to compare their symmetry, established by the shears and pruning knife, to old fashioned Chinese life, bent and bound by convention into a stately and dignified form.

During the Empress Dowager's lifetime there was always a profusion and luxuriance of her favourite flowers at the Summer Palace. Among the rockeries she planted that queer little green orchid, the lan hua, so often copied on her gowns. In front of the audience hall were crab-apple trees whose blossoms made them look like bridal bouquets—trees so long domesticated and caressed by the hand of man that they have, the Chinese believe, acquired souls and strive to show their gratitude, like women loved, by making themselves more beautiful for man's sake. A whole hill known as the "flowery mountain" was a mass of peonies of exquisite blended colours and faint evanescent perfume, a whole lake a carpet of lotuses, shedding a riotous sweetness that plays upon the senses. Oleanders, pink as painted lips, pomegranates, red as wounds, and chrysanthemums, like groups of,ambassadors in full dress, stood outside the latticed windows of the Dowager's own pavilions.

These private apartments are closed and sealed now, in Chinese fashion, with crossed strips of paper. But we may look through the windows at the Old Buddha's bed with its hangings of imperial yellow, nobly embroidered with flying phoenixes, and at her portrait painted by a Dutch artist. On the empty shelves once stood books, ornaments and, of course, clocks— "magnificent jeweled and gold clocks and specimens of all the varieties that were ever made; some with chimes, some with crowing cocks and singing birds, some with running water."

Likewise we may peep into the Audience Hall, through plate glass doors painted with a huge red character meaning "longevity," into an austerely beautiful room furnished with rare specimens of the craftsman's art in carved woods and priceless lacquer.

In this building, standing well back on a terrace decorated with bronze birds and beasts, the ladies of the legations were received by her Majesty at a yearly garden party, and on such gala days the verandahs were shaded with silken awnings while down the handsome marble steps, lapping over them like a blood-coloured river, a crimson carpet poured itself.

"When the guests arrived at the Foreign Office buildings, only a few hundred yards away... they were conducted first to a pavilion on the right of the Audience Hall, where they arranged themselves in the order in which they were to be presented. ... A double line of Princesses led by the Princess Imperial met them on the marble platform, then turned and preceded them into the Audience Hall. Here they separated and stood in a picturesque group on either side of the Throne dais. In the dim obscurity sat the Empress Dowager with the Emperor on her left. Before Her Majesty stood a table with a cover of Imperial yellow reaching to the ground, and set with exquisite porcelain vases containing fragrant fruits and flowers.

"The foreign ladies made three reverences on entering. After the formal presentations were over, the Empress Dowager descended from the dais. One of her chairs, cushioned with yellow satin was brought, and she sat down on the right side of the Audience Hall. The ladies were then collectively presented by Her Majesty to the young Empress and the Princess Imperial, and tea was ordered while the guests stood round the Empress Dowager's chair and she said a few words (through an interpreter of course) to each informally. When tea was finished the ladies, conducted by the eunuchs and accompanied by the princesses, were taken past the palace of the young Empress and across the Old Buddha's court to the pavilion where luncheon was served.

"A row on the lake in one of the state barges or a performance in the three-storied theatre filled up the afternoon. The guests then said farewell to Their Majesties and left the Palace grounds for the Foreign Office where they took their own chairs and carriages for Peking."

How many heartburnings resulted from the wild scramble to get an invitation to these Imperial garden parties! And yet delightful as they were, the understanding visitor is far happier wandering about alone, lingering where he chooses, following the marble terrace along the lake, stopping at the pavilions which accent the indentations of the banks, pausing to admire the famous bronze lions near the ornamental archway.

Legend says they were cast by Sun Ch'uan, one of the princes of the period of the Three Kingdoms (a.d. 221-265) who reigned at Nanking and at Hanyang, but their antiquity is probably exaggerated. It is certain, however, that they were brought to I Ho Yuan by Ch'ien Lung who admired their "five coloured patina"— due to the richness of gold and silver mixed with the bronze—and declared them "of exceeding value." All credit then to the Manchu House for having refused an offer of $2,000,000 made by the Peking Curio Dealer's Guild for these relics of the past, when money was badly needed!

Juliet Bredon

A covered gallery a mile long is one of the features of the Summer Palace and a charming place to linger on a hot summer's day. To the right we get glimpses between the trees of the erstwhile apartments of ladies-in-waiting and of Li Lien-ying, the hated Chief Eunuch, who held in his greedy hands the threads that controlled the dance of the Court marionettes.

To the left lies the lake magically blue. With a sudden intake of breath at its enchanting beauty, we gaze towards the island[213] with the temple that seems part of the rock from which it rises—the temple dedicated to a famous Dragon King.

A seventeen-arched marble bridge connects this floating jewel with a sandy stretch of imitation beach where Ch'ien Lung's bronze cow patiently guards the palace against floods. Further to the west is the quaint "Hunchback Bridge" with its single span thirty feet high, and beyond, leading to the half ruined Fishing Pavilions, a covered bridge that reminds one of Venice.

Indeed, wherever we look there is a fantasy of picturesque tip-tilted roofs and marble terraces. We guess that many an intrigue has taken place amid the profusion and luxuriance of colourful nature; in the blue and gold arbours that seem to play hide and seek among the trees; that tender words have been whispered and vengeful jealousies planned there.

The covered gallery ends at the foot of the Hill crowned by the "Temple of Ten Thousand Buddhas." The climb needs courage and endurance, yet Her Majesty T'zu Hsi frequently mounted the steep steps on her high Manchu heels—heels fixed in the middle of the sole and requiring a perfect balance even on level ground. Urged on by her example and by the glimpse of roofs with polychromatic tiles that promise beauties one dare not miss, we climb laboriously, stopping to rest at Ch'ien Lung's twin bronze pavilions. These, like the stone tablet extolling the view of the K'un Ming Hu (the lake below), defied the fire of 1860 because their pillars, beams and tiles were all moulded in metal cast by the Jesuits.

---

213 This island has now been transformed into a "Nature Hospital" while some of the buildings on the mainland arc rented as Summer Bungalows.

The Summer Palaces and the Jade Fountain

Here we are overtaken by the tourists which our would-be guide has hurried after us. The Girl From Arkansas immediately inquires if she could buy one bronze pavilion. She thinks it would look "real sweet in the garden at home." But her father thinks not—too badly damaged. Something new would be more decorative.

Then the Professor, travelling with them by reason of a strange fascination for this ultra-modern maiden, leads us all enthusiastically in the long, winding climb through rock galleries, while the Girl remarks that any civilised country would insist on the introduction of an elevator. The Professor, though a staid man inclined to be short of breath, waxes eloquent over the lovely picture we look down upon: "Just like a scene from the *Arabian Nights*—this fairy land of quaint-shaped summer houses, soft pink walls, rainbow roofs, lacquered columns, white marble arches and camel's back bridges. Nature and art, my dear, everywhere blended till we cannot tell where one ends and the other begins. It is magic, young lady, that's the only word for it.

We feel by instinct that enchanted princesses have slept under these trees to be awakened by the touch of fairy Princes. We know perfectly well that at any moment a genie may rise in a cloud of heavy smoke from that bronze jar yonder. We are prepared for any number of magic carpets or winged horses to come floating over the wall."

The Professor, who rather fancied himself as a scholar, enjoyed poking around the "Temple of Ten Thousand Buddhas" built of glazed yellow tiles each representing a niche for a seated figure of Buddha. "That's nearly the number of dental parlours in Chicago," the Girl remarked. But the Professor declined to be disturbed by her irreverent comparisons. He had found a slab with a poem on it which he insisted on translating, probably wrongly, judging by the smile of the guide. Anyway it was a pretty poem:

"The shadows up the terrace creep in thick array,
The boy was told in vain to sweep them all away.

Juliet Bredon

> The setting sun had just dispersed the gathering train,
> When lo, the moon would set them up again."

He assured us it was written by a woman, the favourite of an emperor. "Can't you picture her? Her hair was the colour of thunder clouds and mysteriously combed with bands and volutes, with ellipses and convolutions. Phoenix enamelled pins held these in place and decorated the forehead and the part above the ears. Her eyebrow was like a willow leaf, the shape of a new moon; her eyes clear as autumn water, white and black distinctly defined. Golden ear-rings lengthened her face to the shape of a lotus bud. And her garments were worthy of a form supple as a young bamboo. She wore an upper jacket of silk embroidered with a round *p'u tzu* indicating her rank, and her skirts were green and broke in rustling waves about her feet. The buttons which fastened her garments were of pure jade, and on her fingers were rings set with many coloured jewels."

"Some girl!" remarked the Father absent-mindedly as he scrawled figures on a bit of paper. At last he said: "I wish our firm could have had the contract for lighting this place, daughter. I figure a neat little power plant behind the hill would have been a darned sight better than that dinky thing they've got down near the lake. And I guess there must have been some profit on replacing broken globes if Her Majesty's servants were as careless as those we have over at the hotel."

Then we all climbed down again, rather shaky in the knees. The Girl leaned with her back against the wall at the bottom and wondered whether it had been worth while anyway, for there were buildings in New York twice as high. "Yes ma'am," she told me, "twice as high and they have elevators to take you up and down. Now, I guess there's no ice water to be got here!"

There was no ice water but we said you could get luke-warm lemonade on the marble boat, so we all walked there to find "a curiosity, but not a thing of beauty"— the only disillusion in I Ho Yuan! As some witty person remarked: "China wanted a navy, but all she got was a marble boat with a hideous wooden cabin, painted to imitate stone, where tourists buy hot beer or 'soft drinks.'" There we left our companions; Father still

The Summer Palaces and the Jade Fountain

figuring before a glass of mineral water: "Yes, ma'am, I'm on the wagon, have been for two years, makes for efficiency"—the Professor chewing the cud of guide book facts, and the Girl exclaiming: "If I hadn't been born in God's own country, I might have considered being Empress of China and living in this palace. It's mighty romantic and with steam heat and elevators, I guess it would be fine."

We went on to visit the tomb of Yeh-lu Ch'u-ts'ai,[214] and found it outside the palace wall after much difficulty, as hitherto no visitors, save one Japanese savant, had cared to look for it. With inexcusable irreverence, the palace electric light works were installed in a building just in front of the tomb, and one must pass through a room filled with dilapidated and rusty machinery to pay a tubute to the remains of a man who was among China's greatest empire builders. Scion of the house of Liao, born in a.d. 1190, he first served the Chins, and afterwards Genghis Khan. History writes him down as a versatile figure—a governor of Samarkand, compiler of a calendar for the Mongols, author of a history of the Tartar dynasty, originator of paper money in China, and sufficiently disinterested to persuade the emperor to confer a perpetual dukedom on the descendants of Confucius. In fact a Chinese contemporary says: "he was distinguished by a rare unselfishness." All his care and labour had for their sole object the advantage and glory of his masters, whether Chins or Mongols.[215]

When Peking was captured by Genghis Khan, he was governor of the city, and found employment with the conquerors who must have had confidence in him, since he accompanied Genghis in 1224 to subjugate India. In the Karatag, the expedition met with a creature "which resembled a deer, but its head was like that of a horse with one horn on its forehead, and green hair on its body." This monster had power of speech, for it said to the guards: "Bid your master return to his own land." Genghis, troubled by this message, consulted

---

214 See Chapter I.
215 See *A Short History of China*, by D. C. Boulger.

Juliet Bredon

Yeh-lu Ch'u-ts'ai, who replied: "That creature is Kotuan, knowing every language. It appears as a sign that bloodshed is needless at present. For four years the great army is warring in western regions. Heaven, which has a horror of bloodshed, gives warning through Kotuan. Spare the empire for Heaven's sake. Moderation will give boundless pleasure."[216] Genghis listened to the advice of his Minister who, not less by reason of his personality than of his talent, was a striking figure. Eight feet tall, with a long beard, moustaches reaching to his knees and a voice like thunder, he was physically above his fellows. Morally wise and calculating in his plans, he did little, according to the evidence of history, of which he had reason to repent. Of how many men buried in tombs far grander than his simple tumulus in the small bat-infested house with its crumbling roof, can we say as much?

Not far beyond the Summer Palace, within a convenient distance to be visited on the same day, is the lovely park of the Jade Fountain, connected by a canal with Ch'ien Lung's lake. As the water-way is now closed, the visitor is obliged to go by the road that leads across a marble bridge behind I Ho Yuan. It is well worth stopping *en route* at the temple whose gateway is guarded by two fearsome stone animals. These are not the familiar lions, but winged monsters that the Chinese call "*hou*," the "kings of beasts," able to walk or fly, with power over all living creatures. At their unearthly call even tigers obey, hastening like their weaker brethren to inevitable doom, since these bloodthirsty monsters eat every animal they see, ripping open their prey with the horns upon their foreheads, and sucking its blood. Such gluttony so shocked the Heavenly Powers that Shang Ti (the Supreme God) decreed their eyes should be directed skywards for the safety of the brute creation.[217]

---

216 See *A History of the Mongols*, by J. Curtin.
217 The "*hou*" is supposed to be a cross between a fierce Mongolian wolf and a winged tiger. Living specimens are admittedly rare, and it is seldom that they are carved in stone in life size. But miniature statuettes of the "*hou*"— an emblem of one of the constellations in Arius—are found in the row of animals guarding Chinese roofs, and sometimes they arc represented as

The Summer Palaces and the Jade Fountain

This pair guard the temple of Kung Teh Ssu founded under the Mongol dynasty by the Emperor Teh-Temur. He and his successors apparently came here often "not only to perform their devotions, but to revel and to change their clothes"; also to admire from the three towers, which once stood in front of the temple, the fish and flowers in the ponds, where the present day rice-fields are. The Ming emperors likewise came to "inspect the harvest" in this vicinity. But the visit of one of them, Chia Ching, proved unlucky for the monastery. When he went to the tomb of his predecessor Ching T'ai, near by, the local authorities broadened the Chin Shan defile behind the temple for the passage of the Imperial cortege. Now this defile, according to the astrologers, symbolises a white tiger's mouth. When it was enlarged, the tiger's mouth was opened wide enough to swallow the temple—a very bad augury. Moreover, when the Emperor stopped in the pass after his visit to the tomb, he was startled by the terrifying appearance of one of the Deva kings guarding the monastery gates. Angry with himself for his fright, he took the pretext that the buildings were not of the exact dimensions prescribed by the regulations to have the temple closed and the monks committed for trial.

The temple was only restored by Ch'ien Lung in 1770, who endowed it with grants of land and converted it into a lamasery. In his time it gained renown as the place where a miraculous wooden ball had been kept. The ball originally belonged to a famous monk named Pan An, who resided on the site of the Kung Teh Ssu under the T'ang dynasty in a.d. 870. Endowed with the power of locomotion, this ball was employed by its owner for various errands. It used, for example, to trot round the neighbouring villages and collect alms for the monastery. It would run to call the servants and announce visitors, jumping up and down before guests of importance, as if "k'o-towing" to them. Once when a fire occurred, it dived into a pool from which it was rescued unscathed. Such cleverness and initiative caused the ball to be greatly venerated. But Ch'ien Lung, who refers to its existence in his day, expresses doubts as

---

bearers of Buddha's throne.

regards the virtues attributed to it, while observing that it certainly testifies to the undying fame of Pan An. The temple is now in ruins and the ball has disappeared, when or where none can tell, though the remaining Lama priests confirm the legend about it—a legend unique in Chinese folklore. "Nothing is now left to us," they say, "save one old bronze bell and one marble tablet recording Ch'ien Lung's visit in an inscription by his own hand." Perhaps the miraculous ball may trot back some day to its old home and collect alms again to repair the temple. But unless it returns soon, there is great danger that nothing will be left to repair.

Only a few hundred yards from the Temple of the Miraculous Ball stands the entrance gate of the Jade Fountain enclosure. From a glance at the old pagodas crowning the hill one realises that I Ho Yuan, even its older traditions, are things of yesterday compared to Yu Ch'uan Shan. This little park, "The Garden of Peaceful Brightness," has in fact been a pleasure ground for the rulers of the North for 700 years, perhaps more. As far as we know, the original grounds and buildings were planned by the Chin Tartar ruler Ming Ch'ang (a.d. 1193-1208). The Mongols who succeeded his dynasty kept them up; the Mings improved them; the Manchu Emperor K'ang Hsi built temples and pagodas here—one dedicated to Buddha, one to the Spirit of the Fountain, and others to forgotten gods. The loveliest is of solid marble and rises from the ground like a white lily. The base is carved in imitation of the waves of the sea, and the pagoda, seven-storied but of slight build, stands upon a gigantic lotus flower.

More striking is the spire on the highest hill top—the Yu Cheng Pao Tien (or Miao Feng T'a) also erected by K'ang Hsi—and more beautiful, according to Chinese taste, the smaller shaft of green and gold encaustic tiles near the ruined buildings on the western slope.[218]

---

218 Chinese writers declared this the loveliest of the 10,000 pagodas which once existed in and around Peking.

The Summer Palaces and the Jade Fountain

"Marble Boat"—Summer Palace

Juliet Bredon

These were not, as might appear at first, palaces, for no dwelling pavilions existed in this enclosure. In the golden age of Imperial sportsmanship, some of them were used as tiger pits, kennels and falconries. When the brave hunters started in full panoply for the chase, the rendezvous was in this garden and here the big game waited the signal of the Emperor to be loosed in the neighbouring Hunting Park.

Besides these relics—now scarred by fire—of the grand days of old, Yu Ch'uan Shan boasts a tiny lake and many beautiful trees. But its supreme glory remains the pure, sparkling spring which gushes out of the rocks on the hillside. The caves above it, framed in fragrant wisteria blossoms, are full of images. We linger to admire a lovely goddess, with one marble foot dangling, the other showing its sole as it rests upon the opposite knee, the face turned to look over the left shoulder, the chin tilted, the lips parted with a scornful smile. We pause again before Ch'ien Lung's tablet bearing the inscription "The First Spring Under Heaven,"[219] then climb to the rest-house above for a general view.

Truly this is a jade fountain, so deep is its green, so soft the shadows that move across it, when, on summer days, the wind plays upon the water as the old musicians played upon the mn-hsien. The pagodas cast their pointed silhouettes, the little hills[220] look over and smile at their reflections. A queer old Viking barge, with pointed prow, glides lazily through the water weeds, while a Chinese poet in the stern writes characters of praise, smooth-flowing as the ripples in the lake. The wind bells on the shrines above us gossip perpetually from the points of the eaves whenever there is breeze enough "to move three hairs." We wish, how we wish, to understand their chatterings, to know what it is they tell of the emperors and

---

[219] So called because the specific gravity of its water is less than that of any other water in China, except melted snow-water. (*Visite aux temples de Pekin,* "Politique de Pekin," 1921).

[220] The origin of the "stupa" on the hill behind the spring is wrapped in mystery and likely to remain so. Every visitor is curious about a monument so unlike the other pagodas but though it is probably a Buddhist tomb there is no mention of it in any Chinese record.

The Summer Palaces and the Jade Fountain

empresses who once owned this pretty piece of jade-work and came in their barges from Wan Shou Shan, the "Palace of Ten Thousand Ages," to admire it; of the Court poets who compared it to green seas they never saw, or to the lustrous eyes of mythical creatures—to a thousand things of which modern poets have no time to think.

We had reached the point of revery when two little Chinese boys came scurrying up the path. One toppled over and had a bleeding nose in consequence. He howled and rubbed the tears amongst the mess on his face. We gave him our sympathy and a coin, whereupon he instantly recovered, gave chase to the other boy and banged his head against the Chinese gentleman who was leisurely ascending to complete his ode in the rest-house.

After an exchange of courtesies, we inquired about his writing, admiring the large bold characters.

"No, it is not a poem," he made answer, "only an attempt to set down the old legend of the *'Yu Hsi'* or Imperial seal of jade. You noticed Ch'ien Lung's inscription above the spring? This legend explains how it came to be written."

"Please tell us the story."

"Well, once upon a time in forgotten ages, the original piece of jade for this seal was discovered accidentally by a peasant of the feudal kingdom of Ch'u. The countryman was so persuaded of the miraculous qualities of this stone that he did everything in his power to bring it to his prince's notice. He was twice thrown out of the palace for his persistence and the second time his legs were cut off to prevent his ever entering it again. Still at last he managed to convince the sovereign." The stone was tested and broke into three pieces of such marvellous beauty that one was made into the Imperial seal, another into the seal of the "Heavenly Teacher"—the Taoist Patriarch—and the third into an ink slab for Confucius.

The Imperial seal showed its miraculous qualities when Ch'ien Lung calmed a storm on the Yangtze by throwing it into the river—but the talisman of ages was thus lost. Finally one day as Ch'ien Lung, many years later, sat watching the flow of water from the "Dragon Mouth of Yu Ch'uan Shan," he saw to his surprise the current spit up the precious relic. Then in gratitude he erected the inscription "The First Spring Under Heaven."[221] "Perhaps the foreigners honourably think concerning the story that it is foolish?"

"No, elder born, the tale has a charm which surpasses truth."

We bade our friend farewell as he began to climb the jagged rocky path we had lately descended. It was an unusual effort on the part of an Oriental, but he explained that his Chinese guide book ranked Yu Ch'uan Shan first among the eight famous sights[222] of Peking, therefore it must be done. Nowhere but from the highest pagoda could the visitor command a finer bird's-eye view of I Ho Yuan; nowhere so well appreciate its plan; the shape of its lake like a blue-green peacock ruffling sun-gilded feathers, the site of its bridges and its palaces—while at the same time enjoying the panorama of the Western Hills—like masses of cloud nailed against the sky—with Pi Yun Ssu, Wo Fo Ssu and the ruins of the Hunting Park nestling in their valleys.

---

221 The seal is still in possession of the Manchu House.
222 According to Chinese taste, the other seven famous sights are: the Jade Rainbow Bridge across the Palace lakes, the Pai T'a monument in the Pei Hai clothed by the mists of spring, the Marco Polo Bridge (Lu Kou Ch'iao) at the full moon, the panorama of the Western Hills when the setting sun changes them to the colours of flowers, the Golden Terrace with a stone tablet a mile beyond the Ch'ao Yang Men, and the king-fisher coloured rocks of the Nankou Pass.

XV. Temples of the Western Hills

Continue along the road beyond the Jade Fountain to the Western Hills whose slopes are rich in historical associations and musical with the sound of temple bells. The Chinese always loved these peaks, gilded by the sun or silvered by the snow—stainless ornaments of the Eternal Temple in which "neither the hammer, nor the ax, nor any tool was heard while it was building."

When in the 15th century a new flood of faith poured over the land and a new era of temple building began— comparable to, and coinciding in point of time with the great wave of cathedral building that swept across Europe—the Ming emperors delighted to honour the gods throned on these heights. Where they did not build outright, they repaired, decorated and enlarged what earlier dynasties, like the T'angs and Yuans, had constructed, and nearly every sanctuary of importance stands on the site of some other, hundreds of years older.

Hence the difficulty of fixing the age of most of these monasteries in which often only a piece of wall or an angle of roof remains to recall the founder.[223] But those who restored the temples always followed the plan of the original architects— whose names are long forgotten— thus ensuring continuity of design.

Nor were these temples built in a separate mystical or religious style like our churches, but in an "everyday manner common and familiar to everybody." Most of them have the usual series of rectangular courts facing north and south, with the principal edifice in the centre and lesser buildings at the sides, as in a large dwelling house. The gateway is roofed to form a vestibule where the "Diamond Kings" stand on guard. Beyond, either Kuan Ti, represented as a Han Dynasty warrior,

---

[223] This is the history of all Chinese buildings, few of which are really ancient. Our cathedrals withstand the centuries, but Chinese temples, built of less enduring materials, blossom for a while, then wither, and new ones rise from the same roots.

or the Buddhist Messiah,[224] conceived as an obese monk with smiling features, sits enshrined. Passing through this chapel we come to the main courtyard with the principal sanctuary generally dedicated to Sakyamuni, the historical Buddha, who is the central figure of an imposing triad enthroned upon lotus pedestals.[225]

Behind the "jewelled palace of the Great Hero" there may be one or more courts with shrines dedicated perhaps to Kuan Yin, the Goddess of Mercy, or other popular deities. Wing buildings contain figures of the Eighteen Lohans[226] (or Arhats), the treasures of the temple, or portraits and relics of former abbots.

We may find a library or a Buddhist school attached to a monastery, perhaps picturesque gardens or an old pond filled with carp, where the water lies a brownish green under the shadow of the lotus leaves.

Always an outer wall encircles the temple property enclosing sufficient ground to afford space for the higher dignitaries of the establishment, for kitchens and stables, storehouses for fuel and grain, and open pavilions for enjoying the view. Many temples have separate bell and drum towers, lofty wooden masts set in carved stone sockets for hoisting flags and lanterns on festival days, and guardian stone lions. A few have Imperial travelling palaces, called "Hsing Kung" attached to them and all have guest rooms, "K'o t'ang," for the entertainment of strangers and passing pilgrims. In a land where country seats are rare and inns bad, the native gentry spend their holidays in temples and the priests, as in mediæval Europe, are accustomed to receive and lodge all visitors,

---

224 See Chapter IX
225 His companions may be Ananda and Kasyapa, favourite disciples or other Buddhas. See Chapter XI.
226 These are disciples of Buddha (sometimes styled the apostles of the Buddhist Faith) who have reached the stage of emancipation from rebirth but who, through some individual imperfection, have not yet attained Nirvana, the complete merging into Divinity. Thus left in contact with mortals, they assist the earth-bound to free themselves from terrestrial miseries.

including foreigners. In fact travellers' gifts of "tea money" are one of their principal sources of revenue.

If globe-trotters but knew the charms of temple life in these hills which rise ten miles beyond Peking as suddenly as the Alban Hills beyond Rome, they would not be daunted by small difficulties and discomforts in making excursions among them. Such trifles weigh as nothing against the beautiful pictures, the friendly human contacts, the imagination-stirring associations, stored up for after years. Besides the freshness of the air, the soft shade of the trees, the music of chanted "sutras," and the serene views over mountain and plain—all these are a soothing redemption from the sorrows of the 20th century. Here, as on shipboard before the days of wireless, men have time to think and dream and cure their souls of the restless sickness of subways and huge caravansaries supplied with "modern improvements."[227]

Of course, some who follow the paths suggested will feel a shock of disappointment at the dirt, the poverty, the ruinousness of many temples, and "it is quite useless," as Leslie Stephen said of Doctor Johnson's rough sayings, "to defend them to anyone who cannot enjoy them without defence." Other visitors will be glad that time has dimmed the brightness of their colouring to tone with the surrounding hills, and think it more fitting that such sanctuaries should be veiled by the dust of the past. All depends upon the individual taste and viewpoint.

---

[227] Travellers should remember, however, when planning such excursions, that the guest rooms of these Buddhist sanctuaries contain only a wooden table, a bench and a brick "k'ang," or platform, for a bed. To be reasonably comfortable, camp beds with bedding and folding chairs should be sent on a day ahead in charge of a "boy" who is capable of preparing simple meals in foreign style. Chickens and eggs may be bought in the villages, but luxuries like tea, coffee, sugar, bread and meat are unobtainable and must be taken. Those who do not care for the trouble of transporting supplies will find the hotel at Pa Ta Ch'u (foreign style meals and beds, and easily accessible by motor car) a pleasant centre from which to make trips to some of the nearer temples.

Juliet Bredon

Peking residents rent their favourite temples for the season in order to enjoy a picturesque and intimate combination of camp and country life in Buddhist precincts. At Wo Fo Ssu, for example, the Y.M.C.A. has an out-of-town headquarters. This is one of the oldest monasteries in the Western Hills, dating from the T'ang dynasty and boasting, like most well-known temples, a stone tablet inscribed by the Emperor Ch'ien Lung. A fine avenue of old cypresses, doubly appreciated in a country where timber is scarce, leads to the entrance *p'ai lou* of green and yellow tiles, as handsome as the much admired archway of the Hall of Classics. We pass beneath it and cross several sunny courtyards to the hall of the famous Sleeping Buddha. This representation of the Divinity[228] was common among all the Buddhist peoples in the 7th, 8th and 9th centuries, and numerous figures of the Beloved One at rest, generally presented by Tartar converts, survive in various parts of China. It was the Mongols in fact who replaced an earlier wooden figure here by the present replica fifty feet long.

The image with its calm passionless face and closed eyes— an impressive embodiment of dreamless sleep—is fully clothed in robes of state. Only the feet are bare. The pious bring offerings of shoes,[229] large and small, silk or paper according to their means, to place upon the altar— curious and touching witnesses of their faith. Mingling with the sweet, heavy smell of incense, the clang of a bell and the deep hum of a voice reciting the "sutras," are Christian hymns piped by the shrill voices of converts on the hillside. But "Jerusalem the Golden," slightly out of tune, seems to have no power to break the Buddha's

---

[228] Such "Sleeping Buddhas" show the Sage at the end of his earthly incarnations and about to enter the Nirvana paradise only attainable to him "whose senses have become tranquil like a horse well broken-in by a driver; who is free from pride, the lust of the flesh and the defilement of ignorance— to him whom even the Gods envy. Such a one remains like the broad earth, unvexed; like the pillar at the city gate, unmoved; like a pellucid lake, unruffled."—Dhammapada.

[229] Such offerings represent a purely Chinese idea of the Buddha's needs. No Son of Han walks barefoot if he can help it. Therefore it is courteous to place a sleeper's shoes beside him, convenient to his awakening.

sleep. Or if he hears, he is not a jealous god and does not mind the intrusion.

In the next valley to the westward lies Pi Yun Ssu, the "Monastery of the Azure Clouds," the most beautiful temple in the Westefn Hills and one of the most beautiful in China. Here we have an example of how well the Buddhist monks chose the sites of their shrines so that the beauties of nature should enhance the work of the religious architect. From the foot of the valley the dominating marble "stupa" appears, like a ghostly monument, deceptively close in the clear air. Yet we climb two miles of stony pavement before we even reach the outer temple gate guarded by giant Deva kings, huge figures of painted wood and plaster, with arms and legs muscled like the limbs of heroes in Assyrian sculptures. Instinctively there came to mind the story of their apparition as told in the Mahavagga. "On a beautiful night the Four Great Kings entered the holy grove filling all the place with light; and, having respectfully saluted the Blessed One, they stood in the four directions like four great fire brands."

We enter the outermost courtyard to find the buildings falling into decay. The roof of his pavilion has tumbled in upon Maitreya, the Laughing Buddha, leaving the winds and rain to peel off his gilding. But he still laughs and the people envy him because his paunch is filled forever. Such is the Chinese ideal of happiness, and before we criticize the utter materialism of this philosophy, let us stop and remember the millions in an overcrowded land who have only a few cents between themselves and starvation. As Bland says: "the chronic condition of the Chinese with their procreative recklessness born of Ancestor worship and Confucianism, is a struggle for food unequalled in any other part of the world. No wonder then that this struggle has condemned the people te elementary materialism in its business of man-making and man-feeding."[230]

Curious plaster frescoes in a side hall show the delights of Heaven and the tortures of Hell. Heaven is a pale picture of the splendid Buddhist description: "Ten myriad miles to the west

---

[230] *Recent Events and Present Policies in China*, by J. O. P. Bland.

there is an earth called Paradise, the home of Amida, where no creature knows sorrow, neither hunger nor thirst nor nakedness. In Paradise there is neither death nor pain and there is no winter. The flowers in that place never fade and the fruits never fall, and if a man taste of those fruits even but once, he can never again feel thirst or hunger. The Blessed who dwell there eat their rice out of very, very small bowls, but the rice never diminishes within those bowls—however much of it be eaten—until the eater desires no more. And they drink their wine out of very, very small cups, but no man can empty one of those cups, however stoutly he may drink, until there comes upon him the pleasant drowsiness of intoxication.... Glimmering portals close this place and there are seven rows of balustrades, seven rows of precious trees and seven lakes with golden sands round about it. The streets are a compound of silver, pearls and crystal. Six hours of each day and six hours of the night there is a rain of flowers, and every morning the Blessed gather them in their robes and carry them to the Ten Million Buddhas with songs of praise.... Even the birds in Paradise are like none to be seen upon earth; white cranes and golden peacocks and purple parrots with plumage brighter than sunshine. And all these creatures forever chant prayers in unison, because they have no sin.

The representation of Hell makes us shudder with its Oriental crudities and cruelties depicting the ultimate and most solemn fact of human destiny, the Last Judgment, and the punishments meted out to sinners. The dead—noble, priest, and peasant—tremble in an equality of doom. But time is taking revenge on the wicked executioners, pulling the axe and dropping the spear from their bloodthirsty hands.

ARCHWAY—PI YUN SSU

Juliet Bredon

Yet Pi Yun Ssu is not a very old temple compared with many others. It was only founded under the Yuan Dynasty and has had the advantage of many wealthy patrons. Under the Mings a famous eunuch, Yu Ching, favourite of the Emperor Cheng Teh, spent a fortune made by collecting taxes with shrewd business capacity, on the Monastery. When he expiated his squeezing of the people under the next sovereign (who threw him into prison and left him to die in misery) servants secretly buried his official gown and hat in the cemetery attached to the temple where they dared not lay his outcast body.

Other rich courtiers also repaired and enlarged Yu Ching's chosen shrine, notably the equally infamous eunuch, Wei Chung-hsien,[231] "whose memory is to this day execrated by the Chinese people." The life story of Wei Chung-hsien reveals the seamy side of China's Imperial tapestry of statecraft. Careless of repeated warnings from courageous Censors not to allow eunuchs to meddle in government matters, the feeble Emperor of the day, T'ien Ch'i, devoted himself to his hobby of carpentry and permitted Wei to wield such power that he assumed a virtual dictatorship, and, by his evil deeds, contributed more than any other single man to bring about the calamities which finally overwhelmed the dynasty.

After his impeachment, Wei managed to escape from the Palace and fled to Shantung where, "outlawed and abandoned by all his followers, he committed suicide near the grave of Confucius. By order of the Throne his body was subsequently dismembered and his head exhibited at his native city of Ho Chien Fu."[232]

The million dollar sepulchre, ornate as an Imperial tomb, prepared for him at Pi Yun Ssu was never occupied and his

---

[231] More than half of the temples erected or restored under the Mings were the work of eunuchs who built on the pretext of praying for their sovereign lord, the Emperor, but actually for their own glorification and to provide a sanctuary for themselves in time of need.

[232] See *Annals and Memoirs of the Court of Peking*, by Bland and Backhouse.

gifts to the temple remain his only memorial. Thanks largely to his loyal friendship, however, many of the buildings at Pi Yun Ssu are still well preserved. The Hall of the Five Hundred Saints, copied from one at Hangchow, with rows and rows of seated figures larger than life, is quite impressive, and charming is the sanctuary dedicated to Kuan Yin, "She Who Looketh Down Above the Sound of Prayer," where almost any day or hour a few old women may be heard murmuring verses from the Sutra: "Storms and hate give way to Her Name. Fire is quenched by Her Name. Demons vanish at the sound of Her Name. By Her Name one may stand firm in the sky like a Sun."

Ch'ien Lung too was a benefactor of Pi Yun Ssu. It was he who built the yellow-roofed travelling palace, and who commanded the pretty garden, with a raised terrace above a spring, to be made. Shaped and earthed and planted by the monks, Nature herself, working through the centuries, has surpassed the dreams of mortal gardeners, softening the rock faces with lichens, draping ferns over the water, and clothing the tree trunks with moss.

The marble "Stupa,"[233] chief glory of the temple, was also Ch'ien Lung's gift in 1748, and, like Wu T'a Ssu, is a copy of the "Diamond Throne." Through a fine marble archway the seven white pinnacles tower upwards. Flights of steps lead to the high platform of the pagoda from which rise these towers, eighty feet above the ground and capped with bronze. Their sides are covered with carvings showing, like those of the Yellow Temple, unmistakable traces of Indian influence. They represent kings and warriors, gods and goddesses who seem to await the poet that in another Mahabarata or Ramayana shall tell the epics of their loves and wars, sanctities and vengeances.

---

[233] For five years the coffin of Dr. Sun Yat-sen lay in a niche under this "stupa" with an altar table before it, decorated in modern style, with silver cups, memorial shields with inscriptions and paper flowers. On great occasions the coffin was opened to show the embalmed body of China's latest national hero. It was finally removed to Purple Mountain, Nanking.

Marble "Stupa"—Pi Yun Ssu (Western Hills)

Temples of the Western Hills

Happy these gods enshrined in everlasting peace upon their marble pedestals, dreaming away poetic spring days when the wild peach blossoms blush tenderly beside the stern grey rocks; or drowsy summer days, when every crumbling ruin on the hillside bursts into leaf like a garden; or gorgeously colourful days of autumn when the maples don their brilliant dresses of orange and gold. One saintly figure with down-cast eyes—a Kuan Yin doubtless—gazes over the tops of the pines at the cemetery below, where the tombs stand on a carpet of fallen needles like thick brown fur—gazes with pity at the pale boy who sits in the sun upon a grave and coughs his life away.[234]

Near magnificent Pi Yun Ssu is a tiny temple on a hillock called Wan Hua Shan, "Mountain of Ten Thousand Flowers." It has only a single hall with statues of three goddesses, guardians of little children. One appears to be a patroness of eyes, for ex-votos representing eyes are placed upon her altar. But the most curious thing to be seen there is a small figure in a glass case, robed in yellow satin with a handsome blue headdress. The priest explains that it is a mummy of a little girl nine years old. We look closer at the unformed childish features and the gentle smile, while he tells her story. Nearly 200 years ago she lived in the village nearby. When still a baby she was fond of asking questions to which none but the gods knew the answers, and, as she grew older, she loved to climb up to the temple where the old priest of the day gave pretty pious explanations about those things which no man can ever fully understand. Every evening after the lamps had been lighted before the altars, he taught her lips to frame the words of prayer. Now at first, when she wandered away from home, her parents were often anxious about her but they soon learned to know where she could be found, and her father would come and carry her back in his arms. There she would doze off, smiling in her dreams, so he knew that Kuan Yin the Divine was playing shadowy play with the little soul. But one day the parents found that the child had fallen into such a deep sleep that none

---

[234] A sanitarium for tubercular patients has been established lately at Pi Yun Ssu and invalids may often be seen walking under the pine trees.

could waken her. And they wept and mourned until the old priest bade them cease. "It is not kindness to mourn for the dead. Over the River of Tears their silent road is, and when mothers weep, the flood of that river rises and the soul cannot pass but must wander to and fro."

Though they prepared her for burial, five days the child lay fair and sweet as if alive, and they had not the heart to put her away under the fields. The news of the miracle spread far and wide—even into the palace, even to the ears of the Emperor Ch'ien Lung himself. Whereupon he commanded that the little body be embalmed and enshrined in the temple she had loved so well.

Other visitors appeared, and the priest begged to be excused a little while, that he might attend to their wants. We made place for them and they came in—poor peasant folk, who saluted us kindly; an anxious mother desirous to have prayers said for her sick son, a father seeking divine help for a daughter sold far away in famine times, a young wife eager to obtain the pity of the Kuan Yin for her blind boy. The priest spoke caressingly to all, burning some little ex-voto masks for the father, placing a pair of eyes for the mother before Our Lady of Good Sight, and on behalf of each, preparing holy texts. How many innocent prayers are thus being made daily in tumble-down temples, how many fears and hopes and humble sorrows poured out unheard by any, save the gods!

Across the valley lies the Hsiang Shan, "The Perfumed Mountain," or Northern Hunting Park, a wooded enclosure dating from the Chin dynasty. The Imperial preserves of game disappeared when the later Manchu emperors, their spirit of adventure killed by centuries of routine, abandoned the chase. But in the heyday of their dynastic strength, China's sovereigns hunted frequently and with huge retinues. K'ang Hsi, for example, was an enthusiastic sportsman, and Peter the Great's Ambassador, Izmailov, the same who was invited to Yuan Ming Yuan, hunted with His Majesty for deer, pheasants and even tiger, of which last it is reported that he killed one. Ch'ien Lung likewise retained throughout his long life the devotion to the

Temples of the Western Hills

chase which made his forefathers the hardy men they were. With Chia Ch'ing the process of physical and moral degeneration had already begun, and though Tao Kuang fitfully followed the sporting habits of his ancestors, he was the last to do so.

The Hunting Park contains the ruins of a summer palace of the Chin sovereigns (a.d. 1125-1234) and the tomb of the last emperor of the Liaos. There are also remains of a Lama temple and a fine *p'ai lou*. An orphanage and a sanitarium have lately been established in one corner of the Park, but the greater part of the domain remains wild and deserted—a place to learn the art of meditation, to remember yesterday and forget to-day.

In fact, to draw the maximum of pleasure from excursions in the Western Hills, one should ignore what a Chinese friend calls "the little time devil on the wrist." Leave it at home and wander aimlessly while the light lasts as leisurely native travellers do. Take the habit of loafing along with lazy eyes following the shadows of the clouds, or the slow footsteps of a peasant's donkey, whose ribs pierce his sides like sharp elbows, across hills no longer tree clad, as the Sungs knew them, but bare and desolately brown. This loss of green from one-time forests carelessly transmuted into fuel, affects the farmers since it tragically decreases the rainfall. But for us, it has an aesthetic consolation. These burnt-up slopes—a torture to tramp across at high noon when the hot sun beats down upon them—turn towards evening to the most exquisite shades of purple and mauve. Denuded of their drapery of woods, their purity of line shows clearly. Moreover, the dry atmosphere produces light effects of a vigorous beauty that makes us catch our breath.

Follow on foot across these hills, if God made you a good walker, or, if He denied you that quality, by chair or donkey-back from shrine to shrine as fancy leads you. Any passer-by will direct you on your way, not always accurately perhaps but always willingly, and, though nobody has a precise idea of distance, most Chinese you meet will give a cheerful affirmative to your questions just to please you, if not from any previous knowledge.

Give a long morning to Pao Tsang Tzu, the combined temple and eunuch's pleasure house near the Summer Palace. But perhaps you do not care for mornings. Some people don't. Some feel at their best only after noon. Then this is a delightful drowsy hour to visit the little shrine known as the "Temple of Blue Snow" when it was first built by a Thibetan monk in a.d. 1439. In the tiny sanctuary a mysterious tile refuses to be cemented to its neighbours, breaking loose every time it is set in the floor. The priest explains that the site of the temple was formerly a burial ground and the dead monks pry loose the tile so that their ghosts may roam unhindered.

The eunuch who built his retreat beside the temple adored the Empress whom he served. Of course convention did not allow him to tell her what was in his foolish heart. But it did allow him to ask one favour of his gracious Lady—the favour of a visit. She promised lightly, as women do. And half his life he dreamed of buildings to delight her and planned gardens for her pleasure, seeking to tell in every stone and flower what might not be told in words. Then he waited—waited until one summer day, too tired to wait longer, he fell asleep and was laid away in a soft bed on the hillside and the grass raised a little green tent over him. They told the Empress and she wept, for she was a kindly soul and wished to please her faithful servitor. But she had been busy all those years—busy with unessential things as women are, and when she kept her promise at last, she only saw—his tomb.

Shih Tzu Wo, or "the Lion's Nest," is another delightful summer retreat (also built by a eunuch) which lies high up on the sunset side of a hill beyond the Hunting Park. The steep path leading there looks down on the yellow-tiled roof of a once famous Lamasery, part of a Travelling Palace destroyed in 1860; on crumbling watch towers reminiscent of mediaeval alarms; and on Ch'ien Lung's "Miniature Peking" (T'ang Chang). Here are the walls of the former capital reduced in size with gate towers in proportion—the whole forming a model

Temples of the Western Hills

practise ground for the soldiers charged with the protection of the city; here the pavilion where the Emperor himself sat to watch assault and defence and, if mistakes were made, to order the manoeuvres repeated.[235]

Ch'ien Lung evidently believed in preparedness since he also built the queer-looking buildings—like impregnable stone boxes—on the hill slopes further east. They served a double purpose in his day, simulating strong forts (which they were not) to frighten an invader and useful for teaching his soldiers to scale Thibetan strongholds, (of which they were copies) China being at that time at war with Thibet.

The climb to Shih Tzu Wo is far more interesting than the place itself, which is devoid of traditions and poetic associations. But from the gallery (modelled on the one at the Summer Palace) that winds along the hillside, the outlook has beauty and tranquillity, and the view of the plain below which broadens greenly to the distant city, is like a leaf from some old Chinese picture book. In the near foreground, under the very ruins of the British Summer Legation,[236] on an out-jutting knoll below, a farmer and his mule are ploughing the stony soil with a plough of the Period of the Gods, and the wife helps the work with a hoe more ancient even than the Empire of China. All three are toiling with solemn earnestness as though goaded without mercy by the knowledge that labour is the price of life.

"That man we have seen before in the paintings of another century. We have seen him on carvings of a much more ancient date. Exactly the same. Other fashions beyond counting have passed; the peasant's blue gown and straw hat remain. He himself is older, incomparably older than his dress. The earth he tills has indeed swallowed him up a thousand times, but

---

[235] This enclosure has been taken over by the authcrities and planted as a model fruit garden. The deserted Lama temple, and a neighbouring tomb enclosure, conspicuous by its fine avenue of white pines, are likewise being used in connection with agricultural experimental work.

[236] These buildings were hardly finished when in 1900 the Boxers destroyed them. The Minister's family only just escaped into the city in time, not realising till the last moment that these peaceful hills were actually hotbeds of the Boxer movement.

each time it has given back to him life with force renewed. And with this perpetual renewal he is content; he asks no more. The mountains change their shapes, the rivers shift their courses, the stars change their places in the sky; he changes never. Yet, though unchanging, he is a maker of change. Out of the sum of his toil are wrought the ships of iron, the roads of steel, the palaces of stone; his are the hands that pay for the new universities and the new learning, for the telegraphs and electric lights and the repeating rifles, for the machinery of science and the machinery of commerce and the machinery of diplomacy or war. He is the giver of all; he is given in return the right to labour forever, and labouring, to find content."

From Shih Tzu Wo make a leisurely descent into the valley of Pa Ta Ch'u, the "Eight Great Palaces," so called from the eight temples situated one below the other in a cleft between two hills.

The highest, Pao Chu Tung, "Temple of the Pearl Grotto," is remarkable for the magnificent panorama from its terrace and for the handsome granite slab inscribed with the usual poem by Ch'ien Lung and translated by the veteran sinologue and missionary, Dr. Martin, who rented this retreat for many years. Certainly Ch'ien Lung, who wrote more than 30,000 pieces of verse during his long reign, never had a better inspiration for his Muse than when he inscribed here:

"Beneath my feet my realm I see,
As in a map unrolled;
Above my head a canopy,
Bedecked with clouds of gold."

The temple takes its name from a grotto which used to be a favourite place of pilgrimage. Its fame is due to a certain monk who lived in this cavern, dark even at brightest noon, and made himself such a reputation for holiness through forty years of prayer and fasting that K'ang Hsi summoned him to Court to reward him with a purple robe and a poetic inscription: "Even the pigeons on the roofs are converted to the true doctrine (by his example), and even the fish beneath the flowers that overhang the spring are obedient to the Word of the Law."[237]

The oldest of the group of shrines are Hsiang Chieh Ssu (8th century a.d.), Lung Wang T'ang and San Shan An, dating from the Sung dynasty, the last believed to be haunted. The handsomest is Ling Kuang Ssu, "Temple of the Miraculous Light," constructed by the Chins (1162) on the site of a still older temple. The Mings made the usual repairs in their unceasing efforts to keep alight the ancient sense of loyalty to the gods. They had moreover special associations with this valley, since one of their princesses, Tsui Wei, was buried in Ling Kuang Ssu and the hill above named after her—"Tsui Wei Shan." Her tomb has disappeared; likewise the fine white pagoda, a striking landmark of the countryside and the pride of Ling Kuang Ssu, destroyed by the Indian troops after 1900 to punish the priests for harbouring Boxers.

At the foot of the hill is Ch'ang An Ssu, a Ming monastery, historically unremarkable, yet singularly picturesque. The little graveyard attached, where the former abbots lie, is a leafy concert room of insect musicians. A Buddha sits there upon his stone lotus pedestal, half hidden in the long grass, just as he did in the days of Yung Lo. His meditative gaze slants down between half-closed eyelids upon the little railway station (Huang Ts'un) not far away, and he smiles the smile of one who has received an injury not to be resented. Dust and scurf have distorted his features. We are sorry and try to scrape the dirt away from the little symbolic protuberance on his forehead, remembering the ancient text of the "Lotus of the Good Law":

"There issued a ray of light from the circle of hair between the brows of the Lord. It extended over eighteen hundred thousand Buddha fields, so that all those fields appeared wholly illuminated by its radiance, down to the great hell Aviki, and up to the limit of existence. And all the beings in all the six states of existence became visible—all without exception. Even the Lord Buddhas in those Buddha fields who had reached final Nirvana, all became visible."

---

[237] *Visite aux temples de Pekin*, Politique de Pekin, 1921.

Juliet Bredon

Twice daily the trains pass by, nearly shaking him off his pedestal, monsters "without eyes or ears" that roar like storm-breathing dragons, and make the earth quake. Thus the West has burst into the Buddhist peace. Yet the Buddha, All Knowing, knows regret is vain. Therefore he smiles.

Pi Mo Yen, the "Goblin Cliff," another Boxer stronghold, which escaped punishment lightly, lies on the further side of the valley, a little apart from the other monasteries —apart in conception, too, for it resembles an old fortress, rather than a temple, with caves and rock chapels chiselled from the cliffs. The hill on which it stands, the Lu Chin Shan, takes its name from Lu, a celebrated monk of the Sui Dynasty (about the end of the 6th century a.d.). This monk founded a monastery (since ruined) near by, famous under the T'angs and Chins, but he came often to Pi Mo Yen. One day he met there two little boys who served him diligently. It happened to be a season of great drought and while the monk prayed for rain on behalf of the people, the children offered to answer his prayer. Whereupon to his amazement they both jumped down a well and became dragons, while the skies opened and moisture descended on the thirsty land. For this service they were promoted in the Ming Dynasty to the rank of princes and a small altar erected to them close to the well, above which weeping willows droop. The fluff from the trees falls like snowflakes in early spring. Souls are compared to this willow fluff and believed to float upon the earth's surface as the fluff upon water, whence, being nourished, they rise again to make obeisance to the Lord of Heaven. This pretty myth is a popular explanation of the food and drink offered to the spirits of the dead at the graveside, the chief rite of ancestral worship.

The altars of the Pa Ta Ch'u Temples, built so long ago and at the height of their glory when the Wars of the Roses raged in England, are still maintained and Chinese pilgrims visit them yearly. Sitting on a bench in some dim corner of a shrine to admire a beautiful Buddha or a holy picture, the sensibilities of the westerner may be shocked by the slovenly indifference of a priest whose duty it is to prepare for a service. But a ruder violation, not only of religious but of aesthetic feelings, follows the sight of worshippers casually spitting on the temple floor. This disgusting habit is one of the plagues of China and few peasants seem able to abstain from it for more than a few minutes together. It signifies no idea of disrespect, or diminution of devoutness, however, but is just a custom regarded as perfectly ordinary and permissible.

Even if one lingers long in "The Eight Great Palaces," take time and follow round the base of the hill that encloses the valley on the west, and visit little Fa Hai Ssu nestling between the folds of two wooded ridges. The chief attraction here is the setting, not the buildings. Dandelions and grasses grow in the crevices of old stone walls; a knotted tree springs from a cleft rock. Trifles, like these—if one dares call them trifles—proclaim Nature an artist willing to aid man in beautifying his ideals, not merely "a colossal ox blindly pulling at the Plough of Life."

In the dim interior of the Temple, guarded by two white pines, are a series of interesting Ming dynasty frescoes, worth seeing, yet difficult to see.

In this quiet shrine where visitors are rare, pigeons roost unmolested in the eaves. Our presence frightens them and they take flight, circling into the sky, now appearing snow white, now soft grey, as they turn to the glittering sunlight or lie in shadow. Mingling with the melodious whirr of wings, we catch a plaintive note, like the sigh of an Aeolian harp, produced by the rush of air through bamboo whistles attached to their tails.[238]

From Fa Hai Ssu, it is but a short distance to the main road which leads back to Peking via the Ping Tse Men. Let us go slowly lest our car startle the peasants and their donkeys laden with vegetables for market. Even so a string of camels takes

---

[238] The Pekingese make these whistles with eleven different notes so that several flocks of birds flying near one another produce almost the effect of a chime. In the city, where pigeons are liable to stray and be caught by the neighbours, a householder lets his flock out for exercise only at certain hours. A red flag is waved as a signal for their return.

Juliet Bredon

fright at the horn and lumbers in confusion on to a wheat field as we stop before Hsien Ying Ssu, a group of buildings near the village of Hsi Huang Ts'un. They constitute all that remains of the best known nunnery in the neighbourhood of Peking, and are conspicuous for the high tower in their midst. In the days of the Mings a nun named Lu resided here, a wise woman and a prophetess who, with tears in her eyes, implored the Emperor Cheng T'ung (Ying Tsung),[239] not to start on his expedition against the Mongols which ended so disastrously. The emperor neglected her warning with the result that he was taken prisoner by his enemies, and only returned to his throne seven years later. He then remembered nun Lu's counsels and bestowed on her the title of the "Emperor's Younger Sister," also honorific titles on the monastery where she lived, died and was buried. When in a.d. 1527 the Emperor Chia Ching issued a decree ordering the closing of all nunneries owing to the immoral practices which prevailed in them he felt he could not make an exception for this establishment, then known as Huang Ku Ssu, or the "Temple of the Imperial Aunt" though its most famous nun had deserved well of the State. But some unknown patrons obtained the assistance of the emperor's mother, to whose entreaties to spare the temple he finally yielded on certain conditions. This feminine appeal was typical of the influences brought to bear by interested persons in order to shield the pleasure resorts which the nunneries had become. Though the sovereigns were too well aware of their disrepute, all the Imperial decrees ordering them to be closed became dead letters, much to the monarch's regret. In spite of such high protection, however, the Temple of the Imperial Aunt gradually fell into ruin, and was only repaired under K'ang Hsi, to sink once more into material and moral decrepitude. Nowadays the nunnery is poverty stricken, reduced in size and in a ruinous condition. There is only an old abbess left, surrounded by some child novices who live on a miserable pittance in the shadow of the high tower which was once a repository for Buddhist books.

---

239 See Chapter X.

Temples of the Western Hills

Another turn of the road and we reach the historic site of the Huang Ling, the group of yellow-tiled buildings (that no longer exist) in which the coffined bodies of the Manchu emperors were placed while the elaborate ceremonial of the funeral was being prepared, and whence they were taken to the Hsi Ling to be interred.[240]

On the little chain of hills above is a golf course with pretty views over the surrounding country. From one side of the ridge we look back towards Pa Ta Ch'u and the Jade Fountain, from the other, towards Pa Pao Shan. This miniature mountain is crowned by a small Buddhist monastery whose beginnings date from the days of the Chin emperors (a.d. 1194), one of whose numerous country seats was here. Though the real name of this hillock is "Shuang Ch'uan Ssu," or "Hill of the Double Spring"—so called from the two springs at its foot—the popular name of Pa Pao Shan is supposed to originate in the eight kinds of earth to be found in it, representing the "Eight Precious (or magic) Qualities" of the hill.

Quite close to Pa Pao Shan, a little to the north-east of it, is the Hu Kuo Ssu, or "Temple Protecting the State." It is well worth visiting for its associations with the famous eunuch Kang Kung (or Kang T'ieh), whose tomb is behind the temple. Kang, who began his career under the first Ming emperor and valiantly assisted the great Yung Lo in his military expeditions, was a redoubtable warrior, always foremost in danger, so much so that he earned the nickname of "T'ieh" (Iron), or "Kang" (Steel); though his real name was Ping. The spear—weighing a hundred catties[241]—which he is supposed so have wielded, but which would defy the strength of any modern soldier, may be seen in the shrine dedicated to him near his tomb, also his portrait painted from life and a series of pictures (dating from T'ung Chih) in which he and his weapon appear nearly as large as the pony that carries them undauntedly to "deeds of derring do."

---

240 A similar structure for those who were buried at the Tung Ling still exists near the north-eastern corner of Peking.
241 One catty equals roughly one and a third pound.

Juliet Bredon

The Hu Kuo Ssu is an interesting specimen of a eunuch's temple, all the monks being eunuchs who chose to settle near the burial place of their mighty patron. Unlike so many monasteries, it is prosperous, owing to the wealth, perhaps ill-gotten in many cases, of its owners. It enjoyed Imperial favour and distinction to the last days of the Manchu dynasty, and is still kept in good repair, boasting well tilled fields and well filled granaries and stables. Rows of horses and mules stand in the courtyards filling the air with their warm and friendly scent, and labourers are busy threshing millet with a hand-flail, or setting out golden maize to dry in shallow baskets.

A little further on, the handsome red walls and gateway of a temple to Kuan Ti in good repair attract our notice. Beside them, but hidden from view by a lofty curtain of trees, lies a cemetery where many of the eunuchs who served the Ch'ing and even the Ming dynasty are buried.[242] Most of the monuments are identical in form; those of the better class elaborately carved and boasting a set of stone sacrificial vessels standing before their grave mounds. One tomb in a separate enclosure is of a prince and, as a matter of history, it was a prince among his kind who erected it for his last resting place. Here lies the notorious Li Lien-ying[243] who for forty years played a leading part in the Government of China, made and unmade the highest officials of the Empire, and levied rich tribute on the eighteen provinces. The redeeming feature of his character was his unswerving devotion to his Imperial Mistress, the Empress Dowager T'zu Hsi. When she died, his proud spirit broke, nor did he long outlive her, dying himself in 1911 at the age of sixty-nine.

The thirteen storied pagoda of Pa Li Chuang, the largest in the neighbourhood of Peking, casts its shadow near his grave—

---

242 It is unusual in China to find men of different names and clans buried in one graveyard. But eunuchs and priests who have "left the family" (the same euphemistic term is applied to both classes) arc exceptions to the rule.
243 Better known by his nickname of "Cobbler's Wax Li" (P'i Hsiao Li). He was so-called because, before becoming a eunuch at the age of sixteen, he was apprenticed to a cobbler at his native place, Ho Chien Fu in Chihli, from which district most of the eunuchs came.

an auspicious portent. Though the primary object of such pagodas was a repository for relics of the Buddha, many Chinese now consider them as regulators of *feng shui,* or the "influences of wind and water," and they are supposed to bring prosperity to the cities and temples and peace to the tombs that lie within their shadow.

Within the last half century Pa Li Chuang has gone to ruin, and the golden image of the Kuan Yin piously enshrined there by one of the Ming empresses, who built the graceful spire (in the 16th century) and left an inscription of her own composition recording the fact, is no longer on the altar. As worshippers decreased and with them the income of the adjacent monastery, the priests sold their few remaining treasures including the carved woodwork of the temple, bought for fuel by the neighbours. Finding even these sacrifices insufficient to keep themselves alive, the monks in collusion with two obliging villagers, paid a peddler to spread the news that one of the seated Buddhas on the twelfth story of the tower descended from his niche each evening to bless the countryside. Now those who heard of the miracle promptly flocked to the temple, poured offerings into the empty coffers and begged favours of the wonder-working image. Merchants prayed that heavy taxes be abolished, farmers begged for good harvests, girls for rich husbands, mothers for many sons. Strange to say not only the poor and ignorant made the pilgrimage. Rich people arrived in their own limousines dressed fashionably in silks and satins. Venerable old men, bobbed-haired flappers and ragged coolies worshipped side by side, seeking to have their hearts' desires granted, while among the huge crowd of all ages and classes that came to pray for riches in this world and salvation in the world to come, a street vendor offered opera glasses for hire for a few cents in order that the faithful might have a closer view of the miraculous statue.

Unfortunately just as the monks were congratulating themselves on their clever scheme for raising funds, the police arrived on the scene, arrested the conspirators, accused them of deliberately duping the people and unmasked a hoax as simple as ingenious. They had replaced the seated figure of a Buddha in what appeared to be an inaccessible niche high up on the tower, by a standing one, and popular credulity, assisted by good publicity, had done the rest. Alas, the priests paid for their miracle by a term in gaol and now the pagoda of Pa Li Chuang stands desolate and deserted.

Beyond Pa Li Chuang, and about a mile from the P'ing Tse Men, is the temple of Tzu Hui Ssu, popularly known as the Tao Ying Miao, or "Temple of the Inverted Shadow," because there is a hole in the gateway behind the main hall, through which, if light be admitted, objects cast their shadows upside down. This temple was erected in the Wan Li reign of the Ming dynasty by a eunuch— like most of the other temples in the neighbourhood. The walls of the monastery, originally founded for the purpose of distributing tea gratis to the poor, are of irregular stones representing a "tiger's skin," and once enclosed a "stupa," called the Chih Chu T'a, or "Spider Pagoda." An inscription upon it said that its builder, a man of contemplative disposition, used to spend his time studying the "Sutras" with a monk. One morning, in the seventh moon of the year a.d. iooi, as they began to read the "Diamond Sutra" together, a spider climbed on to the altar, faced the image of the god, and made a low bow. When chased away the little creature returned, and when asked if he had come to listen to the Sacred Words, he nodded in assent and remained on the altar. After the reading of the "Sutra" was finished, the spider shed his mortal envelope at the feet of the Buddha and became transfigured, whereupon the holy insect's body was devoutly buried by the monks in a casket over which the pagoda was erected.

Near this temple the city comes out to meet the country. The quiet road turns into a suburban street, an odd confusion of shops and shrines with dark blue draperies made beautiful and mysterious with Chinese ideographs. Children and dogs and chickens dispute our right of way at every step. Bare-limbed peasants, deeply tanned by sun and wind, carry their produce into town, and carters, peddlers and camel caravans block the gate, drawn to the city by the magnet of buying and selling.

Temples of the Western Hills

In the days, not so long ago either, when city gates were closed soon after sundown, it was a fascinating sight for anyone returning late from a country excursion, to watch the scramble of the crowd not to be shut in or out. Then the narrow entrance was a whirlpool of traffic, heavily laden carts, sedan chairs, camel trains, coolies carrying loads, and pedestrians.

Just before dark, half the gate was closed and most of the congestion relieved—only a belated cart, rider, or pedestrian passing now and then with hurried step to enter or leave before the other half of the wooden door was firmly bolted. "When this was done the keys were sent into the Imperial City and latecomers had to spend the night in a miserable inn under the walls, or, if they happened to be without ponies or impedimenta, they might strike a bargain with the man on the ramparts and be pulled up in a basket (after the fashion of St. Paul) and let down the other side at the cost of a dollar for the illegal transaction."

This must be completed without attracting attention from the guards. Fortunately for the tardy, these gentry retired at closing time into their guard houses (on either side of the gate) for a little gamble behind the stands holding sets of old fashioned weapons. The shape of some of these should have been, one would think, sufficiently awe-inspiring to instil a holy fear into the heart of the intending wrong-doer but did not, alas, always do so, as the heads of decapitated criminals were often hung from the gate tower. The crowds of carts and donkeys of the nineties are to-day rapidly being supplanted by motor cars and rickshas, and some of the city gates are open all night long.[244]

---

244 The first attempt to introduce rickshas made about this time was frustrated by the carters' guild who "threw the horrid foreign things, which degraded man to the level of animals, into the Canal."

Juliet Bredon

XVI. Temples of the Western Hills— (Concluded)

The railway that runs to Men T'ou Kou where the coal mines lie[245] is useful to take travellers part-way to another group of temples in the Western Hills. Five miles beyond Huang Ts'un (the station for Pa Ta Ch'u) stands an isolated hill—the Shih Ching Shan, with Buddhists scriptures carved on its cliffs. Trains will stop by arrangement at the base, whence the ascent must be made on foot up a rocky path, between boulders glowing with fiery undertones of red and gold. Hedgehogs hide under the stones. Grass-hoppers, the colour of parched leaves, whirr away from our shadows as we climb. A beetle whizzes by, unfolding wings as blue as if a bit of the sky had been torn off and made more luminous by polishing.

From below, the temple might be some old Italian fortress, might be Licenza itself. This impression increases as we scramble under broken towers, or explore caves cut out of solid rock and gloomy passages suggestive of romantic adventures. Such indeed were common here when this temple-fortress was built in the 16th century. Under the Ming Emperor Cheng Teh (1506-1522) Liu Chin, the chief eunuch and an adopted son of the empress dowager, prompted by an avarice equal to Shylock's and an overmastering ambition surpassing even Wolsey's, formed a cabal among his fellow eunuchs with the object of obtaining supreme power. Part of his scheme included cutting through the Pei Liang barrier of the Hun river whose waters should then flood the capital. At the same time he built the fortress of Shih Ching Shan as a base from which to strike and a last refuge if the worst happened. The plot failed owing to

---

245 The Western Hills and further mountains to the south-west contain valuable coal deposits which Marco Polo refers to as "combustible black stone." But although great geologists like Pumpelly and Richtofen examined and reported upon their richness fifty years ago, the Chinese still work some of the mines with primitive tools, dragging the coal to the surface in basket-sleds fastened to the necks of the native miners who creep on all fours along a narrow run-way near the edge of the veins.

Temples of the Western Hills-(concluded)

a quarrel among the eunuchs, and Liu Chin retreated to Shih Ching Shan where he had hidden a quantity of arms, recently unearthed. Under the mountain many of his faithful adherents were ultimately buried. A walled passage may still be seen in the side of the hill, and legend says that it leads to a subterranean waterway where a marble boat is supposed to float, carrying the ghostly crew of the dead rebels. Whenever a mortal penetrates into the cave, the phantom junk sinks beneath the waters, and whoever looks upon it is immediately stricken dead.

The fortress is now a quaint mediaeval ruin, but the little temple at the top of the hill is better preserved, Its situation is very picturesque, the walls rising from the edge of a steep precipice round which the Hun river circles. From the platform of the "dagoba," said to have been built by Liu Chin's order, we get an incomparable view up a valley enfolded by the blue arms' of the mountains.

Nearly due north of Shih Ching Shan (about four miles distant) is the princely tomb of Lung En Ssu. which once had carved marble gates and the finest avenue of white pines in the vicinity of Peking.[246] They are noble trees, having the strength of a giant and a giant's height, and their crests shiver in the wind like the plumed helmets of warriors marching in triumph. The tomb itself stands on the site of a monastery built by a princess of the Chin dynasty and is the last resting place of one of the great nobles who served the first Manchu emperor. The property of the former Imperial family, this fine sepulchre has lately been sadly despoiled.

Lung En Ssu is only about a mile from the station of San Chia Tien also convenient as a starting point for T'ien T'ai Shan, known among foreigners as the "Mummy Temple"—an easy walk of rather more than an hour. According to a widespread popular legend, "supported by what appears at first sight to be an imposing array of corroborative evidence," the

---

[246] This species of pine (Pinus bungeana) is a native of North China where its immense size and white bark make it the ornament of tombs and temples. See *Chinese Forest Trees and Timber Supply,* by Norman Shaw.

first Manchu Emperor, Shun Chih, did not die in a.d. 1661 as the annals record, but arranged with his ministers to vacate the throne and conceal his identity as the abbot of T'ien T'ai Shan. His decision was supposed to be due to grief at the loss of his favourite wife, the Lady Tung— grief which the native chroniclers of the day naively remark "appears to be genuine, whereby he is greatly distinguished among Imperial husbands who usually rejoice at the death of their consorts." Tung Kuei-fei seems to have been "as good as she was beautiful, and well worthy of an emperor's love. Her brave attempts to control her own grief and to console the emperor when their infant son died, her chivalrous intercession for the empress who had incurred the Imperial displeasure for a grave breach of etiquette, her untiring, and unselfish activity on behalf of those who were her inferiors in rank—all go far to explain why she was loved not only by the sovereign, but also by his mother and by the ladies of the Court." That a gentle and spiritually-minded sovereign should weary of statecraft and long for the tranquil life of a monk, especially when the death of Tung Kuei-fei had destroyed the strongest of the bonds that kept him in touch with the world, is not strange. But Johnston,[247] after a thorough and scholarly examination of the evidence, effectually disproves the pretty story characterised by so much pathos and romance.

Certainly a mummy, or a figure which the priests declare to be a mummy, exists in T'ien T'ai Shan. It differs from the ordinary mummies of Buddhist monks in that it is clad in Imperial yellow robes instead of the usual red "Kachaya" vestments. The "*kang*," or earthenware jar in which this mummy was dried may be seen at any time, and the stone "dagoba" covering a statue of the same figure is still opened once a year for the benefit of the faithful—proof that if the original man so honoured was not indeed the Emperor Shun Chih, he was nevertheless a person of some importance. Johnston identifies him provisionally with a certain lunatic saint who made himself a retreat on this barren T'ien T'ai hill,

---

[247] "The Romance of an Emperor," *New China Review*, 1920.

Temples of the Western Hills—(concluded)

whence his fame soon spread in all directions, owing to the fact that the prayers of those who made supplication to him were promptly answered. "After his death in 1710 it seems likely that his disciples, as often happened in such cases, embalmed his body and set it up in a shrine-that representations regarding the holy man's exceptional merits were made through the proper authorities to the Imperial Court, and that the Emperor Ch'ien Lung, in accordance with numerous precedents, conferred on him a title, 'The Demon-King Monk.'"

In the mountains across the Hun river beyond Men T'ou Kou, lie the two famous temples of Chieh T'ai Ssu and T'an Cheri Ssu, the latter the richest and one of the strictest monasteries near the capital—a very select and exclusive foundation.

The site of Chieh T'ai Ssu, "Monastery of the Ordaining Terrace," is popularly supposed to have been given by Ch'in. Shih Huang Ti to a holy teacher who planned the temple in the 3rd century b.c. It is romantically cradled in a wooded ravine. Leaving Men T'ou Kou we climb gently for two hours, at first among little garden-like farms near the river bed and later up a long stone road, polished by countless feet of men and laden beasts. Fields furrowed in fine streaks spread out from the base of the hills like the ribs of an open fan, tiny thatched hamlets appear trim and tidy from a distance and changing cloud-shapes cast shadows at our feet. How good to breathe this pure air after the dust of the city, how delicious the odours of green things growing out of soft earth, out of hard rock—the smells of strange saps, the queer spicy scents of mould, the perfume of wild begonias that look like pink and white butterflies!

The monastery stands on a high terrace and dates from the T'ang dynasty (7th century a.d.). Under the Liaos it was the residence of the famous monk Fa Chun, who is buried beneath the pagoda (erected a.d. 1075) which may be seen on the right of the entrance to the cloister. Restored from complete ruin by the Mings, Chieh T'ai Ssu is connected with this dynasty by a strange legend.[248] In the reign of the Emperor Ch'eng Hua, the

---

248 See *Environs de Pekin*, G. Bouillard.

saintly abbot Tao Fu obtained miraculous power from the Pussa Wei T'o, warrior-protector of Buddhism. His alms-bowl was carried by magic every day from the temple to the Palace, where it was filled with precious offerings by the Empress Dowager Li, and then returned to its owner. Now one day, when the bowl made its appearance very early in the morning and the Empress was still in bed, Her Majesty jokingly asked it: "Why so early? Is it 500 girls you want now for the 500 monks of the monastery?" At these irreverent words the bowl disappeared and never returned. Fearing the wrath of the Pussa, the Empress inquired from the abbot how she could atone for her sin. Tao Fu answered that there was no way but to carry out her suggestion and send the 500 girls. These were selected accordingly and given lodgings in the little village of Shih Fo near the temple. Their presence, however, proved to be too much of a temptation for the hermits, all of whom ended by succumbing to their charms. Great was the scandal which resulted from this breach of vows, and the abbot was forced to apply the monastic law in all its severity and condemn the 500 monks and their lady-loves to be burned. The execution is supposed to have actually taken place before innumerable crowds, but lo! scarcely had the flames touched the culprits than an invisible force carried them towards heaven, each one embracing his mate. The Pussa had not only forgiven but included the erring monks in the ranks of the Lohans. The Five Hundred Lohans enshrined in one of the temple halls are supposed to represent these servants of Buddha so miraculously saved. A replica of Tao Fu's bowl and the bed of the Empress Li, now used as an altar, may still be seen in the monastery, and a contemporary stela commemorates the details of Tao Fu's life; his tomb is under a pagoda beyond and to the south of Chieh T'ai Ssu.

The monastery buildings were a favourite resort of Ch'ien Lung who left behind him many inscriptions on stone recording his impressions and no less handsome gifts recording his piety—gifts which have enabled the establishment to retain much of its ancient prosperity. As a centre of Buddhist faith

Temples of the Western Hills—(concluded)

and learning, the monastery likewise keeps its importance, standing second only to T'an Cheh Ssu. More than a hundred monks still attend the daily services and, every sixth day of the sixth month, visiting priests arrive to "*liang ching*"—"spread out the classics, to air." The precious manuscripts are kept in a special storehouse, and in case of fire the immediate removal of its contents would be the first duty of the inmates.

While we visit this storehouse, the library, and the hall of assembly, our "boy" tells us the story of a curious ceremony about which the priests seldom speak. This is the "Descent of the Lotus," reminiscent of the "Descent of the Holy Flames" in Jerusalem. A perfect specimen of the summer flower, white and pure, comes down in mid-winter among the monks who have prepared by eighteen hours of prayer and fasting to receive the holy sign. Though it is difficult for us to accept the supernatural theory of this appearance, it is not easy to find a more plausible one to take its place. The abbot, evidently a sincere and honourable man, declares that each devotee is carefully searched before he enters the temple. We can see for ourselves the impossibility of a trap-door in the now empty hall, while a glance is sufficient to make sure no conjuring apparatus could be attached to the ceiling or bare walls. Moreover, during the long hours of waiting no one is permitted to leave the building, not even if he grows faint or ill from exhaustion. But supposing someone should smuggle the lotus into the temple in collusion with confederates outside? That might be possible. Yet, were such the case, how could the flower remain perfectly fresh and uncrushed for nearly eighteen hours? Evidently faith must still have power to work miracles.

Last of all we are taken to the Hall of the Chieh T'ai, or Ordaining Platform, where young postulants make their vows. We have timed our visit to see this service. While waiting for the ceremony to begin, we linger on the terrace with its curious, twisted white pines, one leaning close to the ground, another, called "The Nest of the Phoenix," spreading over the balustrade like a green train. The breath of the hot day, the warm sigh of the dust-laden wind, dies out of the air. The sun goes down and

Juliet Bredon

amethyst light stretches over the spot where the flame vanished. Night comes quickly across the plain as though Buddha is-drawing a veil over his beloved world. Above, the sky is a dark velvet pall and yonder eastward, like the impress of a large finger nail in the blue, rises the new moon. It is the signal for the priests to enter the hall. They fall upon their kness and remain motionless like figures carved from wood. Since dawn no food has touched their lips, no sip of water moistened their tongues. So command the rules, to teach abstinence and hunger-bearing, to nurture self-control by fasting through the scorching hours, without complaint, but only prayers of thankfulness to the Merciful One.

At midnight an acolyte rises from his place and approaches the drum—a huge thing with a mighty power of utterance. "He taps the ancient face and it sobs like waves upon a pebbly breach. He taps it again with a curious monotonous rhythm and it moans like the wind in a forest of pines. Again it roars, again it sobs, alternately crashing like thunder rolling over an abyss, or whispering like throbbing heart-beats." The young monk tilts back his head in ecstasy as if his spirit yielded to the intoxication of the sound. Moving, undulating in waves, the noise has something weird in it, something hypnotic. It ceases suddenly, and the priests bow down in a silence that is frightening after so much clamour. Then again the sound begins, mysterious, oppressive. In the velvety darkness the temple forms are eerie. And suddenly a singular sensation comes over us, a sensation of dream and doubt, as if the roofs and the purple curtain of the sky pricked with stars, and the dragon-swarming eaves, must all vanish presently. These strange peaked gables and Chinese grotesqueries of carving seem too unreal to last, until the drumbeats, regular as a human pulse, finally cease and the "romance of reality" returns.

Now the dawn wind touches the cheek softly like the fingers of a tender woman. The melancholy but melodious sound of Buddhist chants and prayers ends. The service—very solemn and sacramental—is over and the celebrants troop out of the hall to break their fast. A light of exaltation lingers on their faces. We slip away without disturbing them though the abbot has sent a message that he will come to bid us farewell. But judging from his tired eyes, the old man needs rest, so begging him not to trouble himself about us, we start off for the mountain hermitage of Chi Leh Feng Ssu built under the Liao dynasty. We are warned there is nothing to see but the same view down the valley. Still, it is called the "Peak of Perfect Happiness" and every human being should climb that at least once in his life. The founder of Chi Leh Feng Ssu is supposed to have been the man who made the two stone lions that guard Chieh T'ai Ssu. After having completed his work he became a monk and retired to this mountain-peak where he kept a vow of silence for ten years, victoriously overcoming temptations described as similar to those of St. Anthony.

From Chieh T'ai Ssu we decide to walk across the mountains, about three hours hard going up a long winding mountain valley, to T'an Cheh Ssu ("Monastery of the Oak Pool").

On the arch at the outer gate are tablets with the poetical inscriptions: "Purple Hills and Red Springs," "Fragrant Groves and Clean Earth" put up by K'ang Hsi who repaired the temple magnificently. But T'an Cheh Ssu is much older than his reign. The records affirm that it dates from a.d. 400. Very probably they are trustworthy in thus fixing it as the most ancient temple in the Western Hills, because the well-known proverb says "First there was T'an Cheh and afterwards there was Yu Chou" (an old name for Peking). The second character in the name of the monastery, "*cheh*" means a kind of oak used for feeding silkworms. Legend says that in remote antiquity there used to be a pond surrounded by a thousand "*cheh*" on the site of the temple, and here lived two dragons. When the temple was built, the water disappeared and the dragons turned into serpents called "*Ta Ch'ing*" and "*Hsiao Ch'ing*," hence the saying: "The dragon has gone but its sons remain, of a black colour, as large as a bowl."

These serpents dwelt in a red lacquer box with an inscription on the lid: "Kings of Dragons, Guardians of the

Law," but they had complete freedom, climbing upon the altars to rest among the incense burners, leaving the monastery at will and returning to it at the sound of the evening bells. Being the incarnation of the Spirit of the Universe, they had power to alter their form and size at will—a power they manifested when the Emperor Ch'ien Lung, on a visit to T'an Cheh Ssu, expressed doubt concerning their supernatural attributes. No sooner were the irreverent words out of his mouth, than he saw to his amazement the smaller serpent rise in wrath and begin to grow. The tail remained on the altar but the unfolding coils of the body rolled out of the gateway, down the valley and across the hill, while the head pointed towards the Summer Palace. Alarmed, the emperor ordered a service to implore the dragon's pardon according to the rite for the placation of spirits embodied in serpents. After long prayers the serpent began to shrink and finally resumed his normal size. Then, in recognition of their intervention, the emperor ordered the distribution of money to the monks. So numerous was the community in those times that, though the sovereign gave a coin to every one who presented himself, between dawn and dusk on the appointed day, by nightfall the end of the procession of those waiting for alms was not in sight.

The small serpent may still be seen, but visitors are warned to approach him deferentially lest evil befall them.

We also visit, to the west of the temple, the Hall of the Dragon King and a sacred pool[249] of limpid water. Then we tour the spacious grounds, beautifully wooded and immaculately kept. The old "*cheh*" trees have all perished; only a few stumps remain. But there are three famous "ginko" trees[250] of miraculous growth. One sprang full grown' into being, according to the monks, when K'ang Hsi visited the'temple; two during Ch'ien Lung's stay. Others are pointed out as having

---

[249] The dragon is generally associated with water, being, with its congener the snake, an object of frequent worship in time of drought or flood.
[250] The "ginko," (or *Salisburia adiantifolia*) commonly known as the "maidenhair tree," is the most interesting tree in China if not in the world, for it represents the sole surviving link between trees and ferns.

Temples of the Western Hills—(concluded)

been planted by the deposed Emperor Hsuan T'ung and by Yuan Shih-k'ai.

The temple itself is composed of many halls, at least ten large ones—to each of which K'ang Hsi presented an inscription. That dedicated to Kuan Yin contains a picture of the Princess Miao Yen, daughter of Kublai Khan. Weary of the life of Courts she shaved her head and became a nun here, worshipping Kuan Yin day and night with such fervour that the marks of her forehead and her feet may be traced on the flagstone where she devoutly "k'o-towed." During the reign of Wan Li (1573-1620) the Empress Hsiao Ting came to see this and other relics of the temple. She had them packed in a box of precious wood and taken to the Forbidden City but they were later sent back to the monastery. In gratitude for their return, the abbot ordered figures of Kublai Khan and all his family carved and set up in the shrine where his daughter served.

Many sovereigns and famous men have been patrons of T'an Cheh Ssu, leaving behind them proofs of their generosity and their faith. The monument with five "dagobas" (the T'a Yuan) is the gift of some forgotten benefactor in a.d. 600. The pagoda of Yen Shou T'a, or "Great Longevity," a structure over fifty feet high, was erected by Chang Yung, a prince of the Ming dynasty. Tablets dating from the Chins and Yuans and frescoes of the Liao period once embellished the temple, but these have all disappeared. The priests, however, kindly offer to show us a copy of the "*Hsin Ching*" ("Heart Classic") written by K'ang Hsi, together with an essay on the scene and a picture of the landscape, composed and sketched during his stay.

To us the most striking feature of the monastery, rarer even than its treasures, is the devout faith of the monks who.not only hold regular services but appear to lead saintly lives according to their lights. Perhaps their piety and scrupulous observance of their ceremonies is due to the influence of a large community which makes some rule and order necessary, and stimulates its members to activity lest they lose face before one another—an incentive that lonely priests do not have. But no doubt it is also partly due to the fact that the temple is richly dowered and must set an example to its lay patrons. For T'an Cheh Ssu, like Chieh T'ai Ssu, still enjoys the support of rich men and the favour of the princely family of Kung.

While we were there, members of this noble house occupied the spacious guest pavilions that originally formed part of the Emperor K'ang Hsi's "travelling palace." Somebody of the clan was dead and relatives had come to ask masses for his soul. The big bell tolled for the memorial service slowly and regularly; its rich bronze voice echoed over the roofs above the Altar of Infinite Compassion and broke in deep waves of sound against the green circle of the hills.

It is a touching service. It is also a costly ceremony, for many priests take part, chanting and beating wooden fish-head drums to mark the time. And the chant is a magnificent invocation to Kuan Yin.

"O Thou! whose eyes are clear, whose eyes are kind, whose eyes are full of pity and sweetness—O Thou Lovely One with Thy beautiful face, with Thy beautiful eyes:

O Thou Pure One, whose luminosity is without spot, whose knowledge is without shadow—O Thou! forever shining like that Sun whose glory no power may repel —O Thou, sunlike in the course of Thy Mercy, vouchsafe augustly to welcome this Soul."

Before the altar a hundred tapers bow gravely, and incense curls up from handsome braziers that stand beside offerings of fruits and cakes and rice and flowers. On either side of this altar the priests kneel in ranks facing each other—rows of polished heads and splendid brocade vestments. The chanting goes on for hours. Then it suddenly stops. There is perfect silence for a moment followed by a burst of weeping. But this sound of sobs is quickly overwhelmed in one final booming of the fish-head drums, as the high-pitched voices of the chant leaders begin the grand concluding "Sutra of Nirvana," the song of the passage triumphant over the Sea of Birth and Death, while the surging basses repeat the sonorous words: "Transient

Temples of the Western Hills-(concluded)

are all. They, being born, must die. And being born, are dead. And being dead, are glad to be at rest."[251]

Until faith or love shall awaken them again, "they, being dead, are glad to be at rest." Such was our last— and loveliest—memory of T'an Cheh Ssu.

Some distance beyond this monastery is Liang Hsien, an ancient city from which rare visitors make excursions to the ruined tombs of the Chin emperors. Destroyed by the Mings in a petty vengeance against vanquished enemies, they were restored at great expense by K'ang Hsi, because they belonged to men of his own race who once sat on the throne he himself occupied. Permission to worship at the graves was also given by him to their direct descendants. Once during his devotions, a youthful scion of the ancient royal house was startled by a tiger watching him. "Do not fear," said the beast, "though you may not be aware of it, I am deputed to guard these sepulchres. Therefore do not attempt to harm me, and I will continue to protect you and your forefathers." The young man then "k'o-towed" to the sacred animal, and gave orders to his retainers that it should never be molested.[252]

Eleven miles from Liang Hsien a short railway branches off from Liu Li Ho (on the Peking-Hankow line), whence one may make a start for the grottoes of Yuan Shui Tung beyong Shang Fang Shan. This is a long and difficult trip requiring all the usual paraphernalia for a journey into the interior, such as beds, food for several days, etc., and, in addition, a plentiful supply of lamps and candles to explore the caverns. Carts can be used from Liu Ho as far as Hsi Yu Ssu (a fine temple dating from the 6th century a.d.), but from Hsi Yu Ssu to Shang Fang Shan is hard walking. Nevertheless the excursion is its own reward. The stalactites and stalagmites of the caves are

---

251 *Glimpses of Unfamiliar Japan*, by Lafcadio Hearn.
252 The idea of a tiger guarding graves is widespread. A certain mythical animal supposed to prowl around them with intent to eat the brains of. the dead, fears but two foes: tigers and pine trees. Hence the common custom of planting at least one pine tree near an important grave, and the less frequent representation of a stone tiger where his living prototype would not be practical or popular.

magnificent, and the floor of the largest vault reminds one of dragons writhing and twisting towards what looks like, a gigantic Buddha's throne.

There are, besides, several pleasant trips up the valley of the Hun river, notably one to a certain Niang Niang Miao about three hours distant from San Chia Tien.[253] But the best known is undoubtedly that to the Miao Feng Shan, perhaps the most beautiful excursion in the Western Hills. This may be made by any one of five different mountain tracks all through rough country. The easiest way is via San Chia Tien, but only the best and most enduring walkers should attempt even this route on foot.[254]

The road mounts slowly at first, following the river and crossing and re-crossing the beds of tributary streams that become raging torrents in the rainy season. At other times they are simply heaps of dry stones with here and there shallow pools where the subsoil prevents the water from trickling away. These serve as washing places for the country women.

We pass through the hamlet of T'ao Yuan full of so many doll-like babies, with careless noses and flies around their eyes, that one is staggered at the thought of so much birth and begetting. Here also we run a gauntlet of beggars lying in wait for pilgrims. Each has staked a claim of a few dozen yards along the path that climbs, winding and stumbling and twisting, to 2,500 feet above sea level. For two hours and more, the hills to right and left alternately recede and approach. Their blue shapes glide toward us, change to green on nearer view, and slowly drifting past, turn blue again, showing deep pockets of shadow in their shining sides. Then gradually the

---

[253] Niang Niang Pusa, or Holy Mother, is a Taoist deity which vaguely corresponds in some of her attributes to the Buddhist Kuan Yin. Hundreds of shrines are dedicated to her.

[254] Chairs, moderately comfortable, can be procured if due notice is given. But except for steep mountain paths where a chair is the only mode of conveyance, the little grey donkey is universally used for transport in the hills. He has the advantage of being procurable in almost every village at a reasonable hire; is tireless, willing and sure-footed, carrying his rider over stony roads impracticable for ponies, at a steady pace of four miles an hour.

Temples of the Western Hills—(concluded)

whole scene alters. Out of the east a white mist comes rolling up engulfing everything. The distant mountains grow dim, blur to faint outlines and vanish. We are isolated completely in a pale, damp nothingness—a queer sensation and rare in these Western Hills.

Only a few moments it lasts. Then the cold, white roof dissolves slowly as the mist splits and breaks. A gleam of light above us and new peaks are born, playing hide and seek with flying rags of cloud. A ray of sunshine and whole hillsides "are recovered from eternity." For it is the sun that is the key to this country, to its failings and its charms and without the brilliant golden radiance to which one grows accustomed in North China, one feels cheated of what one comes to look upon as a right.

We drop down a little to Chien K'ou, a picturesque village in a valley gay with flowering fruit trees, and immediately ahead towers our goal, a huge dark rock tipped with the monastery of Ling Kan Kung, Miao Fêng Shan, the sacred mountain, stands behind it, silhouetted against the deep blue of the sky like a gigantic milestone marking the end of the world. Our track continues its painful way, climbing another thousand feet in zigzags. Then a final flight of rough rock steps leads to the shrine-crowned summit.

We lodge in the temple whose terrace literally overhangs the valley. Spread out at our feet is an uninterrupted view for a hundred miles over all the surrounding country, including the Hun River Valley, Po Hua Shan, the Nankou Pass and distant Peking—a colossal panorama.

To see this landscape at its fullest beauty we must look on it at sunrise, so aptly called the "Hour of Illusion." Oh, the charm of that first vision of the ghostly colours of the dawn, while the faint scent of rose-bushes on the hillside is wafted down! Before the haze of the day rises, the river shines like a gilded spider's thread, while the villages, still in shadow, are grey dust clinging to the grey-blue valleys and the city is a mere pin-point in the tinted dream of mountain and plain. Much enchantment passes when the sun shoots above the horizon like a golden discus. In the raw clear light we lose the jasper palaces and sails of silver but see only flimsy sheds of mud and thatch and the unpainted queerness of ferry barges. "So perhaps it is with all that makes life beautiful in any land. To, view men or nature with delight, we must see them through illusions, subjective or objective. Happiest he who from birth to death sees ever through some ideal soul haze, which, like the vapours of the dawn, glorifies common things."

None of the temples on Miao Feng Shan have any artistic merit. But they house three Taoist female deities, one of whom confers children on the childless, and they are very sacred. From the 1st to the 18th of the fourth month, when thousands of pilgrims visit them,[255] Chinese women desirous of a son will make the ascent on their knees, prostrating themselves every few yards, to pray before the goddess. Having done this they are confident that their desire will be rewarded.

Returning by way of Ta Chueh Ssu or "Monastery of the Great Awakening," down the slippery stone road paved with huge, flat cobbles from the mountain stream beds, we meet these pilgrims singly or in groups, with flags and drums and bells. We pass again through Chien K'ou, gay now with peddlers and food-vendors, and climb the Yang Shan 3,000 feet high. Thence the descent is terrifyingly steep, skirting the edge of sheer cliffs. The sensation of being carried down in chairs backwards, according to custom, is decidedly unpleasant. A bad slip would mean a fall over the precipice, with little chance of recovery. But we soon find that the chair coolies never make a

---

[255] In planning a trip to Miao Feng Shan it is better to avoid the two weeks (in May) when the pilgrimage takes place, as temples are crowded then and chair bearers difficult to procure. With regard to the best season for hill excursions in general, September and October are on the whole the most pleasant months. April and May, when the fruit trees are in bloom, may be equally delightful, provided there are no high winds to raise the clouds of suffocating dust that make travelling in North China intolerable. In winter the absence of vegetation makes the country look bare, and it is too cold to remain overnight in unheated monasteries, whereas in the middle of summer the rainy season brings with it impossible roads and a host of insect pests.

Temples of the Western Hills—(concluded)

false step, never seem less at ease than they would be walking over flat ground. Their feet always poise upon the stones at exactly the right angle, and they move lightly as birds.

Three hours suffice to reach Ta Chueh Ssu, a parallelogram of buildings lying on the slope of the hill. After travelling steadily since early morning, it is enchanting to rest in this peaceful, aged temple—a scene of quiet tranquillity perhaps more typical of the Western Hills than any other. Outside, the bearers are laughing and shouting, but all is silent here save for the murmur of little streams of clear water (that most priceless boon throughout the hills), and the chatter of magpies in the pines. Once upon a time Ta Chueh Ssu must have been a magnificent monastery, comparable perhaps to Chieh T'ai Ssu. Built on the ruins of an old Liao temple, it became, towards the end of the 12th century, one of the Eight Resting Places of a Chin emperor in the Western Hills. Under the Mings, judging by several inscriptions, and under the earlier Manchus, its prosperity was so great that 200 monks were daily served in the refectory. The guest rooms of the monastery accommodated thousands of pilgrims on their way to Miao Feng Shan, and the huge ovens smoked continuously to feed them.

To-day few fires are lit, and Imperial patrons no longer occupy the little "Travelling Palace." But the melancholy beauty of K'ang Hsi's throne room in a garden court sweet with the scent of peonies and shaded by magnolia trees, is very touching. To feel its soothing atmosphere, one must linger here in solitude amid the beautiful neutral tones of old timbers, the dim shades of wall surfaces, the quaint carvings under eaves— once splendid with lacquer, now faded to the tint of smoke and looking as if about to curl away like smoke and vanish.

Two fine halls in good condition, because extensively repaired a few years ago by certain rich Chinese bankers, are most impressive. The dark interior of the first, which seems somehow cut off from the glowing sunlight of the courtyard, contains a splendid Buddhist trinity and altars decorated with fine pewter incense burners and candlesticks presented by the Emperor Tao Kuang. Along the side walls are figures, larger than life, representing the God (or spirit) of each of the Twenty-Eight Constellations personified by old Indian deities adopted into the Chinese pantheon, and of great interest to the student of comparative religions.[256] In the second hall facing the rear door, which must be opened in order to see her properly, is a figure of Kuan Yin in her role of Protector of Mariners. She is seated on a rock amidst the waves of the sea. Fish swim around her. The Rain Dragon salutes her from a cloud. Her dove perches on a willow branch above her head. Her Vase of Immortality is at hand, and her two disciples stand at respectful attention awaiting her commands.

A superb Ginko tree, said to be more than a thousand years old, is pointed out with pride by the priest. There used to be a pair; now one has yielded to the Tempest of Time. Peking residents, however, make a special trip to see the solitary survivor when autumn tints its leaves and it looks like a multi-millionaire who has hung out all his gold pieces to glitter on the sun. In May, visitors come again to see the wisteria in the temple garden, for then the grand old vines are bent down by the weight of blossoms and while their glory lasts, the bees make holiday. How many noble pilgrims in olden days have loitered beside the spring spouting from a. dragon's mouth into a stone basin fringed with wild iris and violets and ferns, or lingered musing in the pavilion above it, listening to the little "noiseless noises" of the trees? The feet that tread upon the dust and the trodden dust are not so different as they seem. "From the foot of the mountain," says the Chinese poet, "many are the paths ascending in shadow, and many the feet, silk shod or shoeless, that follow them. But from the terrace all who climb behold the self-same moon, and travel to the same ultimate goal."

In this garden the gnarled branches of picturesque pines lovingly entwine an old "sotoba" erected in honour of a famous monk by his disciples in the reign of K'ang Hsi. Legend,

---

[256] Such figures are exceedingly rare as these Star Gods were originally sub-human creatures and are generally represented with composite bodies pardy human and partly animal.

Temples of the Western Hills-(concluded)

however, connects it with Ch'ien Lung. The lucky influences (*feng-shui*) which for centuries assured fame and prosperity for the monastery were said to be embodied in the hill behind this "sotoba"—the hill supposed to resemble a crouching lion. Now, too much luck—for others—always frightened the masterful monarch who feared Heaven might be assisting a rival to his throne. The powerful lion, therefore, looked dangerous to him. So he is supposed to have erected the "sotoba" on the spot where the necromancers said it would rob the king of beasts of his capacity to do harm, and break the spell of his shadow falling upon the travelling-palace. The ruse was successful in averting bad influences from the Manchu House, but, ever since the monument was completed, the records of the monastery show a steady decline, and the abbot does not dissimulate his resentment against a potentate who dimmed the prosperity of his temple.

It is worth while stopping some time at Ta Chueh Ssu just to "get the feel" of the place, and to spend lazy days wandering about in the neighbourhood. On a picturesque cliff to the east of "The Monastery of the Great Awakening" stands a small shrine dedicated to Kuan Ti. In former days this temple was restored by the pious efforts of an old lady named Wang who collected the sums necessary for repairs by selling lanterns and incense year after year to the pilgrims. Having achieved her aim, she settled down here, enjoying a well-earned rest and a fragrant reputation for sanctity. Her tomb may be seen on the road near the temple, bearing the inscription of "Wang Nai Nai," or "Grandmother Wang," and she is known as the patroness of pilgrims.

Continuing in the same direction along -a mountain path, we pass a hill-slope thickly dotted with Buddhist "sotobas"—the monuments of men who were famous churchmen in their day. This locality is called the Hsi Feng Ssu after a temple that once stood there. The ground is now consecrated as a burial place of holy monks and high dignitaries of the Buddhist church, to whatever sect they may belong.

Juliet Bredon

Over one of these graves stands a solitary tower ornamented with bas-reliefs and known as the Ta Kung, or sometimes the Hsuan T'ung Pao T'a, which means "Great Work." This is the tomb of the eunuch Liu Chin whose story has been told in connection with the fortress of Shih Ching Shan. Trustworthy tradition affirms that the year the Ming Tombs were begun, a vast sepulchre was also planned on the site of the Ta Kung, so large indeed that when Yung Lo's mausoleum was completed, the latter was only half built. When Liu Chin's rebellion failed and he himself met an untimely death at the .hands of the Imperial troops, the "Great Work" was abandoned. Nevertheless the peasants believe that the Ta Kung stands over a vast, if unfinished, vault containing elaborate temples, as the larger and more difficult part of the project connected with the tower was supposed to be subterranean. The entrance to this vault may still be seen choked with brambles, but none dare enter this dark doorway for fear of the occult influences known to protect the place.

Above the Ta Kung stands another tower sharply silhouetted against the sky. Some say it marks the resting place of the Ch'in Emperor Ming Chang when crossing the mountains to a favourite retreat on the other side of the range. But the country folk call it the Liu Lang T'a, or "Tower of the Sixth Wolf," because legend, that so often persists after historic fact grows dim, connects it with the sixth son of the celebrated general Yang Chi-yeh,[257] an ardent and valued supporter of the Sung dynasty in their ceaseless struggles with the barbarian invaders from the North. All his sons were distinguished by a valour equal to his own, hence their nickname of "Wolves," and the sixth was especially famous, controlling at one time the country round Peking. This tower is said to have been erected by him about a.d. iooo as a look-out from which he reviewed the movements of his troops. Once upon a time, while climbing on horseback to his pagoda, the Sixth Wolf grew thirsty, whereupon his intelligent and devoted mount struck the rock with his hoof and caused a spring to flow—that same spring

---

257 See Chapter XVIII

Temples of the Western Hills-(concluded)

which is a boon to the half-witted shepherd boy who pastures his flocks on the hillside to-day.

Few men in this lazy age attempt to follow in the footsteps of the Sixth Wolf and his valiant and resourceful charger up that narrow boulder-strewn defile where the breath is torn from one's lips by the wind rushing down through an æolian harp of rocks. But when the heavy shadows close in on this deep walled valley, where the sun rises hours later and sets hours earlier than it does below on the open plains, and dim the burning blue of the wild larkspurs, ghostly shrieks are heard—so the peasants say; war cries of the wild Khitans who knew no law but the sword, no home but the saddle, no faith but the "Black Magic" of their "Shaman" priests.

Many charming places are within easy walking distance of Ta Chueh Ssu. A picturesque and prosperous eunuch's temple, quite near its gates, appears closed and deserted, but knock and the door will probably be opened by a colossal individual stricken with elephantiasis, having an enormous face the colour of mud, and a nose wrinkled like an elephant's trunk. On a late September evening it is pleasant to look at the brocade of autumn tints from the pretty pavilions on the hillside, to linger near the pond where tame goldfish rise to the surface to be fed at the sound of a wooden rattle, to gossip with lonely old men who have cut themselves off from family life by the nature of their calling, but who served Empresses and princesses and remember many things.

Some were connected with Manchu princely families whose properties and tombs are in this neighbourhood. They still make yearly prilgrimages to two graves of their erstwhile masters—that situated in the plain to the east, of the Seventh Prince, and that of the former Prince Regent (Ch'un) father of the deposed emperor which lies high upon the hillside. The latter property combines, in Chinese fashion, a handsome tomb prepared for an owner still alive, and a summer home for his family. The enclosure has a regal approach. Walled villages for retainers and caretakers who still regard the Prince as a kind of feudal chief, give on to a broad avenue shaded by old trees

Juliet Bredon

leading to a marble bridge. Beyond mounts a noble flight of granite steps and a series of pine shaded terraces one above another. The tomb, in a separate walled courtyard, has a wood and a spring behind it, luck-bringing features contributing, like the mountain screen beyond, to the repose of the soul. The travelling palace on the west slope is a little gem set in a garden, laid out in the best artificial Chinese manner. One pavilion contains a throne chair made of twisted roots—a family heirloom presented by Ch'ien Lung. Another is a "poetry pavilion" through which a stream trickles in a channel cut in the stone floor to form the character for "happiness." The old regime may have had its sins both of omission and commission, but it certainly-cultivated refined tastes. Alas, these Manchu grandees—so typical of the faults and virtues of the past—have nothing to offer the new world except a wonderful but unwanted elegance of living which still permits them to accept with calm dignity the fate of failures.

From an upper terrace we can distinguish Ch'ing Shan, the temple with a gushing spring[258] on the way to Miao Feng Shan and one of the prettiest spots to picnic in the neighbourhood. Also Hsiao Chai Ssu perched like an eagle's eyrie under a nearby cliff in majestic and precipitous surroundings.

About an hour's walk from Ta Chueh Ssu, in the opposite direction—to the east—stands the hill called Ch'eng Tzu Shan, capped by an old Taoist temple, the Tung Yueh Miao. Nothing could be more romantic than this solitary shrine on top of a mountain-Tradition, though unsupported by evidence, has it that in the Ming period a man, prompted by a secret vow, appeared in the neighbourhood. This man, whose name is actually on record, chose the site of the temple and not only prepared the materials for it, but is said to have carried them up the hill himself and to have alone erected the shrine. Admiring not only his piety but his energy, we follow in his footsteps up the steep path to the summit, where a flight of stone steps, aslope and broken, leads to two neglected

---

258 A soda water factory occupies part of the premises, yet parts of the temple remain unspoiled.

Temples of the Western Hills—(concluded)

courtyards. The buildings are deserted save for one day in the year, when an incense-burning service is still held in what remains of them by the villagers of the vicinity. We pity the gods who have lost their noses and whose legs have been amputated at the knees. "Verily foxes have their holes, and the fowls of the air have their places of rest, but the gods no longer have shelter over their heads." Time is not always kind to gods—or men. Nature alone resists his ravages, and here, where all else is falling to ruin, the view remains ever fresh, framed in that branch of overhanging pine that curves gracefully like a bent arm. The long spur of mountains, stencilled against the sky reminds one of the best landscapes of the old Chinese artists who rendered their broken magnificence with swift, sure brush strokes.

Close to the foot of Ch'eng Tzu Shan is the charming property of another Manchu, Prince T'ung, well-known as an amateur actor. Such a country seat is rare in the neighbourhood of Peking. Its grounds are full of the peculiar phantasies of Chinese gardens, twisted trees and stones whose shapes are unknown in the West. Its pretty terrace overhangs the plain and keeps a friendly watch over the villages.

The road back to Peking lies round the base of the low hill with an inscription—gift of a Chinese journalist —cut in the rock on the summit, to the Ming Taoist temple of Wen Ch'uan Ssu, famous for its sulphur springs. These cure rheumatism, gout, etc., and the Emperor K'ang Hsi had them enclosed in a granite basin in a.d. 1700. Modern physicians have rediscovered them, so to speak, and a small sanitarium with bath-houses has been built near their site. A rustic festival in honour of the Niang Niang Pussa, combined with a fair, where peddlers did a brisk business in bangles, hair ornaments and ploughs, used to take place here in May. Theatricals were performed in the open pavilion half-way up the hill, and even a village troupe of mummers with soiled and tawdry costumes, made a picturesque effect in such a setting. The temple itself was never of much interest except for the shrine of Chung-li

Ch'uan, eldest and holiest of the Eight Great Teachers, a figure universally revered throughout China.

Chung-li was a mighty warrior in olden days. For twenty years he fought many battles, only, at last, to become the victim of the emperor's suspicions deliberately aroused by jealous enemies at Court. His family was exterminated and his property confiscated. In course of time the emperor's doubts of his loyalty were dispelled, and, on the return of the valiant general from a successful campaign, the sovereign went to meet him at a great distance to explain the mistake, bidding his empress personally serve his guest. Impressed by her unusual beauty, Chung-li on reaching his home was overtaken by a longing that became an illness. As he lay weak and sorrowing unspeakably, he implored the empress to come to see him, whereupon he declared his consuming passion. While gently ministering to the sick man's needs she asked him of what material was the beaker from which she poured wine for him at the Court, and he answered truly, "gold." "And of what material was the beaker from which I poured your wine in your own palace?" she inquired. And again he answered truly, "silver."

Then one last question she put to him. "Was not the wine equally good no matter what the vessel?" The warrior grasped the secret meaning of her words. His oppression suddenly vanished and, bidding farewell to the empress, he rose from his couch, left his home and entered the "Holy Way."

Wen Ch'uan nowadays is much modernised. The temple property has been transformed into a girls' school connected with the Franco-Chinese University in Peking; the theatre pavilion is converted into a summer bungalow, one of several attractive villas for hire to guests desirous of taking the cure. A local "Development Company," largely due to the initiative of a Chinese gentleman educated in France, supervises the sanitation of the baths, plants trees on the hillside, and has started a model farm with vines imported from Europe.

The curious semi-modern building at the base of the hill, which never fails to arouse the curiosity of the passer-by, is a

Temples of the Western Hills-(concluded)

memorial shrine-built by Marshall Feng Yu Hsiang in memory of a friend and companion in arms, General Sun Yueh.

Following the motor road that passes this shrine, over the new stone bridge, pride of the neighbourhood, we come to the Bell Tower marking the beginning of the "Three Li Village (or Pai Chia T'an), so called because its single street of thatched dwellings straggles along for a mile (three *li*). Originally, this village boasted one of the oldest temples in the neighbourhood of Peking, K'ai Yuan Ssu, founded in the K'ai Yuan reign of the T'ang dynasty, about a.d. 700, by a eunuch. It fell into disrepair, but was rebuilt in the reign of Yung Lo by a monk from Ta Chueh Ssu, one of those Buddhist hermits who retired here "to enjoy the mild air, the good water and the sight of peaceful fields." Nothing now remains to mark the site of this historic temple but a stone tablet with an almost illegible inscription and a guardian lion whose features are sadly defaced.

Pai Chia Tan's claim to interest at present lies in the peaceful memorial temple erected to Yung Cheng's brother, Prince Yi,[259] whose bounty is gratefully remembered by the descendants of his tenants in the neighbourhood. In the rear courtyards are four splendid white pines, which might well have inspired Po Chu-yi's lovely verses "The Pine Trees in the Courtyard":

> ...Below the hall
> The pine trees grow in front of the steps...
> And no one knows who planted them.
> Morning and evening they are visited by the sun and moon;
> Rain or fine—they are free from dust and mud.
> In the gales of autumn they whisper a vague tune:
> From the suns of summer they yield a cool shade.
> At the height of spring the fine evening rain
> Fills their leaves with a load of hanging pearls.
> At the year's end, the time of great snow
> Stamps their branches with a fret of glittering jade.
> Of the Four Seasons each has his own mood.

---

[259] See Chapter XVIII.

Juliet Bredon

Among all the trees none is like the other."
(*More Translations from the Chinese,* by Arthur Waley.)

Just beyond the village is the striking landmark of Lone Pine Tree Hill, which the Chinese call Chih Chu Shan, or "Spider Hill," because it resembles a crouching spider with his feet drawn up under him. Once upon a time there lived in this locality two dragons—one on either side of the hill—the White Dragon, at the tiny hidden temple of Pai Chia Shui in the Pai Chia T'an ravine, and the Black Dragon at Hei Lung T'an. Now the sound of this hill's name and its position between the two dragons recalls the well-known Chinese emblem "Erh lung hsi chu," or "the two dragons playing with the pearl"—an emblem reserved for the emperor and used in decorations on the palaces, etc. Popular tradition, which always weaves legends round the name of the great Ch'ien Lung, says that this monarch was much struck by the situation of this hill and these coincidences, just as he was by the "Lion Hill" above Ta Chueh Ssu. "Surely," said he, "here again is an omen of great importance, and a dragon emperor must sooner or later appear at this spot!" By inference, Ch'ien Lung forsaw the overthrow of his dynasty, and the establishment of a new line of monarchs. So he decided to ward off the peril and dispel the inauspicious feng-shui, or occult influence, ruling Chih Chu Shan, by cutting the hill in half. The emperor attained his object, but the wounded hill, divided to this day by a narrow gully, still bears one witness of its mortification and sorrow in the old and lonely pine that crowns the summit. When cut, the roots are still said to shed drops of blood.

Chih Chu Shan guides us to Hei Lung T'an (Black Dragon Altar) whose golden roofs catch and reflect the sunlight like burnished mirrors from the crest of the Hua Mei Shan ("Painted Eyebrows," or "Flowering Eyebrows" Hill). Some say this hillock takes its name from the "flowering eye-browed thrushes"[260] that haunt its trees—others from the black stone

---

[260] This particular kind of thrush, much esteemed by the Chinese, is so-called from the feathery growth over the eyes which does indeed resemble

Temples of the Western Hills—(concluded)

found upon it and used by ladies of the Court under the Chin dynasty, for painting their eyebrows. In any case Ch'eng Hua, the Ming Emperor, made a clever choice when he built upon this site in a.d. 1486.

Our chair-bearers intone a rhythmical chant as we approach the temple, a parody of an old Han dynasty poem:

"When the dragon comes, ah!
The wind stirs and sighs,
Paper money thrown, ah!
Silk umbrellas waved.
When the dragon goes, ah!
The wind also is still.
Incense fire dies, ah!
The cups and vessels are cold."
 (Translation by Arthur Waley.)

On entering the temple precincts we go direct to the bubbling spring to find a lovely pool where the dragon lives. Old trees overhang the water in what seems a perilous balance, while below, the pool, sleek and shining, waits for the falling wisteria and catalpa blossoms with cat-like patience. No wonder this has been a favourite retreat for centuries—that emperors and courtiers without number have walked in the covered gallery overlooking the jade green water.

Because we are hot and thirsty, we drink and we bathe in spite of a warning that we may displease the dragon. The water refreshes us in a most extraordinary way, and seeing no signs of the Hei Lung, we venture to doubt his existence. "It is not wise to say such things," we are rebuked, "lest evil befall. Remember what happened when the Emperor Ch'ien Lung dared to doubt." We do not remember, for we have never heard; therefore the story is related for our benefit.

Once upon a time, His Majesty, on his return from a hunting expedition, spent a day at the temple. When he had rested and partaken of refreshments, he summoned two of his

---

flower petals.

officials and said to them: "We desire to speak with the Hei Lung. Inform him that such is Our pleasure!" The two officials bowed low before him and, hastening to the edge of the pool, addressed the dragon in the following words, each speaking alternately, according to the etiquette of Court: "It is now our duty to inform you that our Master the Emperor desires to see you." As they finished speaking, a voice issuing from the rock replied: "Inform His Augustness that I shall be waiting to receive him." When the emperor proceeded to the spring, spoke gracious words and leaned down to receive the monster, a small creature no longer than his finger emerged among the silver bubbles saying: "I am he whom thou seekest. What dost thou desire of me?" For a moment the sovereign was surprised. He stared at the dragon in a bewildered way and cried aloud: "How strange! I had expected to see a mighty presence, something to strike awe and fear. But, behold! this is not a dragon, only a little creature of no account." Scarcely had these words left his lips than the little creature disappeared. Then the water of the spring boiled fiercely and a rumbling voice thundered; "Hai, was it anything like this that you expected?" and simultaneously, from beneath the rocks, a mighty claw, five pointed, appeared. It grew and grew until it reached the tree tops, and spread like an evil hand over the emperor and the multitude of dignitaries surrounding him, standing splendid and motionless as images. It grew and grew, till at last it reached the sky, and the shadow of those dreadful claws, pointed and menacing, fell upon the temple and upon the hill above, and all the bird and insect voices were hushed as in the stillness before a storm. Then the emperor knew how mistaken he had been in judging by appearances, and he bowed down before the dragon with many exclamations of regret, till, slowly, the claw was withdrawn as the "Hei Lung" became appeased and the sun shone again. But ever since, the spirit of the spring has received the respect which is his due not only from the emperor, but from all the simple people round about. Twice a year the peasants of the neighbourhood pray to him, kneeling at the edge of the pool and begging for plentiful water to ensure

Temples of the Western Hills-(concluded)

good harvests. In dry seasons drums beat in his honour in the villages. Listen, and you will hear them— drums near at hand, and drums from hamlets invisible beyond the parching fields, yet other drums, like echoings, responding.

It is hot and we envy His Majesty the Dragon King, dwelling forever in that marvellous pool, with two tortoises to serve him, and the little shrimps, his courtiers, forming themselves in escorting lines and bowing whenever he appears; hearing himself implored simultaneously in a hundred villages; inhaling the vapour of a hundred offerings; reading the lips of his faithful worshippers making supplication—"O Mighty Dragon, we have burned incense, we have prayed prayers, yet the land thirsts and the crops fail. Deign out of thy divine pity to give us rain!"

Now a kindly god listens to the requests of the people. But once this Black Dragon was deaf to their desires. Then he learned that the power and pleasure even of a god depend upon good behaviour. And the man who taught him this lesson was none other than Ch'ien Lung.

During his reign a terrible drought occurred. The sovereign deeply grieved for the thirsty land, journeyed to Hei Lung T'an to make offerings. But the dragon remained deaf to his entreaties. Then the emperor, in righteous wrath, presented him with an ultimatum in his capacity as Supreme Dragon Sovereign. Either rain should be sent, or the Hei Lung's spirit should be banished from the temple to the arid regions of the far north. When the god still defied him, Ch'ien Lung started to the city carrying the tablet. But no sooner had the procession reached a certain village[261] beyond the temple than the Dragon of the Pool bethought himself of his cool water, and his votive offering; of all the things a deity is pleased to hear and rejoiced to see. And he commanded rain to fall, such bounteous rain as had never before been known. So Ch'ien Lung escorted the image back again, and ever since the Black Dragon has lived in his lovely pool doing his duty, and subjected to no greater

---

261 Still known as the "Village that was Flooded Out."

inconvenience than the visit of an occasional irreverent foreigner who comes to swim in his crystal-clear water.

In token of his repentance Ch'ien Lung ordered yellow tiles made for the roofs of the temple and commanded a painter to record the incident in a series of frescoes. These may still be seen in the highest shrine on the hilltop where, in spite of certain crudities of perspective, the spirited drawing and powerful colouring produce an excellent effect. Two Ming tablets and two of the Ch'ing; dynasty beside this shrine record successful prayers for rain on other occasions.

A group of curious plaster figures, a combination of human and animal forms presided over by the Black. Dragon, or Rain God, are a rare feature of this temple. Lei Kung, the Duke of Thunder, may be recognised by the mallet in his hand and the bandolier of drums across-his shoulders. The "Mother of Lightning," a female figure in parti-coloured robes, holds two mirrors. Various assistants who help pour out the rain water, or control the winds, have a falcon's beak, a pig's head, or wings resembling those of the Indian Garuda bird.

In a little enclosure below with separate gates leading to the pool and the shrine on the hill (an enclosure which could be shut off from the temple proper when the Emperor was in residence), is the small Imperial pavilion where Ch'ien Lung habitually stayed. It was last occupied by the Emperor Kuang Hsu and the Empress Dowager Tz'u Hsi who came in 1892 on their farewell trip to the hills. Since then the place has been disfigured by modern reconstructions in the suburban villa style. A gay company of blue birds still makes its home in the grove of bamboos planted beside the door to ward off earthquakes. A brilliant woodpecker has a cache of berries in the eaves. The little pond in the sheltered garden is swarming with insect life, and inoffensive snakes sun themselves undisturbed on the stones. No Chinese would dream of killing them, partly because of the Buddhist prejudice against taking life and partly because serpents are often sent by the dragon king to announce the coming of the gods. Miraculous snakes of this kind exist at Hei Lung T'an and, though their home is on

Temples of the Western Hills—(concluded)

the Hua Mei Shan, they wander freely through the temple enclosure. Mortals seldom see them. But we are assured that such heavenly messengers have "the face of an ancient man with white eyebrows and wear upon their heads a red mark like a crown."

As we regretfully take leave of Hei Lung T'an and pursue our way through the village beyond the temple, a bubbling chorus which seems to be the very voice of the soil itself, the chant of the frogs in the rice-fields watered by the dragon's spring, follows us.

Continuing westward for about three miles, we reach the macadamised road to T'ang Shan just at the corner where the Po Wang Shan (or Wang Erh Shan), the north-eastern peak of the Western Hills, throws its shadow. This "Mountain of a Hundred Views" is easily distinguished miles away by the ruins of the old temple on top. It is a forsaken place—a shrine stricken dead— only the husk of a temple. We guess, and rightly, that it has a poetic history.

In the year a.d. 1000 the Sungs, who at that time reigned over southern China, were at war with the Liaos, rulers of the northern provinces. The Sung politicians no doubt talked of imperialism and the wonderful opening for young men on the rich plains of Chihli. So they sent a mighty army against Yenching (Peking). The Liao Empress of the day, the famous Jui Chih—a lady of many lovers whose name is still popular in song and story—ordered her troops to advance beyond the city and personally took part in the battle which ended in a crushing defeat for the invaders. After the victory, she built the shrine on Po Wang Shan in memory of her six sons, killed before her eyes in the fierce fight she so nobly led.

Liaos and Sungs have long since disappeared. The Chins defeated them. The Mongols swept over the land. The Mings ousted these northern barbarians. The Manchus waged war and brought the Mings to an ignominious end. But the forlorn ruins of this memorial shrine, symbol of a mother's love and sacrifice, still stand as though challenging the centuries to do their worst, and man to forget the unforgettable.

Juliet Bredon

The road to T'ang Shan strikes out into the plain towards the north. Though monotonous in line, the fields reflect every aspect of the sky and answer every touch of the seasons with their violent contrasts from burning heat to bitter cold. Indeed the South that warms herself all the year at a familiar sun is less voluptuous than these northern plains when at last they feel a quickening pulse in their veins. As they are cold in winter, so in summer they are burning. As they are virginal under snow, equally they are passionate in their short season of growth.

At Sha Ho we cross the old road to the Ming Tombs. A fine 15th century bridge, adapted to modern traffic, spans the river and on our right, behind crumbling walls, lies Sha Ch'eng with the ruins of the Ming travelling palace where the emperors broke their journey. Sha Ch'eng (also called P'ing An, "Quiet Spot," on account of the legend that the T'ang Emperor T'ai Tsung rested here to recover from a severe indisposition on one of his northern campaigns) was once a busy centre, because all the materials used for the construction of the Ming Tombs were brought here by water and loaded into carts to be taken to the building place.[262]

From Sha Ch'eng also, the Mings and the earlier Manchus made their trips to the famous hot springs at T'ang Shan (twenty-two miles from Peking) under the lee of a stone-freckled hill with the picturesque ruins of three old temples silhouetted against the sky-line. K'ang Hsi was especially fond of the place, and to him are due the open air tanks enclosed in marble, each nearly the size of a tennis court. The legend why this pretty spot with its health-giving baths was abandoned, is worth the telling.

---

[262] The modern traveller is struck by the grandiloquent name of "river" when applied to little streams like the Sha Ho and the Hun Ho, nowadays, for the greater part of the year, simply feeble trickles of water. Traditions of traffic, however, seem to indicate that they were once important waterways which have shrunk owing to the deforestation of the surrounding hills—a deforestation that seriously affects climatic conditions and threatens to bring about "a progressive dessication and the gradual encroachment of the sands of the Gobi Desert."

Temples of the Western Hills-(concluded)

The later monarchs of the Ch'ing dynasty, grown superstitious in their decadence, got the habit of consulting soothsayers whenever they started on a journey. On one occasion a certain astrologer, doubtless for some hidden reason of his own, informed the sovereign that it was dangerous to pass through Sha Ch'eng and proceed to T'ang Shan because the Imperial Person is assimilated to a dragon. Now "sand," the Chinese word for which is "sha" and the first character in both Sha Ho and Sha Ch'eng, is as detrimental to the dragon as boiling water, "t'ang," the first character in T'ang Shan. He sinks in the first and stews in the second. When this unpleasant assimilation of hieroglyphics was pointed out to them, the superstitious successors of K'ang Hsi and Ch'ien Lung withdrew their patronage from T'ang Shan which fell into disrepair.

The ground on which the hot springs stand belongs to the Manchu house, however, to this day and is now rented to the T'ang Shan Improvement Company of which the ex-Minister of Finance, Tsao Ju-ling, was the leading spirit. It is to him and to other, members like Lu Tsung-yu, Sun Pao-ch'i and Chin Yun-peng that the new gingerbread bungalows erected in the old park belong. A new hotel (foreign style) with excellent baths, attracts the traveller, especially in late autumn when T'ang Shan is at its best, being one of the few trips outside Peking suitable just before the period of great cold sets in. Moreover, it is a convenient centre for excursions.

There are several picturesque old tombs in the neighbourhood. That of Ch'eng Pei-leh, father of the present Prince Kung, is well kept and handsome, though not to be compared with the magnificent mausoleum of his famous ancestor (the historic Prince Kung) situated a little farther north at the foot of the hills that gird the horizon to the north and protect T'ang Shan from the cold winter winds. Sixth son of the Emperor Tao Kuang, he has a sepulchre resembling in size and grandeur the Imperial tombs at the Hsi Ling, with the difference that the roof-tiles are green instead of yellow.

Juliet Bredon

The ruined temple and weather-worn pagoda of Lung Ch'uan Ssu—the "Dragon Spring Temple," dating from the 10th century a.d.—is also worth a visit. Little remains of the buildings, save one pavilion under whose floor a spring is hidden. The guardian assures visitors that a golden tea-pot, "large enough to serve nine persons," is buried at the source of the water, and a golden mule is entombed in the hill above the temple, though what their connection is, if any, he cannot say. No one has seen these wonderful things, safeguarded by a taboo of sanctity. But the silver spring with its large bubbles, that come sailing majestically up from the little pool and explode quietly in the air, and the swaying water-weeds that seem to have solved the problem of perpetual motion, and the dragon-flies chasing to and fro intent on murder—these are real treasures that all may enjoy.

XVII. The Great Wall and the Ming Tombs

The classical excursion from Peking which no tourist, however hurried, should omit, is to the Great Wall of China via the Nankou Pass. There are many other places where this impressive barrier—the only work of man's hands supposed to be visible from Mars—may be seen, as it stretches for nearly 2,000 miles from the sea coast at Shanhaikuan to the borders of Thibet. But nowhere is the ancient fortification in better preservation, nowhere grander. And Nankou has the advantage of being easily accessible (about twenty-five miles by train on the Peking-Kalgan line) with clean and sufficiently comfortable hotels.

From Peking, the trip to the Wall and back can be done in one day. Including the excursion to the Ming Tombs, it can be rushed through in thirty-six hours, by spending a night at the foot of the Pass. But those who have the time will not regret giving two whole days to the expedition and an extra afternoon to wandering in Nankou itself.

This quaint old walled town is the first link in the chain of defences built across the narrow defile beyond to check barbarian invasions. It also was once, and still remains to some extent, an important stage on the caravan route to Mongolia. A short distance above the town, the hills gather in and we come to the entrance of the gorge guarded by four watch towers. This is the spot where, according to Chinese poets, the visitor should muse at sunset, for "the light falling upon the kingfisher-coloured rocks" is one of the "eight sights of the neighbourhood." Only the brush of a very great artist could reproduce the scene: the narrow entrance to the wild and rugged Pass, water and wind-worn, lying in darkness as if blotted out with ink; the crests of its grim walls slowly turning from flame to sapphire, then to intensest violet against a foreground tinted with delicate purples and blues.

Spur of the Great Wall

The Great Wall and the Ming Tombs

The journey to the Wall at the top of the Pass may be made by train. How prosaic, the stranger exclaims, to view such a renowned sight from a car window! But the railway line itself is interesting. All credit to the Chinese engineer who overcame enormous difficulties in building it—as the steep gradients, the numerous tunnels (one of which goes actually under the Great Wall) and the elaborate stone revetment work, prove.

As the engine slowly puffs up the narrow valley, the steep, bare hills rise higher. We leave behind us the last little farms, so stony that it seems impossible for industry to wrest a living from such poor soil. Walls curving down into the canyon and watch towers standing straight as sentinels give a picturesque sky-line to mountain profiles. Scarred with the traces of many battles between the Chinese and the nomads, these subsidiary defences of the Pass, which now seem so purposeless and disconnected, send fancy roaming back to the days when they were vitally important in keeping out the ancestors of the Turks, the Huns, the Khitans, the Nuchens, the Mongols and other wild tribes who tried to fight their way into the coveted, fertile plans of North China.

The Nankou Pass has been compared to the Khyber, the town itself to Jamrud, the midway fort of Chu Yung Kuan to Ali Musjid; and in its wilder parts this Gateway into China does remind one of the Gateway into India. Though scenically less magnificent, the former is historically a counterpart of the latter. Through one, Genghis Khan and his hordes found their way to the rich Middle Kingdom, and through the other, Greeks, Persians, Afghans and Mongols poured down into the valleys of the Indus and the Ganges.

After an hour's climbing the train stops at the little station of Ch'ing Lung Ch'iao ("Bright Dragon Bridge"). Thence it is an easy walk of half an hour along the old highway to the Pa Ta Ling gate at the top of the Pass (2,000 feet above sea level). The Great Wall crosses the latter squarely here, and through the massive archway, from which the iron-studded gates have disappeared, we get a magnificent view of the plains of Chihli and of the snow-capped mountains in the distance.

On either side, the Wall wanders along the crests of the hills, scaling peaks which it seems impossible even the foot of man could climb. The massive loops of historic masonry classed, and righdy, by the ancients as one of the wonders of the world, are doubly impressive in these mountain solitudes. Not a soul is to be seen save a donkey driver, who has tied his beast to the old cannon lying in the grass (the last of the treasures of antique weapons and armour discovered in one of the towers) and a shepherd who has come up from his village in search of pasturage. He sits watching his flock scrambling among the broken bricks—a pretty sight! The mothers are followed by the little dancing, elf-like kids while the bearded patriarchs, who love to clamber to the most inaccessible heights, stand embossed against the clear sky in triumph and quietude. The stillness is broken only by the occasional whistle of a train softened by distance, or the shrill cry of a hawk pursued by a high-hovering eagle.

To get the prospect in the fulness of its noble grandeur, climb the wall to the highest tower of the eastern spur. So steep is this section that the *terre-plein* takes the form of steps very laborious to mount. But from the casemated embrasures of this huge stone sentry box, twenty-eight other block-houses, each a third of a mile distant from its neighbour, are visible, and whichever way we turn the Wall itself seems to pursue us, writhing like a mighty dragon as far as the eye can reach.

Was it from this same tower that the Chinese philosopher, meditating in the cool of the evening, climbed the silver ladder of a moonbeam to the moon? The legend, one of the many that have clung to the Wall like mosses accumulated through the patient years, says so. Of course, he had amazing experiences when he got to the lunar sphere. First he traversed a succession of glittering halls. Then he found an old man sitting at a table engrossed in a big book, the "Book of Predestined Marriages." Since all marriages in China are supposed to be made in Heaven, the old man was exceedingly busy, but with proper

The Great Wall and the Ming Tombs

courtesy he offered to stop his work and accompany the earth-stranger through the fairy palaces of the moon, built all of silver and mother-of pearl. "High above clouds and rain they stood, high, too, above the winds of sorrow and the chill of death. And they were filled with beautiful women whose robes became them as the petals become the flowers, weaving the patterns of the stars on golden looms."

The sage marvelled greatly at what he saw, but the magical atmosphere was too rare and fine for a mortal to linger in. Just before dawn, therefore, he bade adieu to the venerable ancient, thanked him for his kindly guidance, and descended the moonbeam again. When he reached the earth, he told the neighbours of the wonders he had seen, but they only laughed at him. "If it were true that you had found a country high above clouds and rain, where the winds of sorrow never blow neither the chill of death touches the land, why did you return?" they asked. The sage could not answer their question because he did not quite know himself, so all the people mocked him—all but one wise elder who, divining the unspoken reason, explained: "The sage was drawn back by the remembrance of familiar things, for dearer even than perfection is that to which the heart is accustomed."

Linger on this imposing height and bid imagination re-people the lines of ruined towers with the defenders of bygone ages. Let the mind play cinematograph and give us a moving picture of the history of the mighty rampart in which the Chinese passion for wall construction, manifest to anyone who has been in the country even a few days, finds its grandest expression.

Two centuries before the Christian era Ch'in Shih Huang Ti, contemporary of Hannibal, conceived this giant scheme for keeping the Tartars in their place.[263] For such portions of the

---

[263] It is interesting to note that in still more remote ages, according to Chinese historians, the northern peasants used to plough their fields perpendicularly to the line of foreign invasion, that is to say from east to west. This was a serious deterrent to armies bent on conquest, and using carts for transport. The habit still prevails in some districts. In others, rows of willows were planted to check the advance of cavalry: this is the origin of

Juliet Bredon

Wall as this emperor caused to be built, linking together and extending some previously existing ramparts, he employed 700,000 criminals and prisoners of war. The difficulties at one time seemed so insurmountable that Ch'in Shih Huang Ti consulted a soothsayer. "Never until 10,000 men are buried beneath this wall," he replied, "will it be successfully completed."

Now even so great an autocrat hesitated to entomb 10,000 of his subjects alive for the furtherance of his scheme. So he effected a compromise with the Supernatural Powers by burying one man whose name contained the character "Ten Thousand," and thereafter the work proceeded smoothly.

Other sovereigns of other dynasties carried on or repaired the task of Ch'in Shih Huang Ti. There is a record, for instance, of a Chin monarch who built a section of the wall in ten days by the employment of no less than a million men, numbers of whom died from the results of forced labour. Again there were periods when nothing was done and the barrier fell into disuse. Under the Mongols, who themselves came from beyond it, the Wall, not being required for defence, was left unrepaired and seems to have excited little interest. Marco Polo never even mentions it.[264] But once the Mings ousted the Tartars, the Great Wall again assumed importance, and the new dynasty in the 15th century, rebuilt in granite and brick the section defending the Nankou Pass, innermost of five great loops, begun as earth ramparts in a.d. 555 by the Northern Ch'i. Two are still wholly traceable, one being the wall which passes through Kalgan. The outer walls, of which history says little, are now mere hummocks.

As a matter of fact, during the 2,000 years of the huge racial movements which devastated Asia and even troubled Europe

---

the well-known "Willow Fence," which used to be a prolongation of the Great Wall into Manchuria. Such precautions remind us of the saying, as true to-day as ever it was, that "wars endure but Chinese farmers stick to their tasks."

264 For a detailed history of the Wall throughout its entire length see *The Great Wall of China*, by William Edgar Geil. See also *The Great Wall of China*, by L. Newton Hayes.

The Great Wall and the Ming Tombs

from time to time, China was overwhelmed again and again in spite of the Great Wall. Still, as a rampart against petty raids, it was often valuable and the moral effect on a would-be conqueror must have been tremendous. To invade a country guarded by such a barrier, especially with cavalry, required a stout heart and stupendous preparations. Moreover, there was little hope of slipping through by surprise, as the watch towers in important passes were only a hundred yards apart, and even in remote districts, free from the chronic raids of the nomads, never more than a mile from one another. All of them were manned by small garrisons who had an excellent signal system of beacons by means of which messages could be transmitted from tower to tower for thousands of miles in a remarkably short time.[265] By this means news of an attack at some remote point could be flashed to headquarters in a night, and large armies summoned to keep pace with the movements of the barbarians reconnoitring along the outside of the barrier in search of a weak spot.

Now that the Tartar menace has long since disappeared, the mighty rampart is useless, and there is not so much as a corporal's guard for hundreds of miles, although the "mouths" of the Wall at Kalgan (Chang Chia K'ou), Ku Pei K'ou[266] and other places are still strictly watched and closed at sundown every evening, chiefly, be it noted, to protect the cities near them from bandits. Gone are all those doughty warriors who stood against Genghis Khan; rusty their arms, which antiquarians dig out of the towers; crumbling the towers themselves. Even the Wall in places is slipping down into the valleys, stone by stone, and the waterspouts, cleverly placed on the inside of the barrier so that thirst might add to the difficulties of the invaders, have fallen among the brambles. But at least the strength and glory of the mighty fortification is yielding before no human foe. Only Time, the most powerful

---

265 Such was the object of the numerous Ming watch towers scattered over the Peking plain, and accessible, like the Turkish "*kulehs*," only by ladders from the outside.

266 "*K'ou*" is a Chinese word meaning "mouth."

and invincible enemy, can bring to ruin what no mortal conqueror could destroy.

If you go up to the Wall by train, be sure to come back by road down the Pass. Then you will get a true impression of the old life of the borderland, and understand the full significance of the barrier itself. The journey takes about four hours and must be done by donkey, on foot, or in a chair, making a sharp turn from the top of the defile and proceeding through the T'an Ch'in Hsia or "Playing Harp Gorge" where a little stream makes perpetual music. None can follow this highway without a feeling that he has stepped back several centuries, because as old as the road itself (which for over 2,000 years was the chief artery of intercourse, commercial as well as martial, between the Chinese and the peoples of the North) are the means of travel, the conveyances, the trappings of the animals. One sees the same long strings of soft-footed camels, with the klang-i-klang of bells, that carried freight to Kublai Khan; the same passing herds of sheep "coming in from Tartary"; the same donkey caravans laden with coal; the same droves of shaggy ponies enveloped in a grey dust cloud and driven by quaint Mongols; the same equestrian travellers, sitting short-stirruped on the high accumulation of their baggage. Except for the old garrisons of armoured bowmen and the watchmen patrolling the walls or lighting beacons on the signal towers, we have a perfect picture of the life of the Pass as it was hundreds of years ago.

When the capital of China was moved north by the Ming emperors, a great deal of commerce which formerly followed the southern routes was diverted to this highway, and the opening of trade with the Russian outposts in Siberia, in the 17th century, added considerably to the caravan traffic through the defile. The railway from Kalgan now takes much of this; furs come south, tea goes north and west by other routes. But there still remains a stream of men and beasts up and down the narrow valley sufficiently important to afford us many picturesque impressions and memories.

The Great Wall and the Ming Tombs

The Great Wall.

[Photo by Hartung, Peking]

Near Chu Yung Kuan we overtake a mountain funeral, the coffin suspended from poles resting on the backs of mules. Why the cock tied to it in a basket? On inquiry, we learn that the dead man had been engaged in trading operations in the land of the nomads who live, herd, and think much as their forefathers did in the days of Noah. Every Chinese dislikes to reside, even temporarily, outside the Wall and if he can afford it, invariably provides that should he die "beyond the Mouth," his body shall be brought back and buried within the pale. Lest the spirit lose its way, therefore, a cock accompanies the corpse, so that morning and evening his crowing may guide the soul to follow the mortal remains.

The fortified village of Chu Yung Kuan was always a military outpost and not a trade centre, so that, with the removal of the garrison, it has little life left. Its fortifications, however, remain remarkable monuments to the military genius of the ancients—as substantially built as the Great Wall itself. They turned the Chin Tartars in their time and twice the defenders of Chu Yung Kuan resisted the Mongols, once under the personal leadership of Genghis Khan. Neglect in other quarters, however, cost the people within the Wall an empire, for the great Mongol leader chose another pass, more carelessly guarded, and appeared upon the plain of Peking while the army at Chu Yung Kuan was still waiting for a second assault. Some say the gateway was built in commemoration of this episode; others that it is simply a Buddhist monument put up by the Mongolian Khans, patrons of Lamaism.

The Great Wall and the Ming Tombs

The "Language Arch"—Chu Yung Kuan
(Nankou Pass)

Juliet Bredon

Dated 1345, it is constructed of massive blocks of marble sculptured with Buddhist figures and symbols. On the keystone, a "garuda" bird is carved in bold relief, between a pair of Naga kings with seven cobra heads, and serpentine bodies lost in rich coils of foliage. Within the fifty-foot octagonal passage-way are the four Maharajahs and six inscriptions in six different scripts that have been the subject of much discussion among archaeologists. The languages are: Chinese, Mongol, (written in Bashpa characters[267]), Uigur (derived from the Syriac and parent of the modern Mongol and Manchu) Thibetan, Sanscrit, (in the Devanagar script) and the rare Tangut. The last-named language is the most interesting, both because few samples of it are left, and because it was so long a riddle to scholars. The inscription, which resembles bacilli under a microscope, is a modified form of Chinese characters. When finally deciphered in 1903 by Morrisse of the French Legation at Peking, it proved to be the alphabet of the Hsi Hsia Kingdom (10th to 13th centuries a.d.), a Thibetan state on the upper Huang Ho. Other inscriptions give the names of the restorers of the archway in a.d. 1445, and a tablet added by the Ch'ings describes Chu Yung Kuan as the "First Fortress of the World."

How often must the northern tribes have poured down this rugged causeway in their unrestricted, rapacious hordes to burn the villages inside the wall, to ransack the towns and steal and kill! And what ghastly struggles must have taken place here before the conquering barbarians defeated the defenders and, pausing only to tie the heads of their vanquished enemies to their saddle bows rode away into the valleys. But always the "kindly rains came and washed the blood off the stones, and the sun bleached them clean again, and the shy, wild, green herbs plaited their leaves in garlands to hide the stains and Wounds, and the mountains peeped

---

[267] Bashpa, a Thibetan Lama who was made State Preceptor in a.d. 1260 and recognised by the Khan as supreme head of the Buddhist Church, composed this alphabet, modelled on the Thibetan, for the transliteration of all languages under the sway of Kublai Khan.

The Great Wall and the Ming Tombs

demurely through the gateways with their hints of mists and clouds and vagabond winds and the exquisite astonishments of their tintings— till it seemed as if sorrow and death could never have come that way."

In striking contrast to the wild and savage mood which Nature shows in the Nankou Pass is the peaceful valley about seven miles to the east, where the Ming Tombs lie.[268]

The site of the Thirteen Tombs of the last Chinese dynasty was chosen by the Emperor Yung Lo, when he removed the capital of the Empire from Nanking to Peking. Because of his personal unpopularity in Nanking, he refused even to be buried there near his father Hung Wu, as convention required. But from childhood Yung Lo showed a powerful and violent character and a determination to have his own way. Hung Wu, the founder of the Ming dynasty, of whom Yung Lo was the real consolidator, is said to have had a dream in which he saw a black dragon menacing him from one of the columns of the throne hall. The astrologer consulted on the occasion declined to interpret the dream but advised Hung Wu to observe his own family closely. Then one day, when his twenty-three sons were playing around him, he noticed that the future emperor Yung Lo, least liked by him on account of his intractable disposition and distinguished by an unusually swarthy complexion, did not join in the game but stood watching sullenly with both arms round a column. The dream immediately recurred to his mind. Not long afterwards, the young prince was sent to the distant province of Yen (Peking) where he feigned madness, presumably to ward off the suspicions his domineering nature had created.

When Hung Wu, to maintain the principle of primogeniture[269] which he wished to establish, left the throne to

---

[268] Visitors pressed for time may now visit the Tombs by motor car direct from Peking and return the same day. The trip requires about three hours each way over passable roads.

[269] This principle was not followed by his successors. Later emperors, while claiming the right to choose their heirs, did not necessarily leave the throne to their eldest son but selected the one who seemed to be most suited for the exalted position. Theoretically sound, this system led in practise to family

the eldest son of his eldest son (already dead), the appointed heir found more than his match when he attempted to forestall his uncle's jealousies. In a difficult campaign the latter vanquished his armies and took Nanking, whence the defeated claimant fled to become what Hung Wu had started as—a monk.[270]

Yung Lo's advent to the throne was marked by the most atrocious cruelties against the followers of his nephew. Legend says that one man who dared protest was beheaded in the young Emperor's presence, and the blood gushing from his neck formed the character for "traitor" in the sand—a last revengeful allusion to the despotic ruler. Another who refused to "k'o-tow" to him was placed in a vat of boiling oil, but even in his death agonies he turned his back on the sovereign. A third was skinned alive and his empty skin suspended by a nail from one of the gates of Nanking. Whilst Yung Lo was riding through the gate on a windy day, the dry skin, like a clown's bladder, blew down and slapped him smartly on the face, whereupon the bystanders laughed. This disagreeable incident was the last straw which decided the monarch to leave Nanking where he was so hated and where he had so many unpleasant remembrances. But his subsequent career proved him a great ruler. His military expeditions not only united China, but brought Mongolia and Indo-China under his sway. The death of Tamerlane spared him the test of an encounter with the Terrible Lame One, but Chinese fleets meanwhile dominated the South Sea and the Indian Ocean. The pandects and the great encyclopaedia, bearing Yung Lo's name, the literary and artistic works dating from his reign, complete the glorious record he has left to posterity.[271]

When laying out the tombs for himself and his heirs Yung Lo followed the general plan of Imperial graves which had remained unchanged since the abandonment of the primitive earth pyramid such as marks the burial grounds of the Chou

---

feuds. K'ang Hsi's choice of an heir is a case in point.
270 See Chapter XIII.
271 See Chapter I.

The Great Wall and the Ming Tombs

and Han sovereigns. The T'angs and the Sungs had their triumphant approaches with attendant figures, their tablet-temples where the spirits were worshipped, their evergreen groves, their tower-sheltered vaults cut into the slopes of the hills. Yung Lo had his, only bigger and finer. In fact, before the dethronement of the dynasty, the tombs of the Ming emperors undoubtedly formed one of the largest and most gorgeous royal cemeteries ever laid out by the hand of man. They yield the palm to the Pyramids of Egypt in point of bulk, but certainly not in that of style or grandeur.

One common approach, designated in the Annals as "The Spirit's Road for the Combined Mausolea,"[272] serves for all the tombs dotted about the valley, not in chronological order but wherever each emperor found a site suited to his horoscope. It begins with a magnificent five-arched marble *p'ai lou* (erected a.d. 1541), the finest in China,[273] through whose openings we get a general view along the whole avenue with a background of hills protecting the vale of the dead. In the foreground, a human touch is given by the bronzed farmer leading two grey donkeys with panniers full of persimmons—splashes of golden red and orange, "richer and riper than the golden apples of the fabled Hesperides."

Were we back in Ming days, we should be forced to dismount at the "Great Red Gate" ("Ta Hung Men," a feature of all Imperial necropoli in China) like the retainers who accompanied funeral or sacrificial corteges. Now we may, if we choose, commit the sacrilege of riding up to the second pavilion called the "Tablet House" where stands the huge stone monolith on the largest stone tortoise in North China, a monolith erected by the Emperor Jen Tsung in memory of his

---

[272] Before the overthrow of the Mings, this "Road of the Spirit" was even more impressive than now, because it was lined with stately evergreens. The Tablet House stood in the midst of a park. But notwithstanding orders given by the first Manchu emperors to safeguard the Ming Tombs, the country people cut the trees for fuel and timber as soon as they dared do so.
[273] The height of this impressive archway, measured from the platform on which it stands, is a little under nine metres, the total length a little over ,twenty-one metres.

father (1425), inscribed by Ch'ien Lung with "thirty elegies" in honour of the Ming sovereigns, and guarded by four pillars with sculptured clouds, classically called the "Columns Bearing the Sky."

Here we enter upon the "Triumphal Way," two-thirds of a mile long, paved throughout its length and lined with eighteen pairs of statues of men and animals: two sitting lions, two standing lions, two unicorns rampant and two couchant, two camels kneeling and two standing, four "ch'i lin" (mythical monsters), four horses, four elephants, four civil officials in full robes, four military officials in armour and four "patriotic officials" bearing tablets.

The stately warriors in their sober suits of grey stone are impressive. We guess what valiant men they were from the sternness of their faces. But, of course, everything about them is antiquated and useless from their fantastic helmets to their ponderous boots that are far too heavy to advance or reconnoitre in, or do any of those complicated things modern soldiers have to do. Survivals of their wild, harsh age—the age of tyrants—they stand steadfastly guarding the master they served, reminding us of the old saying: "By day shineth the sun, by night shineth the moon—shineth also the warrior in harness of war."

"To their divinely descended lord, faithful retainers such as they owed everything; in fact, not less than in theory—property, liberty, life itself. Any or all of these they were expected to yield up without a murmur for the sake of that lord. And duty to him, like duty to the family ancestors, did not cease with death. The spirit of the master must continue to be worshipfully served by those who in life owed him direct obedience, and it could not be permitted to enter unattended into the World of Shadows." Thus in early times arose the custom of human sacrifices, at the grave. But finally according to the Records, one compassionate emperor said: "It is a very painful thing to force, or even permit, those whom one has loved in life to follow one in death. Though it be an ancient custom, why continue it if it is bad?" From this time onward the

The Great Wall and the Ming Tombs

suggestion of a court noble, evidently an interested party, that images of men and animals (made of stone, clay, wood and nowadays of paper) be substituted for human sacrifices, was approved. These were sometimes set up at the entrance to the tomb; sometimes placed in the grave chamber; and sometimes burned while the funeral was in progress.

Beyond the last pair of images, the road passes through the triple "Dragon and Phoenix Gate" whence we can distinguish most of the thirteen tombs in their amphitheatre of hills, with the dominating sepulchre of Yung Lo, the Ch'ang Ling, standing out more distinctly than all the rest.

Then the avenue crosses several ruined bridges over mountain torrent beds, dry except in the rainy season, and gently climbs the slope of the hill. Amid such ideally "auspicious conditions" (*feng-shui*) the soul of Yung Lo reposes, and his body lies in a mausoleum more beautiful than any in all the length and breadth of the land.

Three porticoes stand at the entrance to his tomb opening into an outer courtyard with twisted trees. A second gate leads to an inner court with commemoratory stelse and tiled furnaces. The impression culminates in the great sacrificial hall where the rites of ancestral worship have been performed in his honour, not only by his own descendants[274] but also by some of the Manchu sovereigns who conquered the last Ming ruler.

Mark well the majestic aspect of this hall, the largest building in China, full of a grand quietness and reserve. It is worthy of study for the sake of its monumental proportions. Three flights of marble steps lead to the terrace on which it stands, three massive portals with folding doors open into the one vast chamber, seventy yards long by thirty deep—longer than the transept of Westminster Abbey, and about half the length and breadth of Cologne Cathedral. Forty pillars shaped

---

[274] It is curious to note that a direct descendant of. the Ming Dynasty bearing the family name of Chu and occupying a humble position in Peking, used yearly to petition the Manchu emperor for permission to go and sacrifice to the spirits of his ancestors at the Ming tombs. An Imperial Edict was then published in the Court Gazette granting permission and a gift of money for the journey and the ceremonies graciously made.

Juliet Bredon

from tree trunks (*Persea Nan-mu*),[275] each more than twelve feet in circumference and sixty feet high, support the true roof under which there is a lower ceiling about thirty-five feet from the floor. All the magnificence of the empty temple— empty save for a simple wooden table for offerings and the stand for the spirit tablet—is in these columns brightened with vermilion and gold, and sound after nearly 500 years of service, in the heavy cross beams of the roof that they so fittingly uphold, and the ceiling geometrically divided into sunken panels, each worked in relief and lacquered with dragons.[276]

But the tomb itself is not here. It lies beyond the temple and above it. We cross still another court behind, planted, like the preceding, with arbor vitae trees and large-leafed oaks, to the graceful "Soul Tower" containing the tablet inscribed with Yung Loh's posthumous title. Thence a vaulted passage forty yards long leads to the ttimulus, the door of which is closed by masonry. A grey stone stairway climbs among the dark trees to the grave terrace overlooking the mound, classically called the "City of Precious Relics"—an artificial hill more than half a mile in circumference and planted with sombre pines. Beneath this is the huge domed grave chamber where Yung Lo's coffin, richly lacquered and inscribed with Buddhist "sutras," reposes upon its "jewelled bedstead" surrounded by precious stones and metals. Magnificent and elaborate as the tomb buildings are, it is the vault (and remember this is the finest specimen of an Imperial vault in China) upon which most money and labour were expended. The ceiling and sides are lined with blocks of stone so nicely fitted together that supposedly not a drop of moisture can enter. "There is behind the door inside," says Bourne (Proceedings of the Royal Geographical Society, Vol. 5), "a round hole cut in the stone floor and when the door is shut a

---

275 "The '*Nan-mu*' (a species of laurel) is the tallest and straightest of Chinese trees; the grain improves with age, and the wood gradually acquires a dead leaf tint while preserving its aromatic qualities, so that these superb columns of Yung Lo's sacrificial temple, which date from the early pan of the 15th century, still exhale a vague perfume."—*Bushell*.

276 The roof of this splendid hall is now falling to pieces and, unless repairs are made, the building must collapse in a few years.

The Great Wall and the Ming Tombs

large ball of stone follows it and, falling into the hole, by its projecting top prevents the door from ever opening again. Nor could it be opened except by the application of sufficient force to smash it to pieces. When this door has been shut, the deceased emperor is believed to be at peace for evermore."[277]

Nevertheless, despite all these precautions, the Ming tombs were looted by the rebellious soldiers of Li Tzu-ch'eng when the dynasty was overthrown.

Stilled is the turbulent spirit, ended those varied activities which made Yung Lo famous. But we cannot conceive a nobler or more fitting sepulchre for the founder of all that is grand and impressive in Peking. We have so much for which to thank him in the capital he created for China: the wonderful walls he built for it, the palaces he enshrined there, the Temple of Heaven that he called into being! And looking at his tomb we find ourselves thinking that he has even triumphed in some measure over death, for who shall outwit death but "he who creates beauty too beautiful to die?"

Our reverie is rudely broken by a tattered coolie who inquires if we will buy soda water or lemonade. He keeps a little stall of drinks and cigarettes under the shelter of the outer gate. It reminds us of a buffet at some way-station in Europe—only we miss the familiar advertisements of mineral waters and the pictures of the ships by which you ought to go to America, and the hotels at which you ought to stay in Paris. Frankly it jars a little. All the same we buy the lemonade because we feel hot and rather sorry for the coolie who is very poor, since his allowance as caretaker is no longer paid by the poverty-stricken owners of the Ming tombs. But when he offers to sell us a yellow tile from the roof, we refuse to purchase it, much to his amazement. Would we perhaps prefer one more perfect than those which have already fallen like golden leaves as the grass and weeds have pushed the roofs apart? If so, a long bamboo is ready to coax one from the eaves. No, certainly

---

[277] For a detailed description of Imperial tombs see *The Religious System of China*, by J. J. M. de Groot.

not. Let the past tumble down in peace if tumble down it must, though we shudder at the indifference that suffers it.

The other tombs of the group are so greatly inferior to that of Yung Lo, except for the beauty of their situation, that they are scarcely worth visiting.

These tombs are:

The Hsien Ling in which Hung Hsi (posthumous title Jen Tsung) was buried in a.d. 1426 after a short reign of ten months.

The Ching Ling where Hsuan. Teh (Hsuan Tsung) lies, buried in a.d. 1435—a fair and moderate monarch whose peaceful and prosperous reign is famous for the casting of bronzes.

The Yu Ling, sepulchre of Cheng T'ung (Ying Tsung), buried in a.d. 1465, the sovereign who, after a long eunuch regency, was made prisoner by the Mongols, and on being released, found his brother had usurped his throne[278] which he regained—only to fall back under the nefarious influences of the beginning of his reign.

The Miao Ling, tomb of Ch'eng Hua (Hsien Tsung), buried in a.d. 1488 at the height of the Ming prosperity; a benefactor of the people, yet not far-seeing enough to check the growing power of the palace eunuchs.

The T'ai Ling in which rests Hung Chih (Hsiao Tsung), buried in a.d. 1506, a kindly monarch of average abilities and indifferent decision.

The K'ang Ling where lies Cheng Teh (Wu Tsung), buried in a.d. 1522, remembered as a dissolute bon vivant who neglected

---

[278] See Chapters X and XIII.

The Great Wall and the Ming Tombs

state affairs, yet withal a talented personality, a famous linguist, traveller and huntsman.

The Ying Ling, tomb of Chia Ching (Shih Tsung), buried in a.d. 1567, the bigoted Taoist, destroyer of Buddhist temples, whose long but unlucky reign was disturbed by Mongol and Japanese raids.

The Chao Ling in which Lung Ch'ing (Mu Tsung), a promising monarch who died young, was buried in a.d. 1573.

The Yung Ling where Wan Li (Shen Tsung) lies, buried in a.d. 1620. This amiable figure occupied the throne for many years, during which he saw desultory wars with the mighty Japanese captain, Hideyoshi, the dreaded growth of European influence, and the rise of the Manchus. Foreigners chiefly remember him for the famous porcelain made in his time. Historians note the decadence of the dynasty at his death.

The Ch'ing Ling, sepulchre of the kindly T'ai Ch'ang (Kuang Tsung), who died after only a month on the throne (a.d. 1620), presumably poisoned.

The Teh Ling, tomb of T'ien Ch'i (Hsi Tsung), buried in a.d. 1628, called "The Unhappy," and chiefly known to fame as an enthusiastic amateur carpenter. He left the real power in the hands of the corrupt eunuch Wei Chung-hsien[279] and of his foster-mother, both of whom he blindly trusted, while he passed his days with saw and axe. How they misused it may be seen by the rapid downfall of the Mings and by the judgment of K'ang Hsi, who rightly placed the blame on this inattentive emperor and had his tablet removed from the Ti Wang Miao (Pantheon).

The Ssu Ling, erected by the Manchu Emperor Shun Chih, where lies Ch'ung Cheng (Huai Tsung), last of his line, buried here in a.d. 1659. He made a heroic effort to cleanse his court

---

[279] See Chapter XV.

and government but, in spite of all his ambition and energy, it was too late to undo the harm wrought by his predecessors, as he found to his ultimate despair. He is the emperor who strangled himself on the Coal Hill upon the approach of the rebels that brought about the fall of the dynasty and were indirectly responsible for the coming of the Manchus.[280]

By order of Li Tz'u-ch'eng, the conqueror, perhaps in atonement for the desecration of the dynastic tombs when his soldiers got out of hand, two door panels were brought and the emperor's body, together with that of his faithful eunuch attendant, carried to a shop inside the Tung Hua Men. "Here the remains lay for three days while the people were allowed to pay their respects, after which eunuchs were ordered to array the late sovereign in Imperial robes and to dress his hair before laying him in his coffin...."

"On the third of the fourth moon the emperor and his consort were temporarily buried in the grave of the T'ien concubine, but only eunuchs and peasants witnessed the interment. Later, when Li Tz'u-ch'eng had been defeated and the Manchus entered Peking, their Regent, Prince Jui,[281] ordered the building of an Imperial mausoleum and prescribed three days of general mourning. But for the time, the last of the Ming emperors went to his rest unhonoured..."

An account of the burial ceremony, which it is mteresting to quote for its description of a grave chamber, was subsequently given to the Manchu Regent by the minor official who carried it out by command of the rebel Prefect of Peking:[282]

"Seven days after the capture of Peking, I received orders that we were to inter their late Majesties in the grave chamber of the late concubine, the Lady T'ien, and that I was to engage labourers, whose wages would be paid out of the public funds, to open up the passage leading thereto. I therefore engaged

---

280 See Chapters II and VI.
281 See Chapter X.
282 See *Annals and Memoirs of the Court of Peking*, by Backhouse and Bland.

thirty bearers for the Imperial coffin and sixteen for that of the empress, and arranged for their conveyance to Ch'ang P'ing Chou. The departmental treasury was quite empty and as the secretary of Li Tz'u-ch'eng's Board of Ceremonies refused to provide the promised funds, I was obliged to collect subscriptions from charitable persons. Thanks to the generosity of two worthies I obtained the sum of 340 *tiao* (at that time about £6). So I set to work to open up the grave tunnel which was 135 feet long. We toiled three days and three nights before we came to the stone gate opening into the ante-chamber. Inside we found a lofty hall containing sacrificial vessels and many ornaments.

In the centre was a stone vessel whereon stood enormous candles of walrus fat, the so-called 'Everlasting Lamps.' Next we opened the central tunnel gate and found ourselves within a much larger hall in the centre of which stood a stone couch one foot five inches high and ten feet broad, and on it lay the coffin of the Lady T'ien, covered with silk drapery.

"The following day the two coffins were borne through the tunnel and into the grave chamber. We offered sacrifice of a bullock, gold and silver paper, grain and fruits. At the head of the few officials present I proceeded to pay homage to our departed sovereign and we all wept bitterly beside the Imperial biers. Then we placed the coffins on the stone couch, His Majesty's in the central place, that of the Empress on the left and that of the Lady T'ien on the right. The Lady T'ien's death had occurred at a time of peace and, consequently, her coffin had been provided with the customary outer shell. As there had been no means of preparing one in the present case for His Majesty, I had this shell removed and used to cover that of the emperor. The obsequies being over, we refilled the tunnel, banking up the earth so as to conceal the approach. On the following morning we offered libations of wine, and I had a mound erected over the grave by the peasants of the neighbourhood, beside building a clay wall five feet high round the enclosure."[283]

---

[283] The faithful eunuch who followed the emperor to death was buried just

Juliet Bredon

Thus passed the last Ming sovereign from the Dragon Throne and no better epitaph for the dynasty can be found than Boulger's characteristic appreciation:

"When they had driven out the Mongols, the Mings seem to have settled down into an ordinary and intensely national line of rulers.... The Chinese acquiesced in their rule and even showed that they possessed for it a special regard and affection." Yet with the single exception of Yung Lo, "the successors of Hung Wu did nothing great or noteworthy." Of many of these sovereigns we may say that their tombs are more noble than their lives.

---

outside the gate of his Imperial Master's tomb.

XVIII. The Hsi Ling and the Tung Ling

Besides the Ming Tombs there are in the neighbourhood of Peking two other Imperial burial places, rivals in the beauty of their situation and the lavish extravagance of their architecture—the Hsi Ling, or Western Tombs, where some of the Manchu emperors are buried, and the Tung Ling, or Eastern Tombs, where the remainder of the Ch'ings, save only the first two who lie at Mukden, have their sepulchres. Both are more inaccessible than the Ming Mausolea, therefore less known to foreigners. But the Hsi Ling, at least, was not a very long nor a very difficult excursion a few years ago when better railway communications prevailed in China.

The first stage, as far as Kao Pei Tien (84 kilometres) could then be done on the Peking-Hankow line with some hope of regular trains. Near Liang Hsiang Hsien, as one looked out of the car window, a pagoda (the T'a Pao T'a), standing on a mound of red earth, caught the eye. This pagoda dates from the Sung dynasty with which it is connected by a quaint legend. When the first Sung emperors established their sway in K'ai Feng Fu, they found first a dangerous opponent and later a powerful supporter in Yang Chi-yeh, the father of eight gallant youths borne to him by his no less gallant wife, a lady who acted more than once as Commander-in-Chief of her husband's armies. This was just the era—about a.d. 1000—when the Liaos in Peking rose to high fortune under the leadership of the brave Empress Hsiao Tui-chih, the builder of Po Wang Shan, as a monument to her six sons killed on the battlefield.[284] Now in a campaign against old Yang Chi-yeh, she saw him lose all of his sons but one. But while she survived her sorrow, the old soldier succumbed to his. Was it some chord of sympathy, a mother's pity for a father's grief—a human sentiment stronger than the enmity of war—which induced her to honour Yang Chi-yeh's memory by burying his body, that had fallen into her hands, under the T'a Pao T'a? His sole surviving heir, however, could

---

284 See Chapter XVI.

not rest while his father's corpse was in the possession of the conqueror. Failing to recover the aged hero's remains from the empress by force, he enlisted the help of a valiant captain, a man with miraculous power to throw out fire from a magic vessel. They set alight the hill where the pagoda stands by supernatural means, and thus gained access to the sepulchre. Yang Chi-yeh's bones were removed to K'ai Feng Fu, but ever since the earth around the pagoda has remained red as though on fire. Needless to say, this story of filial piety appeals greatly to the Chinese.

Forty miles from Peking, near Cho Chou, we pass a village with large stone monuments. The inscription on one informs us that this is the native place of Liu Pei, founder of the later Han dynasty (a.d. 221). A little further on stands a tablet, erected as a memorial to Chang Fei, a mighty man in his cups.[285] For the Chinese both names have many colourful associations. Their Iliad, the "San Kuo Chih," records the adventures of these heroes, and it is well nigh impossible to attend a theatrical performance at which some incident connected with their lives is not acted. The third member of the famous trio, was Kuan Ti, the warrior-patriot later deified, who entered into the relationship of sworn brotherhood with Liu Pei and Chang Fei by taking the celebrated "Oath of the Peach Orchard."

At Kao Pei Tien, a boundary between the Yen and Chou States in the 3rd century b.c., connection is made with a small branch line, built at the command of the Empress Dowager Tz'u Hsi for the use of the sovereigns when visiting the tombs of their ancestors. This railway runs as far as Liang Ko Chuang whence it is rather more than an hour by donkey to the Hsi Ling.

The site of the Western Mausolea was selected by Order of the Emperor Yung Cheng, who in 1730 despatched Prince Yi[286] and the Viceroy of the Liang Kiang provinces to find a suitable location for his final resting place. They chose well. What could be lovelier than the undulating foothills of the foreground, now

---

[285] See Chapter II and Chapter XI.
[286] See Chapter XVI.

The Hsi Ling and the Tung Ling

concealing secluded valleys, now unveiling them, or than the amphitheatre of purple mountains in the background? There is nothing funereal about the place—no unpleasant reminder of a cemetery. It appears rather as some splendid private domain, which indeed it is, being the property of the Ch'ing House. In the midst of pine forests, carefully preserved for centuries though now being ruthlessly cut down, run mile after mile of well-kept roads which here and there emerge from under the long avenues of sombre trees into broad sunny spaces. Marble bridges cross a winding river starred with tiny yellow pond lilies. A crane perched on an overhanging branch recalls a Japanese cut velvet; a flashing dragon-fly poised over the water might serve as a design for a fan.

Climb the low ridge for a general view of the tombs. Up to the threshold of their sanctuaries, the green forest rolls like a gigantic motionless wave. The blue sky above is without fleck or stain, and "the peace of God which passeth all understanding" is spread as a hand above the tree tops.

Though similar in plan to the Ming sepulchres, these Manchu graves differ in that each has its own avenue of animals, its own "Dragon and Phœnix Portal," its own tablet-house—all on a smaller scale than those of Yung Lo's common approach. This is necessitated by the fact that the enclosure is much larger, being over twenty miles in circumference, and most of the tombs are widely separated from one another. The connecting link is supplied by a wall, surrounding the whole enclosure, with a single entrance gate, the classical "Ta Hung Men," flanked by beautiful marble *p'ai lous*.

It was Yung Cheng's intention that all his successors should lie near him here. But when his son and heir, Ch'ien Lung, came to fix the place of his grave, he decided on the Tung Ling in preference to the Hsi Ling, for he argued that if he were buried beside his father, every succeeding sovereign would follow his example and the tombs of the Emperors Shun Chih and K'ang Hsi be left solitary in the Eastern Mausolea. He therefore expressed a desire that the two sites should serve alternately as the burial places of his successors, his immediate

Juliet Bredon

heir using the Western Tombs, the following sovereign the Eastern, and so on. But the rule thus laid down was not followed by the Emperor Tao Kuang whose grave is at the Hsi Ling instead of the Tung Ling, for he could not bear to be separated from his father even in death.

The Imperial graves in the Hsi Ling are:

The T'ai Ling, tomb of Yung Cheng (posthumous title Shih Tsung), buried in a.d. 1737. This monarch was selected by K'ang Hsi, as the ablest of his many sons, to succeed him, which he did at the age of 45. Though he does not rank either in intelligence or character with his illustrious father or his still more illustrious son, history writes him down as a stern, determined and highly creditable sovereign, equal to his office, worthy of his ract;—in short, entitled to stand among the rulers of China who have deserved well of their country.[287] The Ch'ang Ling, tomb of Chia Ch'ing (Jen Tsung), buried in a.d. 1821, who came to the throne when the Manchu glory had reached its height. Nevertheless a strong hand was required to check the underlying elements of disintegration, and Chia Ch'ing was neither equal to the task nor fitted to realize the expectations of his father, Ch'ien Lung, who abdicated in his favour. His reign was one long period of insurrection, of border risings, and plottings of secret revolutionary societies. Whatever remained of grandeur in his time was due to the great achievements of Ch'ien Lung who left such a profound impression on his age that, even in the eyes of Europeans, China appeared a formidable empire nearly twenty years after his death. "However absurd the pretensions of the Emperor of China to universal supremacy may be," writes a foreign observer, "it is impossible to travel through his dominions without feeling that he has the finest country within an Imperial fence-ring in the world." At his death, aged 61, Chia Ch'ing, the Chinese prototype of Louis XV, left a diminished authority, an enfeebled power and a discontented people. His path had been smoothed

---

[287] For these characteristics see *A Short History of China*, by D. C. Boulger.

for him by his predecessors; his difficulties were raised by his own indifference and the consequences of his spasmodic and ill-directed energy, scarcely less unfortunate than his habitual apathy, mingled with an excessive devotion to pleasure. Boulger aptly sums up his character and reign when he says: "In twenty-five years he had done as much harm to his country as his father had conferred advantages upon it in his brilliant rule of sixty years."

The Mu Ling, tomb of Tao Kuang (Hsuan Tsung), buried in a.d. 1852. Though in every sense a worthier prince than his father, he reaped the consequences of the latter's careless government. The canker so long growing, began to show upon what still appeared a fair and prosperous surface when Chia Ch'ing died. As a young man Tao Kuang had seen his country under his grandfather's wise rule, but a subsequent school of adversity imbued him with the disposition to bear calamity without, however, the vigour to grapple with it. To his credit be it recorded that he realised the extent of the national decay, avoided unnecessary expenditure and never wasted public money on his pleasures or his person—virtues somewhat dimmed by the fact that Tao Kuang was naturally a miser. Despite the simple and manly habits of a lifetime, he died at 70 in the depth of bodily misery and mental indecision, yet still believing that he had borne and tided over the worst crisis—a hope which the next reign was to prove a futile illusion.

The Ch'ung Ling, tomb of Kuang Hsu (Teh Tsung), buried in a.d. 1909. Grandson of Tao Kuang, he was placed on the throne as a child of three—one of the most pathetic, helpless, yet kindly figures in history, a puppet sovereign in the hands of his indomitable aunt Tz'u Hsi who held the Manchu empire together for the last fifty years of its existence.

The finest of all these tombs is the T'ai Ling—"a dream of gorgeous red, orange, and yellow once shrined among groups of firs, and standing sharply silhouetted against a range of barrier mountains, escaped and precipitous, bright as silver where the sunbeams catch upon the outstanding rocks, but shading off into soft blue tones like the bosom feathers of some beautiful bird. The glowing temples in the foreground resemble a covey of golden pheasants; between them and the beholder lie marble bridges and straight stone paths, leading to the sacred precincts of the tomb—the latter, guarded by large square doors of brilliant crimson, brass-bound and studded with gilded bosses, august in the rigidity of their angles, austere in the simplicity of their outlines. Engirdling walls of deep red, a red that shows richly beneath the dark pillars of the pines,[288] surround a mausoleum where the beauties of nature enhance the purest type of Chinese architecture and leave in the memory of the visitor a dignified, yet not a depressing remembrance of the mighty dead.

The "Spirit Hall," raised on a terrace decorated with bronze incense-burners in the shape of cranes and stags, is the culminating point of colour and splendour. What does this temple hold within? Polite attendants open the fourfold doors with odd-shaped keys, climbing a ladder to reach the highest lock far above a man's head, and we enter a room that seems puny in comparison with Yung Lo's massive hall but has the compensating advantage of being in better repair. The high ceiling is upheld by pillars lacquered in gold. Against a background of yellow embroidered curtains, which hide the recesses where the tablets are kept, stand three thrones, draped with yellow brocade. The central throne bears the tablet-stand. Another triple door leads to the tree-planted court before the grave-mound and the tower that conceals the grave entrance. "Soul Tower" and tumulus are again copied from Yung Lo's, only smaller, but the slab closing the tomb is of carved tile-work instead of stone. In nearly all respects, indeed, these Manchu tombs resemble those of the Chinese Ming emperors. There are the same ovens for burnt offerings, built of encaustic bricks, the same solemn groves in the inner courtyard, the same stone copies of sacrificial vessels before the tomb, but low down among the trees and far away. At the Ming Ling, however, all is in ruins; here all is in comparatively good condition.

---

[288] *Round About my Peking Garden,* by Mrs. A. Little.

The Hsi Ling and the Tung Ling

A short distance behind the T'ai Ling is the T'ai Tung Ling, the beautiful grave of Yung Cheng's empress Hsiao Sheng (Niuhulu), mother of Ch'ien Lung. Except that the carvings and embroideries in the sacrificial hall are not dragons but phoenixes, it is practically a replica of the tomb of her husband.

Quite near the T'ai Ling group is the Ch'ang Ling where Chia Ch'ing lies, and associated with it likewise is the grave of his empress consort (the Ch'ang Hsi Ling), mother of the Emperor Tao Kuang. The Ch'ang Ling is exactly like the T'ai Ling only a shade less grand, everything being on a slightly diminished scale. There is just an indication here that times were going down, that Chia Ch'ing, in death as in life, enjoyed neither the power nor the pomp of his forefathers.

The *p'ai lous* at the entrance are missing, and the approach curves off almost informally from the older tomb. A small avenue of stone animals—only one pair of each kind—constitutes the "Spirit Road." Quaint creatures they are too. The man who carved the lions evidently never saw a live model; working from descriptions he made a caricature of the king of beasts with a supercilious smile. As for the camels one might say like Bungay of Bandiloo: "The 'umps allus seemed to me kinder onnateral and oncalled-for like, and calkilated to make folk feel creepy." A tablet-house stands as usual surrounded by four tall stone pillars engirdled by dragons, and griffin-topped. A "Dragon and Phoenix Gate" with handsome insets of tiles faces the buildings. Did ever roofs show their glorious colouring to better advantage than these when surrounded by woods full of poetry and repose?

The Mu Ling differs somewhat from the other tombs. It lies far to the south in a little valley of its own and strikes a note of. originality which one would like to think was due to rebellion against the usual slavish imitation on the part of the builder. To tell the truth, it was nothing of the kind. Tao Kuang who lies here was parsimonious, as we know. He sacrificed the avenue of animals to save money. He skimped on the grave itself, rejecting, the usual expensive tumulus and building a concrete-covered mound, circular in shape and raised on terraces, instead.[289] Then, like so many careful spenders, he burst into sudden extravagance over his sacrificial hall, inscribed as the "Palace of Distinguished Benefits," and constructed the whole of aromatic sandalwood which in its polished simplicity is more effective than brilliant painting.

A very lovely but long excursion may be made from this tomb around to the foot of the mountains which we see from the T'ai Ling and Ch'ang Ling. Here stand three old pagodas, remnants of temples more ancient than the tombs. The hard climb to the two, half-way up the hills, will repay us with a magnificent view. But the peasants in the valley advise against attempting the ascent. A storm is coming, they say, and rightly. No sooner have we reached the top than the tempest bursts, and for over an hour we are in the midst of the broken stormcloud with the crash and roll of thunder all around us. Then it lifts as suddenly as it descended. Already when we start on the downward trail, we see dimly, through the veils of dissipating mist, patches of green earth that appear like mossy stones at the bottom of deep water.

All the way down the valley hosts of little green frogs hop ahead of us along the pathway. The splash as they fall back, startled, into some rivulet is sharp and clear. The rocks are still wet and shining. Big drops of rain still tremble on the thatched eaves of cottages and the crops lie prone as though weary in the little plots of land which the peasants cultivate unrebuked inside the *feng-shui* walls—though theoretically they are forbidden to till this consecrated soil.

But by the time we enter the forest again, the sun is shining brightly and every dripping leaf has become a jewel. The vivid wood-peckers have already resumed work on tree-trunks dark brown with wet. The golden orioles are flashing off in search of provisions, the doves are cooing in the eaves of the tombs; the swallows perch boldly on memorial tablets to dry their wings—hosts of them, all with their heads to the road like curious spectators. They seem in no wise disturbed by our coming but

---

289 This is the common form of the tombs of non-reigning members of the Imperial family.

The Hsi Ling and the Tung Ling

remain quite still looking down upon us as mere passing phenomena, not to be taken seriously.

The Ch'ung Ling, Kuang Hsu's tomb, is practically outside the enclosure and may most conveniently be seen on the way back to the station. Its spotless monuments make an impressive ensemble from a distance. On closer inspection, we find the marble of poorer quality, the workmanship inferior—perhaps because this grave was only finished under the Republican Government which could not be expected to take much interest in an Emperor's resting place, though it did make a special grant of 3,000,000 taels to complete it. The Empress Lung Yu is buried near her husband,[290] which is rather tragic considering that they hated each other in life and kept apart as much as possible. The woman he did love, the unhappy Pearl Concubine,[291] lies on the opposite hill-side in a small, neglected tomb with one lonely poplar growing out of the little tumulous.

The ex-Emperor Hsuan Tung, though still a young man, has his mausoleum in course of preparation on a site to the east, a few *li* distant from Kuang Hsu's burial place.[292] Last of his line and shorn by the irony of fate of mortal possessions beyond the dreams of avarice, even his tomb, on a parched brown slope, is denied the gracious shade of funeral cypresses.

The Tung Ling were, once upon a time, even finer than the Hsi Ling; their enclosure vaster... their forests older and grander, and their situation more picturesque since the Great Wall itself forms the northern boundary—crowning the barrier

---

290 It was customary for an Imperial wife dying before her husband to be buried in his tomb—always built in the sovereign's lifetime. But after the burial of an emperor, the doors of his grave chamber were forever sealed and his widow must therefore have a grave of her own—a very expensive luxury demanded by custom because the Chinese disliked having "superiors" (men) disturbed in their rest by "inferiors" (women).
291 See Chapters V and XI.
292 This custom of building a tomb during the lifetime of the person who is to occupy it—a custom dating from ancient times—is still prevalent, and a site so prepared is given the special name of "Longevity Region."

Juliet Bredon

mountains that "like Giants stand, To sentinel an enchanted land."

The desecration of these tombs in 1928 was a national calamity. But the careless vandalism that ruined their setting—the last and largest forest in North China—is almost as great a tragedy.

Five emperors, including the most famous of the Manchu sovereigns, lie in the magnificent park that used to be heavily wooded and filled with wild creatures of rare species.[293]

The Hsiao Ling contains the mortal remains of Shun Chih, buried in a.d. 1663 with the posthumous title of Shih Tsu—the very same characters given to Kublai Khan. After the first years of consolidation of Manchu power by his famous uncle the Dorgun Amah Wang,[294] Shun Chih took over the reins of Government at fourteen, formed and adapted the new regime, compiled a code of laws, and cemented the ties between China and Lamaist Thibet. His leaning towards religion was so marked that it gave ground to the legends of his abdication and retirement into a monastery. "Quite apart from the delicacy of his constitution, which probably had a share in creating in him a distaste for the wearisome formalities and futilities of a monarch's life, he seems to have been intended by nature to be a pensive student, perhaps even a religious recluse," says Johnston in his *The Romance of an Emperor*. But despite legend, there is no conclusive evidence. that he ever. resigned his responsibilities. Among the founders of Manchu greatness, he deserves full credit for his sincerity of purpose, his moderation, wisdom, and foresight towards a conquered people, thus paving the way for K'ang Hsi to reap, through the love and reverence of his subjects, the allegiance he himself secured through military prowess and a lucky star.

---

[293] For a good map of the Tung Ling region and an accurate description of the various stages of the journey to these Eastern tombs, etc., see "*Voyage d'Etude aux Tongs Lings*, by Captain Dubreuil. Unfortunately travel conditions are difficult at present, roads bad and bandits prevalent, so that only the hardy and adventurous are advised to attempt this expedition to the Eastern Mausolea over a hundred miles distant from Peking.
[294] See Chapters X, XV and XXI

The Hsi Ling and the Tung Ling

The Ching Ling is the last resting place of K'ang Hsi (Sheng Tsu), buried in a.d. 1723, third son of Shun Chih —a most remarkable man in all respects. While still in his teens, he put down a formidable rebellion, and for the greater part of his long reign he was planning or conducting diverse campaigns in Mongolia and Central Asia. Yet he found time to do a great work of internal administration, to build, to encourage literature and art, to write books himself, to win the admiration of those Jesuits whose talents adorned his Court, and the friendship of a kindred spirit in Russia's giant sovereign, Peter the Great, his contemporary. Boulger's appreciation gives life to this historic figure. "The place of K'ang Hsi, among Chinese sovereigns," he says, "is clearly defined. He ranks on almost equal terms with the two greatest of them—T'ai Tsung (of the T'ang dynasty) and his own grandson Ch'ien Lung. Just posterity will beyond doubt assign to this prince a distinguished place among the monarchs of all nations...." "Brave, generous, wise, active and vigilant in policy, of profound and extended genius, having nothing of the pomp and indolence of Asiatic Courts although his power and wealth were both immense..." so de Mailla describes him. In literary attainments he proved the equal, if not the superior, of the learned Chinese scholars of his day. His poems were the most widely read book in China. In addition he knew Latin, Mongolian and Thibetan. The end of the life of this great and good man was marred, however, by domestic troubles and disputes. Yet he died on the summits of splendour and sorrow with supreme dignity and courage.

The Yu Ling is the tomb of Ch'ien Lung (Kao Tsung), buried a,d. 1799, fourth son of Yung Cheng— often called "the greatest monarch of China." As we stand beside his grave, the whole glorious epoch of his reign— the most important in mediseval Chinese history—comes back to mind. The unsurpassed military exploits, the unequalled literary, artistic and administrative achievements of the period would stamp it as an age of unexampled prosperity in any country. How well this monarch established the supremacy of his race, how well he enlisted the co-operation of a great people, how well he employed his resources in extending his dominions from Siam to Siberia and Nepaul to Korea! K'ang Hsi accomplished much, yet he also left much undone. Ch'ien Lung succeeded in everything he undertook and succeeded wholly—so much so that from the military point of view there remained no conquest for the loftiest ambition to accomplish when he at last sheathed his sword and retired into private life. Yet his dream was not to be remembered as a soldier, but rather as the kindly, paternal ruler, father of his people, which is the highest ideal of a Chinese emperor. This too he realised by unremitting attention to the nation's wants, and zeal in furthering what he considered its best interests— realised so well that by common consent the title of Magnificent was attached to his reign. With his death, the vigour of China began to ebb. The blind folly, the feeble-minded vascillation and miserable trickery by which this magnificent heritage was muddled away, is one of the saddest tragedies in the story of nations.

The Ting Ling is the resting place of the fourth son of Tao Kuang, Hsien Feng (Wen Tsung), buried in a.d. 1865, the dissolute, stubborn, narrow-minded heir of an unlucky father. Although at the outstart of his reign he took upon himself, in an official decree, all the blame for the calamities which overtook China, he still secretly kept an exaggerated idea of his own importance with no power to maintain it. The disastrous Taiping Rebellion and the second European war soon proved the hollowness of such pretensions. He died at thirty in the Jehol palace, a fugitive from international justice,[295] leaving the throne to his only son.

The Hui Ling is the tomb of T'ung Chih (Mu Tsung), buried in a.d. 1879. During his minority, some efforts at reform were undertaken by men like Tseng Kuo-fan, Tso Tsung-t'ang and Li Hung-chang under the joint regency of the two empresses. When he took over the Government at the age of seventeen, he was by all accounts a person who wished men well. But two years after his accession he died of smallpox, and was buried with his wife Alute, supposed to have been a victim of the

---

[295] See Chapter XIV.

The Hsi Ling and the Tung Ling

Empress Dowager Tz'u Hsi's vengeful cruelty—a sweet, young figure, "to whom will be given the sympathy of all ages."

Besides the sovereigns, many other Imperial persons are buried at the Hsi Ling—empresses and concubines,[296] those uncrowned favourites who sometimes did much to shape the course of events, notwithstanding the Western idea that' women wield no power in China, and sons and daughters of prolific monarchs like K'ang Hsi and Ch'ien Lung.[297] Such graves, especially those of children who died while still of tender years, are often unimpressive and always so very similar that a detailed description would be superfluous. Yet each one, if we have the patience to seek it out and learn the story of its occupant, forms a piece of the mosaic of the Manchu regime—part of the picture where greatness and misrule are painted together.

Just outside the space reserved for the Imperial family, lie two tombs. One is the resting place of K'ang Hsi's old teacher whom the Emperor so greatly loved and revered that he permitted him to be buried as near the Imperial Person as convention allowed. There is something very touching in the story of the influence of this venerable man over the absolute monarch whose youthful outbursts of anger he could calm with a word, whose generous impulses he could quicken with a smile. For he represents all that was brave, true, and noble in the old order of things, and is an example of that peculiar Oriental relationship between teacher and pupil which often endures throughout the life-time of both—even when the pupil rises in position far higher than his master.

The second tomb beyond the boundaries is that of the upright and fearless Censor Wu Ko-t'u. He protested against the illegal succession of the Emperor Kuang Hsu by committing

---

[296] In the green tiled buildings of the *Fei-li*ng alone are buried the thirty-nine *kuei-fei*, or concubines, of the Emperor Ch'ien Lung and in the Ching Fei-ling the thirty secondary wives of the Emperor K'ang Hsi.

[297] Among the Manchu sovereigns virility and greatness were characteristics that ever went together.

Juliet Bredon

suicide near the mausoleum of T'ung Chih, whose ghost was disinherited by the new nomination to the throne.

It is curious how frequently the Imperial tombs have been the scene of protests and unseemly wrangles, wherein grievances and passions long pent up within palace precincts find utterance.[298] One case of this kind occurred in 1909 on the occasion of the burial of Tz'u Hsi, when the surviving consorts of T'ung Chih and Kuang Hsu, having quarrelled with the new Empress Dowager (Lung Yu) on a question of precedence, refused to return to the city and "remained in dudgeon at the tomb until a special mission under an Imperial Duke was sent humbly to beg them to come back, causing no small scandal among the orthodox."

Even the building of an Imperial tomb at the Tung Ling generally involved squabbles over the percentages which should go into the pockets of the various officials in charge. It was certainly a huge undertaking. Take for example the preparation and labour involved in transporting the large blocks of marble for the effigies of the camels and elephants in the avenues of animals. Rennie, Surgeon of the British Legation, gives an interesting account in his book, *Peking and the Pekinese*, of how one such mass of stone was carried to the spot where it was placed in position and hewn into shape. "In 1862," he says, "I heard of a large block of marble weighing sixty tons which was at that time in course of passing through Peking on a six-wheeled truck drawn by 600 horses and mules. This mass of marble came from one of the quarries about 100 miles from the capital and was on its way to the eastern tombs, there to be cut into an elephant to form one of the decorations of the mausoleum of the late Emperor Hsien Feng. Its dimensions were fifteen feet long, twelve feet thick, and twelve feet broad. The horses and mules were harnessed to two immense hawsers running parallel with one another from the truck, the length of each of them being nearly a quarter of a mile. On the block was hoisted the Imperial flag, and on the truck a mandarin and some attendants were seated. One of the latter had a gong

---

298 See *China Under the Empress Dowager*, by Bland and Backhouse.

which he sounded after each halt when all were ready to start. Other gongs were then sounded along the line, and at a given signal the carters simultaneously cracked their whips, and off started the horses with their unwieldy load. The line was led by a man bearing a flag and all orders were given by signals made with flags."

A description of the burial of Hsien Feng, in 1865, as typical of an Imperial interment, may also be of interest:

"In the autumn of this year took place the burial of Hsien Feng, the preparation of whose tomb had been proceeding for just four years. With him was laid his consort Sokota, who had died in 1850, a month before her husband's accession to the throne and whose remains had been awaiting sepulchre in a village temple for fifteen years[299].... As usual, the funeral ceremonies and preparation of the tomb involved vast expenditure. The emperor's mausoleum alone had cost nominally 10,000,000 taels of which amount, of course, a very large sum had been diverted for the benefit of the Household and others.

"The young Emperor and the Empresses Regent proceeded as in duty bound to the Tung Ling to take part in the ceremonies, and Prince Kung, who had been preparing the funeral arrangements for His late Majesty for five years, was in attendance.

"The body of the Sovereign, in an Imperial coffin of catalpa wood richly lacquered, was borne within the huge domed grave and there deposited in the presence of the mourners on its 'Jewelled Bedstead,' the pedestal of precious metals prepared to receive it. Instead of the concubines and servants who in olden days used to be buried alive with the deceased monarch, wooden and paper replicas of life size were placed beside the coffin. The large candles were lighted, prayers were said and a great wealth of valuable ornaments arranged within the grave chamber: gold and jade sceptres, and a necklace of pearls were placed within the coffin. And when all was duly done, the great door of the chamber was slowly lowered and sealed in its place."

---

299 See footnote 290.

Juliet Bredon

Asleep in his eternal night, Hsien Feng lay tranquil after his unlucky life, in the hollow enjoyment of his wealth.

The "funeral ceremonies of the Empress Dowager Tz'u Hsi, were even more impressive. For four days her enormous catafalque was borne by more than a hundred bearers, over a specially made road, to the silent tomb surrounded by virgin forest and backed by the everlasting hills. Here in the mausoleum built by the faithful Yung Lu for his Imperial mistress, at a cost which stands in the Government records at 8,000,000 taels,[300] Tz'u Hsi, after her splendid, and stormy career, was laid to rest.

Who could forsee that a few years later, Her Majesty would be dragged from her coffin, stripped of her Imperial robes, and left lying naked in her desecrated grave chamber? Though the rifling of Imperial tombs was no unusual act of vandalism—since the graves of every dynasty in China have been looted at one time or another,[301] history records no such organised despoiling. Moreover that such instance of sacrilege should take place in modern times and with modern methods, including the use of dynamite, was a great shock to public opinion.

According to Chinese reports it was a divisional commander who, under orders from a general, broke open the Eastern tombs. Using axes and explosives to force their way into the Mausolea, his soldiers not only stole everything of value from the grave chambers—sufficiently impregnable to resist their efforts for some days—but wantonly destroyed buildings, hacking the lacquer off pillars, and breaking stone monuments.

---

300 Identical in plan but on a smaller scale than the Ting Ling, her husband's tomb, it was in course of construction for over thirty years. Throughout her life-time and particularly in her old age, Tz'u Hsi took a great interest and pride in her last resting-place, visiting it at intervals and exacting the most scrupulous attention from those entrusted with its building and adornment. On one occasion in 1897, when practically completed, she had it rebuilt because the teak pillars were not sufficiently massive.

301 See the valuable memoranda on Chinese Imperial Tombs collected by Mr. Moore Bennett and quoted in *Autumn Leaves* (pp. 248-258) by E. T. C. Werner.

The Hsi Ling and the Tung Ling

No one could trace all the treasures that were actually stolen, though the Chinese newspapers estimated their value—including jewels, jades, four melons made of precious stones known to have been taken from Ch'ien Lung's tomb, etc.—at anywhere from $5,000,000 to $50,000,000 (gold). Though these figures sounded fabulous at the time, they have since been corroborated by the private diary of the chief enunch Li Lien Ying who wrote an account of the burial of Her Majesty Tz'u Hsi and gave a list of what was placed in her coffin.

"Before the Dowager Empress was laid in her coffin," this diary says, "the bottom was spread with a mattress of gold thread seven inches thick, into which was woven an embroidery of pearls. On top of the mattress was laid a lace sheet of pearls with a figure of Buddha. At the head was placed a jade ornament resembling lotus leaves, and at the foot a similar ornament of jade resembling a lotus flower. These were arranged in their places and then the body was lifted into the coffin. The head of the Empress rested on the leaves and her feet on the lotus flower. She was dressed in a ceremonial robe on which pearls were embroidered with gold thread, and over that she wore an embroidered jacket with a rope of pearls, also a rope of pearls encircled her body nine times, and eighteen pearl images of Buddha were laid by her arms. All these were gifts sent by private persons for the Imperial obsequies and were not included in the official list of valuables.

These presents having been so disposed, the body of the Dowager Empress was covered with the sacred *Tolo* Pall, on which are written prayers in Manchu script. A chaplet of pearls was placed in her hand, on her head and by her side were laid gold, jade and gem Buddhas to the number of one hundred and eight. On either side of the feet were placed one water melon and two sweet melons of jade, and jewels carved in the shape of peaches, pears, apricots, dates, etc., to the number of 200. By the left side of the Empress was placed a gem shaped like a lotus root, with flowers and leaves sprouting from the top. On the right there was a coral tree. The interstices were filled with scattered pearls and gems until the whole was level, and over all was spread a network of pearls. As the attendants were in the act of placing the inner lid on the coffin, a certain princess entered and took from a casket a gem ornament of eight galloping horses and another of the Eighteen Buddhist Lohans. She removed the covering and placed these beside the body. She then replaced the pearl quilt and this concluded the ceremony of the en-coffining of the "Old Buddha."

According to the confession of some of the looters caught red-handed by the police, even these vandals were awed by their first sight of the Empress Dowager lying in state on her "jewelled bedstead," looking as if she were alive, "even her hair being in perfect order."

Was it her revengeful spirit which instigated a quarrel among these ghouls over the distribution of the loot —a quarrel which resulted in several deaths among them?

XIX. Peking—The Old Curiosity Shop

When one has seen all the palaces and "done" all the temples and tombs, there still remains a never failing source of interest and amusement in Peking—shopping. The curio shops scattered over the city are the happy hunting ground of the collector in search of things Chinese, rare or fascinating objects which nowhere else in the world are found in such profusion and variety. Few strangers can resist the temptation to bargain for old porcelains, bronzes, embroideries, or whatever appeals to individual taste, and in the resident this habit, sooner or later, develops a special mentality. We shamelessly examine the pictures on each other's walls, turn over our host's dishes at table in search of marks to prove their origin, pick up his lacquer after dinner to feel its weight, boldly inquire the price of his latest acquisition. Such manners, which would be considered ill-bred in Paris or London, are tolerated and understood in the "old curiosity shop," as a witty traveller once called Peking, and if you stay long enough you will acquire them yourself.

There are two methods of shopping—at home, or in the shops themselves. Choose the former and merchants will come to you with blue-cloth bundles which they tirelessly unfold while you sit comfortably back in an armchair. This style of buying is an advantage to the very ignorant, and the very discerning: to the first, because anything appears to them unspeakably desirable; to the second, because, being old customers, the astute salesman knows them and brings the sort of thing they want, thus saving them the trouble of looking over a quantity of trash to find it. But many tourists get no further than the hotel hall where they hover between stalls of knick-knacks, or succumb to the blandishments of a dealer in "very nice Mandarin dance coat, too cheap."

Nevertheless it is a pity not to go to the shops one's self, if only because they are quaint and different from our own. Some have facades of gilded wood so elaborately carved that we feel they should be put under glass as a protection against the dust, but none have show windows. Indeed, few have any windows at all, and the dark, low doorways give little promise of the treasures to be found within. It is fatal to judge, as we would at home, by appearances. Fine feathers do not always mean fine birds. The biggest, and the cleanest shops in Peking may not have the best things. Often a merchant hidden away in a blind alley has the rarest treasures—just as his tiny store has the most high-sounding title. A single-roomed shack is called the "Institution of Felicitous Understanding" and has an old European clock worth $3,000 for sale. A tiny dug-out, known as the "Establishment of Ten-Thousand Glories," offers a most admirable box of Yung-Cheng enamel. In the filthy local "*Cour des Miracles*," east of Ch'ien Men Street, many a good piece has been picked up.

For those strangers with no expert knowledge but a taste for genuine and expensive things, the foreign antiquarians of established reputation are strongly recommended, doubly so to those pressed for time. But given idle hours to while away, the Chinese shops are most amusing and some are really reliable, though the guarantees of others must be taken with a grain of salt. When the big tourist ships arrive, processions of "world-girdlers" rush madly from store to store through the fascinating panorama of the streets gay with lacquered "beckoning boards," showing gilded characters on black or vermilion grounds. These Chinese ideographs, modified for decorative purposes, make a far greater appeal to the eye[302] than our prosaic combinations of letters. They are vivid pictures, they seem to live, to speak, to gesticulate. To them is due much of the local colour of the shopping districts, to them and to the old custom, still followed

---

302 "The picturesque nature of Chinese writing.... demands of those who wish to excel in its practice an education of eye and hand such as are required by draughtsmen. The strokes of the ordinary character are replete indeed, with light and supple touches, sudden stops and -peac0eful curves, waxing energies and gradually waning lines such as only a long apprenticeship of the brush could give. The Chinese *lettré* is firmly convinced that the characters of a perfect writer convey something of their graphic beauty to the ideas they express, and give a delicate, intrinsic shade of meaning to every thought enshrined in them."—*Bushell*.

Peking – The Old Curiosity Shop

by petty tradesmen, of putting images or symbols of their wares over their doors. The shoe-maker's big paper boot, fit for the King of the Mountains, the giant pipe, suitable for his mate, the large gilded coin of the money changer, the hosier's felt stocking hanging from the eaves, the feather duster outside the brush shop, are sighs that never fail to attract the attention of strangers passing by who think themselves in some upside-down wonderland.

To and fro on "Flower Street," in and out of "Donkey Alley," the rickshas file and the sounds of busy bargaining and "last price" offers pursue them as they go. One group stops to buy artificial flowers, embroidered boxes, or barbaric jewellery made of semi- (often *very semi-*) precious stones, another to examine treasures they will hesitate to afford—watches, for example, made in Europe in the 18th century, gorgeously enamelled, wreathed in pearls, studded in diamonds; tiny timepieces set in thumb rings, larger ones such as Chinese princes delighted to hang from their belts in days when belts fitted loosely over satin robes. The prices asked are absurdly high to those who remember how cheaply such jewels were obtainable a few years ago. But newcomers buy, nibbling first gingerly and then, like hungry fishes, swallowing the coveted bait, hook and all, to go boasting afterwards of their excellent meal. *A propos* of watches, a good story is told of how a lovely timepiece broke up a friendship. Two secretaries of Legation, inseparable companions and equally enthusiastic collectors, went together to hunt for watches. They found a treasure which both ardently desired. One, however, thought the curio so much too dear that he relinquished all hope of buying it for himself, though he offered to come back next day and get it for his companion. This was agreed between them, and in the evening, at the club, the would-be owner of the trinket waited eagerly to take possession. "Sorry, cher ami" said the man who had been shopping, "the watch was bought by a tourist this morning." Condolences, vain regrets! But a few weeks later the self-same watch was seen in the cabinet of the secretary who had promised to purchase it for his colleague. Chinese "boys" have an officious habit of setting out what a master carefully hides away when master entertains, in order to make the best impression possible on master's guests. The moral of this little story is: "Never take even your best friend with you to a curio shop. He may want what you want. You cannot decently overbid him—and therefore you risk losing both your curio and your friend."

Quite a number of the best Chinese antiquarians will be found outside Ch'ien Men, in the Liu Li Ch'ang quarter. Here are many shops for the sale of articles indicated by the names of streets like Jade Street, Embroidery Street, Silver Street, Lantern Street, etc. In olden days it was the invariable rule for merchants or artisans belonging to the same Guild to live in the same district. The custom developed partly for the convenience of purchasers but largely to assure mutual protection. Less than than twenty years ago there were still wooden gates topped with iron spikes to close off streets where valuable things were sold, in case of riot or disturbance.

This habit of grouping together is fast dying out and curio shops may now be found all over Peking, on the broad main streets and in the narrow tortuous hutungs as well as in the "specialty streets." The enthusiastic collector hunts up and down the highways and by-ways of the city on the most exciting of all adventures. Sometimes he will search for days and find nothing worth buying, but the hope of drawing a prize in the artistic lottery keeps him interested.

His knowledge may be deficient and inexact, but what he lacks in learning he makes up in love. The stone floors of the shops are cold in winter, he does not notice them; the tiny showrooms stuffy and often an offence to the nose in summer, no matter. The wonders of Chinese art scattered through the museums and collections of Europe, America and Japan, have encouraged people to expect that Peking is an inexhaustible treasure-house, where beautiful works of art at bargain prices may still be easily found. Something, surely, they think, has been overlooked or stolen from the Palace—something, perhaps, remains from the loot of 1860 or 1900,

Peking —The Old Curiosity Shop

Alas, the days of marvellous finds and bargains, at least in genuine old bronzes, the better known porcelains, and the finest pictures, are over. Do not imagine that if by chance a good piece comes on the market, any stranger will pick it up for a song. Whether it appears in Peking itself or elsewhere, a valuable curio is offered first to well-known antiquarians who are waiting for just such opportunities and waiting with ample funds. Yamanaka, the big Japanese dealer, for instance, keeps experts in China the year round. Such men naturally get the best <u>because</u> the dealers know them. They are difficult to cheat because they have years of experience and a perfect familiarity with the books of Chinese critics who have for so many centuries catalogued and described all the masterpieces as they appeared, with a wealth of detail and discrimination unknown elsewhere in the world. At the same time these recognised buyers offer a permanent market, appreciate the value of what is for sale, and are generally willing to pay it.

This by way of warning to the novice who is prone to imagine that in a short time he has become an expert and thinks he may discover what others, who are playing the game ever and always, have overlooked. A real connoisseur of porcelain, let us say, since foreigners are generally interested in porcelain,[303] has a natural gift cultivated by long experience. It

---

303 Porcelain played a great part in the early foreign relations of China. Chinese vases found in Egypt bear the marks of the T'ang and Sung dynasties (*Cathay and the Way Thither*, by Yule-Cordier). Arab trade with the "Middle Kingdom" flourished in the 8th and 9th centuries, and an Arab traveller of that time mentions porcelain vases so transparent that "water is seen through them," as coming from the Land of Sinim. Saladin (1137-1193), Sultan of Egypt and Syria, defender of Acre against the Crusaders, sent forty pieces of fine Chinese porcelain to Nur-ed-din Mahraud, who recovered Syria from the invaders. Marco Polo, writing in 1280, described a visit to a Chinese factory, and stated that the porcelain made there was exported all over the world. Later, when, in the reign of the Ming Emperors Yung Lo and Hsuan Teh a famous eunuch admiral went in command of a fleet of armed junks to India, Ceylon and Arabia, up the Red Sea as far as Jiddah, the port of Mecca, porcelain was included in the list of articles carried by him. Perhaps it was his expedition that brought the celadon vases sent by the Sultan of Egypt in 1487 to Lorenzo de Medici. (See *Chats on Oriental China*,

is a good rule, before buying expensive things, to spend some time studying the genuine works of art in museums or private collections to form the taste and eye. But it is equally essential to read the books of standard authors on the subject, and learn to distinguish the various pastes and glazes, dynastic marks, etc. Unfortunately the name of the potter is rarely attached to his work in China as it is in Japan. Custom required from the Chinese artist, who must begrudge no pains for perfection, a self-discipline sufficiently strong to allow him to merge his personality in a "school," distinguished as a whole by its style, tradition and tendency.

After a little while one becomes, if not exactly expert, at least wise enough to escape obvious pitfalls. Too much dependence, however, must not be placed upon dates (often forged) or decoration, which may have been added later. It is upon the education of the eye that collectors must chiefly rely to judge the general merits of the specimens themselves. No training is so good as the handling of fine pieces—properly authenticated—in which the grain of the porcelain, the colours and the designs can be studied at leisure. The knowledge thus gained becomes the experience which is, above everything else, the necessary equipment for any one who collects old china.

Never forget in the enthusiasm of the moment, when some attractive specimen strikes your fancy, that every trick of Western antiquarians, and a thousand original ones of their own, are familiar to Chinese dealers. They peel their pearls, bury their bronzes to give them a fine patina, dye their furs, smoke their embroideries and ivories, imitate and colour jades, tint rock-crystals, forge date marks and cleverly insert old bottoms in new vases. The temptation to cheat the novice is generally irresistible, in quality, in price, or both, and the most ingratiating and convincing salesman is often the worst offender.

Mended porcelains—and many of the genuine pieces that come on the market nowadays are repaired with a consummate skill that cheats the eye—can often be detected by tapping

---

by J. F. Blacker).

Peking – The Old Curiosity Shop

them with a coin, when the difference in ring between what is whole and what has been replaced is easy to distinguish.

Approach all curios, and most dealers, with caution. A thief may be consided innocent till he is proved guilty, but a first-class K'ang Hsi vase (according to the merchant) should be held guilty of fraud till it is proved to be above suspicion by some one who knows and is disinterested. Such porcelains, if genuine and unbroken are so scarce that there is every reason for mistrust. But if, in addition, the dealer offers the piece as a bargain, telling a hard-luck story about lack of capital, then let caution wait upon enthusiasm. Whenever a Chinese offers to let a good piece go at a sacrifice, be sure that the sacrifice is on the side of the buyer and the victim is the customer, not the shopkeeper. The single season when a large reduction in prices may be expected is just before the Chinese New Year. At this great settling period, every shop-keeper is obliged to pay his debts and, for the ready money which is absolutely necessary to keep up his credit for the next year, he will often sell cheaply to the first bidder.

The few fine porcelains still obtainable in Peking command enormous prices. For people, however, who know enough not to be deceived—unfortunately even experts sometimes disagree—they are an excellent investment. But alas! how seldom we find a real treasure—say a perfect *sang de boeuf* whose luminous red is accounted for by a curious legend.

In ancient days a famous potter received from the emperor an order to make vases the colour of blood. Nine and forty times, with purpose unmoved, did he seek to fulfil the Imperial command. Vainly did he consume his substance, vainly did he expend his strength, vainly did. he exhaust his knowledge. For seven days and nights he fed his furnaces, like another Bernard de Palissy, with all his possessions, while his workmen watched with him the wondrous vases crystallising into being, rose-lighted by the breath of the flame. "Now upon the eighth night,'" say the old chronicles, "the potter bade all his weary comrades retire to rest, for that the work was well-nigh done, and the success assured. 'If you find me not here-at sunrise,' he warned them, 'fear not to take forth the vases, for I know that the task will have been accomplished according to the command of the August.' So they departed. But in that same eighth night the potter entered the fire and yielded up his ghost in the embrace of the Spirit of the Furnace, giving his life for the life of his work, his soul for the soul of his vases. And when the workmen came upon the ninth morning, even the bones of the potter had ceased to be, but lo! the vases lived and glowed with the colour of blood."[304]

Fine *flambés*, whose beauty depends upon a complicated process of firing and re-firing, so that but few potters ever succeeded in blending their colours harmoniously, are equally rare. "The first results were no doubt accidental, though later experience gave certainty to the master-minds of the artists, who were then able to define and measure the combination of the various metallic oxides which would produce exactly the coloration desired." The Chinese call these various splashed or mottled glazes "yao pien," but the better known French name *flammé* or *flambé* is derived from the curious, yet very beautiful, veinings, like flames of fire.[305]

Rarest of all are the Sung porcelains known as "ting-yao," made at Ting Chou in the province of Chihli. This ware of delicate resonant body, invested with a soft-looking fluent glaze of ivory-white tone in the variety known as "pai-ting," or of a yellowish, clayey tint, in that called "t'u-ting," is distinguished by sobriety and severe classical reserve. "The bowls and dishes," says Bushell, "were often fired bottom upwards and the delicate rims, left unglazed, were afterwards mounted with copper to preserve them from injury. Some were clothed in plain white, the glaze collecting outside in tear drops; others were engraved at the point in the paste with ornamental patterns; a third class was impressed inside with intricate and elaborate designs in pronounced relief, the principal ornamental motives being the tree peony, lily flowers and flying phoenixes."

---

[304] See *Some Chinese Ghosts*, by Lafcadio Hearn.
[305] *Chats on Oriental China*, by J. F. Blacker.

Peking – The Old Curiosity Shop

All the more delicate "ch'ai-yao," "thin as paper and clear as a mirror," have long since disappeared, so that we must be content with the literary evidence of Imperial Rescripts to prove their existence.

Even good monochromes dating from the artistic renaissance which took place under the early Manchu Emperors, are hard to find. Beware of copies of the green celadon, the first of the monochromes to be made. This ware is said to have reached its highest development about 1500 when the Turks and Persians bought largely, valuing this self-colour not only for its intrinsic beauty, but because they thought it an infallible test for poison in food.

Good specimens of *clair de lune*, or semi-transparent *blance de Chine* which is supposed to imitate ivory, or the famous "peach-bloom" are practically unobtainable. The latter name is misleading to amateurs who expect the delicate pink of the peach flower, whereas "peach bloom" is actually "a dark reddish brown of unusual but beautiful tone, pierced through its surface in flecks of green and spot* of pink reminding us of the bud when the first touch of spring coaxes it from its dark closed sheath," rather than; the full-blown, rosy blossom.

Middle-class Chinese porcelains are often dearer to-day in Peking than in Paris, New York, London or Tokio. With normal freights, it pays to collect them in the West, ship them back and sell them to globetrotters in China—as has been done. Furthermore, beautiful European imitations of Oriental porcelains, such as those made near Toledo in Spain, have been sent out and put on the local market to deceive the tourist.

Antique bronzes are just as beautiful and valuable as porcelains, though they appeal less to Westerners. But the Chinese themselves are great collectors of bronzes. The sale of Tuan Fang's famous collection, broken up after his death, brought native bidders from every province and caused as great a sensation in the Far Eastern art-world as an auction of Greek marbles would in Europe.

Practically imperishable, this metal has the glamour of great antiquity, for the art of making and decorating bronze was known in China many centuries before Christ. And the shapes in which the early vessels were cast recall the first earthenware jars made by primitive man. Above all a ghostlier value attaches to fine bronzes—faint memories of the half forgotten lives and vanishing beliefs with which they were connected. Sometimes they bring queer fancies to the mind about wrecks of souls, or at least of psychic intuitions. It is difficult to assure one's self that of all the movements and faces which bronze mirrors once reflected, of all the services where the incense burners and wine jars were used, nothing haunts them now. "One cannot help imagining that whatever has been, must continue to be somewhere—that by approaching these old pieces very stealthily, and turning a few of them suddenly face up to the light, one might be able to catch the Past in the very act of shrinking and shuddering away."

While they admit that fine specimens were made in later centuries, native amateurs consider as first class only those bronzes belonging to the Three Dynasties (the Hsia, Shang and Chou 2205-255 b.c.) commonly known as the "San Tai" period. So many vessels were buried at the time of the burning of the books under Ch'in Shih Huang (255-210 b.c.) that they continue to be yielded from the soil, and authentic specimens are still obtainable, though naturally at high prices. Next in value come the bronzes dating from the Ch'in and Han dynasties, while those made under the T'angs and Sungs begin to show less quality. As for the Ming period, when Buddhist influence led Chinese artists to cast gods and goddesses in bronze, its craftmanship is frankly inferior. Indeed no later bronze work rivals the severe forms and simple ornamentations of the Three Dynasty specimens. The latter are recognisable by their chaste shape, their designs, their inscriptions, to decipher which the help of a sinologue is essential, and their beautiful patina. Beware, however, of relying too much on the last as a proof of age. Genuine patina comes from within the metal and depends partly on the presence of gold or silver in the bronze, and partly on the soil in which the piece has been buried—whether damp, or dry and sandy. But artificial patina can be put on with wax

Peking – The Old Curiosity Shop

so cleverly that it is impossible to detect until scratching with a knife or immersion in boiling water exposes the fraud.

Old Chinese pewter and brass, though far less valuable than bronze, are also interesting. Old brass butcher's platters, useful for tea trays, incense burners, and charcoal braziers, if of the rich golden colour that indicates some precious metal with the alloy, are becoming rare. Pewter dishes in those quaint animal shapes which recall the original models of vessels used for sacrificial purposes, are amusing as curios but beware of using them, if new, for serving food as they may cause poisoning.

But there are no art treasures in Peking more fascinating to collect than old Chinese pictures, or more difficult to find, or more expensive when found. Few foreigners, however, care for them because the technique of Oriental artists is so different from our own. Properly to appreciate Chinese painting, as a critic justly observes, the Occidental must throw over his artistic education, his critical traditions, and all the aesthetic haggage that has been accumulated from the Renaissance to our own days. He must especially refrain from comparison of the works of Chinese painters with any of the famous canvases which are in Western collections. Thus and only thus can he escape the influences which blind him to the meaning of Oriental painting.[306]

Probably the first pictures that will appeal to us, after we have learned a little about Chinese paintings, are the fruit and flower pieces. Was it not Whistler who frankly stated that the greatest of the Europeans were clumsy in their portrayals of

---

[306] "The Chinese point of view on pictorial art differs essentially from the Western, and the wide abyss which parts them is proved by the career of the two Jesuits Attiret and Castiglione who were attached as painters to the Imperial Court in the 18th century and tried unsuccessfully to make the Chinese accept European art with its science of anatomy, its modelling, its effects of light and shade, etc.... When Lord Macartney came fifty years later bringing with him several pictures as presents from George III, the Chinese were shocked by the shadows, and asked gravely if the originals of the portraits really had one side of the face darker than the other; the shaded nose was a grave defect in their eyes, and some of them believed that it had come there accidentally."—*Bushell*.

such subjects compared with the Oriental Masters—Whistler, who like Aubrey Beardsley, Grasset, Cheret and Lautrec, acknowledged the influence of Chinese methods on his own work? Alfred Russell Wallace speaks of a collection of Oriental sketches of plants as "the most masterly things" that he ever saw. "Every stem, leaf, and twig," he declares, "is produced by single touches of the brush: the character and perspective of very complicated plants being admirably given and the articulations of stem and leaves shown in a scientific manner." All of which is done "by a genius in the manipulation of the wrist not only unequalled but undreamed of by our old Masters."

Later, we begin to appreciate the landscapes which seem to depict not only a beautiful but an ideal and happy world. Recalling the Western Hills, we realise that Chinese landscape paintings are conventional only in the sense of symbols which, once interpreted, reveal more than our drawing can express—that notwithstanding the weird impression of fantastic unreality which they at first produce they are, nevertheless, a veritable reflection of what exists.

Some Western critics may argue that the meaning of any true art should need no interpretation, and the inferior character of Chinese work is proved by the admission that it is not immediately and universally recognizable. "Whoever makes such a criticism," says Lafcadio Hearn, "must imagine Western art to be everywhere equally intelligible.... But I can assure the reader this is not so." In truth, much of our painting is as incomprehensible to Chinese, as Chinese paintings are to Europeans who have never seen China.

"For an Occidental to perceive the truth, or the beauty, or the humour of Chinese pictures, he must know the scenes which these paintings reflect." They are. not so much an imitation of nature, as a representation of nature which has the imprint of the artists mind upon it. Burne-Jones is unconsciously in touch with Chinese painting when he says: "I mean by a picture a beautiful romantic dream of something that never was—in a better light than ever shone."

Peking – The Old Curiosity Shop

Last of all we come to understand Chinese representations of the human face and figure. Especially in portraits, we must grow accustomed to the lack of detail. When the drawing is on a small scale it is not considered necessary to elaborate feature, and the age or condition is indicated by the style of the coiffure or the fashion of the dress. Here it is "worth while to notice," says Hearn "that the reserves of Chinese art in the matter of facial expression accord with the ethics of Oriental society. For ages the rule of conduct has been to mask all personal feeling as far as possible—to hide pain and passion under an exterior semblance of smiling liability, or impassive resignation. And this suppression of individuality, in life as in art, makes it very difficult for us to discern the personality through the type."[307]

Because they understand the subjective and suggestive principles underlying Chinese art so much better than we do, the Japanese are the largest buyers of fine pictures in Peking. They have, moreover, the advantage of being shown first all the good paintings that come on the market. In London or Paris a rich man will immediately see the best of everything just because he is rich. Not so in the East. Chinese merchants have a proverb: "Do not spread your treasures before everyone." Unless a buyer is known, he will never be shown the really first-class pictures—and the same rule holds true, though to a lesser extent, with all curios because the dealer dislikes to risk having his best wares unappreciated. Only for one who understands will he lovingly turn over the leaves of his beautiful books, with their studies of bird life, insect life, plant life, tree life, where each figure flung from the painter's brush is a revelation to perceptions unbeclouded by prejudice, an opening of the eyes to those who can see, though it be "only a spider in a wind-shaken web, a dragon-fly riding a sunbeam, a pair of crabs running through sedge, the trembling of a fish's

---

[307] The newly arrived Westerner often complains of his inability to distinguish one Chinese from another, and attributes this difficulty to the absence of strongly marked physiognomy in the race. Yet our more sharply accentuated Occidental features produce the very same effect upon the Chinese. Many and many a one has said to me: "For a long time I found it very hard to tell one foreigner from another: they all seemed to me alike."

fins in a clear current, the lilt of a flying wasp, the pitch of a flying duck, a mantis in fighting position, or a cicada toddling up a cedar branch to sing." Only for one who cares will the connoisseur open his *shou-chuan*, those long horizontal scrolls intended to be slowly unrolled and enjoyed bit by bit—one scene following another, completing and resolving that which has just passed.

The difficulty of telling the original from the copy, the genuine from the false, is as great in Chinese paintings as in porcelains or bronzes. Colouring, style, quality of silk or paper, and the seal of the artist are the only means at the purchaser's disposal. Unlike a signature, the Chinese seal—above all a crystal seal—can never be exactly imitated, for, being cut by hand, only the same cutter, and he rarely, could make two identically alike. Therefore, if we carefully examine a genuine seal, it is possible with practice to distinguish imitations easily. An additional aid in detecting forgeries may be derived from the Chinese habit of setting the seals of consecutive owners of a classical picture upon it—often to the point of obscuring the painting. The innumerable hand-written poems, mounted as pictures and having an equal artistic value in native eyes, are peculiarly Chinese.

Besides these standard and expensive curios, the stranger often asks: "What is worth buying in Peking?" This question is difficult to answer because the market is always changing. Several years ago an impoverished Manchu prince sold some very fine old lacquer furniture. To-day it might be difficult to find a single genuine piece. Again a quantity of treasures came out of the temples of Mongolia. They were so quickly bought up that an enterprising dealer had many of them copied in Manchester and sent out to supply the demand in Peking. So the market varies continually, depending on many conditions—whether a fine Chinese private collection is broken up, or poverty obliges monks or eunuchs to sell.

As a rule anything is worth buying that pleases the fancy of the buyer—provided he is getting what he pays for and not "new lamps for old." Things which appeal, rather to the

Peking – The Old Curiosity Shop

specialist than to the general collector are enamels, cloisonne, jades, lacquer, textiles, lanterns, furs, carpets, furniture, barbaric jewellery, iron pictures, glass-ware, embroidered linens, and, of course, knick-knacks of all kinds.

The art of enamelling seems to have been invented at a very remote date in Western Asia whence it penetrated to Europe in the early centuries of the Christian era, but there is no evidence of its having travelled to China till much later. The best examples were made in the reigns of Yung Cheng and Ch'ien Lung. They are very scarce since this work became fashionable in the West. Beware of modern imitations, valueless and often vulgar. Akin to enamel is cloisonne, one of the most characteristic Peking crafts—and very decorative.

Lacquer exists in many colours, qualities and designs—some traceable to the Sung dynasty, some to the Yuan. Being perishable, it is unusual to find a real old piece in good condition, though handsome specimens dating from the Ming dynasty are still to be had. The red lacquer, nowadays much copied, may be judged by colour, depth of carving, and weight. The heavier the piece, the older it is, as a rule. The gold lacquer, of which we see the best examples in palace furniture, screen-frames, etc., is inferior to the Japanese. It is the only art in which these pupils excelled their masters and reached a height of prefection never attained by the Chinese.

Old jades are both valuable and rare. Like bronzes they are sought after by native collectors because they are intimately connected with Chinese culture, and supposed to be endowed with magic properties. In the Chou dynasty (1122-225 b.c.) ceremonial jade ornaments were worn by the Emperor, who also used memorandum tablets of this favourite stone. Jade seals were made in the Han period and jade ornaments buried with the dead. (Beware of new copies of these tomb pieces). Jade astronomical instruments, girdle-clasps, sword-hilts and mirrors were also known in ancient times and in more modern days jade has been used for incense burners, tea-pots, rings, bracelets, ear-rings, pen-rests, sceptres, altar pieces, etc.

Juliet Bredon

Though the oldest specimens are not always strictly beautiful, for they lose their polish with age, a study of them is of great interest and value for the understanding of Chinese psychology and the history of Chinese customs. Even to look at good jade in good condition gives a refreshing sensation of coolness and smoothness. A Chinese connoisseur can tell with eyes closed, from the touch and the temperature, whether a piece is old. Orientals, with their hyper-sensitive finger-tips have developed a new artistic sense which few foreigners ever acquire —the power to judge and enjoy by touch as much as by sight. Of such exquisite perceptions, as J. C. Ferguson points out in his *Outlines of Chinese Art*, we can know scarcely more than we know of those unimaginable colours invisible to the human eye, yet proven to exist by the spectroscope. Our clumsy hands, our untrained sight will hesitate to detect imitations which the Chinese would unerringly discover in jades as in other curios. A few simple rules may, however, help the amateur in his choice of this semi-precious stone:

When buying coloured jades, especially the valuable deep green jewel jade, the yellow, or the black, remember that they are frequently copied in glass. Choose those which have a translucent colour—and then note that a new process has been discovered to produce the fashionable emerald shade—and consult a reliable and disinterested expert before purchasing.

White, or "mutton fat," jades are often imitated in soap-stone. These frauds can generally be detected by their softness, and the finger nail will chip most specimens. The Chinese also have a trick of filling and polishing imperfect pieces of jade with wax to deceive purchasers, so every specimen should be most carefully examined.

Often a stranger, not a curio collector but simply a lover of pretty or portable things, will inquire if there is in Peking nothing that he may buy and enjoy without technique and simply, as Howells says, "Upon condition of his being a tolerably genuine human creature."

Of course there is. Why not embroidery or furs?

Peking – The Old Curiosity Shop

Among the specialties of Peking, embroideries have long been famous—so much so that a certain very effective stitch is known as "*point de Pekin.*" Since the dis-establishment of the Empire, fine throne covers, tapestry pictures, brocades, cut velvets and Court gowns have been stolen or sold out of the Palace or left unredeemed in pawnshops by poor Manchus.[308] But these textiles have such a wide appeal and are so easily packed that they have been bought up by tourists as fast as they came on the market, till very few are left. The genuine old tapestries, *K'o-ssu*,[309] are rare and extremely expensive, but very decorative copies, often palmed off on the unwary as "true Ch'ien Lung," are being made to-day in Hang-chow. They look well mounted as fire screens, cushions and lampshades with their colours softened to restful shades by incense smoke. The genuine reds and blues of the old Ming pieces cannot be imitated because the secret of these dyes are lost, but great care should be taken to avoid bright colours made from aniline dyes—easily distinguishable—and glaring modern gold thread which tarnishes. Textiles should always be bought in a good light.

Sets of throne cushions usually have the dragon motif, but flower and geometrical designs in more than fifty varieties are recorded from the Sung period alone. These like the T'ang Dynasty twill, lozenge and roundel patterns, are familiar to us

---

308 The Chinese pawnshops, distinguished by gilt-topped wooden pillars which remind one somewhat of the Totem poles of the Alaska Indians, are curious, institutions. They differ from those in the West, as they are not receptacles for spare valuables, but simply store-houses. Few Chinese keep their winter clothing at home during summer time or *vice versa*. When the season changes the appropriate clothing is released and that to be pawned put in its place. The usual interest asked is two or three per cent, per month. Pawnshops are a favourite investment of rich men.

309 K'o-Ssu is made by a process which is identical with that by which European tapestry is produced, but the Chinese work is finer in texture and details of design are added in with the brush. "A fine wooden or bone needle is employed instead of a large bobbin and the weft is sometimes beaten in with a hand comb. The material is invariably silk, usually with the addition of gold thread... and sometimes the whole ground of the pattern is formed by the gold thread."

through the work of later times and even copied in silk damasks to this day.

Court gowns may be identified by the wave pattern edging the bottom of the robe and as a general rule, the more shades worked into this border, the more valuable the coat; by the horse-shoe-shaped cuff, and, in the case of a garment destined for the use of the Emperor, by a set of mystical symbols.[310] Tapestry robes command a higher price than satin, and yellow gowns, whatever their material, are the most expensive because this shade was worn only by the Emperor or the Empress. Five clawed dragons denoted that they were used by the former, phoenixes by the latter.

Next in value come the orange gowns worn by princes and princesses, and then the red or blue ceremonial robes of officials. The shorter women's coats embroidered in flowers or butterflies, used by Chinese ladies on festival occasions (weddings, birthday parties, etc.) are especially suitable for adapting as tea gowns and opera cloaks. The temple hangings and priests' vestments often have interest ing ecclesiastical designs including the "Eight Felicitous Emblems":[311] 1. The Wheel of the Law; 2. Conch-Shell; 3. The State Umbrella; 4. The Canopy; 5. The Vase for Relics; 6. The Pair of Fishes; 7. The Lotus Flower; 8. The Chang or Endless Knot; which are seen on most temple altars.

The fur market in Peking for some years has dwindled to comparative insignificance. Under the Empire when courtiers lined their robes with sable, silver fox, ermine, and white fox (the two last in seasons of mourning), a great many fine skins were brought down from Siberia, Manchuria and Saghalin and

---

[310] Among the oldest Chinese designs are these "Twelve Ornaments" worn by the Emperor on his robes of ceremony. They are: 1. The Sun with the Three Legged Bird; 2. The Moon with the Hare; 3. The Stars; 4. Grains of Rice; 5. Fu, a double Figure recalling a key fret; 6. A Pheasant or two Pheasants; 7. Aquatic Grass; 8. An Axe Head; 9. Fire; 10, Mountains; 11. A Pair of Dragons; 12. Two Temple Cups, one decorated with a monkey and the other with a tiger.

[311] These Emblems are found, made of wood, pewter, lacquer, etc., on most Chinese altars.

Peking – The Old Curiosity Shop

sold in the open market or presented to the Throne as tribute. A new tourist demand promises to increase the supply which nearly ceased when Republican simplicity became the rule. Both Russian and Chinese sables are now obtainable in Peking —often at good bargains, and worth several times their price in Europe or America. Sables should be bought with great caution, however. The best Chinese pelt is a golden brown and the dark specimens, so much admired by Westerners, are generally dyed. Beware also of buying old skins. They have suffered from extremes of climate for many years and the hair is liable to fall out. White fox, flame fox, silver fox, if really good, ermine, martin, otter, Manchurian tiger, leopard, wild cat, rabbit, and squirrel, are all comparatively cheap and worth buying if in fine condition.

Peking carpets are becoming famous all over the world. From a small native craft, the industry has grown to such proportions in the last few years that thousands of Chinese rugs are shipped annually to Europe and America. These modern carpets are made to order in any design and Western patterns can be copied satisfactorily. But as they are all woven by hand—the curious process may be seen in any of the little shops outside the Hata Men—and as the manufacturers are generally busy with orders, no work can be finished in a hurry for the passing traveller. The rugs are sold according to the number of threads to the foot, and prices have increased owing to the increased cost of wool. It is, however, worth while to pay for a good quality—at least between 100 and 200 threads to the foot—as thin loosely-woven carpets wear flat in a few months and fall into holes at the first beating. The camel's hair and yak-tail rugs, though attractive, have the disadvantage of a disagreeable caravan odour which remains for months and is overpowering in damp weather. Beware of choosing too complicated patterns, necessitating artificial dyes that fade. The good fast colours are made from Chinese vegetable dyes and the best wearing are the various shades of blue, buff, pink and brick red.

Juliet Bredon

The few remaining K'ang Hsi and Ch'ien Lung carpets and Mongol prayer-rugs made of the inner wool of the Thibetan goat are now very expensive, but sometimes the best specimens resemble the Persian. They may be distinguished by the sheen of the wool, the mellowing-of the colours and by the cotton strands which turn a yellowish brown with age—a shade that cannot be duplicated by dyeing. Old silk rugs, though exceedingly beautiful and valuable, if genuine, should be bought only with the advice of an expert, as hundreds of modern copies are now being put on the market.

There is no more delightful way of spending an afternoon than pottering through "Furniture Street" between the Ch'ien Men and the Hata Men in search of "Chinese Chippendale." Here one may usually find good second-hand pieces. But the best bargains are often picked up in the carpenters' yards before they ever reach the merchants' show rooms. It requires some experience, however, to judge of them when unpolished or in course of repair. A table that at first sight appears only fit for firewood may be, in fact, made of the precious *tzu-t'an*. This is a kind of rose-wood, not ebony as many people think. It has a reddish tinge that darkens with age and exposure to light. Old pieces are quite black and very heavy. The best are made from the part of the tree nearest the ground. The branches and upper trunk also yield a hard wood but of inferior quality. A little experience soon enables one to judge the grain and to distinguish it from that of the *hung-mu* or red wood, of which many fine cabinets, tables, chairs, benches and boxes are also made. Occasionally, a nice specimen of camphor wood, walnut or pear may be found, or the lovely brown *nan-mu*, used not only for furniture but much sought after by rich Chinese for coffins, or of *chi ch'ih mu* ("chicken-track wood," so called from its curious markings) that resembles our maple but is in reality a kind of box-wood.

The simpler forms of decoration, showing a due appreciation of the value of plain surfaces and allowing the full beauty of all these fine woods to appear, are infinitely more attractive than heavy carvings, riots of dragons and clouds, flame and flower designs, such as one finds on the overburdened Cantonese blackwood. True "Chinese Chippendale," sedate and chaste like its Western counterpart, has the advantage of never looking out of place in any surroundings.

In China we are often amazed to find the fingers of the humble craftsman inspired by the soul of an artist. Even common things used by everyday people are often admirable. Common things! Common, perhaps, when compared to the treasures of other ages; common in the sense of being modern and universal, but curious to us Westerners, and positively thrilling when we first arrive.

Who can forget the delicious surprise of his first journey through Chinese streets, unable to make the ricksha runner understand anything but gestures, frantic gestures to stop anywhere, everywhere, since all is unspeakably pleasureable and new. He must not pass by the wizen-faced vendor who has his wares laid out on the ground before him—such quaint sets of dominoes, and water pipes, and brass padlocks. Can he ever discover the row of little silver shops in side lanes where we are promised models of pagodas for salt cellars, and Peking carts, and wheel-barrows, and *p'ai lous* and spider-web menu-holders, and spoons with enamelled handles? Can he take us to see the workers in kingfisher feathers which mount so prettily into combs and hair ornaments—and the native jeweller who stamps the name of his shop inside the soft gold or filigree ring or bracelet, thus binding himself, by guild law and custom, to buy it back at any time by weight, without questioning the quality of the material—and the cloisonne shops where they will copy any design we please—even coats of arms in heraldic colours? He must find the big bazaar that some one recommended as such a curious sight. Did they say outside the Ch'ien Men? Yes, and not one bazaar but several. "The Blue Cloud Chamber," not far from "Snuff Bottle Alley," in Kuan Yin Ssu Street (next to Ta Sha Lan, the "Fifth Avenue of Peking") occupies as three-storied building with dozens of stalls and a very famous tea shop where for ten cents a piece customers may sit and gossip all day. Another bazaar on the same block has an outer wall, a gaily decorated gate and a little courtyard in front with a primitive fire engine and hand pumps. They could not throw a stream as far as the second story but are surrounded by elaborate satin banners with invocations to the Fire God.[312] That is the old Chinese way—to put more faith in charms than in hoses and in this case faith has been rewarded since the merchants proudly boast that their premises have never incurred the enmity of the God of Fire as have most of the other bazaars.

The upper floors are rented to dentists, photographers, barbers and tea shops, but the downstairs booths sell all kinds of curiosities and dainty objects, the redbone chopsticks, a specialty of Peking, embroidered spectacle cases that would almost reconcile one to being short sighted, ladies' shoes for bound feet, enamelled buttons, silks, painted fish-bowls, snuff-bottles and pottery.

It is very distracting to see the Chinese ladies tottering on their "Golden Lilies," and the Manchu matrons in their flowered and gold-barred head-dress deliberating over stuffs for future finery, or choosing gew-gaws, while a rasping phonograph plays Chinese tunes for their edification. We stare unashamed at the men-servants and the maid-servants who accompany them, at the children asleep or breakfasting unconcernedly in the arms of their wet nurses—at the tea and cakes spread out before the whole party, for without tea no sale can be made in China and time is no object. It appears these ladies expect to spend several hours over their purchases as such an outing is one of their rare amusements.

We may look to our heart's content—at the purchasers or at the objects to be purchased. The shopkeepers do not urge us to buy. Because these bazaars, or department stores, are comparatively modern innovations in Peking, they pride

---

[312] It is not uncommon to see charms against fire pasted on the walls of shops. Some have the character for Water enclosed in a circle and a note informing the Fire God that this place has already received the honour of his visit, the inference being that he keep away in future.

There are several temples to the Fire God in Peking (see Chapter X).

themselves on their modern methods. They encourage the sight-seer, like the customer, for the sake of advertisement. When they do sell, they sell at "fixed prices"—"All same America," an attendant informs us proudly.

The premier bazaar of the city, the largest, the busiest, the oldest, is the Tung An Shih Chang, or "Eastern Tranquillity Bazaar," with four gates on Morrison Street and one on Chin Yu Hutung. No visitor should miss seeing "this little town within a town" composed of many buildings and even with streets of its own. Everything one could possibly want is sold here: silk, milk, books, hats, gold-fish, curios, jewellery, and even foreign socks and shirts.

There is also a money-changer on the premises, a regular theatre and a number of tea shops where amateur and professional entertainers, including actors like Mei Lang-fang, appear from time to time.

In addition to everything else, this bazaar is famous for the presence of a fortune teller who calls his office the "Wen Hsin Ch'u," or "Mind Inquiring Place." Great is the reputation of this old man and great the fortune amassed by his successful professional advice which is sought even by foreigners; so great that, gossip says, he rides about town in a motor car and keeps a harem of twenty concubines.

Though all the bazaars sell at fixed prices, in the curio shops, it is usual for most dealers to ask from a quarter to two-thirds more than they hope to receive—sometimes as much as they dare, or believe the customer can be induced to pay. Offer, as a rule, a little more than half what is asked, then, as the merchant gradually comes down in his price, increase very gradually until neutral ground is reached. Finally split the difference, and the bargain is yours. If one is in a hurry or shows any enthusiasm for the article in question, it is impossible to make a cheap purchase. Point out the defects in the piece under discussion and remember the old adage: "It is naught, it is naught," saith the buyer, "but when he hath gone his way then he boasteth." A good plan is to leave the shop when the owner, afraid of losing a customer, runs after you with a last offer—the lowest price, or nearly— that he is prepared to accept.

A Chinese curio-dealer does not expect a daily turnover. A few transactions in the year are enough, owing to the great profits in the business.

We have bargained for days or weeks for a certain thing, passing the shop often. "Not sold yet?" we inquire indifferently. "Not yet," says the shop-keeper with equal indifference. And while we boil with impatience to possess what we want and tremble lest someone else snap it up, he enjoys the bargaining almost as much as the sale. The Chinese, in fact, only appreciate you as a purchaser if you know how to drive a good bargain, whereas we impatient Westerners feel, that the time wasted could be put to a more useful purpose.

Among the Chinese themselves, sleeve bargaining was once the rule. For this curious custom the buyer and seller asked the help of a mutual acquaintance who put one hand up the sleeve of each "and by certain signs indicated when the bargain should be concluded." Another method was the direct quoting of prices from merchant to customer by the pressure of fingers concealed by the latter's cuff, thus ensuring secrecy from the ever-curious bystanders.

This latter custom is still occasionally used at the Thieves Market held before dawn outside the Hata Men. But changing times have dimmed much of its glory and excitement because, whereas "formerly it closed at dawn and buyers and sellers as they bargained with each other were unrecognizable in the darkness," nowadays police regulations permit no business to be done before daylight. This causes considerable inconvenience to the local thieves who find it difficult to dispose of their plunder. In olden times, "a thing of real value might be got for a mere song, but there were many disappointments and the thieves, or their representatives, frequently proved too clever for those whose consciences permitted them to buy anything cheap."[313]

---

313 See *Sidelights on Peking Life,* by R. W. Swallow

Peking – The Old Curiosity Shop

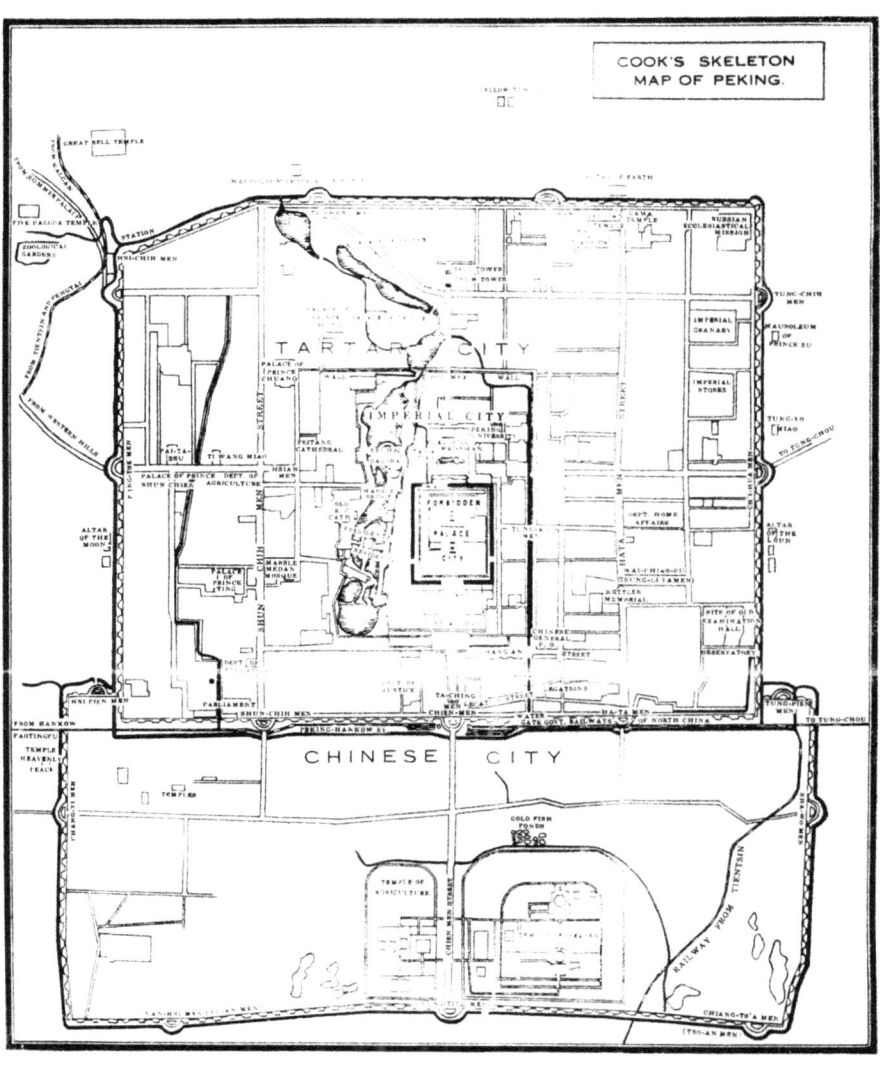

Juliet Bredon

Another interesting sight, alas, no more to be seen, was the fixing of the daily rate of local exchange at a place near the old Mongol Market close to the British Legation. Here at about 4.30 a.m. as soon as the rate was announced, "innumerable carrier pigeons would be thrown into the air with slips of paper on which the rate was written attached to their legs, each one after getting its bearings, making off in a direct line for its own bank."[314] Those, of course, were the days before telegraphs, telephones or even Chinese newspapers, except the old official Peking Gazette which contained chiefly officials reports and rescripts—the days of those bargains in beautiful things of which the modern visitor can only dream.

---

314 See *Autumn Leaves*, by E. T. C. Werner.

XX. The Fun of the Fair

Peking is a city of a thousand activities and industries, though its role in history has been far more important than that of a manufacturing centre. Nevertheless, in many homes whole families work long hours at various handicrafts, and hundreds of small shops are miniacure hives of industry. We must not conclude, however, that "life is all work and no play," or that the Chinese do not care for amusement. The poor clerk or artisan may get little enough of it because he has no leisure—no time of his own except the hours necessary for sleep. He must toil steadily from early morning till late evening. He cannot afford to leave the shop or work bench, except on a rare holiday, night or day for months at a time. Does not the proverb say: "A wise man seeks pleasure only when his rice bin is full," meaning, of course, only when his household is so well provided for that he can afford it? But the prosperous merchants and the rich officials amuse themselves constantly and spend money extravagantly in the tea shops, the theatres, and the restaurants outside the Ch'ien Men.

When play-houses were forbidden by Imperial decree inside the Tartar City, they sprang up just beyond the prescribed boundary, near the "Bridge of Heaven."[315] Soon the best restaurants were established near by, and hotels opened for the convenience of the wealthy visitor. Shops followed to tempt him, pharmacies to cure him,[316] bath houses[317] to cleanse him. These formed the nucleus of the city's "Pleasure Quarter."

---

315 The T'ien Ch'iao, or "Bridge of Heaven," outside the Ch'ien Men, is the old marble bridge, repaired and transformed, that every visitor crosses on his way to the Temple of Heaven. It spans a canal neither fragrant nor clear, and used to be the haunt of repulsive beggars. Hence it came to be associated in the Chinese mind with thievery, beggary and moral corruption. To tell a Chinese to go to the "Bridge of Heaven" was the quintessence of abuse.

316 Here the most curious remedies still find purchasers among the conservative classes—powdered deer's horn and tiger's whiskers, ground fish-bones and oyster shells, dried bamboo juice and cicadas-skins, pounded fossils, and other things too horrible to mention. When drugs failed, the old

Juliet Bredon

It is strange that the haunts of the rich should lie within a stone's throw of the worst slums of the city. Long before the former open their doors, the narrow, sewery lanes a little to the east of them are filled to overflowing with a poverty the more pitiful for its proximity to luxury. The "Flea Market" is held before dawn by torch-light in this neighbourhood. Wares are spread on the street itself, but they are generally of such a character that dirt can do them no harm. Old bottles, broken door-knobs, bent nails, lie by side with frayed foreign collars, dilapidated tennis rackets, rusty corsets, or even threadbare evening slippers that have been thrown into the waste basket of some European house and gathered up by the assiduous rag-pickers who classify the refuse of Peking for this fair. Old clothes' stalls abound, where men bargain fiercely for rags to cover their nakedness, and lodging houses where, for one copper, miserable tatterdemalions sleep on heaps of duck's feathers in evil-smelling hovels. The Abbe Hue describes one of these places and tells how, when customers stole the individual cotton quilts supplied as covering, some one devised a communal bedspread the size of the floor with holes for the

---

style physician resorted to acupuncture and the manikins full of holes exposed in this pharmacist's window were used as charts to indicate where to drive a needle into a patient without fatal results and often with astounding success. The model for these manikins was a famous bronze statue, dating from the Sung dynasty, formerly enshrined in a temple to the God of Medicine on the site of the Russian Compound in the Legation Quarter. After 1900 this statue was taken by Prince Ukhtomsky to St. Petersburg. Another curious aid to the physician is a small bone or ivory figure of a naked woman, used when attending female patients who might not be seen or touched by a male doctor. It was passed between the bed curtains. The sick woman then marked the locality of her pain upon it and handed the figure back, whereupon her medical adviser prescribed accordingly.

317 They are distinguishable in the daytime by the basket used for drawing water, hung on top of a high pole, and at night by a red lantern hoisted as a signal that the bath is hot. The better class establishments, for men only, are reasonably clean. Everybody, except the small minority able to afford a private room, bathes in one large sunken tub where the water is almost at boiling point and the atmosphere full of steam.

The Fun of The Fair

sleepers' heads. It was raised and lowered by tackle, a gong sounding an alarm night and morning to warn the lodgers.

For the stranger both worlds are of compelling interest and help him to understand China as it really is. Let us turn then from the poverty and misery—found alas! in every big city—to the Pleasure Quarter where the crowds begin to gather in the late afternoon.

As soon as the sun goes down, the streets in that part of the city known as "outside Ch'ien Men" are filled with people and present a most animated scene. Indeed the "traffic is too great for the narrow lanes, and the overcrowding aggravated by the fact that numerous vehicles are left standing by the sidewalks while their occupants go inside the various buildings to enjoy their pleasures at their ease." But the East is never in a hurry and in due time the congestion is relieved and traffic moves on again.

Here comes a famous singing girl, in a brass trimmed ricksha with half-a-dozen shining lamps and jangling bells, one of those gaily dressed human butterflies on her way to add to the jollity of a feast. Many men are infatuated by her smile— men old enough to know better. In an expensive motor car, guarded by soldiers, sits a general who is a dictator in his own province. We recognise one of the Living Buddhas passing in his cart. Rumour says he is fond of the play. Yonder, in a carriage whose body is made of mirrors, two women sit sedately; women neither young nor very beautiful, but experienced in the ways of men and confidants of many secrets. They could tell you, only they are too wise, all the gossip of the city. That fat merchant entering a shop is the Chinese Lipton. His refined looking companion was lately in the Cabinet. And the slim youth with the grace and figure of a girl, that both stop to greet, is Mei Lang-fang, the popular actor, on his way to the theatre. So they pass, like figures on a brilliantly set stage— merchants and ministers, soldiers and hetarrae, players all, whether in politics, drama, or emotions.

In olden times even emperors joined the gay throng, incognito. The Ming sovereign Cheng Teh liked nothing better than to visit the book-stalls of the adjacent Liu Li Ch'ang and purchase stories and paintings of the kind to which the dissolute patricians of Peking have always been partial. Ch'ien Lung more than once paid unofficial visits to a certain beautiful lady of the Pleasure Quarter, and T'ung Chih, the unworthy son of the Empress Dowager Tz'u Hsi, frequently slipped out of the Palace, through an opening specially cut in the wall, to idle in "Flower Streets and Willow Lanes." A eunuch's cart, drawn by a fast pacing mule would await him there, and it became a matter of common gossip that the Son of Heaven was frequently mixed up in drunken and disreputable brawls and would return to his throne, even after he had attained his majority, long past the hour fixed for audiences.

Naturally the young Manchu princes were not slow to follow this bad example. The Ta Ago, son of the Boxer leader Prince Tuan, and for a short time heir to the throne, was more distinguished for his exploits outside the Ch'ien Men than for his diligence inside the Palace. Quarrels in eating houses and theatres between the depraved young scions of nobility were of frequent occurrence, and the position of the Chief of the newly established Police Board when dealing with members of the ruling clan, was by no means a happy one. The latter would brook no interference with their whims, though some of these were foolish and unworthy. Such, for instance, was their habit of amusing themselves by dressing up as beggars and parading the streets in this guise. "I remember particularly," says a Manchu official quoted by Backhouse and Bland in *Annals and Memoirs of the Court of Peking*, "one occasion in the dog days of 1892. It was very hot and some friends had invited me to join them in an excursion to the kiosque and garden known as the 'Beautiful Autumn Hillock' outside the gate of the Southern City.[318] This spot is shady and in the middle there is a pond

---

318 In the period of greatest heat, frequenters of the Pleasure Quarter often adjourn to such gardens in the afternoon for a breath of cooler air. The Chiang Chia Feng Yuan, outside the Hsi Chi Men, the Ku Erh Yuan, between the Ch'ien Men and the Shun Chih Men, and the Yi Ch'ang Hua Yuan, outside the P'ing Tse Men, are all well-known resorts for summer evenings. "The water-pavilion in Central Park, the 'Committee Room' in the

The Fun of The Fair

where water lilies and rushes grow. Visitors can take tea quietly at the open-air restaurant.

"At the next table to us sat a young man. His face was black as soot and he looked worn and ill-nourished. His queue was plaited round his head and he had inserted a bone hairpin in his hair after the manner of the Peking hooligan class in summer time. He wore no socks. Stripped to the waist, his only garment was a pair of very shabby short trousers which hardly reached to the knee, all covered with grease and mud; in fact he was scarcely decent.

"Strange to say this miserable looking beggar had on a thumb-ring of green jade worth at least 500 taels (at that time about £8o), and he carried a beautiful and very costly fan with a jade handle. His conversation was full of vulgar oaths and the lowest Pekingese slang. I noticed, however, that the waiters showed him a very particular and eager attention and hardly ever left his side. I was lost in bewilderment and wondering what it meant, when all of a sudden a smart official cart and a train of well-groomed attendants appeared. The servants approached the young beggar carrying a hat box and a bundle of clothes.

" 'Your Highness' carriage is ready,' they told him. 'You have an engagement to dine at Prince Kung's palace to-night. We ought to be starting.' Thereupon the young blade got up, took a towel and washed his face. We were astonished at the transformation. The dirty black had been replaced by a delicate white complexion and, though thin, he had the distinctive features of the Manchu princes. The head waiter whispered to me as he drove off in his official robes: 'That was Prince Tsai.' I replied in amazement: 'What does he mean by such behaviour?

Pei Hai, a newly repaired restaurant in the park of the Temple of Agriculture, and several tea houses in the Zoological Gardens are most popular with local hosts. Anybody who is prepared to pay a reasonable rent, and make the necessary arrangements in advance, will be entitled to have one of these quarters to himself for a whole day or the entire evening. Here he can bring his own cooks, or those of his familiar restaurants. He can even send for an orchestra to play music if his purse permits him to do so." *See Social Life of the Chinese in Peking*, by Jermyn Chi Hung Lynn.

Juliet Bredon

'Ah!' said the man, 'don't you know the latest craze of our young princes in Peking?' He then went on to tell me how Prince Chuang, Prince K'o, Prince Tuan, the *pei-lehs* Lien and Ying, Prince Ch'ing's son Tsai Chen, and many others made a practice of adopting this guise, causing disturbances and street rows, as the police were afraid to touch them... I was horrified to hear this and said: 'Surely this portent is evil to our Empire! Such things occurred just before the Sungs were finally defeated by the Mongols and also at the close of the T'ang dynasty. History is full of similar examples. Mark my words, China will be plunged in dire calamity before ten years have passed.'"

Eight years later the Boxer outbreak happened and most of the princes fell to tramping the streets not as sham, but as real beggars.

"It served them right. They should not have mocked at us," says Tanglefoot,[319] who gets his sobriquet from his habit of wrapping old sacking around his nether extremities. Tanglefoot is a beggar by profession, and a philosopher under his rags. You will generally find him in the Pleasure Quarter running behind a rich man's carriage whining for alms. As the Chinese proverb says: "When the stomach is empty, pride is not strong." Or he will take up his stand outside a shop and make himself so offensive to eyes, ears and nose, that the owner, unable to stand

---

319 Tanglefoot is a very intelligent person and well worth talking to. He can tell, when he pleases, the most remarkable stories of human nature. Some are very terrible, some would make you laugh, and some would make you think. Between himself and the other beggars there is a difference of gentle wood. He comes from a good family who were suddenly stricken by poverty before there was time for him to learn a trade. Now mendicancy is a recognised institution in China, and included in the regular list of profitable professions open to a poor young man entering life. Therefore he said: "Mother, I know there is but one thing now to do. Let me become a beggar." The mother wept silently. Thus he began his career, lucky in his ill-luck, since he succeeded so well that he never needed to resort to the pitiful mutilations—like putting out an eye or cutting off a hand—which are sometimes deliberately undertaken to excite pity. A valuable insight into the seamy side of life in Peking may be obtained from *Peking, A Social Survey*, by Sidney D. Gamble.

The Fun of The Fair

him any longer, will give him. something to go away. "Why does the merchant not call the police to remove you?" we inquire. Having passed him our coppers for many years, we have the privilege of frankness. "He wouldn't dare to do that," is the reply. "I may look ragged and of no account, but I belong to the Beggar's Guild—a powerful organization with a 'king' and thousands of members. Even rich shopkeepers hesitate to offend us,, lest one of our company commit suicide in reprisal on his doorstep and thus involve him in serious trouble and suspicion. Now if you will excuse me," he adds with a courtly bow that shows he has been well brought up,. "I must be going on to the Inn of Heavenly Happiness where several large banquets are taking place. Guests, when well fed and flushed with wine, are most easily moved to enjoy the luxury of generosity."

As provincial visitors enjoy eating "home cooking," there are special establishments where food from all parts of the country is served. A Fukienese may order his native menu of sea foods in Peking, a Shansi man indulge his fondness for vinegar sauces. Natives of Canton patronise places where Cantonese *chefs* are employed, and Honan hosts entertain in houses where their favourite dish of carps is prepared to suit them. Szechuan delicacies for the Szechuaneze are likewise obtainable, also Shantung specialities for the fellow provincials of Confucious, who, legend says, was a connoisseur of food.

Though a full list of the famous "eating shops" in the city is too long to give here, it may be interesting to mention a few of those praised by Chinese gourmets.

The "Tung Hsing Lou" is probably the most patronised restaurant in the city—especially for birthday and funeral feasts. The "Sha Kuo Chu," near the west gate of the Forbidden City which "specialised in pork and kindred dishes but did not provide duck, chicken or fish," used to be a favourite breakfast room for officials after then-audiences at the Palace, and is still fashionable despite the changing times. The "Pai Ching Lou," established two hundred years ago, also keeps its clientele. Equally old and even more reputed is the "Cheng Yang Lou," outside the Ch'ien Men, where mutton grilled on an iron plate is served in winter, and crabs in autumn, each guest being provided with a small wooden hammer to crush bis own crab.

The "Pei I Fang," outside the Shun Chih Men, is one of several places famous for "Peking Duck Dinners," the birds being kept in a dark room and forcibly fed daily until required for the table.

Chinese gentlemen go to all these restaurants, and many others not only to feast—and "for smoothing over difficulties, making up quarrels, or closing a business deal, there is nothing so useful in China as a feast"—but to play cards or Mah Jong, to drink, smoke, discuss politics or lean over the verandahs to watch the crowd. "The pulse of the people," the Chinese say, rightly, "may be felt in the chatter of the balconies." But like the Scotchman visiting Paris, they "do na bring the wife." Custom forbids Chinese ladies to appear in such places with men, even their own husbands, and when a banquet is given, the only women present are singing girls— professional entertainers with no reputation to lose.

Do not imagine, however, that a Chinese dinner party is in any sense an orgy offensive to good taste. No, the Chinese are on the whole a sober and abstemious race, a race of high culture and of ancient civilization. When we were still gorging off half-raw oxen, and drunken with, seven day feasts of mead, they had already acquired one of the hall marks of real civilization—to take "a little" instead of "a lot." Their wine cups hold perhaps two teaspoonfuls, their tea cups three, their pipes a few fleeting whiffs. Drunkenness is exceedingly rare, though it does exist. But the actual quantity of native wine required to produce intoxication for any one bent on it is considerably less than ours because the liquor is served hot and sipped.

Nevertheless wine is an important adjunct to a feast, as witness the familiar phrase used on old fashioned invitation cards, "the wine cups have been polished to await your presence." Also a careful host is most particular that his liquor be of good quality, and of the fifty different kinds of Shaoshing wines, he serves liberally the best he can afford.

Indeed the generosity of a Chinese when he entertains is extraordinary. Neither time nor money are spared and a banquet may consist of thirty or forty courses including ten fried dishes, such as duck's tongues and pig's-loins, ten "big bowls," four cold dishes, several kinds of fruits, and various soups, besides rice, steamed bread and condiments. Everything is ordered in advance, though nothing is fully prepared till all the guests are assembled, and then only after what seems to us Westerners an interminable delay.[320]

A very elaborate menu may cost Mex. $10 or even $15 a plate, but a reasonably good meal may be had for $2. The great difference in price, of course, represents rare delicacies: birds' nests brought from the Southern Seas, shark's fins out of season, bear's paws, early cucumbers from Canton, or other imported vegetables of which the Chinese are very fond. In fact, a vegetarian restaurant is one of the curiosities of the city. Not only is every vegetable obtainable prepared there, but these vegetables are served in imitation of practically every known meat dish. At a recent feast given in this place, twenty-seven different meatless dishes appeared on the table. The roast duck consisted of a preparation made from bean curd; fried eels were the rind of a certain kind of melon cooked in vegetable oils; pork and beef courses were made of bamboo shoots and mushrooms, and so on; the novelty of the entertainment being that the vegetables not only tasted like the various meat dishes but were moulded to look like them also.

First-class restaurants add to their profits by selling their leavings to second-class establishments, these again to third-rate places and so on *ad infinitum*. There is no waste in China, and the scraps that fall from the rich man's table may find their way at last to one of the open-air buffets at street corners, where poor coolies pay a few cents for a bowl of mixed "sweet and sour," including the duck and the dessert emptied into a huge cauldron of scraps by a small boy with a raucous voice, who shouts the equivalent of Mr. Bailey Junior's "The wittles is up" to attract his tattered customers, while pariah dogs prowl

---

320 See *Social Life of the Chinese in Peking*, by Jermyn Chi Hung Lynn.

under the benches to snatch up anything that may fall from the counter.

After a fashionable Chinese dinner party, the guests break ranks with hiccups—considered good style as an expression of appreciation—loosen or discard outer garments, and seat themselves comfortably to enjoy whatever entertainment may be provided, while the cats of the establishment creep in and crunch the bones spat out upon the floor. Singing girls, whose piercing falsetto voices remind us of concerts we have heard on walls or roofs on moonlight nights, may then be sent for, or perhaps, a band of blind musicians. The latter are ugly and their natural ugliness is often increased by the cruel attack of smallpox that destroyed their sight. But when they seat themselves and begin to play upon their quaint flutes and violins, a spell descends upon the company. Then from out of the ugly disfigured lips of the soloist there gushes a charming natural voice, deep, unutterably touching in its penetrating sweetness. No such voice has ever been heard from any singing girl, and no such song. "Who may that be?" queries a bystander. "A peasant only, but a very, very great artist." Truly he "sings as only a peasant can sing, with vocal rhythms learned perhaps from the cicadæ and the nightingales, and with fractions and semi-fractions, and demi-semi fractions of tones never written down in the musical language of the West."

The listeners grow serious, touched by the sad melody and the voice vibrant with all the sorrow and the sweetness and the patience of the blind—plaintively seeking for something forever denied. But when the song is finished and the singer, with the sensitiveness of the sightless, divines that his audience is pensive, he suddenly strikes his violin again and the strings, seemingly of their own volition, dance and quiver into the gayest, liveliest quickstep, into variations of foreign bugle calls which the player has picked up from the buglers of the Legation Guards, mingled with Chinese martial airs and imitations of street noises, squeaking barrows, crowing hens, crying children and quarrelling women, till the guests stare at each other in smiling amazement.

The Fun of The Fair

If it is a new-fashioned dinner party of young people, all may adjourn afterwards to one of the modern dance halls where "pretty partners" are advertised. Such amusement places are one of the most startling innovations in Chinese social life. A few years ago "it was a gross breach of etiquette to touch a woman's hand or even the hem of her garment and the nature of dancing was understood by very few." In fact "jumping to the piano" (or orchestra) was attributed only to other than aesthetic motives.

Sometimes a host may choose to entertain his friends at a theatre, possibly at the "Ti I Wu T'ai" on Chang Yi Men Street, a fine building in semi-foreign style, cleanand comfortable, a great improvement on the old fashioned playhouses which are often draughty, unattractive and dirty. Posters of red paper several feet long, pasted on the outside wall, announce what plays are going on. But in China there is no need to hurry over dinner to catch the rising curtain, no danger of late-comers being shut out until the next act. The performances last half the day and most of the night—sometimes, in the case of a series of popular historical or mythological plays, even three or four days—and the audience is continually coming and going. Nobody thinks of keeping silent; in fact, discussions are held constantly by convivial parties who sit around tables either in the pit or the wide galleries,[321] eating sweetmeats and drinking tea. Nobody *appears* to listen to the actors shrieking themselves hoarse, but a fine feat of acrobatics or a graceful posture never fails to elicit shouts of "Hao, hao!" (good, good) and the approving gesture of upturned thumbs, reminiscent of Roman amphitheatres.

Scenery is scarce or merely suggestive, and the stage-appears bare and unadorned, much as ours did in Shakespeare's time. To compensate, the costumes are

---

[321] In modern style theatres like the "Ti I Wu T'ai," "Kai Ming," etc., where Mei Lang-fan acts, men and women may sit together in any part of the house-and seats are reserved. In the old fashioned playhouses women may sit in. boxes only and places cannot be reserved, but are sold by attendants who expect a tip for their trouble in addition to the price of the seat.

wonderful, and the head-dresses, decorated with pheasant feathers, mirrors, and wired silk pompoms, very gorgeous. The actors are always men, or young boys, for the female roles,[322] and some of the technique of the tragedians appears to us grotesque. Imagine painted warriors, with deep purple or white circles like goggles round their eyes, entering with an artificial strut that would shame a peacock, yelling at each other in high pitched voices, then waving their arms, striding to and fro across the boards and in desperate moments turning somersaults, with a property man behind each to rearrange his robes afterwards, while the drums and cymbals of the band bang violently! The comedians, however, are often really amusing, bringing out clever puns and repartees, though rather highly spiced for our taste.

A third variety of theatrical representation, combining the best elements of both tragedy and comedy with scenic effects and costumes worthy of the Russian ballet, is being developed by that remarkable interpreter of female roles, A Mei Lang-fang. His popular plays, or pantomimes we might call them, since mimicry and graceful gesture are more important than plot or language, arouse the enthusiastic admiration of Chinese and foreigners alike.

Beyond the Ti I Wu T'ai, the Pleasure Quarter is spreading in the direction of the Temple of Agriculture. New restaurants have sprung up, and an Amusement Garden, the Ch'eng Nan Yu Yi, south of the Tartar City wall—especially charming in warm weather—caters to fashionable idlers.

The poorer people seek their amusements in the open space between the T'ien T'an and the Hsien Nung T'an, (the Temple of Heaven and the Temple of Agriculture). Here are mat-shed theatres, stilt walkers, acrobats and story-tellers somewhat similar to the Italian "improvisatore." These men are immensely nimble of breath and full of slang expressions and

---

322 Men and women seldom act together in the same play, as the Chinese consider it improper. A few companies composed exclusively of women and having their own theatres exist, but they are considered second class by native spectators.

witticisms to draw a laugh from the crowd. Often they work themselves into a perfect frenzy, gesticulating till the sweat pours down their faces. Then, at the psychological moment, they refuse to go on with the story till they have taken up a collection, after an appeal much as follows, "My Gods of Riches and Stars of Long Life, all my performance is a mockery and of no value, but my labour is genuine and my work hard. Therefore I ask you to be generous and throw your copper cents to me in quantities."

Here are open tea-stalls with samovars heated by balls of coal dust and damp clay. Here are peddlers selling big yellow slabs of cake with plums stuck in them. A pleasant odour rises from chestnuts roasting in open cauldrons. Millions of flies buzz round a travelling butcher's barrow so thickly you cannot see the mutton for the flies, but the Chinese do not seem to mind. Whole families take their evening meal alongside one of these travelling kitchens, which a ragged coolie carries, stove and all, by a bamboo pole slung over his shoulder. He provides a rough bowl, a pair of chopsticks and a bone ladle, and his menu consists of soup, coarse macaroni, strips of cabbage sizzling in frying fat, or sweet potatoes sputtering in dishes of hot bubbling syrup. These he advertises with a musical cry: "One copper cent for a big hot potato. Warm your hands with it first and eat it afterwards."

Beyond these primitive pleasure-haunts there used to be a riding course much patronised by horse-dealers and gentlemen jockeys who liked to show off their pacing ponies before the admiring crowd. Their mounts, specially brought from Mongolia, were worth much more than a good trotter would fetch. The Chinese do not care for the latter and indeed their high saddles, ridden with exceedingly short stirrups, are less comfortable at this pace. It was a pretty sight when these miniature horses, with brass-studded harness and bits of bright cloth braided into manes and tails, came down the straight at full tilt, singlefooting as fast as the ordinary pony can gallop, while the rider stood up in his stirrups turning sideways, and the crowd applauded vociferously.

Juliet Bredon

Near-by, in a sunny open space, the bird fancier may still be seen taking his singing thrush for an airing. This has always been considered a most dignified pastime for a Chinese gentleman, besides being a necessity for the health and happiness of the pet. Many varieties of feathered singers, such as larks and "Flowering Eye-Browed Thrushes," mope and refuse to sing unless taken out regularly and their cages swung gently to and fro. Others must be set at liberty and fed with berries thrown into the air. We may smile at the pastime as an amusement for grown men, and a recent "regulation" forbids the habit as "conducive to idleness and waste of time." But, after all, it argues a refined and poetic trait in the national character, and the tiny feathered creatures chirping in their cages, or flying with grace and fearlessness to alight on the hand or the forked twig held out for them, are very pretty and amusing.

Like the Frenchman, the Chinese is a born boulevardier. He loves a crowd and he delights in an excursion to some public park where lie can stand about in leisurely dignity, sunning himself in indolent attitudes. Almost every fine afternoon, streams of carriages and rickshas, filled with well-to-do pleasure seekers, used to wend their way to the Botanical and Zoological gardens outside the Hsi Chih Men. Before the Pei Hai and the Nan Hai were opened, this resort, founded by an official of the Department of Agriculture as an Experimental Station, was a popular promenade. A great attraction was the menagerie started for the Empress Dowager Tz'u Hsi with wild animals presented to her, but most of them, having died, are now in the museum—stuffed. The grounds are spacious and well kept, with pretty lakes and pleasure boats for hire and dainty tea-houses overhanging lotus ponds. Sometimes the water is hidden by the large plants which stretch like a silvery green lawn right up to the balconies, and amid the heavy leaves, lying lazily at angles of rest, the flowers seem to rise on their stalks like great cups, each holding in its stately heart a lump of gold.

The Fun of The Fair

In olden times, when no public gardens existed, the people's only out-of-door distractions were the temple fairs. The habit of holding such fairs dates from great antiquity and has always had the highest patronage. To mention but one instance, Ch'ien Lung used to order booths erected at the New Year along the main road of his Summer Palace for the amusement of the Court. There were stalls with curios, embroideries, etc., and exhibitions of pictures in charge of eunuchs, the articles for sale being supplied by the merchants in Peking through the supervisor of the Octroi, who selected what goods should be sent. Everything was done just as at a real market fair. Even peddlers and hawkers were allowed to come and ply their trades, and waiters and attendants were brought from the best restaurants of the city to serve *al fresco* meals. As His Majesty passed through the bazaar, the waiters would shout the menus for the day, the hawkers would cry their goods and the clerk call out the figures which they were entering in the books. The bustle and animation delighted the Emperor and his guests, the high officials and their wives invited to make purchases. The bazaar continued daily till the end of the first moon when the stalls were taken down.[323]

The most picturesque public fair was that formerly held In the Mongol Market, near the British Legation. Here Mongol traders offered for sale war trumpets, Buddhist images, prayer wheels, tea-pots and rough silverware inlaid with turquoises. The crowd was always interesting with its curious intermingling of racial types. No stranger could help staring at the women of the steppes with their stiff padded epaulettes and long plaits of hair braided with strings of coral and se ni-precious stones. No shrewd Chinese merchant could help swindling their genial but stupid spouses, squat and almost square in their sheepskin-lined clothes and felt riding boots. The Mongol men have ever been to the Pekingese what the Auvergnats are to the gamins of Paris, or the country bumpkins

---

[323] The Empress Dowager Tz'u Hsi revived this picturesque custom at the new Summer Palace during the period (before the *coup d'etat* of 1898) of her retirement from state affairs.

come to London for the cattle-show to the cockney cabbies—the butt of popular jokes, invariably cheated wherever they go.

Of the quaint fairs that still continue, the best known and the most frequented are the Lung Fu Ssu, the Hu Kuo Ssu and the Liu Li Ch'ang. The Lung Fu Ssu is held three times a monih—on the 9th, 10th, 11th, 12th; 19th, 20th, 21st, 22nd; 29th, 30th, 1st and 2nd—in the courts of a dilapidated Ming temple near the "Eastern Four P'ai lous. The "Eternal Happiness" monastery, from which it takes its name, was built at great expense in a.d. 1451, and its five line sanctuaries were served by Lama priests. Under the region of Yung Cheng the fair was inaugurated to celebrate the temple festival and it has been continued ever since, even after the disastrous fire in 1901 which destroyed the grandeur of the establishment.

Cheap wares of all kinds are sold here. At the outer gate, one is besieged by men with Pekingese puppies. Some of them look like imitation dogs. They ought to have green wheels and red flannel tongues.

Within, modern brasses and trays, or odds and ends of curios are spread out on the ground or on stalls. One corner of the large court is given over to the sellers of crickets in bamboo cages and gold-fish—beautiful creatures with triple and quadruple tails. We should like to buy them all and put them in big bowls with clear water. But the peddler explains that if we did, they would die; they prefer the murky liquid to which they are accustomed.

A whole row of artificial flower stands are crowded with women in search of hair ornaments. It is fascinating to watch their slender figures moving with pliant elegance like willow branches bending in a light breeze.

We follow the crowd to the inner courtyard. More stalls here; stalls where false hair is sold in long tresses; stalls with red ceremonial candles boxed in pairs for weddings; comb stalls; stalls with dozens of tiny but unusually sharp knives for shaving cheeks, nose, brows and chin; with bamboo back-scratchers shaped like baby's hands; stalls that all sell ribbons to wind about the ankles and keep the trousers in place; stalls innumerable for every Chinese requirement.

In the midst of them are booths with steaming food where, weary shoppers stop to rest and ply their chopsticks in the open air. The money-changer sits beside them with lines of cash in grooved wooden trays. The seal-cutter has established himself not far off. The herb-seller has chosen a corner where his wares will not be trampled on. A "guaranteed dentist" near by has a stock of tempting teeth neatly extracted, and ready for customers, also gold caps to fit over sound molars just to look expensive. The fortune-teller and chooser of lucky days is also ready to be consulted. He has the usual bamboo tube containing sticks of various lengths. This he shakes by request till a stick falls out. It it long? That means luck to his customers. No, alas it is a short one. Pass on please and try again another day. The sound of the little gong with which he advertises his presence brings to mind a childish verse:

> "Elijah was a prophet who attended country fairs,
> And advertised his business by a troupe of dancing bears."

Even a prophet, you see, will never get credit for prophecy unless he uses good publicity.

The spectacle mender, the razor grinder, and the cheap jeweller, all are present, plying their trades as busily as if they were in their own shops. The cloth auctioneer must be positively irresistible to the native matrons as he pulls his calico to show its strength while singing its praises in rhyme:

> "Ten cents, ten,
> Or a bit more.
> Here you have a stuff never seen before.
> Only ten a foot, strong and handsome too,
> Here's what you want. Just the thing for you."

The words of his chant may be partly rendered by this free translation. But the gestures, the voice tones, the cadence are inimitable.

Juliet Bredon

We tear ourselves away from his amusing pantomime. What could we do with the hideous flowered percale he holds out so invitingly? There is perhaps too little merit in resisting it.

But we fall shamefully when we get as far as the toy stalls. Every foreigner is struck by the astonishing ingenuity by which Chinese toy-makers achieve at a cost too small to name, almost the same results as we do at great expense. Poverty, ages ago, taught them the secret of making pleasure the commonest instead of the costliest of experiences—the divine art of creating the beautiful out of nothing. A group of little paper figures standing on horse hairs are made to dance on a brass tray by a light tap on the edge, the whole delightful contrivance costing only a few cents. A flock of geese will fly up and down a thread by loosening or tightening the bent bamboo attached to it—all for a copper. Butterflies of paper flutter on light osier twigs. Artificial blossoms attached to real branches deceive the eye. Always the cheapest materials are used—paper, bamboo, straw, clay, bits of wood, or feathers. But whether the doll's furniture, so cleverly copied on Chinese Chippendale models, be made of scraps of old cigar-boxes, or the insects of dried mud, or the pink-cheeked goddesses of sugar, or the weird, mythical animals of painted cloth, or the figurines, as pleasing in their way as those of Tanagra, of clay, each thing is so cleverly done—so expressive, often so humorous—that one is forced to buy.

The Hu Kuo Ssu fair, second in importance to the one held at Lung Fu Ssu, also takes place three times a month (on the 7th and 8th, 17th and 18th and 27th and 28th days of the Chinese calendar) in a Lama temple designated for this purpose by Kublai Khan. Thibetan Living Buddhas used to reside here under the Mings, but it is now in ruins. The fair, held in the courtyards, is for the supply of the ordinary household needs of simple folk: brooms, feather clusters, scissors, spoons, peanuts heaped in little piles, the frailest of toys, the cheapest of glass jewellery. The street leading to the temple is filled with flower shops. One at least dates from Ming times324 and the dealer shows with pride two historic palms, planted in that dynasty, of a variety known to the Chinese as the *T'ieh Shu* ("iron tree"). They flower only once in a century or more and, according to the records kept by his family, they have blossomed but twice since the advent of the Manchus. The foreign visitor will be interested in inspecting the winter plant houses of wattle and dab, with mud walls on three sides, mud roofs and thick white paper pasted over the skeleton poles of the southern exposure. They make warm, dry shelters for the plants, keeping them at a safe and even temperature through the bright but bitter winter season. Some of these hot-houses have underground flues that force the plants appropriate to the New Year to bloom on time. If the festal blossoms lag behind in the last week of grace, cauldrons of boiling water furnish clouds of gentle steam-heat that open the most obstinate peonies, and gild the fruits of the dwarf orange trees and the curious "Buddha's Fingers"—a symbolic fruit of the lemon family shaped like a hand. All these favourite New Year gifts for friends are then packed in paper-lined baskets, warmed with hand braziers and, thus snugly protected from frost which would otherwise wither them in an instant, are transported to the home of the purchaser to add to the decoration of house or shop at this joyous season.

In Peking, the New Year (according to the Lunar calendar) is a time of universal rejoicing—the one holiday lasting several weeks, the one occasion of unbounded festivity and hilarity, as if the whole population threw off the old year with a shout, and clothed itself in the new with a change of garments. It is celebrated by the most famous of all Peking fairs held at the Liu Li Ch'ang.

---

324 Several firms in Peking boast of equally ancient beginnings, for example the T'ung Jen T'ang Pharmacy in the Ta Sha La'rh outside the Ch'ien Men. This establishment still uses the valuable Ming jars, bought when it first opened, to hold drugs and herbs.

Shop in Lantern Street

The Fun of The Fair

Let us go by all means if we have a chance. The "boy" says we must pass through Lantern Street, though it is round-about way, just to see the crowds. Very well. Our rickshas hardly move faster than a walk; because the traffic is so great. But we do not complain, for the streets have the effect of an infinitely diverting theatrical performance, and a slow pace gives us better opportunities to look at the shops thronged with purchasers. Everybody buys a lantern for the festival and the choice is positively bewildering. Some are of horn or gauze, painted with characters signifying lucky wishes, or with the owner's name. Some are of paper and some of silk mounted in carved wood, and some have curious shapes of birds, or crabs, or figures of jointed beetles and bumblebees. These are very inexpensive, really nothing but toys since they give no light. But in these days of cheap electricity, the lantern is not so much a necessity as a decorative adjunct to Chinese life.[325]

A little further and we find ourselves in the thick of Booksellers' Street, the great resort of the literati who spend hours, much as their European colleagues do in Paris at the little stalls along the Seine, searching for treasures; old books, rubbings of famous inscriptions, scroll pictures. There are poems, mounted upon silk, which are wonders of calligraphy. And there are charming landscapes—glimpses of snow-covered mountains, rice-fields with birds darting over the grain, trees crimsoning beside tremendous gorges, ranks of peaks draped with clouds, all none the less charming because frankly modern and costing from one dollar to twenty.

The outdoor fair with the usual booths of all kinds, quacks, mountebanks, jugglers and puppet shows, is held in a large open space bounded by fine wide roads newly opened up. But in a narrow lane leading off from it is the old Temple of the Fire God where pearls, jades and porcelains are for sale. Here is temptation personified. And what a crowd! At first it seems impossible for anybody to move in it. Nevertheless all are moving or rather circulating from stall to stall. "There is a

---

[325] In bygone days lanterns were carried by all classes. Even sentries used them when on duty, also umbrellas and fans.

general gliding and slipping as of fish in a shoal, but with patience and good humour one finds no difficulty in getting through the apparently solid press of heads and shoulders."

We notice that prices are absurdly high until the last day of the fair—in fact, prohibitive. But the merchants hardly expect to sell. Things are really placed here on exhibition to attract the attention of buyers who will later go to the shops to bargain in private for what they have seen and admired. Nevertheless, even to look at such things as are exposed is an education.

Outside in the street, the poorer classes spend their coppers at the fruit stalls where mounds of white Peking pears, large purple grapes that the Chinese know how to keep for a year by burying them underground in pottery jars on an ancient cold storage system, rosy cheeked apples, and orange persimmons, show bright spots of colour. Dear to the children is the crab-apple man with the prickly broom on his shoulder, every bamboo stick dotted with little red apples preserved in honey. His recipe came originally from the Mongols who wear these fruits, prepared in this same way, strung on strings around their necks, and often take a bite from their necklace as they ride or bargain. It was in fact the Mongols who developed the sweet tooth of Asia, carrying their love of sugared dainties with them in their conquests and passing it on to the Turks, the Persians and all the peoples of the Orient, so that by their sweets one may still trace the path of the once-powerful Khans. The famous candy shops of the Liu Li Ch'ang made their reputation by improving on the original recipes, and they put up not one, but a hundred varieties of delicious preserves in green-glazed jars for eager customers.

The two favourite dissipations of the Pekingese, as some one justly remarks, are sweets and fire crackers. As we return, crackers are flashing all around us, celebrating the end of the happy holiday. It has all passed like a pleasant dream. And now the little plum trees, gifts of felicitation in every house, are losing their flowers.

Another year of toil must pass before they bloom again. But the joyous spirit of the feast still seems to haunt the guest rooms. Perhaps it is only the perfume of pleasures so deeply enjoyed, because so rare, for the busy, toiling multitude; perhaps an ancestral memory, some Lady of Past New Years who lingers on the threshold awhile as if loath to leave, "for the sake of Auld Lang Syne."

Juliet Bredon

XXI. Western Landmarks

Here and there in the native city or suburbs of Peking some Western landmark, a church or chapel, a school or hospital, inscribed in French or English, or a cemetery marked with a cross, offers a striking contrast to its Far Eastern environment. These properties belong to various Christian Missions, and serve to remind us of a romantic chapter in the history of foreign relations with China, and the extraordinary part played by missionaries in early days.[326]

Setting aside the dim legend that St. Thomas, the doubting Apostle, himself preached the Gospel to the Chinese, it is certain that Christian teachers visited them in very remote ages.[327] The first, probably, were Manichaeans. We know for certain that two Nestorian monks carried silkworm's eggs to Justinian in the 6th century, and that their order had been proselytising in China, since the reign of the great T'ai Tsung (T'ang Dynasty) several hundred years before the arrival of the first papal embassy. The Nestorians were an important community in Peking as late as the 14th century, and their last activities were reported to Ricci as having been wiped out in North China by a persecution about a.d. 1540.[328] But while their influence lasted, they were powerful enough to prevent the permanent establishment of any other Christian sect.

John of Montecorvino, sent by Pope Nicholas IV in the 13th century to the Court of Kublai Khan, is the first of the Roman Catholic fathers to thrill our imaginations. We read how he was kindly received at Khanbalig (ancient Peking), where he remained, as he says so affectingly, "twelve long years without any news from Europe"; how he built a church "which had a steeple and belfry with three bells that were rung every hour to summon the converts to prayer"; how he baptised nearly 3,000

---

326 See *A History of Christian Missions in China*, by K. S. Latourette.
327 The birth of Christ is recorded in the Chinese chronicles as having taken place in the reign of Hsiao P'ing Ti (Han dynasty), on the fourth day of the "Tung Chih festival," in "Teh-ya"—(Judea).
328 Yule-Cordier, *Cathay and the Way Thither*.

Western Landmarks

persons and "bought 150 children whom he instructed in Greek and Latin, composing for them several devotional books"; and how, after an "outward life that was good, and hard, and rough," he died in a.d. 1328 an Archbishop, and more than forty years an exile from his home. The whole city mourned for him, Christian and heathen alike rending their garments and making pilgrimages to his tomb.

Doubtless much of his success was due to the complete toleration of the Khans towards all religions.[329] Mangu, the predecessor of Kublai, defined their attitude when he said: "We Tartars recognise one God at whose beck we live and die, and to whom our hearts are always converted. But just as God has given men several fingers on their hands, so has he granted them many ways leading to celestial bliss." For others, less tolerant than himself, this sovereign arranged a field day when the Nestorians, Catholics, Mohammedans, Taoists and Buddhists were invited to appear and settle their disputes. Rubruquis, a Dutch priest sent out by the French King St. Louis, was the victorious champion of the first two bouts, but at a later one held in 1256, the doughty Christian pleader being absent, Mangu decided for Buddhism, "the thumb," as against Christianity, Mohammedanism and Taoism which he styled mere "fingers"—and this despite the fact that his own mother, as Friar Odoric, who visited Karakorum in search of Prester John, attests, was a Christian.[330]

Later, the teaching of the Gospel in China was discontinued for many years. By the end of the 16th century, however, the Jesuits began to exercise an influence which very nearly overwhelmed all their rivals. St. Francis Xavier had marked China as the field of his special labours. He himself, however, never succeeded in reaching the capital, "for when once his

---

[329] "In the quarters of the infidels," says Brother Peregrine in a letter written in a.d. 1317, "we can preach freely, and we have preached several times in the Saracens' mosque for their conversion.'
[330] For a full description of Mangu Khan's religious tournaments see the account, bristling with unconscious humour, of Brother Rubruquis himself. *The Journey of William of Rubruck to Eastern Parts of the World* 1253-1255. Translated by W. W. Rockhill.

destination became known, formidable wheels of opposition were set in motion by the Portuguese....whose traders were from the start inimical to all missionary work, foreseeing danger to their business if any collision with the Imperial authorities should result from it."[331] St. Francis died in 1552 of fever, near Macao, without personally realising his dream. But his mantle fell upon a worthy successor in Father Ricci, to whom, when he reached Peking after overcoming a thousand difficulties, the Ming Emperor Wan Li showed special favour.

The Order continued to hold its high position in the early days of Manchu rule owing to the pre-eminent abilities of another great leader, Father Schall, who enjoyed even more consideration under the Manchu Emperor Shun Chih than under the last Mings, receiving the appointment of Tutor to the Heir Apparent and a free gift of the site of the house near the Shun Chih Men, where Ricci had lived, for a church. On this land the Nan T'ang, or Southern Cathedral, was built in 1650.[332] These honours excited the jealousy of the Chinese officials, as Schall warned Shun Chih they would, and when this Emperor died, the famous missionary was thrown into prison together with his companion, Verbiest. For six long years they suffered the horrors of a Chinese gaol! Finally the four Regents, into whose hands the administration had fallen after Shun Chih's death, incurred the displeasure of the youthful heir (K'ang Hsi) by their harsh treatment of these Roman Catholic priests, towards whom his father had shown himself well and kindly disposed. In fact, it was largely due to their persecution of his old tutor that in 1667 the young Monarch dismissed them and assumed control of the Government at the age of thirteen.

---

331 "A Study of Roman Catholic Missions in China," by Hollis W. Hering, *New China Review*, 1921.
332 Gloriously associated with the names of Ricci, Schall and Verbiest, decorated with handsome statues imported from Europe and paintings done by the skilful brush of Castiglione, the Nan T'ang as a place of worship survived the recall of the Jesuits and the expulsion of the Lazarists, only to be burned by the Boxers during the fanatical outbreak of 1900.

Western Landmarks

K'ang Hsi honoured the Jesuits in every way, accorded them official rank and consideration at Court, built them dwelling houses and a church—the original Pei T'ang Cathedral, on ground actually within the Palace enclosure, given in 1693 as a reward for His Majesty's cure from a fever by quinine, or "Jesuits' bark" (then new in Europe), administered to him by Fathers Gerbillon and Visdelou.[333]

In return, these sayants placed their scientific knowledge at the disposal of the Emperor, and very useful it was to him too. Verbiest corrected the inaccurate calculations of the native astronomers. Gerbillon, his successor, was sent by K'ang Hsi to Russia to help the conclusion of the Nerchinsk Treaty, and, as a reward, the Emperor published, on March 22nd, 1692, his great "Edict of Tolerance," permitting Christianity to be preached freely throughout the Empire.[334] Schall reformed the calendar and cast cannon which, "with much ceremony and robed as for mass, he blessed in the presence of the Court, sprinking them with holy water and giving to each the name of a female saint which he had himself drawn on the breech." Other Fathers surveyed and mapped the Empire, personally engraving the plates.

This was undoubtedly the golden age of the Jesuits in Peking. They had three churches in the city, besides a church for women, which the ladies of the capital were especially zealous in ornamenting with their jewels. It is doubtful, though, whether this church had much influence, since Ripa tells us that it was only open once in six months. Yet that it was allowed in the capital at all is significant.

---

[333] "Les Missionaries Europeens sont admis a chaque grande ceremonie, ou ils ont leur rang. L'Empereur leur a fait souvent l'honneur de leur adresser la parole et de leur dire des choses pleines de bonte, a la face, pour ainsi dire, de tout l'Empire," *Memoires Concernant les Chinois, par les Missionaires de Pekin. Paris,* 1776-1791.

[334] See H. W. Hering, *A Study of Roman Catholic Missions in China*

The Catholic University

"The story of Ricci, Schall, Verbiest and their companions," says Freeman-Mitford,[335] "teaches one great truth too often ignored in later days. If missionaries are to be successful in China, it must be by the power of masterly talent and knowledge. They can only work on any scale through the lettered classes, and in order to influence them must be able to give proof of superior attainments as the old Jesuits did... With courage, devotion, self-sacrifice our [Anglo-Saxon and Protestant] missionaries are largely endowed. They have given proofs of these even to the laying down of their lives, but these qualities are as nothing in the eyes of the cultivated Confucian. One such convert as Schall's friend, the Prime Minister Su, or his daughter, the saintly Candida, would do more towards christianising China than thousands of poor peasants. To make such converts, however, needs qualifications which are rare indeed. Above all things, an accurate and scholarly knowledge of the language is necessary. There have been not a few excellent scholars among our missionaries. But there are many more whose ignorance has been fatal, covering themselves and the religion they preach with ridicule. Fancy a Chinese Buddhist mounting on the roof of a hansom cab at Charing Cross and preaching Buddhism to the mob in pidgin English! That would give some measure of the effect produced on a Chinese crowd by a missionary whom I have seen perched upon a cart outside the great gate of the Tartar City at Peking, haranguing a mob in bastard Chinese delivered with a strong Aberdeen accent. The Jesuits knew better than that." In fact the Jesuits, when they found the Chinese hostile to their missionary efforts, fell back on Western scientific knowledge to overcome this opposition. "It was," says Hering, "by their high scholarship that the great leaders—Ricci, Schall, Verbiest— worked their way literally step by step to the capital, and there entrenched themselves."

How well their methods of elevating and purifying the minds of men and turning their thoughts to God by a knowledge of His marvellous works, succeeded, is patent to all.

---

335 See *The Attache at Peking*.

Juliet Bredon

K'ang Hsi's mother, wife and half the Court were baptised Christians, and the Emperor only hesitated himself because of the cult of his ancestors. Therein laythe difficulty. It would never have proved insuperable if these tolerant, sensible, far-seeing Jesuits had been left alone or sustained by an intelligent Pope during the enlightened reign of K'ang Hsi.[336] But when they urged the Pope to recognise the Imperial ancestors and thus do away with the one obstacle to the Sovereign's conversion, envious Dominicans and Franciscans reported to Rome that the Jesuits were sanctioning heathen customs[337] and leading lives of pomp and wordly splendour. Thereupon the Pope sent legates to make inquiries and, naturally, trouble with the Jesuits ensued. K'ang Hsi resented the Holy Father's interference and, wearied with the bickerings of the new priests, would have nothing more to do with their religion or its teachers after Clement XI launched his bull supporting the Dominican contentions and denouncing ancestor worship as a heathen practice.[338]

---

[336] It is interesting to note that the present Pope has, within the last five years, officially confirmed the attitude of his predecessor towards Chinese ancestral worship.

[337] What would these protagonists of Christian purism have said of the fact, proved by scholars, that St. Iosaph, or the Holy Prince Josaphat (canonised by the early Christian Church on the testimony of St. John Damascene), whose very name is a corruption of the word "Bodhisatva" and whose feast in the Roman Catholic calendar is on the 27th of November—corresponded in life to Sakyamuni Buddha? (See Yule-Cordier, *The Book of Ser Marco Polo*, 3rd ed.).

[338] "The East has been tolerant of all creeds that do not assault the foundations of its society, and if Western Missions had been wise enough to leave these foundations alone—to deal with the Ancestor Cult as Buddhism did, and to show the same spirit of tolerance in other directions, the introduction of Christianity on a very extensive scale should have proved an easy matter. That the result would have been a Christianity differing considerably from Western Christianity is obvious... but the essentials of the doctrine might have been widely propagated without exciting antagonism... To demand of a [Chinese] that he cast away or destroy his ancestral tablets is not less irrational and inhuman than it would be to demand of an Englishman or a Frenchman that he destroy his mother's tombstone in proof of his devotion to Christianity." —*Lafcadio Hearn*.

The Emperor of China had no intention of sacrificing the peace of his Kingdom to Christianity."

The opportunity slipped by, never to return, and the golden age of Jesuit influence in China passed with the passing of their greatest men and the remarkable sovereign they served.

Yung Cheng, successor of K'ang Hsi, was an ardent Buddhist, in spite of the fact that in his youth he had a priestly preceptor, Father Pedrini, of whom he was very fond.[339] Intending to make it quite plain that he was master in his own Empire, and annoyed when some of the Jesuits took sides in his family quarrels, he wrote several direct "orders" to the Pope, abolished the Court rank of Roman Catholic missionaries, and tolerated them only as directors of works and art industries. He even confiscated the Pei T'ang and turned it into a hospital for plague patients. The next Emperor Ch'ien Lung was more gracious. He sat to Attiret for his portrait. He entered into correspondence with Voltaire through Father Amiot, and took an interest in the painters who were embellishing his palace at Yuan Ming Yuan.

But toleration ceased altogether with his reign and after disfavour, neglect and, finally, open persecution, the Jesuits—whose Order had, meanwhile, been suppressed by the Pope—were replaced in 1783, at the request of the King of France, by the Lazarists. The Jesuits returned to Peking only after the war of 1860. Then Bishop Mouly, who may be regarded as the second founder of the Mission, assumed public charge of his. flock, and the Abbe Delamarre slipped into the Chinese version of the Peking Treaty (without the knowledge of the French Minister) that famous clause which secured full rights and immunities for Christian Missions.

Once again, the Roman Catholics regained possession of their cherished Cathedral, the Pei T'ang. The original building was sold by order of the Emperor Tao Kuang in 1826 to a prince

---

[339] Father Pedrini appears to have been a worthy man, devout and generous. He built the Hsi T'ang, or Western Cathedral, at his own expense in 1723. But he had neither the opportunity nor the capacity to wield the influence of his predecessors.

who allowed this church, that had been in the hands of the missionaries for more than a century, to fall into ruin. When it was returned, the priests found the iron grille, presented by Louis XV, still hanging on its hinges at the entrance. They immediately installed a provisional chapel and here, on October 29th, 1860, in the sanctuary re-opened after thirty years, a Te Deum was sung in honour of the victories of Napoleon I.

It was not long destined, however, to resound with Christian thanksgiving. After Kuang Hsu reached his majority and the Empress Dowager Tz'u Hsi established herself in the Sea Palaces, she found the minster so near to her dwelling quarters that the towers spoiled the *feng-shui* of her gardens. The priests were accordingly persuaded to accept a new site further away. But the building remained standing in the Imperial domain, and foreigners often remarked on the strange anomaly of a Christian church in the precincts of an Oriental potentate. It long served as a kind of museum where, among mustysilks and carpets, Father Armand David's wonderful collection of stuffed birds and animals was left to be gradually eaten by insects. In 1900, when the French entered this old Pei T'ang (pulled down in 1909), they discovered, among other things, the remains of a mounted lion. Tradition says that while Father David was in Paris during the Siege of 1870 and people were eating the animals in the Zoological gardens, he obtained and mounted a skin for his collection in Peking, and that it was this same lion, victim of the Siege of Paris, whose pelt was found by the troops who came to relieve the Siege of Peking.

The present Pei T'ang is closely associated with the name of Bishop Favier, worthy successor of the early Jesuit fathers, who died in 1905 and is buried in one of the side chapels. Under his inspired leadership the enormous establishment which, in addition to the church, comprises an orphanage, a printing press, several schools, a cemetery, etc., weathered the Boxer outbreak of 1900. In fact, with only thirty-one French Marines and eleven Italians to reinforce the native converts, it sustained a siege lasting from June 15th to August 13th, even more remarkable than that of the Legations. There were 400 victims out of 3,000 Christian refugees, besides one French officer killed, and nearly half that gallant little band of defenders either killed or wounded.³⁴⁰

In *Round About My Peking Garden*, Mrs. Archibald Little describes a visit to the half-ruined Pei T'ang shortly after the Relief. "When we look at its façade riddled with shot, its aisles propped up by beams, the trees in the grounds with their bark gnawed off, the tumble-down masses of brick and mortar behind the broken walls, the great pits where the mines exploded engulfing children by the hundred, we recall memories of heroism and of suffering so bravely endured that our hearts ache.... ' There,' says a young Portuguese Sister, her big brown eyes luminous with the recollection, 'there is where the Italian lieutenant was buried by a shell and for three hours we could not dig him out. No... " He was alive and only bruised. Ah, the young French lieutenant, that was sad! He was so good. We could but grieve over his loss.'³⁴¹ Then we pause by the grave of the Sister Superior who lay dying as the relief came in, 'too late for me,' as she wrote—her one thought for days past: 'What can I give them to eat to-morrow? What can I give them to eat? There is nothing left,' ... haunting her to the end. ' The poor soldiers,' said another Sister, ' they suffered so from hunger, although they tightened their belts every day! I tore all my letters into bits and made cigarettes of them. Burnt paper is better than nothing. And they had nothing to smoke. That is so hard for a soldier.' Next we pause by the great pit where so many children, blown up by a mine, lie buried.... The Sisters are great authorities on mines and shells now.. They know, too, which leaves are poisonous and tell how the Chinese Christians

---

340 "De toutes les defenses organisees pendant le siege de Pekin," said Monsieur Pichon (the well-known French statesman who was Minister for France in Peking at the time), "celle du Peitang est pent-etre la plus etonnante et la plus remarquable."

341 In *L'Ame Bresonne*, Le Goffic pays, under the title of "Trois Marins," a touching and beautiful tribute to this young hero who had a presentiment that the Pei T'ang would be saved, but he himself would die there. His simple journal, published after his tragic death, gives an excellent picture of this remarkable siege.

swelled and suffered trying to sustain life by eating them. They present the remainder of their school children. 'While the cannonading was going on, we nuns moved about the compound with the tail of our children after us to any shelter where the firing seemed less dangerous,' said the young Portuguese Sister.

"We paid a call upon the Bishop. 'Did any of your Christians recant?' we asked. 'A few, very few. I think 12,000 Converts lost their lives' [rather than deny their faith], replied Monseigneur Favier, 'besides three European and four Chinese priests, also many of our Chinese sisters. One priest hung, nailed on a cross, for three days before he died. Monseigneur Hamer they killed by cutting his arms and legs to the bone, filling the cuts with petroleum and setting them alight. What saved us? Oh! a series of miracles, nothing else.'

"Once again we stood outside the Cathedral. It was a beautiful bright Sunday morning this time, and the soldiers were streaming out from the Te Deum sung in honour of the deliverance—soldiers of all nationalities. We looked back at the shot marks on the ruined facade and realised that those shots were the call which summoned this great gathering of the nations to the Imperial City of Peking, right into its heart, straight into its forbidden precincts. How little the Chinese dreamed this would be the result when they fired them!"

Instead of wiping out the Pei T'ang as they hoped, the besiegers lived to see it repaired and decorated more handsomely than before, with a special chapel added in remembrance of their failure and two guns, inscribed "1606 Rotterdam," taken from the Boxers, placed beside the gates.

The Roman Catholics to-day have several other churches[342] and chapels in Peking, besides schools for both sexes and orphanages in charge of Sisters of Charity, who also serve as nurses in the Hospital of St. Michel, built by Bishop. Favier on the site of the old Board of Rites, and next door to the former offices of the Imperial Physicians. But the oldest and most

---

342 Such as the Tung T'ang, many times rebuilt, and, in the days of. the Portuguese Jesuits, the finest church in Peking.

Western Landmarks

interesting of their ecclesiastical property is at Sha La, outside the P'ing Tse Men, best known for its famous cemetery, where the early scholars and propagandists lie in consecrated soil originally given by the Ming Emperor Wan Li for the tomb of his protege Ricci in 1610.[343] Likewise, this sovereign commanded that an avenue of stone figures, such as we see at princely graves, embellish the tomb of the only Westerner, except Sir Robert Hart, who received the honour of having not only himself but his parents and grandparents ennobled.

When Schall and Verbiest died, K'ang Hsi buried them here at his own expense in costly tombs of Chinese style, and testified in Latin and in Chinese to their virtues on turtle-borne tablets. Dr. Edkins has preserved in his account of Peking[344] a description of the funeral of Father Verbiest, in which Chinese and Christian rites were curiously combined. He says that near the grave stood a great stone crucifix with altar-tables below it adorned with Buddhist emblems, the conventional vases, candlesticks and incense burners such as appear at important heathen tombs in China, and points out how significant these emblems are of the toleration of early evangelists, and the compromises in faith's mere ritual and externals which they conceded for conversion's sake.

In 1900 the Boxers burned Sha La and violated the tombs, of which there were originally more than eighty. Much of their grandeur was ruined beyond repair, but, wherever possible, the old monuments were set up again. One can still decipher on cracked slabs the battered inscriptions that mark the last resting places of that illustrious company.

The tradition of Catholic culture and unselfish effort towards the Chinese people—a Christian tradition, alas, too often ill-repaid by cruelty and martyrdom—is also carried on in the new "Catholic University" just completed in Peking. Outgrowth of a suggestion placed before the Pope by the late

---

[343] This land once belonged to a rich eunuch who had intended it for his own sepulchre, but, having committed some crime, was condemned to death and his property confiscated.

[344] Published as an addendum to Williamson's *Journeys in North China*.

Mr. Vincent Ying, a Chinese scholar and teacher, this institution was founded by the Benedictines and embodies the characteristic spirit of their Order inasmuch as "it reconciles the old with the new, adapting traditional Chinese forms to the needs of modern school architecture."

The handsome new buildings, in the form of a small walled city with corner towers, stand on the site of the former Prince Tsai T'ao's palace in the West City and provide an admirable answer to Kipling's statement that "east is east and west is west, and never the twain shall meet." Here they do meet, and merge in a thoroughly satisfactory manner, thanks to the broad-minded plan conceived by Don Adalbert Gresnigt, a Dutch Benedictine Father who has many notable churches in Europe, South America, and China to his credit.

Side by side with the most modern class rooms, laboratories, dormitories, etc., for the thousand and more students who attend the University and Middle School, are the purely Chinese buildings where the monks live, also a unique one-storied chapel, painted and decorated in Chinese style. Wherever possible the picturesque features of the original gardens, such as open pavilions, galleries, and artificial ponds, have been sympathetically preserved so that the students, after a football game on the excellent modern campus, may return to the peaceful atmosphere of old traditions. This combination of influences should surely do much to advance, and at the same time to steady, the new generation, or that part of it which has the luck to profit by such well-balanced and harmonious surroundings.

Scarcely less romantic than the story of the early Catholic Fathers is the history of the Russian Ecclesiastical (Greek Orthodox) Mission in Peking. Its beginnings may be traced back to that little band of Albazine prisoners[345] who brought their own priest, Father Leontieff, and the holy Icon of St. Nicholas with them to Peking in 1685 and worshipped in a small Chinese temple specially fitted up for their services in the Tiorth-east corner of the Tartar City—near the locality where

---

345 See Chapter II.

the Russian Guards were given grants of land in the 14th century.

Ten years after the arrival of these Albazines, the Metropolitan of Tobolsk, in sending a communion cloth and recognising the little congregation, ordered that preaching among the Chinese in general should begin and prayers be offered for their emperor. "Pray thus," writes he quaintly, "after the petitions for the Tsar: 'We pray to our Lord that He may spare His servant (name), His Bogdokhanic Majesty (as his titles are), and increase the years of his life and give him noble children for his succession, and deliver him and his boyars from all sorrow, wrath and need, all ailments of the soul and of the body, and open to him the light of the Gospel, and forgive him all sin, voluntary and involuntary, and unite him to the Holy Universal Apostolic Church, so that he may receive the Kingdom of Heaven.'"

The old priest who accompanied the Albazine Bannermen and shared their joys and sorrows, even following them on a Chinese expedition against the Kalmuks, died in 1712. The first Mission which came to replace him, under the leadership of the Archimandrite Hilarion, was received with much honour. But before it was permanently established, Hilarion died and the Li Fan Yuan requested that a successor be sent to Peking. Peter the Great planned to appoint a bishop but gave up the idea, some say in consequence of the intrigues of the Jesuits who were then getting into trouble in China against their own judgment, and were not in a position to contend against competitors who might prove dangerous. Subsequently, having lost fear of possible rivalry on the part of the Russian priests (who once nearly supplanted them in their posts on the Astronomical Board), the representatives of both creeds came to be on most cordial terms. Many mutual courtesies were shown in the course of their relations. As already stated, the Jesuit Father Gerbillon was of great assistance in concluding the celebrated Treaty of a.d. 1689 between Russia and China,[346]

---

[346] One of the three texts of this Treaty is even written in Latin.

just as the Greek Orthodox Father Gouru in 1860 proved a valuable mediator during the second foreign war in Peking.

Looking back to earlier days, we see the Roman Catholics asking and getting an Icon from the Russian envoy Nicholas Spather in 1676 to be put up in the Nan T'ang for the convenience of Greek Christians who came to Peking with the Russian caravans long before the Albazines arrived, or they had a church of their own. This kindness was generously repaid when, after the bitter persecutions of Chia Ch'ing's reign, a Russian Archimandrite took charge of that same Nan T'ang (from 1826 to 1860).

When the Russian Ecclesiastical Mission was officially recognized by the Kiakhta Treaty of a.d. 1727, the friendliness of the Chinese Government towards the priests was shown in many ways; by grants of official rank, land, etc. Old records relate that the Chinese even went so far as to recommend the priests for Russian decorations and at one time undertook to pay them a yearly allowance in silver and rice, according to a promise made to Father Hilarion. This astonishing engagement was faithfully observed until the Tientsin Treaty of 1858.

It was not because of sympathy with their creed, for they hated Christianity in all its forms, that Yung Cheng and his heirs assisted the Russian monks while at the same time persecuting the Jesuits, but rather because, during the hundred and seventy-five years that the former had then been in Peking, there was never a single serious anti-orthodox missionary outbreak. Only one slight ripple disturbed the smooth surface of their relations with the Chinese when, for a few years, about 1760, the priests were confined in the Mission owing to a temporary estrangement in Russo-Chinese political relation.

The reason these priests escaped the ill-will manifested towards the Roman Catholics was undoubtedly due to the fact that they did not meddle in state affairs, and were men sufficiently modest not to invite jealousy; sufficiently wise to be reasonable in their attempts at proselytising, sufficiently tactful never to try by means of religious doctrine to bring the

Western Landmarks

Chinese under the political wing of the Church, while at the same time often discharging diplomatic services to mutual advantage. The work of the Mission was, in fact, less evangelistic than literary and scientific. A succession of distinguished students and Archimandrites have written books which are still among the best authorities on the social life of the Chinese, the tribes of Central Asia, the history and geography of China, Mongolia and Thibet as well as many studies on various religions, Taoism, Nestorianism, Buddhism, Mohammedanism, including in these last years a history of the Russian Orthodox Mission in China.[347]

Father Hyacinth Bitchurin, to name the most striking among the scholars, had exceptional capacities blended with a temperament so fiery that it could not adapt itself to monastic discipline and routine. During his long residence in Peking as head of the Mission (1808-1821), his many weaknesses, upon which the highest Chinese authorities looked with fatherly solicitude, were far more notorious than his studies. Returning to Russia in disgrace, the vast knowledge he had collected finally rehabilitated him in the eyes of his superiors, who recognised that in twenty-five years he had accomplished a stupendous task in translation and original commentary, and at last achieved a right to the admiration[348] of posterity.

The buildings of the Pei Kuan, or "Northern Hostelry," where the Mission established itself after the Russian Legation took over its old site, were blown up by dynamite in the Boxer disturbance of 1900. Most of the native Christians, descendants of the Albazines, were thrown down a well (still to be seen in the garden) vainly crying out for mercy. "Kill, kill! burn, burn! let not one Christian remain alive, nor one remembrance of

---

347 Many of them also taught in the official Russian Language School established by the Chinese Government in the 18th century. Unfortunately their valuable and scholarly works are nearly all inaccessible to persons unversed in Russian.

348 In the Alexander Nevsky monastery at Petrograd, the Chinese epitaph on his tomb reminds those who visit it of the land he loved so well, the land where he lived, failed, struggled and succeeded, the land from which his genius drew its inspiration.

him!" shrieked the fanatics, as they passed on to set the torch to the priceless library accumulated through two centuries by men like Hyacinth, Polycarpus, and Palladius—a library including a collection of books acquired at the request of Anglo-American Missionaries in connection with plans for a Union of Churches. This represented one of the first steps towards a fine ideal. Who knows what it might not have meant to Christianity had it been realised![349]

Happily the famous Nicholas Icon was preserved and may be seen, blackened by age, in the new church. Together with a few treasures of the Monastery, the monks carried it with them to the Yung Ho Kung where they lived temporarily. They went back afterwards to their same property, enlarged now by the purchase of the Palace of the Fourth Prince. Undaunted, undiscouraged, they gradually built up their establishment again into a typical Russian monastery, save that the bishop's house, remodelled from one of the princely palace halls, gives an unmistakable Far Eastern note to the picture. Besides the Cathedral, rebuilt on the site of the old Church of the Assumption or of Saint Nicholas (first consecrated in 1696), the priests erected a commemorative church over the remains of the martyrs, and various other buildings—schools and quarters for priests and nuns. Following the Russian monastic custom, they also added all that was required to make the community self-supporting. The whir of a flour mill may be heard in one corner of the park. Scattered under the trees are bee-hives. The lowing of cattle denotes the presence of a dairy not far off. A busy printing press provides for the intellectual needs of the flock.

The whole impression is one of monastic calm, joined to unhurried industry, so strongly reminiscent of old Russia itself,

---

349 The jealousies of the different sects of Christianity have enormously increased the difficulties in the way of China's conversion. A highly educated Chinese gentleman once appealed to Freeman-Mitford on the subject. "How is it," he inquired, "that if I go to one teacher and talk to him of what I have learned from another, he answers me: ' No, that is not right. That is the doctrine preached by So-and-So. If you follow him, you will go to hell.' " Is it any wonder that the inquirer grows suspicious and confused?

so close to Earth and yet so near to Heaven, so patient and so capable when dealing with things that feed the souls and bodies of men.

Associated with the Mission is the picturesque Russian cemetery between the An Ting Men and the Yellow Temple, close to the spot where the Allies intended to breach the north wall of the city in 1860. Many of the first members of the Mission lie in the shadow of the little chapel with its characteristic gilded cupola and, strange to say, some British Protestants, men massacred by the Chinese in 1860, were kindly granted sepulchre here. Here, too, urns containing the remains of the late Czar and members of his family, so foully murdered in Siberia, were kept for some months before being sent to relatives in Europe.

Not till long after the Roman Catholics and the Orthodox priests were established did Protestant Missionaries begin to work in Peking. They, too, profited by the surreptitious clause in the French treaty and came to the capital shortly after the Chinese Government was forced to receive foreign diplomats at the Court after 1860. Times had changed since Wan Li welcomed Ricci and the Chinese Ministers took a paternal interest in the morals of Father Hyacinth, aiding him to overcome temptation by placing over his gate: "Undesirable persons must not enter here."

The Protestants were offered, even though they might have refused it, no official rank. They were presented with no princely palaces, earned no gratitude save the gratitude of the poor and sick, and not always that, for the people were so ignorant that they mistrusted unselfish motives. They had, in a word, but two privileges—their faith and their sacrifices.

The Protestant pioneers in Peking were members of the London Missionary Society, who made their headquarters at first in the British Legation itself, because in those early days it was very hard for the Missions to secure property. If it were known a piece of land was about to be sold to the Christians, this was a signal for a small riot in which the owner might suffer personal violence and have his house torn down over his head. In some cases where a place was finally bought, it was necessary for the foreigners to remain personally in possession lest it be wrecked by their unwilling neighbours.

The Church of England work was begun in Peking in 1862 by members of the Church Missionary Society. On its present property in the West City, near the "Elephant House Bridge," stands a large school for boys and a handsome Cathedral, planned by the universally-beloved Bishop Scott, who died a few years ago.

In 1863, Dr. W. A. P. Martin, the well-known sinologue, arrived and started the work of the American Presbyterian Mission in the north city, and in 1864 the Rev. Henry Blodget established the American Board Mission (Congregational).

The first Methodist Episcopal Church followed in 1869, and the compound around it served as the refuge of many foreigners and Chinese before they went into the British Legation during the Boxer trouble.

Other sects followed till now we find churches and chapels, ministering to almost every shade of Christian belief, scattered over the city. Moreover, workers combining special forms of social service with religion, such as the Salvation Army and the Y.M.C.A., have come to serve the Sons of Han.[350]

Most of these Missions and societies have a large central compounds, with subsidiary chapels or branches under their control, established in places where business or pleasure cause the Chinese to congregate. Their doors are open every day and passers-by are invited to come and listen to the Gospel preaching.

How much is accomplished from the religious standpoint no layman dares state. The Roman Catholics claim to make 100,000 converts a year, mostly of course, children rescued from destitution and brought up in their schools and orphanages. What success attends the various Protestant sects in their work

---

350 The Y.M.C.A. has a large building on the Hata Men Street, the gift of John Wanamaker, the merchant millionaire of Philadelphia, and the Salvation Army —a fine hall, built in Chinese style, in the Wang Fu Ching Ta Chieh.

Western Landmarks

of conversion we cannot say, having no available figures to judge by—if such results may indeed be judged entirely by figures.

But one fact is patent to the most casual observer, and that is the good which schools and hospitals in charge of missionaries have done the Chinese people.

More powerful even than the schools, as witnesses for Christianity, are hospitals, where all creeds and classes are given careful and attentive treatment. In such institutions where the first physicians in their attempts to heal were hindered by ignorance and prejudice, conditions are slowly changing for the better. A surgeon who cuts off a woman's leg to save her life is no longer expected to provide for her during her remaining years because public opinion considers he has interfered with fate. Wards are not wrecked because some evil person spreads a report that children's eyes are being used to make medicine, though cases of families demanding reprisals on foreign doctors for the death of relatives under their care occur even nowadays. Suspicion and unjust accusations, rooted in a dislike of even those foreigners who honestly desire to help China, still make disinterested scientific work difficult, but, on the other hand, the primitive conditions and lack of proper appliances against which physicians contended in early days have given place to modern apparatus and conveniences.

The old Peking Union Medical College, founded in 1906 "following the disorganisation of Mission work that resulted from the Boxer outbreak," and now taken over by the China Medical Board of the Rockefeller Foundation, is, for example, as fine an up-to-date hospital as can be seen anywhere. Outwardly its nineteen buildings with green tiled roofs[351] are an artistic adaptation of Chinese Palace architecture. Within, they contain the latest devices to mitigate suffering, advance research,[352]

---

351 Their tiles were made at the old Imperial tile works (Liu Li Chu) on the Hun river, opposite the village of San Chia Tien.
352 For full details on the aims and the work of the Rockefeller Hospital see the *Annual Announcement* of the Peiping Union Medical College.

and, above all, to train young Chinese, both men and women, as physicians and nurses to serve their own people.

The site of this splendid institution is historic. On it once stood the Palace of Prince Yu, a senior member of the Manchu Imperial House, but according to a popular report, the ground originally belonged to Wu San-kuei, the famous Chinese general who deserted the Mings to join the Manchus.

A curious legend says that the stone lions in front of the Yu Wang Fu, as the Chinese still call the Rockefeller Hospital, once marched off to the Sea Palaces and created a disturbance there. Brought back with difficulty to their places, these beasts were tied down to prevent further escape.

When excavating the foundations of the new buildings, the remains of an iron helmet, or head-dress, encrusted with gold and jewels, was found, though whether it was part of Wu San-kuei's armour, as it may well have been, is not proved. The fragments picked up by the workmen were turned over to the Yu family in accordance with an agreement made with them that any treasures discovered on the property should be given back to its former owners.

That the Chinese are not slow to see the business advantages of a foreign education nowadays is evidenced by the hundreds of students who attend the Peking University attached to the Methodist Mission near the Hata Men—grown from the small beginnings of the Wiley Institute founded in 1885 for advanced Students and chartered as a full fledged University in 1890 by the State of New York. Whether the westernised system of education will prove in the long run as well suited to the Chinese character as the old Confucian system, time alone can show. China unquestionably needs newer and higher forms of teaching, but many think that these must be evolved from the ancient standards—from within and not from without. It is certain, however, that the education offered by the Christian schools and colleges aims at making the students morally more compassionate and beneficent to their fellow-beings, and physically more manly by encouraging healthy sport with its lessons in fair play, unselfish

Western Landmarks

subordination to the rules of the game, and combined effort. This will be especially beneficial in the case of the girls and young women, whose activities, mental and physical, have long been cramped by bound feet and confined lives.

The majority of the higher schools founded in China of late years are intended to prepare students for advanced courses in the Universities of Europe and America. This is the case with the Tsinghua College to the north-west of Peking, near the site of the old Summer Palace, built on part of the ground that once belonged to Prince Tuan; fifth son of the Emperor Tao Kuang. When it was found that the amount of the Boxer indemnity paid to the United States exceeded the sum required to make good the losses sustained in 1900, it was decided to pay back the balance to China on condition that the money be used in founding an institution to prepare students for further study abroad. To-day, this college appears like a miniature modern town. Its buildings represent the utilitarian architecture of the 20th century: they might be situated equally well in Chicago or Cleveland. All that the most modern western college could wish for may be found here: a campus, a fully equipped hospital, a fine library, a splendid gymnasium and a swimming tank. The professors, some of whom are Americans, direct the 300 students in modern courses of study and inspire their leisure, encouraging glee Clubs and college magazines, such as they themselves knew at home. But the president has always been a Chinese and he outlines the general policy of the institution which shows a steady tendency to raise the standard of the curriculum to the university grade of work. Many thoughtful Chinese themselves believe that it is better for their growing generation not to go abroad while still young, hence the desire to provide higher education at home. The West, with its vast difference of outlook and standards, is apt to prove unsettling to men and women who must come back and spend their lives in China—unless they are old enough to have sound mental balance and clear judgment.

Not far from Tsinghua is Yenching University, whose main gate one passes on the way to the Summer Palace. It seems singularly appropriate that the garden on which the picturesque semi-Chinese style buildings of Yenching stand was designed towards the end of the Ming dynasty by a Chinese scholar—one of the four greatest calligraph-ers of his day—after his retirement from official life as Keeper of the Imperial stables.

His retreat, modelled after the pleasaunces of Southern China so much admired in his lifetime, was for several centuries the meeting place of scholars, artists and poets, who sang its praise in graceful verses like the following:

> "When I leave the Imperial City and come to the Villa of Breeze and Mist,
> Seeing its pavilions and pagodas everywhere mirrored in the clear lake water,
> I dream that I am once again under the shady trees of Kiangnan in autumn time,
> Hearing the songs of the Soochow girls as they scull their boats on the river."

Even the names of the striking features of this historic garden reflect the scholarship of the original owner and serve, doubtless, to inspire the modern student. The old records mention one lake "which bore the title of the Stream of Literature and of a library, shaped like a boat which stood beside it and was known as 'The Vessel of Persistence.' " An islet was poetically called, "Pine Breezes and Moonlit Water." There was a "Fairy's Raft Ford," "An Embankment of the Forest Dweller" and a little bridge airily designated as "A Fringe of Cloud."[353]

When the Ming dynasty collapsed, the "Villa of Breeze and Mist" fell into the hands of the Manchu nobles of the new regime and remained in their possession, suffering, like the old Summer Palace, from the bombardments in 1860. At the time that the university bought the ground, few of the original garden ornaments—the curious rocks, and carved marbles—

---

353 One of the original pines on this islet is still standing. For further details about this picturesque property see *A Guide to Yenching University*.

remained. But the ex-Emperor Hsuan Tung presented Yenching with the fine pair of mythological animals and two winged marble pillars. Other old stone monuments have been bought or given with the idea "not only of preserving for China relics that might otherwise have perished during recent unsettled years" but of restoring the beauty of the gardens designed and executed with such skill and care so many centuries ago.

Of the original monuments of this "Villa of Breeze and Mist" nothing now remains but one old gateway, which is supposed in Ming days to have faced a temple, and a Marble Boat—a smaller edition of the one in the new Summer Palace.[354]

Of the new buildings, that devoted to the Administration is said to be the largest two-storied building under a Chinese roof and the big auditorium on the upper floor seats 1,200 people. The Dean's residence and the administration building of the Women's College are modelled after the twin towers of the Meridian Gate (Wu Men) in the Forbidden City and here it is interesting to note how the architect has solved the problem: "where can smoke emerge from a roof that was never designed to have a chimney?" The Po Ya pagoda near the lake, a new copy of an old monument in the nearby city of Tung-chow, has been cleverly adapted to modern requirements, though no one could guess that it serves as a water tower.

Many of the buildings, etc., are gifts of individual foreigners, friends of China, a fact interesting to remember at a moment when it is the fashion to dwell on the harm, or supposed harm, that Western institutions and westerners have done to this country. Faults in the dealings between Occident and Orient there have been of course, faults on both sides—lack of sympathy, double-dealing, aggressiveness, failure to understand. But of what use for races to dwell constantly on

---

[354] Interested visitors who care to look over the grounds and buildings of Yenching University should address themselves to the "President's Office" in the Administration Building where one of the "Self Help students" will conduct them around. They may also avail themselves of the Yenching buses which run to and from Peking several times a day.

differences, due to heredity and custom, since, willy-nilly, we all have to live in the same house of nations, so to speak, now that quick communications make us close neighbours?

To decry the educationalists, and still more the Missionaries, who have their faults like other people and who—let us hasten to admit—often complicate the policies of Foreign Offices, is also a popular pastime.

But would it not be well for all critics, Chinese as well as foreign, to remember those first Mission schools where new ideals of cleanliness were taught side by side with Bible texts, those first kindergartens where babies learned to keep their noses clean, as well as to lisp Christian hymns, those first hospitals where disinfectants bore, in addition to technical labels, the text "Love One Another."

Why should we forget, in the bitter clash of present day ideas, all the years of patient work done by foreigners and mostly by Missionaries, which has justly entitled them to a high place in the affections of the Chinese people? Surely whatever their errors, much should be forgiven those devoted men and women who have given their lives to care for the sick as for their own sons. Nor must we forget that for the last two hundred and fifty years the Catholic and Greek Orthodox Missionaries, and for the last hundred years the Protestants, have been working to spread education, and overcome superstitions on lines not unlike those suggested by modern Chinese politicians. "La critique est aisee mais l'art est difficile." Therefore, leaving aside the moot point whether the Chinese ever become good Christians or even desire to, let us admit that foreigners, both missionaries and laymen, have undoubtedly helped to set a higher standard of hygienic living in China, alleviated much suffering, given much in charity, taught many that were ignorant and at the same time, through sympathetic scholarship, vastly contributed to correct many of the world's erroneous judgments regarding the Land of Sinim.

XXII. Appendix I The Dynasties of China

LEGENDARY PERIOD.
About 3000-2205 b.c..

Fu Hsi

Shen Nung, the first Farmer who taught the people to till their fields.

Huang Ti ruled for 100 years, invented wheeled vehicles, armour, ships, etc.

Yao, known as one of the Perfect Emperors, lived during the Chinese deluge.

Shun, also known as a Perfect Emperor and one of the 24 classical examples of filial piety.

Yu, the Great.

THE HSIA DYNASTY
17 SOVEREIGNS.
Capital Honan-fu (Lo Yang), 2205-1766 b.c.

THE SHANG DYNASTY
28 SOVEREIGNS.
Capital Honan-fu, later Sian-fu (Ch'ang An & He). 1766-1122 b.c.

THE CHOU DYNASTY
37 SOVEREIGNS.
Capital Sian-fu, then Honan-fu, 1122-255 b.c

The Feudal Age. The later period of this dynasty is famous as the era of the philosophers, Lao Tzu, Confucius and Mencius.

THE CH'IN DYNASTY.
4 SOVEREIGNS
Capital Hsi An Fu. 255-206 b.c.

The founder of this dynasty was Ch'in Shih Huang Ti, sometimes called the Napoleon of China. He built the Great Wall and, having unified the Empire, adopted the title of Supreme Ruler. After his death his dynasty soon collapsed and was succeeded by the famous Hans.

THE HAN DYNASTY (Former or Western).
14 SOVEREIGNS.
Capital Hsian-fu. 206 b.c.—-a.d. 25.

THE HAN DYNASTY (Later or Eastern).
14 SOVEREIGNS.
Capital Honan-fu. a.d. 25-220.

THE PERIOD OF THE THREE KINGDOMS.
a.d. 220-265.

VARIOUS MINOR DYNASTIES followed which are of little interest or importance to the general reader.

THE T'ANG DYNASTY
20 SOVEREIGNS.
Capital Hsian-fu. a.d. 618—907. This is often called the Golden Age of Chinese Learning.

PERIOD OF THE FIVE DYNASTIES
13 SOVEREIGNS, a.d. 907-960.

None of these ephemeral dynasties exercised control over the whole of China, and the country not being in a position to present a united front to a foreign foe was the more easily conquered by the Tartars.

THE LIAO (Khitan, Tartar) DYNASTY.

Dynasties of China

9 SOVEREIGNS.
Capital Peking a.d. 915-1125.

THE CHIN Nuchen Tartar DYNASTY.
10 SOVEREIGNS.
Capital Liao Yang then Peking, a.d. 1125-1234. These dynasties in the north were contemporary with the SUNG DYNASTY in the south, the Chins being first the allies and then the conquerors of the Sungs. The Mongols finally swept in, overthrew the Chins, and eventually the Sungs also.

THE SUNG DYNASTY (Northern and Southern).
18 SOVEREIGNS.
Capital K'aifeng-fu then Nanking and Hangchow. a.d. 960-1260 (1279).

THE YUAN (Mongol) DYNASTY.
10 SOVEREIGNS.
Capital Peking, a.d. 1260-1368. Shih Tsu or Kublai Khan, who reigned from a.d. 1260 to 1294, was the first of the descendants of the great Genghis Khan to establish supremacy over the whole of China and to fix his capital at Peking. In his title as Emperor of the Mongols, his sway was recognised from Borneo to the Carpathians.

THE MING DYNASTY.
16 SOVEREIGNS.
Capital Nanking, then Peking, a.d. 1368-1644.

Hung Wu	T'ai Tsu	1368 -1398
Chten Wen	Hui Ti	1398 -1402(deposed)
Yung Lo	Ch'eng Tsu	1402 - 1424
Hung Hsi	Jen Tsung	1424 - 1425
Hsuan Te	Hsuan Tsung	1425 - 1435
Cheng T'ung	Ying Tsung	1435 - 1449 and again from 1457 - 1464
Ching T'ai	T.u Tsung	1449 - 1457

447

Juliet Brecon

Ch'eng Hua	Hsien Tsung	1464 - 1487
Hung Chih	Hsiao Tsung	1487 - 1505
Cheng Te	Wu Tsung	1505 - 1521
Chia Ching	Shih Tsung	1521 - 1566
Lung Ch'ing	Mu Tsung	1566 - 1572
Wan Li	Shen Tsung	1572 - 1620
T'ai Ch'ang	K uang Tsung	1620 Reigned only one month
T'ien Ch'i	Hai Tsung	1620 - 1627
Ch'ung Chen	Huai-Tsung	or Chuang Lieh Ti 1627 – 1644

THE CH'ING (Manchu) DYNASTY.
10 SOVEREIGNS.
Capital Peking, a.d. 1644-1911.

Shun Chih	Shih Tsu Chang Huang Ti.	1644 - 1661
K'ang Hsi	Sheng Tsu Jen Huang Ti	1661 - 1722
Yung Cheng	Shih Tsung Hsien Huang Ti	1722 - 1735
Ch'ien Lung	Kao Tsung Ch'un Huang Ti	1735 Abdicated 1796. Died 1799.
Chia Ch'ing	Jen Tsung Jui Huang Ti	1796 - 1820
Tao Kuang	Hsuan Tsung Ch'eng Huang Ti.	1820 - 1850
Hsien Feng	Wen Tsung Hsien Huang Ti.	1850 - 1861
T'ung Chih	Mu Tsung Yi Huang Ti	1861 - 1874
Kuang Hsu	Teh Tsung Ching Huang Ti	1874 - 1908
Hsuan Tung	Abdicated 1912 in favour of the Republic.	

The first name given is the title of the reign, the second, the personal posthumous title of the emperor.

XXIII. Appendix II - The Principal Festivals and Fairs in Peking

(All these festivals and fairs are held by the old Chinese— lunar— calendar, according to which their dates are given.)

First Moon, 1st-5th.
New Year festivities, including illuminations and the pasting of new "lucky" pictures and inscriptions on walls and doors. Sacrifices are made at this season to the Gods of Luck and of Riches. Festival of the Buddha Maitreya.

First Moon, 1st-15th.
Fair at the Bell Temple (Ta Chung Ssu).

First Moon, 3rd-16th.
Liu Li Ch'ang fair.

First Moon, 13th.
"Devil Dance" at the Yellow Temple. Festival of Kuan Ti.

First Moon, 14th-16th.
"Lantern Festival" (teng chieh)—a continuation of the New Year festivities) and various lantern fairs.

First Moon, 18th.
End of "Lantern Festival." This is supposed to be the day on which rats marry, and everybody must go to bed early for fear of disturbing them and being annoyed by them in revenge throughout the whole year. Star Festival (chi hsing)

First Moon, 19th.
"Gathering of the Hundred Gods" Fair at Po Yun Kuan.

First Moon, 30th.
"Devil Dance" at Lama Temple (Yung Ho Kung).

Second Moon, 2nd.
"Lung t'ai t'ou" the day on which the "Dragon raises his head." Festival of the Patrons of villages.

Second Moon, 3rd.
Birthday of Erh Lang "the Prince of the Heavenly Tao."

Second Moon, 19th.
One of the three birthdays of the Kuan Yin Pusa (Avalokiteshvara). Services at all her temples.
Formerly the Spring ceremony at the Temple of Confucius took place about this date, but it has now been abandoned.

Third Moon, 1st-3rd.
Festival of the Hsi Wang Mu. Fair at the P'an T'ao Kung.

Third Moon, 15th-28th.
Festival of the Spirit of Mount T'ai Shan at the Tung Yueh Miao.
The Ch'ing Ming—the Spring Festival (the date is variable). On this day the graves of parents are repaired and offerings are made at them.
Fair at the Ch'eng Huang Miao (in the Chinese City).

Fourth Moon, 1st-18th.
Pilgrimage to Miao Feng Shan, to the shrines of the three Niang Niang Pusa ("The Heavenly Mother"), "Our Lady of Many Sons" and "Our Lady of Good Eyesight".

Fourth Moon, 8th.
Birthday of Buddha. Washing of images in Buddhist temples.
Fair near the Kao Liang bridge, connected with the temple of the Pi Hsia Yuan Chun "the Princess of the Coloured Clouds."

Principal Festivals and Fairs of Peking

Fourth Moon, 13th.
Festival of the Yao Wang, the God of Medicine.

Fourth Moon, 14th.
Festival of the Taoist Immortal Lu Tsu and the Fire God. (The third and fourth moons are the season of peonies, and fairs are held in most of the temples of which peony gardens are a feature).

Fifth Moon, 5th.
"The Dragon Boat Festival" or "Festival of the Fifth Moon", coinciding with the Summer Solstice. The most popular Chinese festival after the New Year. Of old the amusements on this day were diversified by many quaint sports. For instance, a special game of polo took place inside the Palace, with the Hsi Hua Men serving as a goal. Frog-hunting expeditions were undertaken to the Southern Hunting Park (Nan Hai Tzu), etc.

Sixth Moon.
Coincides with the beginning of the three periods (fu) of summer heat. Sacrifices are made on the 22nd to the Dragon Kings of springs and wells, such sacrifices being also offered in the second and eighth moons.

Seventh Moon, 7th.
"Meeting of the Cowherd and the Weaver" (Niu Lang and Chih Nu, the latter being the patroness of needlework. The God of Literature is also honoured on this day.

Seventh Moon, 15th.
"All Souls' Day" (chung yuan chieh) set aside for the summer visit to ancestral tombs.

Eighth Moon, 15th.

"The Harvest Moon Festival" (chung ch'iu chieh), coinciding with the Autumn Equinox—the third great Chinese popular festival in the year. Offerings which must be round in shape and consist mostly of vegetables are made on this day to the Moon, the Heavenly Matchmaker ("The Old Man of the Moon") and to the benign Moon Hare. Numerous figures and pictures of the latter may be seen on sale for presents to children. The vegetable markets are particularly animated on this day.

Sacrifices to Confucius.

Tenth Moon, 1st.
Winter offerings to the dead, consisting mostly of representations of clothing.

Twelfth Moon, 30th.
All the Buddhas visit the Earth.
Every Moon, 9th, 10th, 11th, 12th; 19th, 20th, 21st, 22nd and 29th, 30th, 1st, and 2nd.
Fair at Lung Fu Ssu.

Every Moon, 7th-8th, 17th-18th and 27th-28th.
Fair at Hu Kuo Ssu.

Every Moon, 3rd, 6th, 13th, 16th, 19th, 23rd, 28th and 29th. "Night Market" (yeh shih) outside the Ch'ien Men.

Every Moon, 2nd, 5th, 8th, 12th, 15th, 18th, 22nd, 25th and 28th.
"Night Market" outside the Hata Men.

Every Moon, 2nd and 16th.
Pilgrimages to the small temple of the God of Riches (Ts'ai Shen Miao) outside the Chang Yi Men.
Fairs at the T'u 1 i Miao , between the Liu Li Ch'ang and the Chang Yi Men, and outside the Hata Men, the latter being

Principal Festivals and Fairs of Peking

known as the "Flower Market" (hua erh shih). These fairs are held several times a month and their dates are variable.

Many pages would be required to give even an outline of the innumerable customs and superstitions that mark the days of the old Chinese lunar calendar but interested readers may consult Henri Dore's great work, Recherches sur les Superstitions Chnoises, The Moon Year, by Bredon and Mitrophanow, etc.

Some of the older festivals are dying out, and many legendary saints being rapidly forgotten. Nevertheless the Lunar New Year, the Dragon Boat Festival, the Moon Feast, etc., still are important holidays in the life of the Chinese people despite the efforts of the new Government to stamp them out of existence.

Juliet Bredon

ROMANIZATION ERRATA

Ch'eng Hu; read Ch'eng Hua
Ch'eng Pei-leh read Ch'eng Pei Lo
Ch'ung Cheng read Ch'ung Chen
Hsieh Fang-teh read Hsieh Fang-te
Hsuan Teh read Hsuan Te
Kuan Yo Miao read Kuan Yueh Miao
Kung Teh Ssu read Kung Te Ssu
T'an Cheh Ssu read T'an Che Ssu
Tsung Hsiao Ssu read Ch'ung Hsiao Ssu
Tsui Wei read Ts'ui Wei
Tsui Wei Shan read Ts'ui Wei Shan
Yung Lu read Jung Lu

XXIV. Index

Albazines, 32, 433, 434, 435
Altar of Earth, 8, 40, 66
Altar of Harvests (see Che Chi T'an), 98, 101, 102
Altar of Heaven, 8, 80, 136, 138, 140
Alute, Manchu Empress, 364
America, 29, 35, 58, 347, 374, 389, 393, 432, 441
American, 5, 19, 35, 36, 142, 149, 253, 436, 438
American Board Mission, 438
American Legation, 5, 35
American Presbyterian Mission, 438
Amherst, Lord (British Ambassador), 241
Amiot, Father, 427
An Lu-shan (General of the T'ang period), 3, 208
An Ting Men (gate), 6, 14, 212, 220, 437
Ancestor Worship, 231
Arhats (Lohan), 181, 272
Attiret, Father, 248, 381, 427
Banner organisation, 14, 32, 158, 433
Bashpa (Mongol scholar and Mongol script), 340
Belgian, 35
Bell Temple (Ta Chung Ssu), 2, 6, 212, 449
Bell Tower (Chung Lou), 6, 48, 214, 319
Benoist, Father, 249
Bitchurin, Father Hyacinth, 7, 123, 178, 435
Black Temple (Hei Ssu), 218

Blue Temple (in the Nan Hai Tzu), 234
Booksellers, 417
Boxers, 18, 22, 29, 37, 115, 197, 285, 287, 422, 430, 431
Bridge of Heaven (see T'ien Ch'iao), 136, 397
British, 29, 33, 34, 35, 241, 250, 285, 366, 396, 411, 437, 438
British Legation, 33, 34, 35, 366, 396, 411, 437, 438
British Summer Legation, 285
Buddha Maitreya, 163, 164, 165, 275, 449
Buddha Sleeping (see Wo Fo Ssu), 274
Buddha, Sandal Wood, 196, 206
Buddhagaya, 218
Buddhism, 152, 153, 156, 164, 166, 300, 421, 425, 426, 435
Buddhist, 8, 7, 22, 36, 45, 79, 80, 102, 117, 120, 126, 152, 154, 166, 168, 177, 182, 185, 192, 195, 201, 206, 207, 215, 227, 237, 268, 272, 273, 274, 275, 288, 290, 291, 298, 300, 302, 308, 311, 313, 319, 324, 338, 340, 346, 349, 370, 380, 411, 425, 427, 431, 450
Canal, Grand (see Grand Canal), 27, 186, 234
Castiglione, Father, 87, 249, 381, 422
Central Hospital, 197
Central Park (Chung Shan

Juliet Bredon

Park), 40, 102, 103, 104, 105, 400
Chai Kung (see Hall of Abstinence), 137, 139
Chamot, 33, 36
Chang Fei (hero of the Three Kingdoms' period), 354
Chang Hsun (General), 30, 40, 138, 139
Chang Yi Men (gate), 16, 153, 407, 452
Chao Hsien Miao (see Lei Shen Miao), 176
Chao Hsuan Ti, T'ang Emperor, 206
Chao Jih T'an (see Temple of Sun), 222
Chao Ling (Ming Tombs), 349
Ch'en, Lady (Concubine of the Ming period), 9
Chinese (Outer) City (Wa, 14
Cheng T'ung (Ying Tsung)—Ming Emperor, 179, 238, 290, 348, 447
Cheng Yang Men (see Ch'ien Men), 14
Chi Shui T'an, 186, 187
Chi Shui T'an (Lake), 186, 187
Chi, City of (ancient Peking), 2, 5, 101, 186, 187, 229, 303, 353, 400, 405
Chia Ch'ing—Manchu Emperor, 55, 110, 241, 283, 356, 357, 359, 434, 448
Chia Ching—Ming Emperor, 16, 106, 149, 222, 265, 290, 349, 448
Chiang Ts'o Men (see Yu An Men), 16
Chiao Min Hsiang (Legation Street), 30
Chieh T'ai, 210, 299, 301, 303, 306, 311

Chieh T'ai Ssu (alias Wan Shou Ssu—Western Hills), 299, 303, 306, 311
Chien K'ou (Western Hills), 309, 310
Chien Wen—Ming Emperor, 237
Chih Chu Shan (Spider Hill—Western Hills), 320
Chin (or Nuchen Tartar) dynasty, 4, 5, 17, 33, 63, 162, 204, 226, 229, 230, 240, 265, 266, 282, 283, 288, 291, 297, 307, 311, 314, 321, 327, 334, 338, 393
Chin Chung Miao (temple), 204
Chin Shan (defile, Western Hills), 162, 265, 288
Ching Ling (Ming Tombs), 348, 363
Ching Ling (Tung Ling), 348, 363
Ching Shan (see Coal Hill), 297
Ching T'ai (Tai Tsung)—Ming Emperor, 179, 219, 238, 265, 447
Cho Chou (Peking-Hankow Railway Station), 354
Chou dynasty, 61, 69, 170, 385
Chou Yen-ju (Prime Minister), 20
Christians, 63, 72, 103, 135, 211, 274, 333, 385, 420, 421, 426, 427, 428, 429, 431, 435, 438, 440, 444
Chu Yuan-chang (see Hung Wu), 7, 11
Chu Yung Kuan (Great Wall), 331, 338, 340
Chueh Sheng Ssu (see Bell Temple), 212
Chung Hai, 113, 114, 116, 117

456

Chung Ho Tien (palace hall), 70
Chung Hua Men (Dynastic gate), 40, 65
Chung Shan Park (see Central Park), 40, 98
Chung Tu (ancient Peking), 4, 5
Chung-li Ch'uan (Taoist Immortal), 318
Church Missionary Society, 438
Clement XI, Pope, 426
Coal Hill (Ching Shan or Mei Shan), 8, 17, 20, 28, 36, 39, 73, 90, 98, 106, 108, 109, 110, 111, 126, 350
Colour symbolism, 142
Confucian Temple (Wen Miao or Ta Ch'eng Miao), 166, 170, 173
Confucianism, 152, 168, 169, 275
Confucius, 22, 103, 135, 168, 169, 170, 172, 173, 263, 269, 278, 445, 450, 452
Dalai Lama, 120, 126, 157, 182, 214, 216
David deer, 234
David, Father Armand, 428
Dog Temple (see Erh Lang Miao), 193
Dorgun Amah Wang (Prince Lui), 179, 362
Dragon Boat Festival, 451, 453
Dragons, 128, 303, 388
Drum Tower (Ku Lou), 6, 48, 192
Dutch, 32, 241, 258, 421, 432
Dynastic Gate (see Chung Hua Men), 39, 50, 66
Eastern Tombs (see Tung Ling), 353

Erh Lang, 192, 193, 194, 450
Erh Lang Miao (Dog Temple—Tartar City), 194
Examination Halls, 27, 28
Fa Chun, monk, 299
Fa Hai Ssu (Western Hills), 289
Fa T'a Ssu (pagoda), 203
Fa Yuan Ssu (see Sung Chu Ssu), 182, 183, 206, 207
Fa Yuan Ssu (temple), 182, 183, 206, 207
Fairs, 449, 452
Favier, Bishop, 7, 1, 428, 430
Feng Hsien Tien (Private Ancestral Hall), 99, 109
Festivals, 99, 118, 449
Fire God, 192, 392, 417, 451
Flea Market, 398
Flower Market, 453
Flowers, 80, 119, 215, 281
Forbidden City, 7, 8, 14, 20, 39, 41, 63, 64, 67, 70, 73, 78, 79, 80, 84, 85, 90, 92, 94, 98, 99, 106, 109, 111, 113, 116, 121, 123, 139, 140, 176, 177, 199, 215, 233, 253, 256, 305, 443
France, 26, 35, 139, 251, 318, 429
French Legation, 34, 340
Fu Ch'eng Men (see P'ing Tse Men), 14
Fu Yu Ssu (Lama temple), 176, 177
Gardens, 40, 79, 89, 124
Genghis Khan, 4, 126, 226, 230, 263, 331, 335, 338, 447
Gerbillor, Father W, 423, 433
Ginko (Maidenhair) tree (Salisburia adiantifolia), 80, 312
God of Medicine, 398, 451

457

God of Rain (see Fu Yu Ssu), 176
God of Riches, 192, 452
God of Thunder (see Lei Shen Miao and Ning Ho Miao), 176
God of War (see Kuan Ti), 188
God of Writing, 223
Goddess of Mercy (see Kuan Yin), 19, 195, 272
Grand Canal, 27, 186, 234
Great Wall, 229, 329, 331, 334, 335, 338, 361, 446
Hai Tien (village), 180, 241, 244
Hall of Abstinence (Chai Kun), 99, 137, 138, 139
Hall of Classics (Kuo Tzu Chien), 173, 274
Halliday, Captain, 35
Hamer, Bishop, 430
Hammam (bath house—Museum), 73
Han dynasty, 2, 19, 87, 321, 354, 420
Han Lin College, 34, 208
Han Yu (T'ang period poet), 170, 172
Happy Valley, 233
Hart, Sir Robert, 36, 431
Harvest Moon Festival, 452
Hata Men (Ch'ung Wen Men—gate), 14, 22, 25, 26, 30, 54, 156, 193, 389, 390, 394, 438, 440, 452
Hei Lung T'an (Chinese City), 205, 320, 323, 324, 325
Hei Lung T'an (Western Hills), 205, 320, 323, 324, 325
Hilarion, Archimandrite, 433, 434
Ho Shen (Minister of the Manchu dynasty), 54, 55, 56
Holland (see Dutch), 29
Hotei (sec Pu Tai), 159
Hou (mythical animal), 14, 192
Hou Men (gate), 14, 192
Hsi An Men (gate), 14
Hsi Chih Men (gate), 14, 38, 123, 186, 212, 243, 410
Hsi Feng Ssu (Western Hills), 313
Hsi Hua Men (gate), 65, 72, 177, 451
Hsi Ling (Western Tombs), 180, 291, 327, 353, 354, 355, 356, 359, 361, 365
Hsi Pien Men (gate), 16, 226
Hsi Wang Mu (Taoist divinity), 202, 450
Hsi Yu Ssu (Western Hills), 307
Hsi Yueh T'an (see Temple of Moon), 222
Hsiang Chieh Ssu, 287
Hsiang Shan (Hunting Park—Western Hills), 282
Hsiao Chai Ssu (Western Hills), 316
Hsiao Ling (Tung Ling), 362
Hsiao Sheng (Niuhulu)—Manchu Empress, 359
Hsiao Ting—Ming Empress, 305
Hsieh Fang-te (Sung period scholar), 208, 454
Hsien Feng—Manchu Emperor, 9, 241, 244, 251, 252, 364, 366, 367, 368, 448
Hsien Ling (Ming Tombs), 348
Hsien Ying Ssu (Nunnery, Western Hills), 290
Hsin Ching (Heart Classic, Western Hills), 305
Hsin Hua Men, 73, 114
Hsiung Nu, 2

Index

Hsu Ching-ch'eng (Official), 201
Hsu T'ung (Imperial Tutor), 37
Hsuan Jen Miao (temple, Imperial City), 178
Hsuan Te—Ming Emperor, 14, 58, 73, 79, 173, 177, 178, 188, 199, 227, 305, 314, 348, 357, 361, 375, 443, 447, 448, 454
Hsuan T'ung—Manchu Emperor, 58, 73, 79, 173, 177, 188, 199, 305, 314
Hsuan Wu Men—(see Shun Chih Men), 14
Hu Kuo Ssu (temple and fair), 291, 292, 412, 414, 452
Hu Kuo Ssu (Western Hills), 291, 292, 412, 414, 452
Hua Mei Shan (Western Hills—Hei Lung T'an), 320, 325
Huang Ch'eng (see Imperial City), 14
Huang Chi Tien, 83
Huang Ku Ssu (Temple of the Imperial Aunt—see Hsien Ying Ssu), 290
Huang Ling (Western Hills), 291
Huang Ssu (see Yellow Temple), 214, 218
Huang Ts'un (Railway Station), 287, 290, 296
Hui Ling (Tung Ling), 364
Hui T'ung Tzu, 187
Hun river, 229, 296, 297, 299, 308, 439
Hundred Gods, gathering of, 228, 449
Hung Chih—Ming Emperor, 348, 448
Hung Jen Ssu (temple), 197, 206
Hung Wu (Chu Yuan-chang) Ming Emperor, 124, 125, 341, 352, 447
Hunting Park (see Hsiang Shan), 234, 268, 270, 282, 283, 284, 451
Icon of St Nicholas (Russian Mission), 432, 434, 436
Imperial Carriage Park, 34
Imperial City (Huang Ch'eng), 14, 178, 295, 430, 442
Imperial Granaries, 27
Imperial Guard (see Banner Organisation), 14, 145
Imperial Tombs —(see Tombs Ming Tombs, Hsi Ling, Tung Ling), 368
India, 171, 219, 227, 263, 331, 375
Industrial Museum, 43
Inner (Tartar or Manchu) City (Nei Ch'eng), 14
Italian, 35, 47, 123, 159, 181, 241, 296, 408, 429
Italy, 8, 29, 53
Izmailov (Russian Ambassador), 240, 282
Jade, 29, 61, 111, 113, 122, 123, 240, 249, 250, 264, 266, 270, 271, 291, 374, 385
Jade Canal, 29
Jade Emperor (see Yu Huang), 111
Jade Fountain (Yu Ch'uan Shan), 29, 113, 240, 249, 250, 264, 266, 271, 291
Jade Rainbow Bridge (Sea Palace), 122, 270
Japan, 29, 46, 47, 94, 159, 172, 177, 192, 201, 231, 253, 307, 374, 376
Japanese, 37, 47, 159, 185, 263, 349, 355, 375, 383, 385
Jesuits, 26, 152, 249, 260, 363,

459

Juliet Bredon
  381, 421, 422, 423, 425, 426, 427, 430, 433, 434
Jui, Prince (see Dorgun Amah Vang), 179, 180
Kalgan (Chang Chia K'ou)_, 329, 334, 335, 336
Kang Kung (Kang T'ieh), 291
Kao Miao (temple), 188
Kao Pei Tien (Hankow-Peking Railway Station), 353, 354
Kao Tsung—Sung Emperor, 189, 363, 448
Khanbalig (ancient Peking), 5, 6, 7, 420
Khitan Tartars (see Liao dynasty), 3, 5, 171, 446
Kiakhta Treaty, 32, 33, 434
King of France, 427
Korea, 6, 159, 208, 209, 228, 364
Koreans, 30, 36
Kuan Ti (God of War), 19, 20, 22, 188, 189, 190, 192, 204, 271, 292, 313, 354, 449
Kuan Ti Miao (temple), 19, 192, 204
Kuan Yin (Goddess of Mercy), 19, 195, 207, 272, 279, 281, 282, 293, 305, 306, 308, 312, 391, 450
Kuan Yo Miao (temple, Imperial City), 188, 190, 454
Kuang Chi Ssu (or Hung T'zu Kuang Chi Ssu), 195
Kuang Hsu—Manchu Emperor, 9, 20, 22, 28, 73, 85, 92, 110, 116, 121, 135, 188, 238, 244, 250, 257, 324, 357, 361, 365, 366, 428, 448
Kuang Hua Ssu (temple, Imperial City), 192
Kublai Khan—Mongol Emperor, 5, 7, 11, 13, 26, 123, 125, 130, 153, 186, 196, 212, 220, 226, 305, 336, 340, 362, 414, 420, 447
Kung Te Ssu (temple), 454
Kuo Tzu Chien (sec Hall of Classics), 173
Labrousse, Rue, 37
Lama Temple (Yung Ho Kung), 156, 208, 449
Lamaism, 156, 159, 164, 165, 166, 338
Lamas, 152, 156, 157, 158, 162, 163, 164, 166, 177, 214, 218
Lantern Festival, 449
Lao Tzu (philosopher), 222, 445
Laughing Buddha (Pu Tai), 159, 275
Lazarists, 422, 427
Legation Quarter,, 24, 29, 132, 398
Legation Street (see Chiao Min Hsiang), 30, 37
Legations, 9, 24, 28, 29, 30, 31, 33, 35, 36, 37, 115, 127, 201, 428
Leontieff, Father, 432
Li Hung-chang (statesman), 7, 364
Li Lien-ying (eunuch), 117, 260, 292
Li Pai Ssu (see Mosque), 153
Li Tz'u-ch'eng (Ming General), 8, 179, 350, 351
Liang Hsiang Hsien (Hsi Ling), 353
Liang Ko Chuang (Hsi Ling), 354
Liao (Khitan Tartar) dynasty, 214, 303
Ling Kan Kung (Western Hills), 309
Ling Kuang Ssu (Western

Hills), 287
Lithographic Bureau (Ministry of Finance), 43
Liu Chin (Ming period eunuch), 296, 297, 314
Liu Lang T'a (Tower of the Sixth Son—Western Hills), 314
Liu Li Ch'ang, 202, 207, 374, 400, 412, 415, 418, 449, 452
Liu Li Ho, 307
Liu Pei (hero of the period of the Three Kingdoms), 354
Liu Po-wen (Minister under the Ming dynasty), 16
Living Buddhas, 156, 157, 182, 215, 216, 399, 414
Loch, H. B., 188
London Missionary Society, 437
Lone Pine Tree Hill (Chih C'hu Shan—Western Hills), 320
Louis XIV, 26, 139, 249
Louis XV, 87, 356, 428
Lu Kou Ch'iao (Marco Polo bridge), 230, 270
Lung Ch'ing—Ming Emperor, 349, 448
Lung Ch'uan Ssu (pagoda), 328
Lung En Ssu (tomb—Western Hils), 297
Lung Fu Ssu (temple and fair), 412, 414, 452
Lung Wang T'an (Western Hills), 287
Lung Yu—Manchu Empress, 361, 366
Ma Shen Miao (Temple of the Protector of Horses), 192
Mahakala Miao (P'u Tu Ssu, Lama temple), 179, 180, 182, 238
Manchu, 2, 6, 8, 9, 10, 13, 14, 16, 19, 25, 30, 31, 32, 33, 37, 39, 50, 51, 54, 67, 72, 78, 79, 81, 83, 85, 90, 91, 92, 98, 99, 109, 113, 121, 125, 135, 145, 153, 159, 163, 177, 178, 179, 180, 182, 190, 192, 197, 199, 214, 228, 229, 240, 252, 259, 260, 266, 270, 괨282, 291, 292, 297, 298, 313, 315, 317, 327, 340, 343, 345, 349, 350, 353, 355, 356, 357, 358, 362, 365, 369, 379, 384, 392, 400, 401, 422, 440, 442, 448
Manchu City (see Inner City), 14
Manchu dynasty (see Ch'ing dynasty), 19, 37, 67, 81, 83, 92, 98, 99, 179, 197, 292
Mangu Khan, 421
Manichaeans, 420
Marco Polo, 6, 26, 123, 124, 230, 234, 270, 296, 334, 375, 426
Marco Polo Bridge (see Lu Kou Ch'iao), 230, 270
Marriages, 332
Martin, Dr W A P ,, 286
Mei Shan (see Coal Hill), 106
Men T'ou Kou (Western Hills), 296, 299
Meng Tzu (philosopher), 172
Methodist Episcopal Church, 438
Miao Feng Shan (Western Hills), 308, 310, 311, 316, 450
Miao Feng T'a (Miao Kao T'a—Jade Fountain Pagoda), 266
Miao Ling (Ming Tombs), 348
Miao Yen (Princess of the Mongol dynasty), 305
Ming Ch'ang—Chin Emperor, 266

461

Ming dynasty, 28, 40, 57, 124, 125, 149, 237, 289, 292, 294, 305, 341, 385, 442
Ming Tombs, 252, 314, 326, 329, 341, 343, 353
Missions, 152, 420, 422, 423, 426, 427, 437, 438
Mohammedan, 54, 114, 152, 153, 155, 234
Mongol dynasty (see Yuan dynasty), 56, 124, 173, 219, 223, 265
Mongol Market, 34, 396, 411
Mongolia, 5, 6, 32, 125, 126, 157, 172, 179, 182, 215, 218, 227, 329, 342, 363, 384, 409, 435
Mongols, 4, 5, 7, 16, 27, 30, 40, 53, 125, 126, 156, 158, 179, 180, 218, 238, 263, 264, 266, 274, 290, 325, 331, 334, 336, 338, 348, 352, 402, 418, 447
Montecorvino, Archbishop John de,, 420
Mouly, Bishop, 427
Mu Ling (Hsi Ling), 357, 359
Nan Hai (Sea Palaces), 113, 114, 115, 116, 125, 127, 234, 410, 451
Nan Hai Tzu, 234, 451
Nan T'ang, 422, 434
Nanking, 3, 7, 42, 130, 259, 279, 341, 342, 447
Nankou Pass, 270, 309, 329, 331, 334, 341
Nan-mu, 346
National Library (see Library), 41
National Museum, 72, 78
Nei Ch'eng (see Inner or Manchu City), 14
Nerchinsk Treaty, 32, 423
Nestorians, 420, 421
New Year, 34, 67, 69, 70, 92, 94, 99, 377, 411, 415, 419, 449, 451, 453
Niang Niang Miao, 308
Nien Hua Ssu (temple, Tartar City), 191, 192
Night Market, 452
Ning Ho Miao (temple, Imperial City), 176, 178
Ning Shou Kung, 83, 84
Nuchen Tartars (see Chin dynasty), 171
Nurhachi—Manchu Emperor, 8, 9, 110, 179
Observatory, 26, 27, 28
Odoric, Friar, 123, 124, 421
Old Buddha (see Tz'u Hsi), 83, 85, 110, 116, 117, 119, 120, 125, 127, 128, 199, 200, 220, 239, 253, 256, 257, 258, 259, 370
Old Summer Palace (see Yuan Ming Yuan), 240, 244, 246
Outer City (see Chinese City), 14
Pa Li Chuang (pagoda), 292, 293, 294
Pa Ta Ch'u (Western Hills), 273, 286, 288, 291, 296
Pa Ta Ling (Great Wall), 331
Pai Chia T'an (see Three Li village), 319, 320
Pai Lin Ssu, 185
Pai T'a Ssu (Lama temple), 195, 197
Palace Museum, 78, 86, 112
Pan An, monk, 265
Pao Chu Tung (Western Hills), 286
Pao Ho Tien, 70
Parkes, Sir Harry (British Plenipotentiary), 31, 188
Parliament, 70, 119, 169

Pearl Concubine (see Chen, Lady), 85, 199, 361
Pei Hai, 4, 41, 83, 113, 115, 122, 124, 125, 127, 128, 130, 165, 196, 197, 206, 228, 270, 401, 410
Pei Kuan (see Russian Mission), 32, 435
Pei P'ing Fu (ancient Peking), 7
Pei T'ang, 423, 427, 428, 429, 430
Peking Gazette, 136, 208, 396
Peking Treaty, 427
Peking University (see University), 192, 440
Persia, 153
Persians, 331, 379, 418
Peter the Great, 32, 130, 139, 240, 282, 363, 433
Pi Hsia Yuan Chun (Taoist Goddess), 224, 450
Pi Mo Yen (Western Hills), 288
Pi Yun Ssu (Western Hills), 270, 275, 278, 279, 281
Pi Yung Kung (see Hall of Classics), 173
Pictures, 90
Po Chu-yi, poet, 50, 319
Po Wang Shan (or Wang Erh, Shan—Western Hills), 126, 325, 353
Po Yun Kuan (or Ch'ang Ch'un Kung—Taoist temple), 4, 126, 212, 226, 228, 449
Porcelain, 375
Portuguese, 32, 192, 422, 429, 430
President, 9, 30, 40, 70, 114, 115, 119, 138, 173, 443
Prison, 224
Protestants, 437, 444
Pu Tai (see Buddha, Laughing), 159, 208

Race Course (P'ao Ma Ch'ang), 229, 231
Republic of China, 70
Republican, 25, 30, 38, 40, 119, 138, 173, 200, 361, 389
Ricci, Father Matteo, 420, 422, 425, 431, 437
Ripa, Father, 423
Rockefeller Foundation, 439
Roman Catholic, 164, 420, 422, 423, 426, 427, 430, 434, 437, 438
Rubruquis, Brother, 421
Russia, 31, 32, 109, 125, 130, 139, 152, 240, 363, 423, 433, 435, 436
Russian Legation, 31, 32, 33, 435
Russians, 25, 31, 33
Sacrifices, 135, 149, 231, 449, 451, 452
Sakyamuni (see Joseph, St), 181, 195, 197, 214, 216, 219, 220, 272, 426
Salvation Army, 438
San Chia Tien (Peking-Hankow Railway Station), 297, 308, 439
San Kuan Miao (American Legation), 36
San Shan An (Western Hills), 287
San Ta Tien, 70, 90, 91
Schall, Father, 26, 422, 423, 425, 431
Scott, Bishop, 438
Sea Palaces, 8, 84, 92, 113, 114, 117, 118, 119, 121, 122, 130, 428, 440
Seals, 91
Sha Ch'eng (town), 326, 327
Sha Ho (river), 326, 327
Shang Fang Shan (Western

Juliet Bredon

Hills), 307
She Chi T'an (Altar of Harvests, Central Park), 98, 101, 102
Shen Nung, 148, 149, 445
Shen Wu Men, 65, 73, 90, 106, 108
Sheng An Ssu (temple, Chinese City), 205
Shih Ching Shan (Western Hills), 296, 297, 314
Shih Fo (Village, Western Hills), 300
Shih Pa Yu (see Temple of Punishments), 225
Shih Tzu Wo (Western Hills), 284, 285, 286
Shou Huang Tien (Coal Hill), 109, 111
Shuang Ch'uan Ssu (see Pa Pao Shan), 291
Shuang T'a Ssu (pagoda), 201
Shun Chih Men (gate), 14, 30, 187, 400, 404, 422
Shun Chih—Manchu Emperor, 14, 20, 30, 67, 92, 110, 126, 179, 187, 214, 298, 349, 355, 362, 363, 400, 404, 422, 448
Siege of Peking, 428
Sokota—Manchu Empress, 367
Sor, 163, 164
Soul Tower (Imperial Tombs), 346, 358
Spider Pagoda (see Tao Ying Miao), 294
Spirit Hall (Imperial Tombs), 358
Spirit Road (Imperial Tombs), 359
Spirit Screen, 56, 120
Ssu Ling (Ming Tombs), 349
Star Festival, 118, 449
Stranger Concubine (see Mohammedan Concubine), 73, 85, 114
Su Wang Fu (Legation Quarter), 37
Summer Palace (Yi Ho Yuan or Wan Shou Shan), 5, 31, 38, 180, 218, 220, 238, 240, 241, 244, 250, 253, 256, 257, 260, 264, 284, 285, 304, 411, 441, 442, 443
Summer Palaces, 240
Sun Ch'uan, Prince of the period of the Three Kingdoms, 259
Sung Chu Ssu (Lama temple), 182
Sung dynasty, 3, 5, 41, 170, 204, 287, 314, 353, 385, 398
Sungaria, Princess of (see Mohammedan Concubine), 172
Ta Ago—Manchu Prince, 400
Ta Ch'eng Miao (see Confucian Temple), 168
Ta Chueh Ssu (Western Hills), 310, 311, 313, 315, 316, 319, 320
Ta Chung Ssu (see Bell Temple), 212, 214, 449
Ta Fo Ssu (see Ta Hui Ssu), 219
Ta Hui Ssu (temple), 219
Ta Hung Men (Imperial Tombs), 355
Ta Kao Hsuan Tien (palace), 111
Tao Fu, monk, 300
Tao Kuang—Manchu Emperor, 135, 241, 283, 311, 327, 356, 357, 359, 364, 427, 441, 448
Tao Ying Miao (Tz'u Hui Ssu—Temple of the Inverted Shadow), 294
Taoism, 152, 168, 222, 421, 435
Taoist, 7, 8, 102, 111, 122, 126,

Index

152, 155, 168, 202, 223, 225, 226, 228, 269, 308, 310, 316, 317, 349, 451
Tartar City (see Inner City), 2, 6, 13, 14, 16, 26, 33, 65, 92, 178, 185, 186, 192, 223, 232, 397, 408, 425, 432
Te Sheng Men (Tartar City gate), 14, 187
Teh Ling (Ming Tombs, 349
Temple of Agriculture (Hsien Nung T'an), 19, 40, 70, 101, 132, 148, 149, 151, 205, 401, 408
Temple of Earth (Ti T'an), 142, 220
Temple of Heaven (T'ien T'an), 19, 24, 40, 66, 98, 101, 115, 119, 132, 135, 136, 138, 141, 142, 144, 145, 148, 149, 204, 220, 347, 397, 408
Thibet, 126, 156, 157, 158, 159, 160, 166, 172, 180, 182, 198, 200, 201, 206, 209, 214, 215, 218, 250, 284, 285, 329, 340, 362, 363, 390, 414, 435
Thibetans, 30, 156
Ti An Men (see Hou Men), 14
Ti T'an (see Temple of Earth), 220
Ti Wang Miao (Chinese Pantheon), 197, 199, 200, 349
Tiao Yu T'ai (see Wang Hai Lou), 228
Tientsin Treaty, 32, 434
Ting Ling (Tung Ling), 364, 368
Tombs, 212, 326, 341
Tseng Tzu (philosopher), 172
Tsinghua College, 441
Tso An Men (gate), 16, 203
Tsung Hsiao Ssu (temple, Chinese City), 206, 207, 454
Tung An Men (gate), 14
Tung Chih Men (gate), 14, 238
Tung Hua Men (gate), 65, 72, 350
Tung Ling (Eastern Tombs), 291, 353, 355, 359, 361, 362, 366, 367
Tung P'ien Men (gate), 202
Tung Yueh Miao (Taoist temple), 212, 223, 224, 225, 316, 450
Tung Yueh Miao (Western Hills), 212, 223, 224, 225, 316, 450
Tzu Ssu (philosopher), 172
University, 41, 318, 431, 432, 440
Victoria, Queen of England, 80, 165, 205
Victory Monument (Central Park), 103
Visdelou, Father, 423
Voltaire, 427
Wai Ch'eng (see Chinese City), 14
Walls, 13, 138, 331
Wan Fo Lou (Pei Hai), 128
Wan Hua Shan (Western Hills), 281
Wan Li—Ming Emperor, 186, 219, 220, 294, 305, 349, 422, 431, 437, 448
Wan Shou Hsing Lung Ssu (temple, Imperial City), 177
Wan Shou Shan (see Summer Palace), 253, 256, 269
Wan Shou Ssu (see Chieh T'ai Ssu), 212, 213, 220
Wan Shou Ssu (temple), 212, 213, 220
Wang Ch'eng-en (Ming eunuch), 108

465

Wang Erh Shan (Western Hills—see Po Wang Shan), 325
Wang Hai Lou, 228, 229
Water Gate (City Walls), 24, 29, 30
Wei Chung-hsien, (Ming eunuch), 278, 349
Wen Ch'uan Ssu (Western Hills), 317
Wen Hua Tien, 72
Western Tombs (see Hsi Ling), 353, 356
White Dagoba (see Pai T'a), 4, 122, 125, 126, 197
Williams, Dr Wells, 35
Winter Palace (see Forbidden City), 6, 118
Wo Fo Ssu (Western Hills), 270, 274
Wu Lung T'ing (Pei Hai), 127
Wu Men (palace gate), 65, 66, 67, 72, 73, 78, 136, 443
Wu San-kuei (General), 8, 10, 179, 440
Wu T'a Ssu, 218, 219, 279
Wu Wei-yeh (poet), 180
Wu Ying Tien (palace), 72
Xavier, St Francis, 421
Y.M.C.A., 274, 438
Yang Chi-yeh (Sung General), 314, 353
Yang Shan (Western Hills), 310
Yao Shih Fo, 195
Yeh-lu Ch'u-ts'ai (Mongol statesman), 263, 264
Yellow Temple (Huang Ssu), 214, 216, 218, 279, 437, 449
Yen Shih-fan, 57
Yen Sung, 57
Yen Tso Ssu (temple), 229
Yen Tzu (philosopher), 172
Yenching University (see Yen Ching), 3, 441, 442, 443
Yi, Prince, 319, 354
Ying Ling (Ming Tombs), 349
Ying T'ai (Ocean Terrace, Sea Palaces), 115
Ying T'ai Island, 115
Ying Tsung—Ming Emperor (see Cheng T'ung), 290, 348, 447
Yo Fei (hero of the Sung dynasty period), 188, 189, 190, 204, 205
Yu An Men (gate), 16
Yu Ching (Ming eunuch) (Pi Yun Ssu), 278
Yu Chou (ancient Peking), 3, 303
Yu Ch'uan Shan (see Jade Fountain), 29, 240, 266, 268, 269, 270
Yu Huang (The Jade Emperor), 111
Yu Ling, 348, 363
Yu Sheng Ssu (temple, Tartar City), 192
Yuan Ch'ang (Official), 201
Yuan dynasty, 188
Yuan Ming Yuan (Old Summer Palace), 240, 241, 246, 247, 250, 251, 252, 253, 282, 427
Yuan Shih-k'ai, President, 9, 38, 58, 70, 102, 114, 116, 119, 120, 122, 128, 137, 138, 143, 169, 188, 190, 191, 250, 305
Yuan Shui Tung (grottoes, Western Hills), 307
Yueh Hsia Lao Erh (Old Man of the Moon), 224
Yung Cheng—Manchu Emperor, 72, 110, 158, 159, 172, 195, 210, 240, 319, 354, 355, 356, 359, 363, 385, 412, 427, 434, 448

Yung Ho Kung (see Lama Temple), 22, 128, 156, 157, 158, 164, 166, 185, 218, 234, 436, 449
Yung Ling (Ming Tombs), 349
Yung Lo—Ming Emperor, 9, 7, 8, 11, 16, 26, 27, 46, 48, 64, 98, 101, 113, 139, 140, 173, 213, 214, 219, 233, 237, 243, 287, 291, 314, 319, 341, 342, 345, 346, 347, 348, 352, 355, 358, 375, 447
Yung Lu (Manchu statesman), 234, 368, 454
Yung Ting Men (gate), 16, 30, 148, 234
Zoological Gardens (San Pei Tzu Hua Yuan) (see also Agricultural Experimental Station), 401

www.ingramcontent.com/pod-product-compliance
Lightning Source LLC
Chambersburg PA
CBHW051415290426
44109CB00016B/1310